Sadlier

We
Live Our
Faith

As Disciples of Jesus

Volume I

Sadlier

A Division of William H. Sadlier, Inc.

The Ad Hoc Committee to Oversee the Use of the Catechism, United States Conference of Catholic Bishops, has found this catechetical series, copyright 2007, to be in conformity with the *Catechism of the Catholic Church*.

Nihil Obstat
✠ Most Reverend Robert C. Morlino

Imprimatur
✠ Most Reverend Robert C. Morlino
Bishop of Madison
October 3, 2006

The *Nihil Obstat* and *Imprimatur* are official declarations that a book or pamphlet is free of doctrinal or moral error. No implication is contained therein that those who have granted the *Nihil Obstat* and *Imprimatur* agree with the contents, opinions, or statements expressed.

Acknowledgments

Scripture excerpts are taken from the *New American Bible with Revised New Testament and Psalms* Copyright © 1991, 1986, 1970 Confraternity of Christian Doctrine, Inc., Washington, DC. Used with permission. All rights reserved. No part of the *New American Bible* may be reproduced by any means without permission in writing from the copyright owner.

Excerpts from the English translation of the *Catechism of the Catholic Church* for the United States of America, copyright © 1994 United States Catholic Conference, Inc.— Libreria Editrice Vaticana. English translation of the *Catechism of the Catholic Church: Modifications from the Editio Typica* copyright © 1997 United States Catholic Conference, Inc.—Libreria Editrice Vaticana.

Excerpts from the English translation of *Rite of Baptism for Children* © 1969, International Committee on English in the Liturgy, Inc. (ICEL); excerpts from the English translation of *Lectionary for Mass* © 1969, 1981, 1997, ICEL; excerpts from the English translation of *The Roman Missal* © 1973, ICEL; excerpts from the English translation of *The Liturgy of the Hours* © 1974, ICEL; excerpts from the English translation of *Rite of Penance* © 1974, ICEL; excerpts from the English translation of *Rite of Confirmation, second edition* © 1975, ICEL; excerpts from the English translation of *Pastoral Care of the Sick: Rites of Anointing and Viaticum* © 1982, ICEL; excerpts from the English translation of *A Book of Prayers* © 1982, ICEL. All rights reserved.

English translation of the Glory to the Father, Lord's Prayer, Apostles' Creed, Nicene Creed, by the International Consultation on English Texts (ICET).

Excerpts from the English translation of the *Compendium of the Social Doctrine of the Church* copyright © 2004 Libreria Editrice Vaticana—United States Catholic Conference, Inc., Washington, DC (USCCB); excerpt from *The Challenge of Peace* copyright © 1983 USCCB; excerpt from *Stewardship: A Disciple's Response* copyright © 2002 USCCB; excerpt from *God's Mercy Endures Forever: Guidelines on the Presentation of Jews and Christians in Catholic Preaching* copyright © 1988 USCCB. All rights reserved.

Excerpts from *The Documents of Vatican II*, Walter M. Abbott, General Editor, copyright © 1966 by America Press.

Pacem in terris, Peace on Earth, Encyclical Letter, Pope John XXIII, April 11, 1963.

Sollicitudo rei socialis, On the Social Concern of the Church, Encyclical Letter, Pope John Paul II, December 30, 1987.

Excerpt from *Chicken Soup for the Preteen Soul* copyright © 2000 by Jack Canfield and Mark Victor Hansen. Health Communications, Inc., Deerfield Beach, FL.

Excerpt from *The Little Prince (Le Petit Prince)*, by Antoine de Saint-Exupéry, translated from the French by Richard Howard, copyright © 1943 by Harcourt, Inc.; copyright renewed ©1971 by Consuelo de Saint-Exupéry; English translation copyright © 2000 by Richard Howard.

Excerpt from *Julian of Norwich: Showings*. Translated and introduced by Edmund Colledge, OSA, and James Walsh, SJ. Preface by Jean Leclercq, OSB. Copyright © 1978 by Paulist Press, Inc., Mahwah, NJ.

Excerpt from *The Desegregated Heart*, by Sarah Patton Boyle, copyright © 1962 by Sarah Patton Boyle. Originally published by William Morrow, New York, 1962. 2001 edition reprinted by the University of Virginia Press, Charlottesville, VA, by arrangement with William Morrow, an imprint of HarperCollins, New York, NY.

Excerpts from *The Way of Perfection (Camino de perfección)* by Saint Teresa of Ávila. Translated and edited by E. Allison Peers from the critical edition of Silverio de Santa Teresa. Originally published by Sheed & Ward, London, 1946. 1991 Image Book edition published by Doubleday, a division of Bantam Doubleday Dell Publishing Group, Inc., New York, NY. First Image Books edition published in 1964 by special arrangement with Sheed & Ward, Inc.

Excerpt from *If You Don't Like the News . . . Go Out and Make Some of Your Own*, by Wes Nisker. Copyright © 1994 by Wes Nisker. Published by Ten Speed Press, Berkeley, CA.

Excerpt from *The Story of a Soul (L'Histoire d'une âme)*, by Saint Thérèse of Lisieux, edited by Rev. T.N. Taylor, Burns, Oates & Washbourne, Ltd., London, 1912; eighth edition, 1922.

Excerpt from *The People's Choice, from Washington to Harding: A Study in Democracy*, by Herbert Sebastian Agar. Originally published by Houghton Mifflin Company, Boston, 1933. 2001 edition reprinted by Simon Publications, Phoenix, AZ.

Excerpt from *Jean Donovan: The Call to Discipleship*, updated, 2005 (Peacemaker Booklet Series), by John Dear, SJ., copyright © 2005 Pax Christi USA.

Excerpt from *Cartas con la señal de la cruz* by Manuel Lozano Garrido. Originally published in 1967 by Ediciones Mensajero, Bilbao, Spain. 2001 edition published by Edibesa, Madrid.

Excerpt from *Middlemarch*, by George Eliot (Mary Ann Evans), 1871.

Excerpts from *What Is to Be Done?* By Leo Tolstoy, 1883.

Excerpt from *Chapters from a Life*, by Elizabeth Stuart Phelps Ward, 1897.

Excerpt from *Optimism*, by Helen Keller, 1903.

Excerpt from "'Dolly' Is a Pearl of Great Price," Joan Barthel, *The New York Times*, Arts & Leisure, November 26, 1967; copyright © 1967, *The New York Times*.

Excerpts from "Why I Forgave My Assailant," by Steven McDonald, copyright © 2004 by Steven McDonald. Reprinted from the *Bruderhof Forgiveness Guide*.

Excerpt from *The Hiding Place*, by Corrie ten Boom and John and Elizabeth Sherrill, as reprinted in "I'm Still Learning to Forgive," *Guideposts*, November 1972. Copyright © 1972 by Guideposts.

Quotation from C. Smith Sumner, from www.zaadz.com, a Web site maintained by Zaadz, Inc., Topanga, CA.

Quotation from César Chávez, from the César E. Chávez Foundation, Glendale, CA.

Quotation from Saint Joan of Arc, from The Saint Joan of Arc Center, Albuquerque, NM.

Quotation from John F. Kennedy's address at Rice University, September 12, 1962, from *Public Papers of the Presidents of the United States*, volume 1, 1962, as issued by the U.S. Government Printing Office.

Quotation from Lillian Dickson from the Billy Graham Center Archives at Wheaton College, Wheaton, IL.

Quotation from Tom Taylor from Universal Press Syndicate, Kansas City, MO.

Quotation from Mohandas K. Gandhi from the Navjeevan Trust, Ahmedabad, India.

Adaptation of "A Prayer for Healing" by the priests and brothers of the Sacred Heart, Sacred Heart Monastery, Hales Corner, WI.

Adaptation ("Do It Anyway") from "The Paradoxical Commandments" by Dr. Kent M. Keith, copyright © 1968, 2001 by Kent M. Keith.

Lyrics from the song "Beggars at the Feast," from the musical *Les Misérables*, by Herbert Kretzmer, Alain Boublil; music by Claude-Michel Schönberg. Copyright © 1987 Alain Boublil Music Ltd., New York.

"Await the Lord with Hope," copyright © 1996 Bob Hurd. Published by OCP Publications, 5536 NE Hassalo, Portland, OR 97213. All rights reserved. "Three Days," copyright © 1999 M. D. Ridge. Published by OCP Publications. All rights reserved. "Christ is Here," copyright © 1998 Christopher Walker. Published by OCP Publications. All rights reserved. "This Is the Day," text, irregular, based on Psalm 118:24, adapted by Les Garrett. Copyright © 1967 Scripture in Song, administered by Maranatha! Music, c/o The Copyright Company, Nashville, TN. All rights reserved. International copyright secured. "Hosea," copyright © 1972, The Benedictine Foundation of the State of Vermont, Inc., Weston, VT. All rights reserved. "This Day God Gives Me," copyright © 1969, James D. Quinn, SJ. Published by Selah Publishing Co., Inc., Pittsburgh, PA 15277.

S® is a registered trademark of William H. Sadlier, Inc.
We Live Our Faith™ and **We Believe**™ are registered trademarks of William H. Sadlier, Inc.

William H. Sadlier, Inc.
9 Pine Street
New York, NY 10005-1002

ISBN: 978-0-8215-5677-1
9 /11 10

The Sadlier *We Live Our Faith* Program was developed by nationally recognized experts in catechesis, curriculum, and adolescent development:

Catechetical and Liturgical Consultants

Dr. Gerard F. Baumbach
Director, Center for Catechetical Initiatives
Concurrent Professor of Theology
University of Notre Dame
Notre Dame, Indiana

Carole M. Eipers, D.Min.
Vice President, Executive Director of Catechetics
William H. Sadlier, Inc.

Curriculum and Adolescent Catechesis Consultants

Sr. Carol Cimino, SSJ, Ed.D.
National Consultant

Joyce A. Crider
Associate Director
National Conference of Catechetical Leadership
Washington, D.C.

Kenneth Gleason
Director of Religious Education
Cincinnati, Ohio

Saundra Kennedy, Ed.D.
National Religion Consultant
William H. Sadlier, Inc.

Mark Markuly, Ph.D.
Director, Loyola Institute for Ministry
New Orleans, Louisiana

Kevin O'Connor, CSP
Institute of Pastoral Studies
Loyola University Chicago
Long Grove, Illinois

Gini Shimabukuro, Ed.D.
Associate Professor
Institute for Catholic Education Leadership
School of Education, University of San Francisco

Scriptural Consultant

Reverend Donald Senior, CP, Ph.D., S.T.D.
Member, Pontifical Biblical Commission
President, The Catholic Theological Union
Chicago, Illinois

Media/Technology Consultant

Sister Jane Keegan, RDC
Senior Internet Editor
William H. Sadlier, Inc.

Catholic Social Teaching Consultants

John Carr
Secretary, Department of Social Development and World Peace
United States Conference of Catholic Bishops
Washington, D.C.

Joan Rosenhauer
Coordinator, Special Projects, Department of
Social Development and World Peace
United States Conference of Catholic Bishops
Washington, D.C.

Sadlier Consulting Team

Michaela Burke Barry
Director of Consultant Services

Kenneth Doran
National Religion Consultant

Inculturation Consultants

Reverend Allan Figueroa Deck, SJ, Ph.D.
Executive Director
Loyola Institute for Spirituality
Orange, California

Kirk P. Gaddy, Ed.D.
Principal
St. Katharine School
Baltimore, Maryland

Dulce M. Jiménez-Abreu
Director of Spanish Programs
William H. Sadlier, Inc.

Theological Consultants

Most Reverend Edward K. Braxton, Ph.D., S.T.D.
Official Theological Consultant
Bishop of Belleville, Illinois

Reverend Joseph A. Komonchak, Ph.D.
Professor, School of Theology and Religious Studies
The Catholic University of America
Washington, D.C.

Most Reverend Richard J. Malone, Th.D.
Bishop of Portland, Maine

Writing/Development Team

Rosemary K. Calicchio
Vice President, Publications

Blake Bergen
Editorial Director

Melissa D. Gibbons
Director of Research and Development

Joanne McDonald
Senior Editor, Project Director

Mary Ann Trevaskiss, Supervising Editor
Maureen Gallo, Senior Editor
William Beebe, Ph.D.
Joanna Dailey
William M. Ippolito
Allison Johnston
Mary Ellen Kelly
Regina Kelly
Daniel Sherman

Publishing Operations Team

Deborah Jones
Vice President, Publishing Operations

Vince Gallo
Creative Director

Francesca O'Malley
Associate Art Director

Jim Saylor
Photography Manager

Design Staff

Debrah Kaiser, Sasha Khorovsky, Maria Pia Marella

Production Staff

Diane Ali, Brent Burket, Robin D'Amato, Tresse DeLorenzo, Maria Jimenez, Joe Justus, Vincent McDonough, Yolanda Miley, Maureen Morgan, Jovito Pagkalinawan, Julie Riley, Gavin Smith, Martin Smith, Sommer Zakrzewski

Contents

We Live Our Faith!

Welcome to the *We Live Our Faith* program! Each chapter will help us to grow as disciples of Jesus by:

GATHERING . . . BELIEVING . . . and **RESPONDING**

We Live Our Faith As Disciples of Jesus centers on Jesus' life, his teachings, and the sacraments he instituted. It presents Jesus' call to each of us to become his disciple and the ways in which his teachings, his sacraments, and his Church nourish us for discipleship.

Hi!
My name is James.
Come with me as I walk through a chapter of *We Live Our Faith*.

Let's start with the **GATHERING** section.

Prayer helps me to focus my energy and to reflect on God's presence in my life.

I do a survey, quiz, puzzle, or game with my friends and classmates.
I check with other students my age at **www.weliveourfaith.com**.

I respond to a Big Question about life.

The goals help me to see how this chapter will engage my mind, my heart, and my actions in living my faith.

There is always an interesting story, profile, current event, or report, plus an activity in this section.

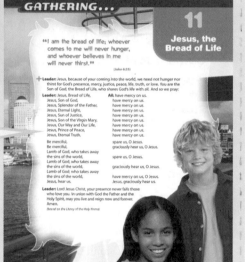

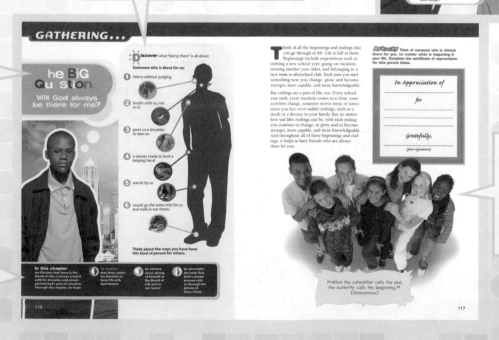

Jesus prepares his disciples for all that is to come.

One day, on the way to a region called Caesarea Philippi, Jesus questioned his disciples. He tried to find out what they were thinking about him. Jesus' disciples told him that some people said that he was "John the Baptist, others Elijah, still others Jeremiah or one of the prophets" (Matthew 16:14). Jesus asked them again, "But who do you say that I am?" (Matthew 16:15).

It was his Apostle Simon, also called Peter, who replied for all of the disciples. Peter said, "You are the Messiah, the Son of the living God" (Matthew 16:16). Jesus blessed Peter for recognizing this truth. But Jesus, knowing that his role as Messiah was not yet clear to the people, warned all of the disciples not to tell anyone about this for the time being.

Yet the disciples continued to witness Jesus' ability to help people to live full and holy lives. They saw him bring this "fullness of life" to those he spoke to, ate with, prayed with, forgave, and healed. They saw and heard Jesus invite all future events of his life might not seem so "full of life" to his disciples. He knew that people would oppose him, question his teachings, and threaten his life. He knew that his mission of salvation would require him to suffer and die. His disciples would find all of these events difficult to understand. So, Jesus began to prepare them for all that was to come.

Jesus told his disciples that his suffering and death were coming. But he also told them that on the third day he would rise. He would fulfill the promise that had been made to God's people throughout the ages. Through his life, death, and rising from the dead, Jesus would save all people from sin and the power that sin has over humanity, and save them for fullness of life with God.

Jesus challenged his disciples to live their lives in complete commitment to his Gospel message. Jesus taught that a life lived in true discipleship leads to **eternal life**, a life of happiness with God forever.

Faith Word
eternal life

Activity Based on what you have learned about Jesus, how was he "always there" for his disciples?

Jesus tells his disciples he will always be with them.

Jesus focused his public ministry on enabling people to have life, both here and hereafter. Jesus spoke the following words to his disciples, telling them about the new life that only he, as God's divine Son, could give:

"I am the bread of life; whoever comes to me will never hunger, and whoever believes in me will never thirst." (John 6:35)

"I am the living bread that came down from heaven; whoever eats this bread will live forever; and the bread that I will give is my flesh for the life of the world." (John 6:51)

"Whoever eats my flesh and drinks my blood has eternal life . . . Just as the living Father sent me and I have life because of the Father, so also the one who feeds on me will have life because of me." (John 6:54, 57)

Jesus wanted his disciples to know that belief in him is needed in order to have life with God.

By calling himself the Bread of Life and the Living Bread, Jesus was telling his disciples that he was truly the Son of God and sent to bring God's life to them.

Jesus taught that his disciples would have life with God forever if they truly believed that he was the Son of God and if they lived as his disciples.

Only Jesus could satisfy people's hunger and thirst for God—he was all the food they needed for eternal life. But when Jesus spoke of himself as the Bread of Life and as food and drink, many people were troubled by his words. They asked themselves, "How can this man give us [his] flesh to eat?" (John 6:52). But at his last meal with his disciples on the night before he died, Jesus shed new light on the meaning of his words.

At that meal, known as the Last Supper, Jesus gave his disciples a special way to remember him and to be with him. Jesus "took the bread, said the blessing, broke it, and gave it to them, saying, 'This is my body, which will be given for you; do this in memory of me.' And likewise the cup after they had eaten, saying, 'This cup is the new covenant in my blood, which will be shed for you'" (Luke 22:19–20). Jesus' breaking of the bread and sharing of the cup was an offering of himself for our salvation. It was the Eucharist, Jesus' gift to all of his disciples.

Through the Eucharist Jesus could remain with his disciples forever because Jesus is wholly and completely present in the bread and wine that become his Body and Blood. This true presence of Jesus Christ in the Eucharist is called the **Real Presence**. Through the Eucharist, the Son of God, the Bread of Life, joins the lives of those who receive him to the eternal life and presence of God—Father, Son, and Holy Spirit.

"The bread that I will give is my flesh for the life of the world." (John 6:51)

Activity Write and title a poem about Jesus, who is always present to us in the Eucharist.

Faith Word
Real Presence

Truly present

During Mass the priest does and says what Jesus did and said at the Last Supper. Through the priest's words and actions, and by the power of the Holy Spirit, the bread and wine are changed into the Body and Blood of Christ. Jesus truly becomes present to us in the Eucharist under the appearance of bread and wine. This change that the bread and wine undergo is called transubstantiation. *Trans* means "change"; *substantia* means "substance"; *tion* means "the act of." What the bread and wine really are—their substance—becomes the Body and Blood of Christ, yet what they look like and taste like—their appearances—remain the same.

Each time you receive Holy Communion, remember that Jesus is truly present in what looks like bread and wine, but is really his Body and Blood. You are receiving Jesus himself.

CATHOLIC IDENTITY

An activity helps me to apply what I have learned to my own life and relationships.

Specific aspects of the Catholic faith strengthen my identity as a Catholic.

In the BELIEVING section, I learn more about the Catholic faith and about Jesus' call to me to live as his disciple.

Great photos and beautiful artwork help me to understand the Catholic faith.

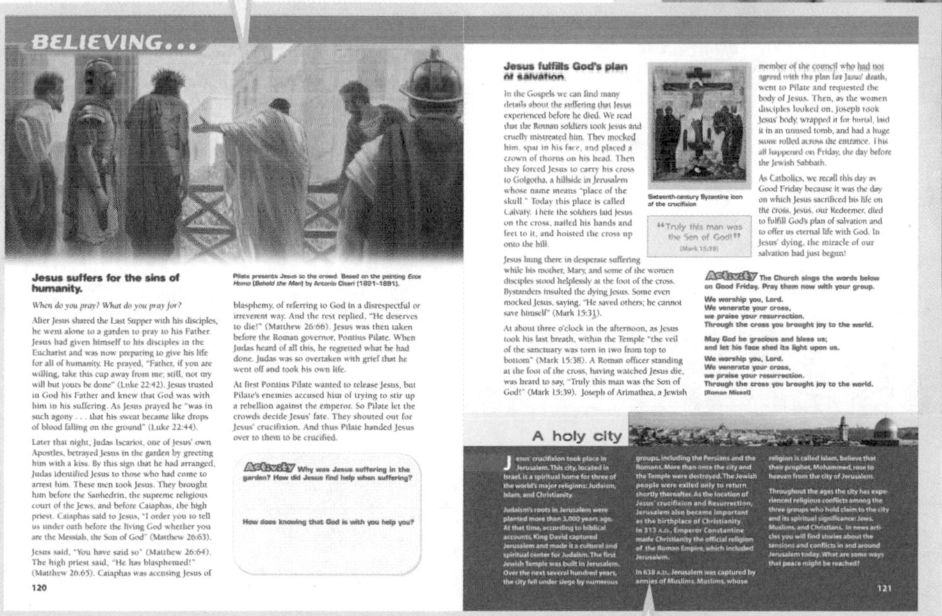

Jesus suffers for the sins of humanity.

When do you pray? What do you pray for?

After Jesus shared the Last Supper with his disciples, he went alone to a garden to pray to his Father. Jesus had given himself to his disciples in the Eucharist and was now preparing to give his life for all of humanity. He prayed, "Father, if you are willing, take this cup away from me; still, not my will but yours be done" (Luke 22:42). Jesus trusted in God his Father and knew that God was with him in his suffering. As Jesus prayed he "was in such agony . . . that his sweat became like drops of blood falling on the ground" (Luke 22:44).

Later that night, Judas Iscariot, one of Jesus' own Apostles, betrayed Jesus in the garden by greeting him with a kiss. By this sign that he had arranged, Judas identified Jesus to those who had come to arrest him. They then took Jesus. They brought him before the Sanhedrin, the supreme religious court of the Jews, and before Caiaphas, the high priest. Caiaphas said to Jesus, "I order you to tell us under oath before the living God whether you are the Messiah, the Son of God" (Matthew 26:63).

Jesus said, "You have said so" (Matthew 26:64). The high priest said, "He has blasphemed!" (Matthew 26:65). Caiaphas was accusing Jesus of blasphemy, or referring to God in a disrespectful or irreverent way. And the rest replied, "He deserves to die!" (Matthew 26:66). Jesus was then taken before the Roman governor, Pontius Pilate. When Judas learned of all this, he regretted what he had done. Judas was so overtaken with grief that he went off and took his own life.

At first Pontius Pilate wanted to release Jesus, but Pilate's enemies accused him of trying to stir up a rebellion against the emperor. So Pilate let the crowds decide Jesus' fate. They shouted out for Jesus' crucifixion. And thus Pilate handed Jesus over to them to be crucified.

Pilate presents Jesus to the crowd. Based on the painting *Ecce Homo (Behold the Man)* by Antonio Ciseri (1821–1891).

Activity Why was Jesus suffering in the garden? How did Jesus find help when suffering?

How does knowing that God is with you help you?

Jesus fulfills God's plan of salvation.

In the Gospels we can find many details about the suffering that Jesus experienced before he died. We read that the Roman soldiers took Jesus and cruelly mistreated him. They mocked him, spat in his face, and placed a crown of thorns on his head. Then they forced Jesus to carry his cross to Golgotha, a hillside in Jerusalem whose name means "place of the skull." Today this place is called Calvary. There the soldiers laid Jesus on the cross, nailed his hands and feet to it, and hoisted the cross up onto the hill.

Jesus hung there in desperate suffering while his mother, Mary, and some of the women disciples stood helplessly at the foot of the cross. Bystanders insulted the dying Jesus. Some even mocked Jesus, saying, "He saved others; he cannot save himself" (Mark 15:31).

At about three o'clock in the afternoon, as Jesus took his last breath, within the Temple "the veil of the sanctuary was torn in two from top to bottom" (Mark 15:38). A Roman officer standing at the foot of the cross, having watched Jesus die, was heard to say, "Truly this man was the Son of God!" (Mark 15:39). Joseph of Arimathea, a Jewish member of the council who had not agreed with the plan for Jesus' death, went to Pilate and requested the body of Jesus. Then, as the women disciples looked on, Joseph took Jesus' body wrapped it for burial, laid it in an unused tomb, and had a huge stone rolled across the entrance. This all happened on Friday, the day before the Jewish Sabbath.

As Catholics, we recall this day as Good Friday because it was the day on which Jesus sacrificed his life on the cross. Jesus, our Redeemer, died to fulfill God's plan of salvation and to offer us eternal life with God. In Jesus' dying, the miracle of our salvation had just begun!

Sixteenth-century Byzantine icon of the crucifixion

"Truly this man was the Son of God!" (Mark 15:39)

Activity The Church sings the words below on Good Friday. Pray them now with your group.

We worship you, Lord.
We venerate your cross,
we praise your resurrection.
Through the cross you brought joy to the world.

May God be gracious and bless us;
and let his face shed its light upon us.

We worship you, Lord.
We venerate your cross,
we praise your resurrection.
Through the cross you brought joy to the world.
(Roman Missal)

A holy city

Jesus' crucifixion took place in Jerusalem. This city, located in Israel, is a spiritual home for three of the world's major religions: Judaism, Islam, and Christianity.

Judaism's roots in Jerusalem were planted more than 3,000 years ago. At that time, according to biblical accounts, King David captured Jerusalem and made it a cultural and spiritual center for Judaism. The first Jewish Temple was built in Jerusalem. Over the next several hundred years, the city fell under siege by numerous groups, including the Persians and the Romans. More than once the city and the Temple were destroyed. The Jewish people were exiled only to return shortly thereafter. As the location of Jesus' crucifixion and Resurrection, Jerusalem also became important as the birthplace of Christianity. In 313 A.D., Emperor Constantine made Christianity the official religion of the Roman Empire, which included Jerusalem.

In 638 A.D., Jerusalem was captured by armies of Muslims. Muslims, whose religion is called Islam, believe that their prophet, Mohammed, rose to heaven from the city of Jerusalem.

Throughout the ages there have been experienced religious conflicts among the three groups who hold claim to the city: Jews, Muslims, and Christians. In news articles you will find stories about the tensions and conflicts in and around Jerusalem today. What are some ways that peace might be reached?

Features give interesting details about an aspect of the chapter.

Turn the page for more exciting features!

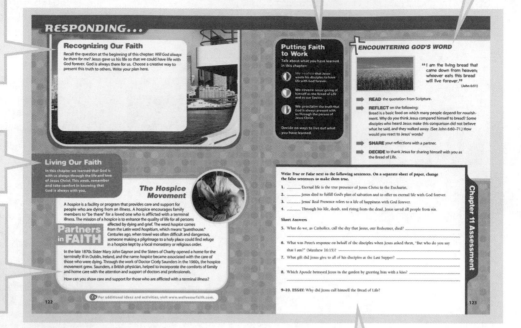

I answer the Big Question in light of what I have learned and do a group activity.

I decide on ways that I will live out what I have learned.

I pray, using a passage from Scripture.

I'm called to witness to my faith.

I learn about saints, groups, and holy people who are models of discipleship for me.

I have the opportunity to demonstrate my knowledge and understanding of the chapter.

In the RESPONDING section, I integrate and apply what I've learned in the chapter to my life.

I evangelize at home and with my friends by sharing what I have learned.

I connect the chapter material to the ritual prayer and action of the liturgy.

I plan further research and visit www.weliveourfaith.com.

I decide on ways to live out Catholic social teachings.

Throughout the year we will learn about many saints, holy people, and Catholic organizations, including:

Saint Paul

Saint Jerome

Blessed Julian of Norwich

Saint Teresa of Ávila

The Catholic News Service

Pope John Paul II

Venerable Matt Talbot

Saint Joseph

Jean Donovan

Blessed Francis Xavier Seelos

The Hospice Movement

Saint Mary Magdalene

Oliver Messiaen

Marla Ruzicka

Blessed Miguel Pro

Catholic Relief Services

Saint Peregrine

Pope Benedict XVI

Blessed Laura Montoya

Saints Raphael, Gabriel, and Michael the Archangels

Sean Devereux

Jesuit Volunteer Corps

Venerable Catherine McAuley

Saint Teresa de Los Andes

We Live Our Faith has many great features that will help us to grow as Jesus' disciples.

We visit **www.weliveourfaith.com** to find:

surveys

quizzes

games

chapter resources

magazines

community outreach

. . . and much more!

We Live Our Faith is filled with great activities, including:

discussions and reflections

games

role-plays

timelines

quizzes

polls and surveys

puzzles

teamwork

outreach projects

artwork

creative writing

prayer services

We pray by using:

Scripture readings

meditations

prayers from the Mass and the sacraments

traditional Catholic prayers

prayers from many cultures

prayer in our own words

psalms

songs

We learn more by using these helpful resources:

Bible Basics

Prayers and Practices

Glossary

Index

Now let's get started!

Unit 1

Who Is God?

Chapter 1
The Source of All Life
The Big Question:
How do I know God is present in my life?

Chapter 2
The Truth Revealed
The Big Question:
In what ways can I find truth?

Chapter 3
The Blessed Trinity
The Big Question:
Why do relationships matter to me?

Chapter 4
God, Our Loving Father
The Big Question:
How do I know God loves me?

Chapter 5
Jesus Christ, the Good News
The Big Question:
What is the good news for me?

Chapter 6
Holy Spirit, Helper and Guide
The Big Question:
How do I find my way?

10

GATHERING...

"You shall seek the LORD, your God; and you shall indeed find him."

(Deuteronomy 4:29)

Leader: Lord, may we recognize that even as we seek your presence in our lives, you are always seeking *us*.

Reader 1: A reading from the Acts of the Apostles

"The God who made the world and all that is in it, the Lord of heaven and earth, does not dwell in sanctuaries made by human hands, nor is he served by human hands because he needs anything. Rather it is he who gives to everyone life and breath and everything."

(Acts of the Apostles 17:24–25)

Reader 2: "People might seek God . . . though indeed he is not far from any one of us. For 'In him we live and move and have our being.'"

(Acts of the Apostles 17:27–28)

Reader 3: God of heaven and earth, be with us as we seek you.

All: For you are not far from any one of us.

Reader 4: God of heaven and earth, help us to find you in our lives.

All: For in you we live and move and have our being.

Leader: God, our Father, we ask this through our Lord Jesus Christ, your Son, who lives and reigns with you and the Holy Spirit, one God, for ever and ever.

All: Amen.

@ Visit www.weliveourfaith.com to find appropriate music and songs.

11

The BiG QuEstion:

How do I know God is present in my life?

Discover how you view God. Take this short quiz to discover how you experience God in your life.

1 Of the following things in nature, _____ would make me think of God's presence the most.
- (a) the warmth of the sun
- (b) the ocean waves crashing on the shore
- (c) pets and other living things
- (d) other: _____

2 My strongest reminder of God's love is probably
- (a) my relationship with people who have raised or mentored me.
- (b) nature and the world around me.
- (c) my friendships, my community, or the Church.
- (d) other: _____

3 Which definition of prayer means the most in your life today?
- (a) Prayer is asking God for help or to take care of me.
- (b) Prayer is offering my thoughts and feelings to God.
- (c) Prayer is having a conversation with God.
- (d) other: _____

4 I begin to think of God when
- (a) I'm in trouble or need help.
- (b) everything gets quiet at night.
- (c) I'm spending time with my family or friends.
- (d) other: _____

Scoring:

If your answers were mostly:	you experience God:
a's	as a parent, one who cares for you.
b's	as a powerful and limitless presence.
c's	as a close friend.
d's	in your own specific ways.

Do you experience God in only one way or in more than one of the ways described above?

In this chapter
we explore how we come to know God. Our answer leads us to an understanding of who we are, how we should live, and why our lives have meaning. Through this chapter, we hope

 to understand that God created us to know him, reveals who he is, and gives us the gift of faith

 to accept that Jesus Christ is the fullness of God's Revelation

 to respond to the gift of faith by following Jesus as members of the Church.

As human beings, we have a natural sense of curiosity. We are always asking questions: What's life all about? Why does anything exist? Where did everything come from? Why is it designed the way it is? How did it all get started?

These kinds of questions have led to the development of hundreds of sciences, from anthropology to zoology. Through science, we investigate how, when, and why things have come to be. But science cannot explain everything, nor can it answer all of our questions.

Think of the questions that arise when we experience the overwhelming beauty of creation. Think of the joy that we experience when we feel the love of family and friends. So many of our everyday experiences prompt us to search for a source and a purpose behind everything, including ourselves. And we ask: What is that purpose? Who is that source? To answer these questions, we must move beyond science to faith.

Activity Design a screensaver that shows something in life that helps you to know that there is a source and purpose behind everything that exists. Share your design and explain your choice.

"There is a God-shaped hollow in the human heart that nothing else can fill" is a quote widely attributed to Blaise Pascal (1623–1662), a French mathematician and scientist.

Who needs proof?

Aristotle

Aristotle was a Greek philosopher who lived about five hundred years before the time of Jesus. He developed ways to know that God exists. In the thirteenth century Saint Thomas Aquinas, a Catholic theologian, used Aristotle's work to develop his own "proofs" for God's existence. Here is a summary of these proofs:

1 The world is full of motion—for example, the earth's rotation, the tides of the ocean, the movements of the planets, and so on. But no inanimate thing can move by itself. There must be a "prime mover."

2 Everything in existence must be caused by something. The world and everything in it could not have just happened by chance. There must have been a "first cause."

3 There are many things that could have existed. So much was possible. There must be a "necessary" being who first decided what would exist.

4 Human beings constantly evaluate things as either good or bad, true or false, beautiful or not beautiful, and so on. There must be an "ultimate beauty, goodness, and truth" by whose standards we measure things.

5 There is an amazing design and pattern within creation. For example, think about your eyes as they read this page. How remarkable, complex, and efficient they are! You can say the same about your entire being and everything in creation. Everything has such a detailed design. There must be a "designer."

If you were trying to help someone recognize that God exists, which of these proofs would you use? Which proof do you find most persuasive? Are there any other proofs that you can think of?

God created us to know him.

Our questions about life eventually lead us to recognize that there is a greater presence, one who *transcends*, or goes beyond, everything. This "greater presence" that we sense in life—the one who transcends everything and is the source of it all—is *God*. And the questions that we ask about life are really part of our search for God. But why do we even have these questions? Why *are* we searching for God?

In Scripture we read that God created us
". . . in his image;
    in the divine image" (Genesis 1:27).

And when God created us, he gave us his own breath of life: "The LORD God formed man out of the clay of the ground and blew into his nostrils the breath of life" (Genesis 2:7). In other words, God not only created us—God created us to reflect who he is. We are alive because God gave us his own life. Therefore, to understand ourselves and our lives, we need to know God, who is the source of our whole life and being. So, we are constantly searching for God.

God wants us to search for him. God loves us and wants us to know him. Of course, God is greater than anything we can comprehend or explain and will always remain a mystery to us. But we continue to search for God because we are created by him and for him, and because God will never stop calling us to know him and to love him.

Activity God created us in his image—we reflect who God is. Today, how can you be a reflection of God for other people in your life?

God's Plan Unfolds

God creates the universe.

Humankind is created.

The great flood covers the earth.

God calls Abraham.

OLD TESTAMENT

Moses receives the Law on Mt. Sinai.

God makes himself known.

It is part of our human nature to search for God. According to the *Catechism of the Catholic Church*, "The desire for God is written in the human heart" (*CCC*, 27). Yet God's desire for us is even stronger—God is always searching for *us*. God takes the initiative, reaches out to us, and makes himself known. God's making himself known is called **Divine Revelation**.

God revealed to humanity his great love and unfolded his plan for us. According to biblical accounts, over time God communicated with people, performed powerful deeds, and helped people to know how to live as God's own people. In the beginning God created the first humans and spoke to them. Later, God called a man named Abraham and his wife Sarah and chose to form a special relationship with them and their descendants. God made their descendants his "chosen people." God helped free these chosen people, the Israelites, from their slavery in Egypt. Then, by giving them the Ten Commandments, God revealed how they were to live.

> **"The desire for God is written in the human heart."**
> (*CCC*, 27)

Through these and other events in the Bible, God gradually revealed who he is and how much he loves humankind. And, as we read in Scripture, "In times past, God spoke in partial and various ways to our ancestors through the prophets; in these last days, he spoke to us through a son" (Hebrews 1:1–2). His Son is Jesus Christ. Jesus fulfilled God's plan for humanity.

Jesus died for all humanity and offers to all people **salvation**, the forgiveness of sins and the restoration of humanity's friendship with God. It is through Jesus' words and deeds that we encounter God among us, as one of us. And it is through the power of God the Holy Spirit that Jesus' saving words and deeds continue to be effective for us today. Thus, the one we search for is always here among us. He reaches out to us through Divine Revelation and fully reveals who he is in the words and deeds of his Son, Jesus Christ.

Faith Words
Divine Revelation
salvation

Activity Think of some major events or milestones in your life, from your birth to the present, and list them below. Make a timeline of these events on a separate sheet of paper. Now, looking at each event, think about the ways God has reached out and made himself known to you.

God is worshiped in the Temple.

Jesus redeems humanity.

Pentecost: the Church begins.

The work of Jesus continues.

NEW TESTAMENT

BELIEVING...

God gives us the gift of faith.

Do you think of yourself as "religious"? Why or why not?

Throughout time people have responded to God through worship, prayers, rituals, and other religious practices. Archeological evidence shows that since ancient times almost all peoples have practiced a religion of some kind. In fact, we can say that human beings have a natural tendency to be religious. Our tendency to respond to God through religion is part of God's plan to invite us to live by faith.

Faith is the gift from God that enables us to believe in God, to accept all that he has revealed, and to respond with love for God and others. Faith is certainly a great gift. Without it, we would be lost in uncertainty. We would be overwhelmed by our questions about who we are, how we should live, and what the meaning of our lives is. But faith enables us to go beyond our doubts or concerns about life and to believe that God is always with us.

Faith Word
faith

Faith is even more than believing in Jesus Christ and believing that God exists, however. Faith is a way of life. It involves trusting that God has created us, loves us, cares for us, is merciful toward us, and wants justice for everyone—and it involves sharing love, care, mercy, and justice with others.

Though God gives us this gift of faith, he does not "program" us with faith as if we were computers. Rather, God enables us to choose freely how we are going to respond to him. So, God invites us to live by faith. It is our choice to freely say yes or no to God's invitation.

Activity Think about a time when the gift of faith helped you to get through a period of uncertainty in your life. In the space below, write a short prayer thanking God for his love and care.

Share this prayer with someone who needs God's gift of faith today.

Who are God's people?

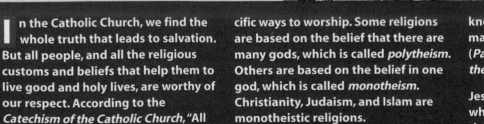

In the Catholic Church, we find the whole truth that leads to salvation. But all people, and all the religious customs and beliefs that help them to live good and holy lives, are worthy of our respect. According to the *Catechism of the Catholic Church*, "All religions bear witness to men's essential search for God" (2566).

Most religions have three features in common: a set of beliefs; values or moral laws; and prayers, rituals, or specific ways to worship. Some religions are based on the belief that there are many gods, which is called *polytheism.* Others are based on the belief in one god, which is called *monotheism.* Christianity, Judaism, and Islam are monotheistic religions.

As Catholics we share the bond of Baptism with other Christians. But we also trust that people of other religions who follow their conscience and live their faith as they know best can be saved by the dying and rising of Jesus Christ. "The Holy Spirit in a manner known only to God offers to every man the possibility" of salvation (*Pastoral Constitution on the Church in the Modern World*, 22).

Jesus wants all of his followers everywhere to be united. Jesus prayed "that they may all be one" (John 17:21). The Catholic Church's effort to create goodwill among Christians everywhere is called the *ecumenical movement.*

What can people of faith around the world do to show more respect for one another? How can you help?

CATHOLIC IDENTITY

16

The Church gives witness to God's presence.

The full revelation of God comes to us through the life of Jesus Christ. Jesus is God the Son, the second Person of the Blessed Trinity, and his entire life was a *yes* in response to God, his Father. In Jesus, "the whole of God's truth has been made manifest" (*CCC*, 2466). Jesus taught, loved, and cared for all people, especially people in need. Jesus showed us how to be loving, merciful, caring, and just. Jesus showed us perfectly how to live by the gift of faith. And Jesus gathered followers, or disciples, who, as a community, worked together to live as Jesus lived.

> In Jesus, "the whole of God's truth has been made manifest" (*CCC*, 2466).

We are Jesus' disciples in the world today. We follow Jesus together as a community—in the Catholic Church. The **Church** is the community of people who believe in Jesus Christ, have been baptized in him, and follow his teachings. Members of the Church support one another in faith, guided by the pope and bishops who govern in Christ's name. We work together to live as Jesus' disciples.

At Baptism we accept the gift of faith from God and become Jesus' disciples. We become part of the Church. At Baptism we also receive another gift from God, the gift of grace. **Grace** is a participation, or a sharing, in God's life and friendship. Grace helps us to respond to God with love. It leads us to want to know God better and to live as God wants us to live. It gives us the strength to live as Jesus' disciples.

Faith Words
Church
grace

It is a great blessing to be baptized into the Catholic Church. Living as followers of Jesus and members of the Church, we can live as the image of God that we were created to be, giving witness to God's presence in the world.

Activity Think of three ways to follow Jesus and live out your discipleship this week.

17

RESPONDING...

Recognizing Our Faith

Recall the question at the beginning of this chapter: *How do I know God is present in my life?* Make up a billboard advertisement that answers this question. Design your billboard in the space above.

Living Our Faith

In this chapter we learned that we were all created in the image of God. Think of one thing that you can do at home, at school, or in your neighborhood to respect the image of God in others.

Partners in FAITH

Saint Paul

The life of Saint Paul gives us an amazing example of recognizing and responding to God's presence. Paul, originally named "Saul," lived in the first century at the time of Jesus. But at first Saul did not have faith in Jesus. In fact, after Jesus' death and Resurrection, Saul did all he could to stop Jesus' followers—even punishing and killing them! But one day Saul was surrounded by a great light. He heard the voice of Jesus telling him to change his ways. Saul responded by being baptized, changing his name to Paul, and traveling extensively to teach others about Christ. Paul founded many communities of Christians, to whom he wrote many *epistles*, or letters, which are found in the Bible. After years of being punished for spreading Christianity, Saint Paul was *martyred*, or killed for his faith. On January 25 the Church celebrates Saint Paul's conversion to Christ, and on June 29 the Church honors him, with Saint Peter, as a founder of the Church.

Saint Paul called Christians to realize the nearness of God in their lives. In what ways can you help people realize that God is present in their lives?

Putting Faith to Work

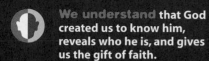
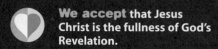

Talk about what you have learned in this chapter:

We **understand** that God created us to know him, reveals who he is, and gives us the gift of faith.

We **accept** that Jesus Christ is the fullness of God's Revelation.

We **respond** to the gift of faith by following Jesus as members of the Church.

Decide on ways to live out what you have learned.

✝ ENCOUNTERING GOD'S WORD

From a burning bush, Moses heard God tell him to help the Israelites to escape their slavery in Egypt. Moses asked for God's name so that he could tell the Israelites who sent him. God replied:

> "I am who am . . . Tell the Israelites: I AM sent me to you. . . . This is my name forever; this is my title for all generations."
>
> (Exodus 3:14, 15)

➡ **READ** the quotation from Scripture.

➡ **REFLECT** on these questions:
If you were Moses at the burning bush, what would God's words mean to you? What about God's sacred name, "I AM"?

➡ **SHARE** your reflections with a partner.

➡ **DECIDE** how you can show that you truly believe that *God is.*

Write the letter of the answer that best defines each term.

1. _____ Divine Revelation

2. _____ faith

3. _____ Church

4. _____ grace

a. a participation, or a sharing, in God's life and friendship

b. God's making himself known

c. the gift from God that enables us to believe in God, to accept all that he has revealed, and to respond with love for God and others

d. the natural tendency to be religious

e. the community of people who believe in Jesus Christ, have been baptized in him, and follow his teachings

Write *True* or *False* next to the following sentences. On a separate sheet of paper, change the false sentences to make them true.

5. _____ God created us to know him.

6. _____ God reaches out to us through the Church and fully reveals who he is in the words and deeds of Abraham.

7. _____ Faith is not a way of life.

8. _____ Grace gives us the strength to live as Jesus' disciples.

9–10. ESSAY: What does Jesus help you to know about God?

RESPONDING...

Sharing Faith with Your Family

Discuss the following with your family:
- God created us to know him.
- God makes himself known.
- God gives us the gift of faith.
- The Church gives witness to God's presence.

Start a family gratitude journal. You can use any type of notebook or journal. You may first want to decorate it together. Then invite family members to write about experiences that remind them of God's presence in their lives. Make time each month to have a family member read something he or she wrote in the journal. Then thank God together in prayer.

The Worship Connection

Look and listen. You are inside your parish church. What are some things that help you to experience God's presence?

More to Explore

Work together on an Internet search for Catholic groups and organizations that show God's presence in the world through their good works. Share your findings.

Catholic Social Teaching ☑ Checklist

Theme of Catholic Social Teaching:
Call to Family, Community, and Participation

How it relates to Chapter 1: As Catholics we are called to participate in public life, working for the good of the community and making God's presence known through our actions.

How can you do this?

☐ At home:

_____

☐ At school/work:

_____

☐ In the parish:

_____

☐ In the community:

_____

Check off each action after it has been completed.

"Your word is truth."
(John 17:17)

✝ **Leader:** Almighty God, we receive so much information in our lives—from books, the Internet, radio, TV, newspapers, magazines, our conversations, and our classes. Help us to distinguish truth from opinion, to sort fact from fiction, to tell right from wrong, and to live by your truth.

All: "Guide me in your truth and teach me, for you are God my savior."
(Psalm 25:5)

Reader 1: "I wait for you, O LORD;
I lift up my soul to my God.
Make known to me your ways, LORD;
teach me your paths."
(Psalm 25:1–2, 4)

All: "Guide me in your truth and teach me, for you are God my savior."
(Psalm 25:5)

Reader 2: "Good and upright is the LORD,
who shows sinners the way,
Guides the humble rightly,
and teaches the humble
the way."
(Psalm 25:8–9)

All: "Guide me in your truth and teach me, for you are God my savior."
(Psalm 25:5)

Leader: May God help us to know and to live by the truth.

All: Amen.

GATHERING...

The BiG QuEStion:

In what ways can I find truth?

Discover whether you can separate fact from fiction by marking each statement below as true or false. Then turn the page upside down to see the answers.

1 McDonald's Filet-O-Fish® Sandwich was developed in 1962 to draw Catholics to the popular hamburger restaurant on Fridays when they could not eat meat.

2 The Bible is the best-selling book of all time.

3 Early Christian burial sites were called *catacombs* because the deceased were buried with their pet cats and their favorite hairbrushes.

4 The United States has the most Catholics of any country in the world.

5 Popes originally began wearing pointy hats to keep their heads warm during the winter.

Answers:

1. True. Louis Groen, who owned several McDonald's restaurants in Cincinnati, Ohio, came up with the idea for the sandwich to prevent losing Catholic customers on Fridays.

2. True. Every day an average of forty-seven Bibles are given out or sold around the world. That is an average of 1,410 Bibles per month and 17,155 Bibles per year!

3. False. The word *catacomb* comes from the Greek words *kata kumbas*, which mean "near the low place." Early Christian graves were located in the low place between two hills outside Rome.

4. False. Brazil is the country with the most Catholics in the world, Mexico is second, and the United States is third.

5. True. Small pointy hats were fashionable at the time, and popes began wearing them to keep their heads warm in the winter. Years later the hats were designed to be pointier and were worn for ceremonial purposes.

Discuss things that you have heard about history, society, politics, or life in general that you suspect might not be true. Share with one another why you think this information might be false. Suggest ways to find out what's true.

In this chapter we learn that we find the truth in Scripture and Tradition. Through this chapter, we hope

 to understand that God reveals the truth, his Divine Revelation, to us through Scripture and Tradition

 to trust that Scripture and Tradition can guide us in knowing how to live

 to listen to God's word in Scripture and follow the guidance of Tradition.

Discovering the truth can be a powerful experience. It can help us to make important decisions. It can help us to determine what to believe, what to remember, and how to live. But how do we discover the truth? Out of everything we read, see, and hear, how do we know what's true and what's simply a rumor, an opinion, or downright false?

Activity In the puzzle find and circle ten things that people might consult for the truth. (Some may be found backwards or diagonally.) List the ten items on the lines.

When you finish the puzzle, think of some other sources of truth, and write them on the lines provided. With your group discuss the reliability of each listed item as a source of truth.

```
V T F E Q G E M T E Y T R N A
F F E N T C X E N N Z S E M T
X R I N N X E A C Y W A V Y
Y W I E R T U T L Y S B X S G
R A I E B E L G B C Y I Q R C
O C P O N K T V P L C B M E B
S Z O E T D V N A O I L X H A
P K C D X S S Y I P H E R C C
S P A R E N T S Y E D S F A Z
C U L F X L Q N S D X P Q E N
C G D S V U W T G I B P L T X
G W E B E N U O I A A J Z F I
X E L M C R S O S Y C I Y Q R
N O I G I L E R O M P N F F N
S B S I U L P O M M M C K H V
```

1. _____

2. _____

3. _____

4. _____

5. _____

6. _____

7. _____

8. _____

9. _____

10. _____

Other: _____

Other: _____

BIBLE, ENCYCLOPEDIA, FRIENDS, INTERNET, NEWS, PARENTS, RELIGION, SCIENCE, TEACHERS, TEXTBOOKS

66 The spirit of truth and the spirit of freedom—they are the pillars of society,99 wrote Henrik Ibsen (1828–1906), Norwegian playwright.

The truth that matters most

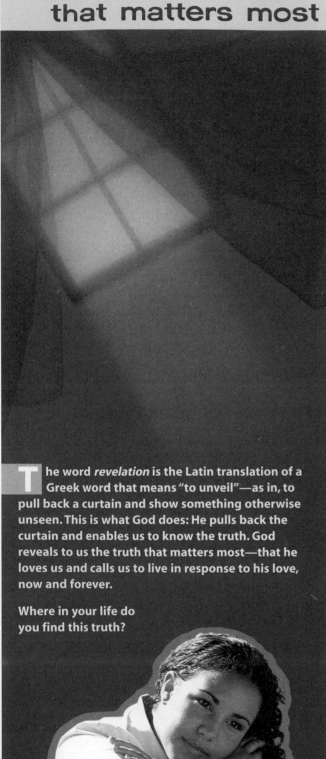

The word *revelation* is the Latin translation of a Greek word that means "to unveil"—as in, to pull back a curtain and show something otherwise unseen. This is what God does: He pulls back the curtain and enables us to know the truth. God reveals to us the truth that matters most—that he loves us and calls us to live in response to his love, now and forever.

Where in your life do you find this truth?

Scripture and Tradition reveal the truth.

Throughout our lives God makes himself known, revealing the truth of how much he loves us and of how we can respond to his love. God reveals the truth, his Divine Revelation, through Scripture and Tradition.

Scripture, also referred to as Sacred Scripture or the Bible, is the written account of God's Revelation and his relationship with his people. It is God's word, written by human authors under the inspiration of the Holy Spirit. The special guidance that the Holy Spirit gave to the human authors of the Bible is called **divine inspiration**. It guarantees that the Bible contains God's saving truth without error.

Tradition is the Revelation of the good news of Jesus Christ as lived out in the Church, past and present. Tradition, therefore, includes the teachings and practices handed on from the time of Jesus through his Apostles to the whole Church. Tradition consists of all that the Church has learned with the guidance of the Holy Spirit, including her teachings, her documents, and her worship, prayer, and other practices. Tradition is the source of the Church's ongoing understanding of the meaning of Revelation and the ways to apply it to our lives.

> **Faith Words**
> Scripture
> divine inspiration
> Tradition

So, God's truth is communicated through both the written word of Scripture and the living message of Tradition. Together Scripture and Tradition are like a fountain of truth pouring into our lives. As Catholics, we accept and honor both. They are both inspired by the Holy Spirit and are both essential for teaching us how to live as God's people.

Activity God reveals the truth to us through Scripture and Tradition. With your group compose a prayer thanking God for his Divine Revelation. This week pray this prayer with family and friends.

The truth is written in Scripture.

Throughout history God has made himself known to people and revealed the truth to them. What God revealed to human beings eventually came to be shared with all people, for all time, in the writings of the Bible. The Bible is a collection of 73 books written over a span of almost 2,000 years. (For a complete listing of the books of the Bible, see "Bible Basics" on pages 310 and 311.)

> Catholics are and have always been "nourished and ruled by sacred Scripture"
> (*Dogmatic Constitution on Divine Revelation*, 21).

The development of the Bible began with the ancient Israelites, also known as the people of Israel or the Hebrews. They were God's people and our ancestors in faith. When God made himself known to them, they shared their faith in God with one another. By word of mouth they told stories about their experiences of God and about living as God's specially chosen people. For a long time they shared their faith with their descendants in this manner. In time the Holy Spirit inspired some of them to put their experiences in writing. Later, people would meet to study these inspired writings in **synagogues**, gathering places for studying Scripture. These writings are preserved in the Bible, in the Old Testament.

The New Testament developed in a similar way—from religious experience to word of mouth to inspired writing. Jesus' Apostles heard what Jesus preached, saw his miracles and healings, and witnessed his death and **Resurrection**, his rising from death to new life. Strengthened by the Holy Spirit,

they went forth and taught about Jesus. They proclaimed that Jesus Christ was the Son of God, our Lord and Savior. They gathered followers to live as Jesus' disciples. Communities of Christians were formed, and these communities continued to tell others about Jesus. Certain disciples, such as Saint Paul, wrote **epistles**, letters found in the New Testament to the early Christian communities about God's Revelation in Jesus Christ. And, as people who knew Jesus firsthand began to die, the **Gospels**, the accounts of God's Revelation through Jesus Christ, were written. The Gospels and the epistles, along with the Acts of the Apostles and the Book of Revelation, make up the New Testament.

Though we don't know the identity of every Old Testament and New Testament writer, we believe that the Holy Spirit guided each one to write the truth that God wanted to communicate to the world. For this reason Scripture helps us to find the truth that we need for life. As Catholics, we are and have always been "nourished and ruled by sacred Scripture" (*Dogmatic Constitution on Divine Revelation*, 21).

Faith Words

synagogues
epistles
Gospels
Resurrection

Activity Name your favorite story or passage from the Bible. Discuss the truth that God reveals through it. What other truths does God reveal in your life?

More about the Bible

The Bible is the word of God. As Catholics, we believe that God, working through human authors, is the Bible's true author. However, this does not mean that we believe God actually dictated the words of the Bible or personally wrote them down. Rather, the Bible was written by inspired human beings. They communicated God's truth using the language and expressions of their times. They also used symbolism and other storytelling devices. Therefore, we cannot interpret their writings literally, as if the Bible is an exact, scientific record of things. Instead, the Bible is meant to teach us not scientific facts but the great truths of our faith. The Bible's account of creation, for example, expresses the great truth that God created everything and made human beings in his image.

Do you know any other truths that you learn from the creation story? Reread it (Genesis 1:1—2:4 and Genesis 2:5–25) and discuss the possibilities!

CATHOLIC IDENTITY

25

The truth is handed down in Tradition.

What are some things that are handed down in your family?

Imagine that you've received a letter from a distant relative. You've heard this relative's name mentioned in family conversations, but you don't really know him or her. Nevertheless, you open the letter and begin to read it. You find that you don't understand all of it because it refers to people in your family that you've never heard about—or moments in your family history you've never known about. So you bring the letter to an older family member who gives you the background you need to understand the letter. Gradually, the meaning of the letter becomes clear.

Well, Scripture is like that letter, and Tradition is like the personal message that helped you to understand the meaning of the letter. No written record, not even Scripture, can pass from generation to generation and capture all that it means to live as a disciple of Jesus. Even the Gospel of John states, "There are also many other things that Jesus did, but if these were to be described individually, I do not think the whole world would contain the books that would be written" (John 21:25). Scripture cannot stand alone; it needs Tradition to shed light on its meaning, and the Church needs both Scripture and Tradition to understand and live the truth.

Tradition actually existed before the writing of the New Testament and helped in its formation. When the early Christians handed on what they had learned from Jesus' Apostles, they were handing on Tradition. And it has been handed down to the present day and continues to lead us to the truth.

Through Tradition we constantly learn the truth about ways to live as Jesus' disciples. Tradition is an essential part of our lives as Catholics and a treasure of truth on which the Church continually relies.

Activity There are many ways the truth is made known to us within Tradition. In the chart below, the parts of Tradition are shown in the first column. Fill in the second column by writing examples for these parts of Tradition. Some examples are provided.

PARTS OF TRADITION	EXAMPLES
The teachings, customs, and practices handed down from Jesus through the Apostles, whether by word of mouth or in writing	Baptism
The creeds, the statements of the beliefs that we profess as Catholics	
The teachings of the pope with the bishops of the Church, through their gatherings at councils and through their documents and other communications	Second Vatican Council (1962–1965)
The teachings of the Church Fathers, scholars who helped to explain and hand on the Christian message during the first centuries of the Church	The writings of Saint Ignatius, bishop of Antioch, Syria, during the first century A.D.
The life and experience of the Church as she gathers together to worship God, celebrating the sacraments and listening to God's word	

How would you explain God's Revelation through Tradition to a younger Catholic?

The Church lives by the truth.

Scripture and Tradition are "one sacred deposit of the word of God" and flow "from the same divine wellspring" (*Dogmatic Constitution on Divine Revelation*, 10, 9). Together they make up the deposit of faith. The **deposit of faith** is all the truth contained in Scripture and Tradition that Christ revealed and entrusted to the Apostles and thus to their successors, the bishops, and to the entire Church. The deposit of faith helps the Church to always live by the truth.

The Church grows in knowledge of the truth as a community—when gathered for worship, when hearing God's word in Scripture, when praying together. It is within our community of faith, the Church, that we truly discover the truth. And to guide us in understanding the truth, we depend on the **Magisterium**, the living teaching office of the Church, consisting of the pope and the bishops. In Jesus' name and with the help of the Holy Spirit, the Magisterium interprets both Scripture and Tradition. The Magisterium teaches us how to apply the message of Scripture and Tradition to our lives today.

Through letters, statements, and documents for the whole Church, the Magisterium continually teaches us about the truth. And when the Church encounters new circumstances, questions, and issues, the Holy Spirit guides the Magisterium and the whole Church to develop her understanding of Divine Revelation in Scripture and Tradition. It is said that Scripture, Tradition, and the Church "are so linked and joined together that one cannot stand without the others" (*Dogmatic Constitution on Divine Revelation*, 10).

So, in each generation, the whole Church continues to share and build upon the faith of the Apostles, believe and live the faith, and pass the faith on to the next generation. In this way the Church's faith is always developing, and God's Revelation is living and active in the Church. And the Church hands on to the world all the truth that has been received through God's Revelation.

Faith Words

deposit of faith
Magisterium

> Scripture and Tradition are "one sacred deposit of the word of God" and flow "from the same divine wellspring"
>
> (*Dogmatic Constitution on Divine Revelation*, 10, 9).

A meeting of the United States Conference of Catholic Bishops

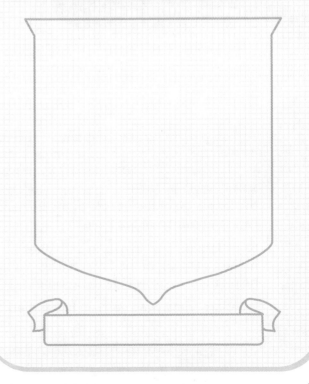

Activity Scripture and Tradition are an essential part of your heritage as a Catholic. Make an emblem or a crest that stands for your family's heritage. Be sure to include symbols for both Scripture and Tradition. How will your family crest remind you and your family to live out the truths of your faith?

RESPONDING...

Time Capsule

Recognizing Our Faith

Recall the question at the beginning of this chapter: *In what ways can I find truth?* Imagine that you are putting together a time capsule that will show future generations how to find truth. List some things that you would put inside the time capsule.

Living Our Faith

Find a Scripture quote or a Catholic prayer that deals with some aspects of truth. By your actions this week, try to be faithful to its meaning.

Partners in FAITH

Saint Jerome

Saint Jerome is the patron saint of Scripture scholars. He was born in approximately A.D. 347 in the Roman province of Dalmatia. When he grew up he traveled to Rome to study literature. In Rome he became a Christian and was baptized. He began to study *theology*, the study of God and God's relation to the world, and to think about ways to live his faith. Seeking a way to get closer to God, he moved to a desert near Antioch to live the life of a hermit. In the quiet of the desert, Jerome worked on a series of religious writings. His greatest work was his translation of the Bible into Latin. Latin was the language of the people of the Roman Empire. Jerome's work is still the Church's official Latin translation of the Bible.

Saint Jerome died in 419, in Bethlehem. In addition to being declared a saint, Jerome was named a Doctor of the Church. This is a special honor given to holy people whose writings help others to grow in faith. Jerome's feast day is September 30.

What are some ways you can help others to grow in faith?

 For additional ideas and activities, visit www.weliveourfaith.com.

Putting Faith to Work

Talk about what you have learned in this chapter:

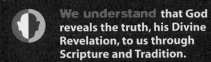 **We understand** that God reveals the truth, his Divine Revelation, to us through Scripture and Tradition.

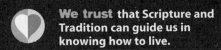 **We trust** that Scripture and Tradition can guide us in knowing how to live.

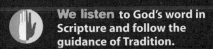 **We listen** to God's word in Scripture and follow the guidance of Tradition.

Decide on ways to live out what you have learned.

✝ENCOUNTERING GOD'S WORD

❝Do not take the word of truth from my mouth,
for in your edicts is my hope.
I will keep your teachings always,
for all time and forever.❞

(Psalm 119:43–44)

➡ **READ** the quotation from Scripture.

➡ **REFLECT** on these questions:
What might "take the word of truth" from you? How can you keep close to the truth "for all time and forever"?

➡ **SHARE** your reflections with a partner.

➡ **DECIDE** to do all that you can to live by the truth.

Circle the letter of the correct answer.

1. _____ is the written account of God's Revelation and his relationship with his people.

   a. Tradition   **b.** Scripture   **c.** Divine Revelation   **d.** Divine inspiration

2. The special guidance that the Holy Spirit gave to the human authors of the Bible is called _____.

   a. the New Testament   **b.** the Old Testament   **c.** divine inspiration   **d.** Divine Revelation

3. _____ is the Revelation of the good news of Jesus Christ as lived out in the Church, past and present.

   a. Tradition   **b.** Scripture   **c.** The deposit of faith   **d.** Divine inspiration

4. The _____ is the living teaching office of the Church, consisting of the pope and bishops.

   a. synagogue   **b.** deposit of faith   **c.** Bible   **d.** Magisterium

Short Answers

5. What is an epistle? _____

6. What are the Gospels? _____

7. There are many ways the truth is made known to us within Tradition. List three examples.

   _____

8. What is the deposit of faith? _____

9–10. ESSAY: How does God reveal the truth, his Divine Revelation?

RESPONDING...

Sharing Faith with Your Family

Discuss the following with your family:

- Scripture and Tradition reveal the truth.
- The truth is written in Scripture.
- The truth is handed down in Tradition.
- The Church lives by the truth.

With your family, designate an area in your home as a family prayer space. Place the following items in the prayer space: a Bible, a crucifix, and pictures or icons of Jesus and favorite saints. You might also include prayer cards and a prayer intention jar. Encourage your family to carry on a tradition of praying together in your prayer space. Make readings from Scripture a part of your family prayer, especially the readings that are proclaimed at Mass.

The Worship Connection

Look around your church for images depicting stories from the Bible. After Mass talk about these images as well as the Scripture readings that were proclaimed.

More to Explore

Find some examples of ways that technology is being used for sharing the truths of the Bible today. Share your findings with your group.

Catholic Social Teaching ☑ Checklist

Theme of Catholic Social Teaching:
Option for the Poor and Vulnerable

How it relates to Chapter 2: Scripture, Tradition, and the Magisterium of the Church call upon us to care for those who are poor and in need.

How can you do this?

☐ At home:

_____

☐ At school/work:

_____

☐ In the parish:

_____

☐ In the community:

_____

Check off each action after it has been completed.

3
The Blessed Trinity

"The grace of the Lord Jesus Christ and the love of God and the fellowship of the holy Spirit be with all of you."

(2 Corinthians 13:13)

✛ **Leader:** Almighty God, you reveal yourself as one God in three Divine Persons. In your loving relationship of Father, Son, and Holy Spirit, be with us as we explore the mystery of who you are—the mystery of the Blessed Trinity.

All: The Mighty Three
my protection be,
encircling me.
Come and be
around my land, my home,
encircling me,
O Sacred Three.

Leader: Praise to the Father,

All: praise to the Son,

Leader: praise to the Spirit,

All: Trinity blessed.

Leader: Praise the Almighty,

All: Three ever One. Amen.

(traditional Celtic prayers)

Visit www.weliveourfaith.com to find appropriate music and songs.

The BiG QuEStion:
Why do relationships matter to me?

iscover the ingredients of a good relationship with friends or family. Use each letter of the word *relationship* to list the elements of a good friendship or family relationship. One example is provided.

R
E
L
A
T
I
Openness
N
S
H
I
P

Choose one of these elements and discuss ways to make it part of one or more of your relationships.

In this chapter we review the Catholic belief in the Blessed Trinity. Through this chapter, we hope

 to learn that that the Blessed Trinity is the mystery of the loving relationship of one God in three Divine Persons: Father, Son, and Holy Spirit

 to appreciate that our faith in the Trinity calls us to loving relationships with God and one another

to live our faith in the Trinity through loving relationships.

One hundred years from now, it won't matter
how you did on a test
Or how popular you were.
No one will care about how many hits you got in a
baseball game.
It won't matter if you miss a day of school
Or what you got for your eleventh birthday.
Your highest score on a computer game won't be
remembered
Or if your family had a swimming pool.
No one will care who came in first in that one race.
It won't matter if your handwriting was messy
Or if all your artwork wasn't the best.

But, if you made life a little better
for just one other person

That's what will be remembered.
That's what will matter.

(Sydney Miller, age twelve)

What message about relationships
does this poem express?

Activity What message about relationships would you like to tell others? Write your
own poem, short story, or skit that conveys
this message.

"I have friends to find and so many
things to learn," wrote Antoine de
Saint-Exupéry (1900–1944), in
the book, *The Little Prince*.

God is Father, Son, and Holy Spirit—the Blessed Trinity.

The Blessed Trinity is the central mystery of our Catholic faith. The **Blessed Trinity** is the three Divine Persons in one God: God the Father, God the Son, and God the Holy Spirit.

Reading about Jesus in the Gospels helps us to understand the mystery of the Blessed Trinity. In the Gospels, Jesus Christ makes it clear that he is the only *Son* of the *Father*, whom the Father sent to save the world, through the power of the *Holy Spirit*. The Gospels clearly reveal that:

Faith Word

Blessed Trinity

God the Son became man and lived among us in the person of Jesus Christ.

When Jesus was baptized by John the Baptist, "heaven was opened and the holy Spirit descended upon him in bodily form like a dove. And a voice came from heaven, 'You are my beloved Son; with you I am well pleased'" (Luke 3:21–22).

God the Father, our creator, was at work in everything Jesus said and did.

Jesus raised his friend Lazarus from the dead, praying, "Father, I thank you for hearing me. I know that you always hear me" (John 11:41–42).

God the Holy Spirit empowered Jesus to teach and to share God's love.

"Jesus returned to Galilee in the power of the Spirit, and news of him spread throughout the whole region. He taught in their synagogues and was praised by all." (Luke 4:14–15)

But how can God be *one* God and *three* Divine Persons at the same time? And how can God be a relationship of Father, Son, and Holy Spirit? As human beings we are unable to fully understand or express how this is possible. It is a mystery of our faith, a truth of our faith that we know only because God has revealed it to us.

Believing in this revealed truth of the Blessed Trinity also means recognizing God's love for us: "God's very being is love. By sending his only Son and the

Spirit of Love in the fullness of time, God has revealed his innermost secret: God himself is an eternal exchange of love, Father, Son, and Holy Spirit, and he has destined us to share in that exchange" (*CCC*, 221). This loving relationship of Father, Son, and Holy Spirit is perfect unity, and what God desires for us is to reflect the same unity through truthful and loving relationships with others.

Activity Work with your group to make a large poster encouraging people around the world to live in the unity and love that God desires for us. Jot down some ideas for your poster here. Share them with your group before you begin your work. Discuss ways that you can put these ideas to work in your own life.

The mystery of the Blessed Trinity is central to our faith.

All of our beliefs as Catholics revolve around the mystery of the Blessed Trinity because it is the mystery of *who God is*. The truth of the Blessed Trinity reveals the very nature of God and thus the way that we are called by God to live. The truth of the Blessed Trinity sheds light on all of our beliefs and guides us in all areas of our lives. The whole life of the Church revolves around our belief in the Blessed Trinity:

> **"By sending his only Son and the Spirit of Love in the fullness of time, God has revealed his innermost secret: God himself is an eternal exchange of love, Father, Son, and Holy Spirit."**
>
> (*CCC*, 221)

- In the Sign of the Cross, we pray, "In the name of the Father, and of the Son, and of the Holy Spirit."

- We conclude our prayers with "We ask this through our Lord Jesus Christ, your Son, who lives and reigns with you and the Holy Spirit, one God for ever and ever."

- We pray: "Glory to the Father, and to the Son, and to the Holy Spirit: as it was in the beginning, is now, and will be for ever."

The words *Father*, *Son*, and *Holy Spirit* express the relationship between the three Divine Persons of God and are essential to our relationship with God. We are baptized "in the name of the Father, and of the Son, and of the Holy Spirit" (Rite of Baptism). And just as the Father, Son, and Holy Spirit are one, all who are baptized become one with God and one another.

The grace that we receive, a sharing in God's life, unites us to the Blessed Trinity and to all the other believers who share in God's life, too. Thus, the Church, the community of faith, is one with the Blessed Trinity and one with all of her members.

God continues to be with us and is active in our lives as Father, Son, and Holy Spirit through the grace of all the sacraments that we receive. And in our prayer and liturgy—especially in the Mass—we become one with the Father, Son, and Holy Spirit, and our unity with one another is strengthened.

Activity Write your own prayer praising God—the Father, the Son, and the Holy Spirit. Share your prayers with one another.

The Trinity and the Sign of the Cross

In the second century A.D., Christians traced a small cross over their foreheads with their thumbs before prayers, during the Sacrament of Baptism, at times of temptation, or at the beginning of each day. This was a way to acknowledge Jesus' presence and ask for his protection. Over the centuries, Christians began to trace a larger cross over themselves—from forehead to chest, and then from shoulder to shoulder.

Sometime after the fourth century, the words *In the name of the Father, and of the Son, and of the Holy Spirit* were added to the gesture. Since belief in the Trinity had been widely misunderstood in the fourth century, the words may have been a way to acknowledge faith in the Church's teachings about the Trinity.

Today, as Catholics, we pray the Sign of the Cross when we begin and end our prayers, bless ourselves with holy water, or ask for God's blessing. Tracing a small cross is still part of the Sacrament of Baptism as it was in early Christian times. It is also part of Confirmation, Anointing of the Sick, and Holy Orders. In these sacraments, a small cross is traced on the forehead or on the hands.

Find time today to ask for God's blessing by praying the Sign of the Cross.

World Youth Day, 2002

God calls us to live our faith through loving relationships.

How can you share God's love with others?

God has demonstrated his love through the Blessed Trinity by sending his Son to be the Savior of the world and by giving us the Holy Spirit. And God, who reveals himself as the loving relationship of Father, Son, and Holy Spirit, created us in his image. So, made in his image, we are meant for loving relationships. We are meant to love God and to experience God's love for us. And we are also meant to love ourselves and one another, too.

Jesus himself called us to this love when he gave us the Great Commandment: "You shall love the Lord, your God, with all your heart, with all your soul, and with all your mind. . . . You shall love your neighbor as yourself" (Matthew 22:37, 39). Jesus even taught that we must love the very people who are difficult to *like*. He said, "Love your enemies, do good to those who hate you, bless those who curse you, pray for those who mistreat you" (Luke 6:27–28). As Jesus' disciples, we are called

to loving relationships with everyone—at home, at school, in the parish, in the neighborhood, in the nation, in the world. This is how we live our faith in God, the Blessed Trinity of loving relationships.

Activity Name ways to help your relationships with friends and family become more reflective of God's love. Make these ways part of your personal life-plan by implementing them today and in the future.

God calls us to share his love with the world.

Did you know that at the moment you were baptized in the name of the Blessed Trinity, you were changed forever? You were set apart to carry on a mission—Jesus' mission of sharing God's love and salvation with the world. You were given the power to carry on the mission of evangelization. **Evangelization** is the sharing of the good news of Jesus Christ and the love of God with all people, in every circumstance of life. And that mission is the mission of the whole Church.

> "Love your enemies, do good to those who hate you, bless those who curse you, pray for those who mistreat you."
>
> (Luke 6:27–28)

Evangelization takes place in our daily lives. It is bringing our faith to the world and the world to our faith. We evangelize when we:

- speak and act in ways that reflect God's love
- tell others about the wonderful things that Christ has done
- show, through our words and actions, what it means to be a disciple of Jesus Christ
- share our faith with those who have not yet heard the message of Jesus Christ
- encourage others who already believe in Jesus Christ to continue to grow in their faith.

Evangelization is so important that recent popes have spoken about it to the whole Church in letters and in other documents. In 1975 Pope Paul VI wrote that the Church actually *exists* to evangelize. However, evangelization does not happen automatically. To evangelize, we must know our faith and the teachings of the Church. But beyond that, evangelization is sincerely believing and practicing the faith we want to share. It is being a living example of God's love for everyone we meet. The Church's mission of evangelization calls us into a loving relationship with the whole world.

Faith Word

evangelization

What are icons?

The painting shown here is called an *icon*. An icon is a special kind of Christian religious painting. It has a sacred purpose—to express the beauty of the mystery of God and all that he has revealed. It invites us into prayer and reflection.

Artists who paint icons follow a set of rules about the colors, the materials, and the style of painting that they can use. Parts of icons are painted with a very thin covering of gold. Most often, icons depict Jesus, Mary, or other saints and holy people. The icon here is known as *The Icon of the Trinity*. Painted by Andrei Rublev in 1410, it shows three angels, representing three visitors who came to Abraham in Genesis 18:1–15. But the painting also has greater meaning for Christians as an icon representing the three Persons of the Blessed Trinity.

If you were painting an icon, how would you represent the Blessed Trinity? Explain the reasons for your choice.

Activity At each stage of life we are called to evangelize. How can people in each of these age groups share with others the good news of Jesus Christ and the love of God?

Stages of Life	Ways to Be Evangelizers
children	
teens	
young adults	
adults	
seniors	

How will you try to evangelize this week?

Recognizing Our Faith

Recall the question at the beginning of this chapter: *Why do relationships matter to me?* Give three reasons why relationships matter, based on what you learned in this chapter.

1.

2.

3.

Living Our Faith

Think of one thing that you can do in your daily life to live your faith in the Blessed Trinity through loving relationships. Then act on it.

Partners in FAITH

Blessed Julian of Norwich

"Suddenly the Trinity filled my heart full of the greatest joy. . . . For the Trinity is God, God is the Trinity. The Trinity is our maker, the Trinity is our protector . . . the Trinity is our endless joy and our bliss." A woman we know as Julian of Norwich, who lived in England during the late fourteenth century, wrote these words after an illness during which she experienced visions about the love of God. After recovering, she became an *anchoress*, a woman who lived in prayer and seclusion, usually in a small shelter, or cell, at a church. She took her name from the church in Norwich, England, where she lived—St. Julian's. She was devoted to daily prayer and meditation, and many people visited her cell to seek her advice, which combined spiritual insight with common sense.

Julian is probably the first woman to write a book in English. Her *Revelations of Divine Love*, about her visions, continues to help people grow in faith and love. The Church celebrates the life of Blessed Julian of Norwich on May 13.

Blessed Julian of Norwich invites us to rejoice in the love of the Blessed Trinity. How can you celebrate this love today?

Putting Faith to Work

Talk about what you have learned in this chapter:

 We learned that the Blessed Trinity is the mystery of the loving relationship of one God in three Divine Persons: Father, Son, and Holy Spirit.

 We appreciate that our faith in the Trinity calls us to loving relationships with God and one another.

 We live our faith in the Trinity through loving relationships.

Decide on ways to live out what you have learned.

✝ ENCOUNTERING GOD'S WORD

"The Spirit itself bears witness with our spirit that we are children of God, and if children, then heirs, heirs of God and joint heirs with Christ."

(Romans 8:16–17)

➡ **READ** the quotation from Scripture.

➡ **REFLECT** on the following:
What do you think you inherit from God as an heir of God and a joint heir with Christ? Pray for the Holy Spirit's help in answering this question.

➡ **SHARE** your reflections with a partner.

➡ **DECIDE** how you can open yourself to the Spirit, live as a child of God, and follow the example of Jesus Christ.

Complete the following.

1. The Blessed Trinity is the three _____.

2. Evangelization is the sharing of _____.

3. All of our beliefs as Catholics revolve around _____.

4. God calls us to live our faith _____.

Underline the correct answer.

5. (**God the Father/God the Son/God the Holy Spirit**) became man and lived among us in the person of Jesus Christ.

6. (**God the Father/God the Son/God the Holy Spirit**) empowered Jesus to teach and share God's love.

7. (**God the Father/God the Son/God the Holy Spirit**), our creator, was at work in everything Jesus said and did.

8. The (**New Commandment/Great Commandment/Blessed Trinity**) is "You shall love the Lord, your God, with all your heart, with all your soul, and with all your mind. . . . You shall love your neighbor as yourself" (Matthew 22:37, 39).

9–10. ESSAY: In what ways is the mystery of the Blessed Trinity central to our faith?

Sharing Faith with Your Family

Discuss the following with your family:

- God is Father, Son, and Holy Spirit—the Blessed Trinity.
- The mystery of the Blessed Trinity is central to our faith.
- God calls us to live our faith through loving relationships.
- God calls us to share his love with the world.

Work on strengthening the loving relationships within your family. Plan a weekly family night or a special activity with a parent.

The Worship Connection

At Mass this weekend, every time you make the sign of the cross, ask God to bless not only yourself but someone you know.

More to Explore

Search the Internet or other resources for examples of the Blessed Trinity represented in art. Share your findings.

Catholic Social Teaching ☑ Checklist

Theme of Catholic Social Teaching:
Solidarity of the Human Family

How it relates to Chapter 3: Solidarity is the unity that binds all people together as one human family. As Catholics, we are called to foster loving relationships with all people.

How can you do this?

☐ At home:

_____

☐ At school/work:

_____

☐ In the parish:

_____

☐ In the community:

_____

Check off each action after it has been completed.

GATHERING...

God, Our Loving Father

"**The LORD is gracious and merciful,
slow to anger and abounding in love.**"
(Psalm 145:8)

Leader: God, our Father, you are merciful and loving to all people, in every generation.

Reader: A reading from the Book of Psalms

"Lord, you have been our refuge
through all generations.
Before the mountains were born,
the earth and the world brought forth,
from eternity to eternity you are God.
Fill us at daybreak with your love,
that all our days we may sing for joy."
(Psalm 90:1–2, 14)

Leader: Father, with joy, we praise you for your love:
From the rising of the sun until its setting,

All: Praised and glorified be the name of God.

Leader: From the south to the north,

All: Praised and glorified be the name of God.

Leader: From the north to the south,

All: Praised and glorified be the name of God.

Leader: From one side to the other,

All: Praised and glorified be the name of God.

Leader: From dawn until evening,

All: Praised and glorified be the name of God.

Leader: From night until day,

All: Praised and glorified be the name of God.

Leader: From noon until noon,

All: Praised and glorified be the name of God. (from a Jewish prayer of praise)

Leader: Amen.

All: Amen.

 Visit www.weliveourfaith.com to find appropriate music and songs.

41

The BiG QUESTION:

How do I know God loves me?

iscover whether you can guess which of the following quotations about God come from the Bible. To determine whether or not you were right, turn the page upside down to see the source of each quotation.

1 "God loves each of us as if there were only one of us."

2 "To love another person is to see the face of God."

3 "All things are possible for God."

4 "I know God will not give me anything I can't handle. I just wish that he didn't trust me so much."

5 "God loves a cheerful giver."

6 "God heals and the doctor takes the fee."

7 "No God, know fear. Know God, no fear."

8 "God is love."

Answers:

1. widely attributed to Saint Augustine (A.D. 354–430) 2. *Les Misérables*, the musical based on the novel by French writer Victor Hugo (1802–1885) 3. The Bible (Jesus in Mark 10:27) 4. widely attributed to Blessed Teresa of Calcutta (1910–1997) 5. The Bible (Saint Paul in 2 Corinthians 9:7) 6. *Poor Richard's Almanac* 7. Anonymous 8. The Bible (1 John 4:8)

In the space below write your own quotation about God. Cut it out, and exchange quotations with your group. Discuss the meaning of each quotation.

In this chapter we consider the deep love that God has for all people. Through this chapter, we hope

 to understand that God has shown his love for humankind throughout the ages

 to appreciate God's love for all of us

 to respond to God's love by following Jesus.

Think about your day. Perhaps it went something like this: The alarm clock sounded or a family member woke you up. You dragged yourself out of bed. You got ready. You grabbed your books, rushed out of the house, went to school, saw your friends, took notes, had lunch, took quizzes, attended club meetings or team practice, went home, did homework, helped with chores . . . and probably much more.

Now "rewind," playing back your day again. This time, see if you can remember your feelings as you went through your day. Try to remember moments when you felt that you were cared about or loved. Remember times when *you* cared about someone else. Recall times when you felt appreciation for something in your life or concern about someone or something in your life. Though you may not have realized it, you were sharing and experiencing love in various ways throughout your day.

"Service . . . is love in action," said Sarah Patton Boyle (1906–1994), U.S. civil rights activist and author.

Activity In the electronic planner, list some things that you may experience tomorrow that might remind you that you are loved. For example, someone might help you with your homework. Try to be aware of your experiences as you go through your day tomorrow.

43

God loves all he has created.

Though you may not always realize it, you share and experience God's love throughout each day. Whether you are in the cafeteria at school, at home doing homework, out with your friends . . . or even if you're having a bad day, God's love is always present.

God's love for human beings is everlasting. It is behind all that God has done, beginning with his creation of life itself. The two accounts of creation that are found in the Old Testament show life as a gift that God gives us out of great love. They reveal that God is our creator who loves us and has a plan for us.

The first account of creation, Genesis 1:1—2:4, opens with these words:

"In the beginning, when God created the heavens and the earth, the earth was a formless wasteland, and darkness covered the abyss, while a mighty wind swept over the waters.

"Then God said, 'Let there be light,' and there was light" (Genesis 1:1–3).

In other words, God created the universe by his own power, out of nothing. In this story God simply says, "Let there be . . . ," and every part of creation comes into being: light, sun, moon, stars, sky, water, earth, sea, fish, plants, animals, and finally human beings, who are made in the image and likeness of God. And God looks at all that he has made and sees that it is good.

In the second account of creation, Genesis 2:5–25, God creates human beings first and makes them his partners in caring for creation. They are to enjoy and develop what God created, take good care of it, and, by doing so, reflect the love that God has for the world he created.

These two accounts of creation in the Old Testament really have the same message: God loves all that he has created, and humanity is the peak of his creation. Though each of these accounts is unique, both of them help us to recognize that God is our loving creator who has a plan for all that he has created.

Michelangelo's ceiling painting in the Sistine Chapel in Italy

Activity Michelangelo was the greatest artist of his time (1475–1564). But when the pope asked him to paint God during the act of creation for the ceiling of the Sistine Chapel in Italy, Michelangelo tried to avoid it. He feared he would fail. Yet the result of his four years of hard labor, working by candlelight on a wooden scaffold, is a great masterpiece that thousands of people come to see each year.

Michelangelo's work of art is shown above. Explain how your image of creation would be similar or different.

God invites us into a loving relationship with him.

Throughout the ages God has expressed his love by calling humankind into friendship and partnership with him. God wants people to know him and to experience a loving relationship with him. In the Old Testament we read that God called people into such a relationship again and again. God invited people to share in his love and to be part of a *covenant* with him. In the Bible, a **covenant** is a solemn agreement between God and his people.

> **"I am God the Almighty. Walk in my presence and be blameless."**
> (Genesis 17:1)

Throughout the Old Testament there are accounts of God's covenants with people, beginning with the story of Noah in the Book of Genesis. Although this particular story may not be literally true, it was used to teach the great truth of God's everlasting love for human beings. God called Noah at a time when human beings were not showing love for God and one another. But Noah was a good man who loved God. God told Noah to build an ark, a kind of ship, and to take his wife and family, along with two of every living thing, on board. Then a great flood destroyed all life outside the ark. After the flood, God made a covenant with Noah, his family, and every living creature. In this covenant God invited human beings to experience his love and forgiveness, promising that a flood would never again destroy life on earth. Through this covenant with Noah, God was making a lasting covenant with all of humankind.

Faith Word
covenant

In the Old Testament we also read that God made a covenant with a man named Abraham. At a time when people were worshiping many different gods, God called Abraham to worship him alone. God said, "I am God the Almighty. Walk in my presence and be blameless. Between you and me I will establish my covenant, and I will multiply you exceedingly" (Genesis 17:1–2). Even though Abraham's wife, Sarah, was too old to have children, God promised that Abraham's descendants would become a great nation and that Abraham and Sarah would have a son. In return, God asked Abraham and Sarah to serve and worship God alone. Abraham and Sarah obeyed and trusted God completely. As God promised, they were blessed with a son, Isaac, and the descendants of Abraham and Sarah went on to become a great nation—the Israelites.

As the Old Testament continues, God again and again renews his covenant with human beings and deepens his relationship with them. The message of these Old Testament accounts of God's covenant is that God loves us, wants the best for us, and invites us to respond by living as he calls us to live.

Activity Fill in the speech bubbles below.

Noah

I LIVE MY COVENANT WITH GOD BY

Abraham

I LIVE MY COVENANT WITH GOD BY

How do you live your covenant with God?

שלום What's in a word?

Most of the Old Testament was originally written in Hebrew. The following Hebrew words were used in the Hebrew version of the Old Testament. They can help us to recognize the greatness of God's love for us.

hesed (CHEH sehd): a word used to describe God's undying love, tender care, and generous mercy. The English language cannot even express the full meaning of *hesed*, but the term "loving kindness" comes close. We are called to have faith in God and in his loving kindness.

shalom (sha LOHM): a word that is often translated as "peace" but means much more. It includes all the best values that we can imagine—holiness, peace, justice, forgiveness, freedom, truth, faith, hope, and, above all, love. The Hebrew word *shalom* was meant to describe all the good that God desires for human beings.

What are some words that could help you to remember God's love for you?

God is merciful and gives us laws out of love.

Why are laws and rules important?

Throughout time God has always been faithful to humankind. Unfortunately, human beings are not always as faithful to God. But God continues to love us and is always ready to forgive us. God rejoices when people turn back to him. In the Old Testament there are many accounts of God's **mercy**, his forgiveness and love.

In the Book of Exodus we read the account of God's freeing the Israelites from slavery in Egypt. God called Moses and helped Moses to lead the Israelites out of Egypt. Then the Israelites journeyed through the desert and came to a mountain, Mount Sinai. God called Moses up this mountain and spoke to him. God told Moses that he wanted to make a covenant with the Israelites. God said that the Israelites should worship God alone as their one, true God, and that in return God would make the Israelites his special people. Moses told the people what God was asking of them, and they agreed to it.

The Ten Commandments

I	I am the LORD your God: you shall not have strange gods before me.
II	You shall not take the name of the LORD your God in vain.
III	Remember to keep holy the LORD's Day.
IV	Honor your father and your mother.
V	You shall not kill.
VI	You shall not commit adultery.
VII	You shall not steal.
VIII	You shall not bear false witness against your neighbor.
IX	You shall not covet your neighbor's wife.
X	You shall not covet your neighbor's goods.

After this, God gave Moses the Ten Commandments on Mount Sinai. God gave the commandments to the people out of love. The commandments would lead the people to true freedom because following these laws would free them to be faithful to God.

Faith Word

mercy

Forty days and forty nights passed before Moses finally came down the mountain carrying two stone tablets on which the commandments were written. But while Moses was away, the Israelites had already forgotten their one, true God. Moses found them worshiping a false god, a golden calf that they had made from melting down their gold jewelry. When they realized how terrible their actions were, they were fearful and sorry. Lovingly, God forgave them when they turned back to him. God told Moses that he was "a merciful and gracious God, slow to anger and rich in kindness and fidelity" (Exodus 34:6).

Always another chance

As Catholics, we believe that God always forgives us and continues to love us, despite the mistakes we make. In fact, when Moses came down from the mountain and saw the Israelites worshiping the golden calf, he actually threw the stone tablets to the ground in anger and broke them. (See Exodus 32:19.) Yet God, always merciful, told Moses: "Cut two stone tablets like the former, that I may write on them the commandments which were on the former tablets that you broke" (Exodus 34:1). Moses cut two new stone tablets and returned to the top of Mount Sinai to receive the commandments for a second time. So, actually, God gave the commandments to Moses twice!

Privately recall a time when you did something wrong but were given another chance. Think about how that felt. How do you offer another chance to others?

CATHOLIC IDENTITY

Activity The Ten Commandments, when followed, help us to have safe, loving, and peaceful relationships with God and others. Using the commandments as a basis, develop rules for improving friendships and family relationships.

Christ II, a photomosaic by Robert Silvers (contemporary artist)

Jesus Christ is the greatest sign of God's love.

As we have seen, there are many examples of God's love in the Old Testament. God created the world out of love and made human beings partners in caring for creation and for one another. God formed a covenant with humankind and revealed ways to be faithful to that covenant. And throughout the ages, God has shown his mercy when people have turned away from him.

All of these expressions of God's love are part of God's *providence*. **Providence** is God's plan for and protection of all creation. In his plan of salvation for humankind, God promised to send someone who would save human beings from sin. When the right moment in human history came, God sent his only Son, Jesus Christ, into the world as the promised Savior. Jesus is the greatest sign of God's love among us. In the New Testament we read: "In this way the love of God was revealed to us: God sent

Faith Word

providence

his only Son into the world so that we might have life through him" (1 John 4:9).

As the Son of God, Jesus forgave people's sins as only God could forgive them. He healed people who were suffering. By the way that he lived, he taught people how to be faithful to God and how to treat everyone with respect and love. And he gave up his own life so that we would have life forever. Jesus said, "For this is the will of my Father, that everyone who sees the Son and believes in him may have eternal life" (John 6:40). Everything that Jesus said and did showed the love that God has for us.

> ❝In this way the love of God was revealed to us: God sent his only Son into the world so that we might have life through him.❞
>
> (1 John 4:9)

There is no greater sign of the Father's love than Jesus Christ. As Jesus' disciples, we too can become examples of God's love. By helping those who are suffering, by forgiving those who hurt us, and by treating everyone with respect, love, and justice, we allow our lives to become an answer to the question "How do I know God loves me?" It is through our actions that we can share God's love with others.

Activity Be an example of God's love. Make an encouraging e-card for someone, including a message about God's love and providence.

RESPONDING...

Recognizing Our Faith

Recall the question at the beginning of this chapter: *How do I know God loves me?* With your group, work on a computer-generated slide presentation that answers this question. Write your ideas below.

Living Our Faith

Make a list of ways to show God's love to others through actions, not words. Try one or two of your ideas this week. Notice the effect(s) that your action(s) have.

Saint Teresa of Ávila

Teresa was born in 1515 in Ávila, Spain. As a teenager, Teresa entered a convent for her education. She began to grow closer to God. In 1535 she became a Carmelite nun. But in time Teresa discovered problems within her religious community. She felt that the nuns needed to simplify their lives and become more focused on God's love. So, in 1560 Teresa established a reformed order of Carmelite nuns known as *Discalced*, or "barefooted," Carmelites. This religious order was focused on living simply, praying, and sharing God's love together as a community.

Teresa loved to pray and believed it was important to reflect on God's love often. In her book, *The Way of Perfection*, one of her many writings, Teresa wrote, "[God's] love for those to whom He is dear is by no means so weak: *He shows it in every way possible.*"

In 1970 Pope Paul VI named Saint Teresa a Doctor of the Church. The feast day of Saint Teresa of Ávila is October 15.

How can you, like Teresa, encourage others to share God's love?

@ **For additional ideas and activities, visit www.weliveourfaith.com.**

Putting Faith to Work

Talk about what you have learned in this chapter:

 We understand that God has shown his love for humankind throughout the ages.

 We appreciate God's love for all of us.

 We respond to God's love by following Jesus.

Decide on ways to live out what you have learned.

✝ ENCOUNTERING GOD'S WORD

❝Can a mother forget her infant . . . ? Even should she forget, I will never forget you.❞
(Isaiah 49:15)

➡ **READ** the quotation from Scripture.

➡ **REFLECT** on the following question:
How do you feel about the fact that God loves you as a mother loves her infant child?

➡ **SHARE** your reflections with a partner.

➡ **DECIDE** on one thing you can do today to show gratitude for God's love.

Write *True* or *False* next to the following sentences. On a separate sheet of paper, change the false sentences to make them true.

1. _____ Jesus Christ is the greatest sign of God's love.

2. _____ In the Bible, providence is a solemn agreement between God and his people.

3. _____ God's plan for protection of all creation is called a covenant.

4. _____ God is merciful and gives us laws out of love.

Short Answers

5. What did God promise in his covenant with Abraham? _____
_____

6. What happened while Moses was away on Mount Sinai for forty days and forty nights? _____
_____

7. How did Jesus show the love that God has for us? _____
_____

8. What is the message of the two accounts of creation found in the book of Genesis? _____
_____

9–10. ESSAY: In the Old Testament, how did God show that he is our loving Father?

Sharing Faith with Your Family

Discuss the following with your family:

- God loves all he has created.
- God invites us into a loving relationship with him.
- God is merciful and gives us laws out of love.
- Jesus Christ is the greatest sign of God's love.

As a reminder of the love shared in your family, spend time together looking through family photo albums or viewing home movies. You might also make a collage of family photographs to place in your family prayer space. (See "Sharing Faith with Your Family" in Chapter 2.)

The Worship Connection

The first reading at Sunday Mass is usually from the Old Testament. This week listen closely to the first reading and the responsorial psalm for descriptions of God's love. Talk about what you heard.

More to Explore

Make a list of TV shows or novels that portray friendships. Write a plus sign by the ones that show loving relationships and a minus sign by the ones that do not. Share your findings.

Catholic Social Teaching ☑ Checklist

Theme of Catholic Social Teaching:
Care for God's Creation

How it relates to Chapter 4: God, our Father and creator, loves all that he has created and makes us his partners in caring for creation. We are to take care of the environment, our resources, and all living things.

How can you do this?

☐ At home:
_____

☐ At school/work:
_____

☐ In the parish:
_____

☐ In the community:
_____

Check off each action after it has been completed.

GATHERING...

5
Jesus Christ, the Good News

"He journeyed from one town and village to another, preaching and proclaiming the good news."

(Luke 8:1)

✚ **Leader:** Let us thank God for all of the good news in our lives.

Reader: We thank you for the family and friends who care for us.

All: We thank you, God.

Reader: We thank you for the people and organizations helping those who are suffering in the world.

All: We thank you, God.

Reader: We thank you for your great love for us.

All: We thank you, God.

Reader: And we thank you for the good news that you sent your only Son, Jesus Christ, into the world.

All: We thank you, God.

Leader: Take time now to silently say your own thank-you prayer to God for all that is "good news" in your life.

(silent meditation)

All: May we all become "good news" to others. Amen.

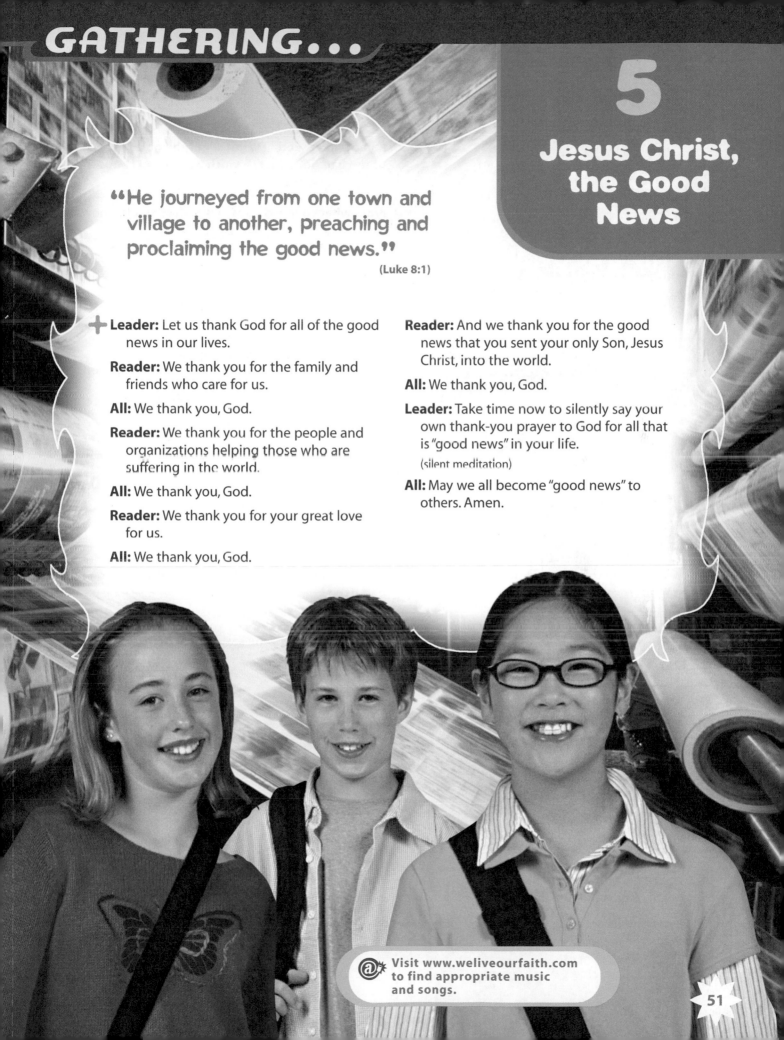

@ Visit www.weliveourfaith.com to find appropriate music and songs.

GATHERING...

The BiG QuEStion:

What is the good news for me?

:D: iscover your attitude about the news that you hear each day. Answer the following questions.

1 If you were asked, "Do you want the good news first or the bad news first?" which would you choose?

good news　　　　　bad news

2 From what source do you most often get the news?

| TV | newspapers | radio |
| Internet | magazines | word of mouth |

other: _____

3 What one factor makes you choose this news source more often than you do other news sources?

reliability　　　convenience　　　speed

detailed information

design or graphics　　　　　inclusion of opinions

4 Circle the statement that best describes your feelings about the news.

I can't live without the news—I need to know
　　what's going on.
The news bores me.
The news interests me.
The news depresses me.
The news gives me something to talk about.
I don't trust the news.

5 Do you think that the news media report too much bad news?

yes　　　　　　　　no

6 Do you agree with the statement "No news is good news"?

yes　　　　　　　　no

Results:

With your group conduct a poll to find out how everyone responded to the questionnaire above. Share your reasons for your answers. Your group might also poll family members and friends and then share findings at a later session.

Discuss what good news you would like to hear and how you can make it happen.

In this chapter
we learn about the good news: that God loves us so much that he sent his only Son into our world to save us and to show us how to live. Through this chapter, we hope

 to recognize
the good news that God sent his only Son, Jesus Christ, to save us and to show us how to live

 to trust
that the four Gospels will help us to come to know Jesus

 to share
the good news with others.

WORLD PEACE ACHIEVED — BILLIONS REJOICE

POVERTY ENDS — WORLD ECONOMY THRIVES

ENVIRONMENT RECOVERS — POLLUTION DISAPPEARS

Wouldn't it be great if these news headlines were real? Sometimes it seems as if all we hear about is bad news. Some people refuse to watch or read the news for this reason. A recent survey found that 44 percent of people in the United States said that the news actually made them feel depressed (The Pew Research Center for the People and the Press, 2004). Whether or not we agree, there's no denying that news can have a powerful effect on us.

> **"**If you don't like the news . . . go out and make some of your own.**"**
> (quotation attributed to American journalist Wes Nisker, born in 1943)

Activity Rewrite the three headlines below to turn them into good news.

BUDGET CUTS TARGET HOMELESS

OIL SPILL HARMS WILDLIFE

GANG VIOLENCE HITS LOCAL NEIGHBORHOOD

Good news on prime time!

TIME
THE WEEKLY NEWSMAGAZINE

BISHOP FULTON J. SHEEN
No Easter without Good Friday.

Archbishop Fulton J. Sheen (1895–1979) has been called the greatest Catholic evangelist of the electronic age. An *evangelist* is someone who proclaims the good news of Christ by what he or she says or does. Archbishop Sheen used the media—pamphlets, books, radio, and television—to proclaim the good news to millions of people. But it was especially through television that he took the world by storm. He captivated audiences with his 1950s primetime show, *Life Is Worth Living*. With faith, enthusiasm, and a sense of humor, Archbishop Sheen spoke to his TV audiences about God's love. He offered Christian answers to life's problems. His only props were a piece of chalk and a blackboard (and a "guardian angel" who would erase the board during commercial breaks). *Life Is Worth Living* won an Emmy, and Archbishop Sheen appeared on the cover of *TIME Magazine*. His magnetic personality drew many people to enter or to return to the Catholic Church. An effort to have Archbishop Sheen declared a saint is underway.

How could the good news be proclaimed in the media today?

We meet God in his Son, Jesus Christ.

Through Jesus Christ, God expressed his love for humanity in the most extraordinary way: In Jesus Christ, we meet God "in the flesh." *Incarnation* is a word that means "having become flesh," and the truth that the Son of God, the second Person of the Blessed Trinity, became man and lived among us is called the **Incarnation**. By becoming one of us in his only Son, Jesus Christ, God fully reveals who he is, shows us how he wants us to live, and offers us forgiveness and salvation. Out of all the news that we could ever receive, this is truly the good news.

Jesus Christ came to proclaim this good news to everyone, especially those who were poor, hungry, sick, lonely, homeless, or treated unfairly. His good news had a powerful effect on all people—no matter what their situation in life. So, the coming of Jesus Christ is good news for all people and for all time.

Jesus Christ changed human life forever. He taught us how to live in complete love and friendship with God. He saved us from anything that could keep us from fully experiencing God's love and friendship. He could do all of this because he is divine, God's only Son. And yet Jesus was also human. He was like us in every way, except that he did not sin. He felt joy and pain and all of the other emotions that we feel. When he preached, he spoke as one who completely understood human life. He was one with us in our human experience. Jesus Christ is both truly divine and truly human at the same time—*true God* and *true man*.

> **Faith Word**
> Incarnation

Activity With your group, enact a news report telling of the good news of Jesus Christ. Write your plan here.

We meet Jesus in the four Gospels.

The word *gospel* means "good news." During Jesus' time *gospel* meant good news for the people of a society, such as the news that a ruler was excusing people from taxes. In time Christians began to use the word *gospel* to mean the good news that God sent his only Son, Jesus Christ, into the world. The four Gospels in the New Testament are written accounts of this good news. They are the most important written accounts of Jesus Christ that we have.

> It is Jesus "himself who speaks when the holy Scriptures are read in the Church"
> (CCC, 1088).

The development of the four Gospels followed these steps:

(1) Jesus, the Son of God, lived, taught, and worked among us, and then died and rose to new life to save all humankind.

(2) Eyewitnesses to Jesus' life and teachings shared the truth that Jesus was the Son of God who saved all people, and by word of mouth this good news began to spread.

(3) The authors of the Gospels, inspired by the Holy Spirit, wrote the good news of Jesus that had been handed down. Each emphasized different details because he was writing for his own community.

Each of the four Gospels, the Gospels of Matthew, Mark, Luke, and John, gives us a unique perspective on Jesus, but they all express the same truth. They all give us the same good news.

As we hear the Gospel reading at every Mass, Jesus continues to teach us. The *Catechism of the Catholic Church* states, "It is he himself who speaks when the holy Scriptures are read in the Church" (1088). In these written accounts of Jesus' life, then, we *meet* Jesus. He reaches out to us, inviting us to become his disciples. He guides us and gives us an example to follow. He draws us into prayer. He preaches to us, and no matter how often we hear his teachings, they always have meaning for our lives.

Activity What would you highlight or emphasize if you were writing your own Gospel about Jesus today? Make an outline for your Gospel below.

Jesus as the Good Shepherd, sculpture

Compassionate Christ, contemporary portrait of Christ by Father John Giuliani

Ecce homo, 1937–1941, portrait of Christ by Georges Rouault

55

The synoptic Gospels tell the good news from a similar viewpoint.

If you were introducing Jesus to someone for the first time, what would you say?

The Gospels of Mark, Matthew, and Luke are the **synoptic Gospels**, which present the good news of Jesus Christ from a similar point of view. Symbols for these three Gospels are shown at right. The word *synoptic* comes from the Greek word *synopsis*, which means "a viewing together." The synoptic Gospels share many of the same details. They all emphasize Jesus' divinity, but also focus on Jesus' human nature, showing the disciples recognizing his divinity only gradually. The synoptic Gospels also show Jesus using parables to teach. A **parable** is a short story with a message.

About thirty years after Jesus Christ's death and Resurrection, a Christian disciple known as Mark wrote the synoptic Gospel considered to be the first of the four Gospels. The other two synoptic Gospels, Matthew and Luke, may have been based on Mark. The Gospel of Mark is the shortest of the four Gospels. It is a fast-paced account of Jesus' words and actions. Mark was probably writing for **Gentile**, or non-Jewish, Christians being persecuted for their faith in Christ. Mark urges them to hold on to their belief in Christ, especially in times of suffering. Jesus is portrayed as one who suffers with humanity and shares God's love with humankind.

The Gospel of Matthew was written between A.D. 70 and A.D. 90 for Jewish people who became followers of Christ. Matthew emphasizes Jesus' humanity by including a story about his birth and early life. Matthew also shows Jesus welcoming everyone to share in God's love and identifying with those who are poor, lowly, and suffering. Jesus' Jewish heritage is also highlighted. Jesus is shown to be a descendant of Abraham and of the Israelites' King David. Jesus is also shown to be a "new Moses." Just as Moses received God's laws on Mount Sinai, in Matthew's Gospel Jesus teaches people how to follow God's laws in the "Sermon on the Mount." In Matthew's Gospel it is clear that Jesus fulfills the promises that God made to his people in the Old Testament.

The Gospel of Luke was written for Greek Gentiles, probably between A.D. 80 and A.D. 85. Luke may have been a disciple who traveled with Saint Paul to spread Christianity. Like Matthew, Luke includes details about Jesus' birth and early life. Luke also emphasizes Jesus' concern for all human beings. Luke's Gospel is the only Gospel that includes Jesus' parables about the lost sheep, the lost coin, and the lost son—all parables about God's love and forgiveness toward humankind. And Luke includes many examples of Jesus' welcoming attitude toward all—reaching out to both men and women and to everyone who is outcast, troubled, rejected, or poor.

Thus, in the synoptic Gospels we see Jesus as one who understands the human condition and shows God's love to everyone. In these Gospels, no one is excluded from the good news that Jesus has to share.

Faith Words
synoptic Gospels
parable
Gentile

Activity The synoptic Gospels each include a story about Jesus healing a paralyzed man. Read the story in Matthew 9:1–8, Mark 2:1–12, and Luke 5:17–26. How are these accounts alike? How are they different? Discuss your ideas.

The Gospel of John explores the mystery of the Incarnation.

The Gospel of John was written about A.D. 90. The symbol for John's Gospel appears at right. Unlike the synoptic Gospels, it contains much poetic language and imagery. This picturesque language is meant to give the reader a deeper insight into the meaning of Jesus' words and deeds. It also helps to emphasize the great mystery of the Incarnation.

The major theme of John's Gospel is that Jesus Christ is the *Word of God* who became a human being and lived among us. The **Word of God** is the Son of God, the most complete expression of God's word. At the very beginning of John's Gospel, John explains that Jesus Christ is the Word of God who *is*, and has always been, with God, and who *is* God. As John's Gospel continues, Jesus' disciples recognize from the beginning that Jesus is God's Son. John portrays Jesus' miracles as dramatic signs that he is the Son of God, and people who experience these

Faith Word

Word of God

> "As the Father loves me, so I also love you."
>
> (John 15:9)

miracles are called to faith. The stories of Jesus' miracles are long, with lots of dialogue and explanation.

John's Gospel also stresses Jesus' many teachings about love. Among these teachings is Jesus' call to follow his own example of love. Jesus teaches the New Commandment, calling us to love one another in the same way that he loves us. Jesus teaches us that if we love one another as he loves us, then we become signs of God's love, because Jesus loves as *God* loves. Jesus explains, "As the Father loves me, so I also love you" (John 15:9).

Sometimes John's Gospel focuses on tensions between Jesus and Jewish authorities. This was probably because, when John's Gospel was written, Jews who accepted Jesus and Jews who did not were in conflict. But John's Gospel always moves us to profess our faith in Jesus as God's Son—and as the most powerful example of God's love on earth.

Activity Design an Internet ad that invites people to recognize that Jesus is God's Son.

How do we pray with Scripture?

Lectio divina (LEHK see oh dee VEE nah) is the Latin name for a way of praying that Christians have practiced for many centuries. *Lectio divina*, which means "divine reading," usually involves the following steps:

Read a Scripture passage. As you read, reflect, noticing parts of the text that stand out to you.

Meditate on the same reading as you read it again. To meditate is to try to understand what God is revealing, perhaps by imagining that you are

part of the story or scene, or by silently talking to God about what you have read.

Pray to God, speaking what is in your heart.

Contemplate by choosing a word, phrase, or image from the Scripture passage, focusing on it with your whole heart and mind, and feeling God's great love for you.

Decide on a way to respond to what you have read, and act on it.

Try praying this way using a passage from one of the Gospels.

RESPONDING...

Recognizing Our Faith

Recall the question: *What is the good news for me?* Together with your group design a cartoon that can answer this question.

Living Our Faith

Decide on a way to tell others the good news of Jesus Christ this week. You might wish to write your own "good news" newspaper and distribute it to friends and family.

The Catholic News Service

Established in 1920, the Catholic News Service (CNS) continues its mission to spread the good news of Jesus Christ using current technology and media. Staffed by professional journalists, CNS serves the faithful by reporting news about the involvement of the Church in the world. This source of international news and information about the Church and the lives of Catholics living out the faith is a division of the United States Conference of Catholic Bishops (USCCB), based in Washington, D.C.

More than 170 Catholic newspapers in the United States and news organizations in more than 35 countries use CNS as their primary source of news related to the Church. Look inside your diocesan newspaper or on a Catholic Web site—there is bound to be a news article from CNS.

How can you find the news that is happening in your parish? How can you become more involved in its programs to help people and to share the good news?

@✶ For additional ideas and activities, visit www.weliveourfaith.com.

Putting Faith to Work

Talk about what you have learned in this chapter:

 We recognize the good news that God sent his only Son, Jesus Christ, to save us and to show us how to live.

 We trust that the four Gospels will help us to come to know Jesus.

 We share the good news with others.

Decide on ways to live out what you have learned.

✝ ENCOUNTERING GOD'S WORD

The Apostles **"** set out and went from village to village proclaiming the good news and curing diseases everywhere **"**

(Luke 9:6).

➡ **READ** the quotation from Scripture.

➡ **REFLECT** on this question:
What does it mean to proclaim the good news everywhere?

➡ **SHARE** your reflections with a partner.

➡ **DECIDE** with your group how you will share the good news wherever you go.

Write the letter that best defines each term.

1. _____ Word of God

2. _____ Incarnation

3. _____ parable

4. _____ *gospel*

a. good news

b. the Son of God, the most complete expression of God's word

c. the truth that the Son of God, the second Person of the Blessed Trinity, became man and lived among us

d. a short story with a message

e. the Gospels of Mark, Matthew, and Luke, which present the good news of Jesus Christ from a similar point of view

Write the name of the Gospel described in each statement.

5. The Gospel of _____ portrays Jesus as one who suffers with humanity and shares God's love with humankind.

6. The Gospel of _____ emphasizes Jesus' concern for all human beings.

7. The Gospel of _____ explains that Jesus Christ is the Word of God who became a human being and lived among us.

8. The Gospel of _____ highlights Jesus' Jewish heritage.

9–10. ESSAY: Explain why the coming of Jesus Christ is good news for all people and for all time.

Chapter 5 Assessment

Sharing Faith with Your Family

Discuss the following with your family:
- We meet God in his Son, Jesus Christ.
- We meet Jesus in the four Gospels.
- The synoptic Gospels tell the good news from a similar viewpoint.
- The Gospel of John explores the mystery of the Incarnation.

Look for ways your family can live out the good news of Jesus Christ by helping someone in your parish or neighborhood. You may want to check your parish bulletin for volunteer opportunities.

The Worship Connection

At Mass, pay attention to the ways in which honor and respect for the Gospels are shown. Share your observations with your family.

More to Explore

In this chapter we learned about the good news of Jesus Christ. This week, see if you can find any stories that reflect the good news of Jesus Christ in TV programs or in other forms of media.

Catholic Social Teaching ☑ Checklist

Theme of Catholic Social Teaching:
Life and Dignity of the Human Person

How it relates to Chapter 5: As we learned in this chapter, God loves all of us so much that he sent his only Son, Jesus Christ, for the salvation of us all. And God calls us to recognize one another's dignity and to share his love with all people.

How can you do this?

☐ At home:

_____

☐ At school/work:

_____

☐ In the parish:

_____

☐ In the community:

_____

Check off each action after it has been completed.

GATHERING...

6

Holy Spirit, Helper and Guide

"When he comes, the Spirit of truth, he will guide you to all truth."

(John 16:13)

✚ **Leader:** Holy Spirit, you guide us to the truth and help us to live as Jesus' disciples. Jesus said, "The holy Spirit that the Father will send in my name—he will teach you everything and remind you of all that [I] told you" (John 14:26).

All: Come, Holy Spirit, fill the hearts of your faithful.
And kindle in them the fire of your love.
Send forth your Spirit and they shall be created.
And you will renew the face of the earth.
(Prayer to the Holy Spirit)

Leader: God our Father,
let the Spirit you sent on your Church
to begin the teaching of the gospel
continue to work in the world
through the hearts of all who believe.

All: We ask this through our Lord Jesus Christ, your Son,
who lives and reigns with you
and the Holy Spirit,
one God, for ever and ever. Amen.
(collect, Mass During the Day, Pentecost)

@ Visit www.weliveourfaith.com to find appropriate music and songs.

GATHERING...

The BiG Question:

How do I find my way?

iscover your opinions about how to find your way when making decisions. Conduct the following poll with your group.

If you were not sure whether something you were going to do was right or wrong, which one of the following would most influence your decision?

A. doing what would make me happy

B. doing what would help me to get ahead

C. following the advice of a parent or a teacher

D. doing what God would want me to do

Results:

Count how many people selected each possible answer. Figure out the percentage of the group that chose each response. Then chart your findings on the bar graph.

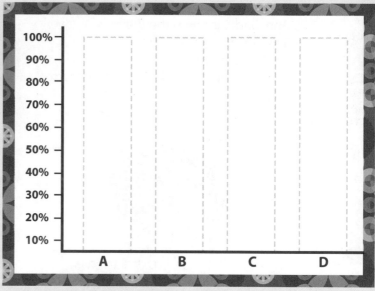

Discuss what can help you to make the best decisions as a disciple of Jesus.

In this chapter
we learn that the Holy Spirit helps us to live as Jesus' disciples and to continue the mission of Jesus. Through this chapter, we hope

to understand that the Holy Spirit is present and active in God's plan of salvation

to trust the Holy Spirit to guide the life and teachings of the Church

to rely on the help and guidance of the Holy Spirit.

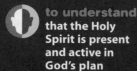

Help from Hannah

Dear Hannah,

My friend Corey has always been a great friend—outside of math class, that is. He's always trying to cheat during math quizzes. The other day he copied all of my answers on a quiz and we ended up with the same score. I feel bad about saying anything to him because he's my friend, but I don't feel good about what's going on, either. I need your help. What should I do?

Sincerely,

All Quizzed Out

Have you ever had to find your way out of a dilemma or a difficult situation? How did you find your way? Who or what helped you? What kind of guidance would you give to "All Quizzed Out"?

Activity Write a response to "All Quizzed Out" below. Then share responses with your group. Explain your reasons for your answer.

> "Life is too complicated and there is too much at stake to even think about trying to handle it all without the guidance of the Spirit," said C. Smith Sumner (1933–   ), an American entrepreneur and computer executive.

The Holy Spirit is always present with the Father and the Son.

In the Old Testament, we find examples of the Holy Spirit bringing life, order, and goodness to all of creation. In the Book of Genesis we find the Holy Spirit at work in creation. The Holy Spirit moved among creation as the very wind, breath, and spirit of creation. When God began to create, "a mighty wind swept over the waters" (Genesis 1:2).

The Holy Spirit was also active in God's relationship with our ancestors in faith, the Israelites. During the Exodus, God led the Israelites through the desert in a column of cloud and fire. Thus, the power of the Holy Spirit guided the Israelites forward. (See Exodus 13:21–22.) After the Israelites reached their promised land and established their

kingdom, it was through the Holy Spirit that the prophets began to teach and to guide them. A **prophet** is someone who speaks on behalf of God, defends the truth, and works for justice. The Holy Spirit spoke through the prophets, teaching the Israelites to remain faithful to God. And through the prophets, the Holy Spirit revealed God's plan to send the **Messiah** to save the people from their sins.

The word *Messiah* comes from a Hebrew word that means "Anointed One." Anointing was a Hebrew custom; kings and priests were anointed with oil as a sign that God had appointed them to their special roles. So too would the Messiah be anointed. But he would be anointed with the Holy Spirit, and he would be appointed to bring mercy, peace, and justice to the world. Describing the Messiah, the prophet Isaiah once said:
"The spirit of the LORD shall rest upon him" (Isaiah 11:2).
And that promise of the Messiah was fulfilled with the coming of Jesus Christ, who actually read those words of Isaiah as he began his public ministry, or his work among the people.

The presence and guidance of the Holy Spirit throughout time is one of the ways that God has expressed his love for humanity. Yet it was not until God fully revealed his plan for salvation—in Jesus Christ—that the presence and the power of the Holy Spirit truly became known.

Faith Words
prophet
Messiah

Who is the Holy Spirit?

As Catholics we believe in one God in three Persons—the Father, the Son, and the Holy Spirit. At times it can be difficult to put into words exactly who the Holy Spirit is. Catholics sometimes say that the Holy Spirit is "the love shared between God the Father and God the Son." This way of speaking about the Holy Spirit was handed down to us by Saint Augustine of Hippo (A.D. 354–430). It expresses the Holy Spirit's complete unity with both the Father and the Son. Yet even though the Father, the Son, and the Holy Spirit are one, each plays a particular role in the salvation of humankind. The Holy Spirit *sanctifies* us, or makes us holy. The Holy Spirit helps us to become holy by making the truth clear to us, reminding us of Jesus' teachings, helping us to understand God's word, and helping us to do good and avoid sin. The Holy Spirit inspires faith within us and gives us the power to live by it.

CATHOLIC IDENTITY

How can the presence of the Holy Spirit be experienced in your day-to-day life? Answer this question in a drawing, a poem, a song, or a story.

Activity Compose a prayer to the Holy Spirit that you can say when you need guidance.

The Holy Spirit is active in God's plan of salvation.

The Holy Spirit is active in God's plan of salvation. It was through the power of the Holy Spirit that Mary, a young Hebrew woman chosen by God, conceived and bore God's Son, Jesus Christ, our Savior. And the Holy Spirit continued to be with Jesus throughout his life. Even before Jesus began his public ministry, the Holy Spirit came upon Jesus at his Baptism, strengthening him: "The holy Spirit descended upon him in bodily form like a dove" (Luke 3:22).

> 66 The Holy Spirit is at work with the Father and the Son from the beginning to the completion of the plan for our salvation. 99
>
> (CCC, 686)

Through the power of the Holy Spirit, Jesus taught, healed, and worked miracles. Jesus also shared the life of God with all people and saved them from sin. All of Jesus' words and actions were carried out with the strength and guidance of the Holy Spirit. "The Holy Spirit is at work with the Father and the Son from the beginning to the completion of the plan for our salvation." (*CCC*, 686)

Activity The Holy Spirit is continually at work in our lives. Imagine that you have been asked to design a stained-glass window for your parish church that represents the Holy Spirit at work in Jesus' life. Sketch here what your window would look like. For ideas, you might wish to look in the New Testament for verses about the Holy Spirit.

Holy Spirit window, St. Peter's Basilica, Rome

The Holy Spirit came to the disciples at Pentecost.

Who is someone you look to for guidance? Why?

Jesus told his disciples that the Holy Spirit would empower them to continue the work he had begun. Jesus said, "I will ask the Father, and he will give you another Advocate to be with you always, the Spirit of truth . . . . When he comes, the Spirit of truth, he will guide you to all truth" (John 14:16–17; 16:13). After Jesus died, rose, and returned to his Father in heaven, the disciples were gathered in Jerusalem during the Jewish Feast of Weeks, which was known as "Pentecost." And on the day of **Pentecost**, which now marks the beginning of the Church, the Holy Spirit came to Jesus' first disciples as Jesus promised: "Suddenly there came from the sky a noise like a strong driving wind, and it filled the entire house in which they were. Then there appeared to them tongues as of fire, which parted and came to rest on each one of them. And they were all filled with the holy Spirit and began to speak in different tongues, as the Spirit enabled them to proclaim" (Acts of the Apostles 2:2–4). Even though the

visitors to Jerusalem did not all speak the same language, because of the Holy Spirit they all could understand the good news that the disciples were proclaiming.

Faith Word
Pentecost

Then the Apostle Peter gave a powerful speech to the crowds, explaining that Jesus Christ died, rose, went back to his Father in heaven, and sent forth the Holy Spirit. When the people who were listening to Peter asked what they should do next, Peter told them, "Repent and be baptized, every one of you, in the name of Jesus Christ for the forgiveness of your sins; and you will receive the gift of the holy Spirit" (Acts of the Apostles 2:38).

As baptized members of the Church, we all have received the Gift of the Holy Spirit. The same Holy Spirit who empowered Jesus' ministry now helps us to continue Jesus' work in the world. The Holy Spirit helps us to have a deeper understanding of the truth that Jesus preached and to remember all that Jesus taught. And the Holy Spirit enables us to share Jesus' teachings and love with all people everywhere.

Activity Imagine that you are one of the people in the crowd gathered at Pentecost. Write about your experience below.

How does the Holy Spirit help you in your life today?

The Holy Spirit is always guiding the Church.

As Catholics we constantly proclaim our faith in the living presence of the Holy Spirit. At Mass, for example, we pray in the Nicene Creed: "We believe in the Holy Spirit, the Lord, the giver of life, who proceeds from the Father and the Son. With the Father and the Son he is worshiped and glorified." The Holy Spirit is eternally present with the Father and the Son and is at work in the Church. The Holy Spirit is at work:

> "I will ask the Father, and he will give you another Advocate to be with you always, the Spirit of truth."
>
> (John 14:16–17)

- in Scripture, which the Holy Spirit inspired and which we read and interpret with his help

- in Tradition, helping us to express and live our faith

- in the Magisterium, guiding its teachings for the Church

- in the words and symbols of all the sacraments and worship in the Church

- in prayer, helping us to listen and be heard

- in all of the many gifts and ways of serving that members of the Church live out each day

- in the efforts to share our faith with the world through evangelization

- in the saints who have given witness to the good news of salvation.

The Holy Spirit is and has always been the life of the Church—the source of her strength and all of her gifts. The first Christian communities "were all filled with the holy Spirit and continued to speak the word of God with boldness" (Acts of the Apostles 4:31). In the Church today, the Holy Spirit continues to help us to do the same.

Activity Make a pamphlet that could be used to teach younger students about the Holy Spirit's role in the Church.

Symbols of the Holy Spirit

The Coming of the Holy Spirit (Acts 2:1–12), Soichi Watanabe, Japan

Many different symbols have been, and still are, used to represent the Holy Spirit in paintings, stained glass, and other works of art.

The dove is perhaps the most common of these images. According to the Gospels, when Jesus was baptized, the Holy Spirit descended in the form of a dove. A dove can be seen as a sign of freedom, a sense of purity, and the peace that the Holy Spirit gives to us and that remains in the hearts of the baptized.

Fire is another common symbol for the Holy Spirit. In Scripture, it is said that, at Pentecost, the Holy Spirit came upon each of Jesus' disciples as a flame. In paintings of Pentecost, fire is shown above the heads of the disciples, signifying the presence of the Holy Spirit. The flames represent the Holy Spirit's ability to completely transform God's people. Fire is also symbolic of the light and love that we experience, through the Holy Spirit, in our relationship with God.

Water is associated with Baptism and has been used in art to symbolize the Holy Spirit's power to renew, refresh, and give new life.

Research other symbols that have been used for the Holy Spirit. You might even draw your own symbol and share it with your group.

RESPONDING...

Recognizing Our Faith

Recall the question at the beginning of this chapter: *How do I find my way?* Write a poem about the Holy Spirit that answers this question.

Living Our Faith

How can you share Jesus' teachings and love today? Reflect silently, and then ask for the Holy Spirit's help in carrying out your plan.

Partners in FAITH

Pope John Paul II

Pope John Paul II, a man of the Spirit, was born Karol Jozef Wojtyla on May 18, 1920, in Wadowice, Poland. As a youth he was an avid student, athlete, and actor. He studied for the priesthood during the Nazi occupation of Poland and became a bishop at the age of thirty-eight—the youngest bishop in Polish history. Nine years later he became a cardinal. The College of Cardinals elected him pope in 1978. He was the first non-Italian pope in 456 years and, at fifty-eight years old, the youngest pope of the twentieth century.

Pope John Paul II traveled to more places than any other pope in Church history. He was dedicated to equality, solidarity, human rights, and the "new evangelization," spreading the good news in the modern world. His papal letters and other writings fill more than 150 volumes. He also authored an autobiography, poetry, and prayer. His death on April 2, 2005, brought hundreds of thousands of pilgrims to Rome for his wake and funeral.

Just as John Paul II was a man of the Spirit, how can you be a person of the Spirit by respecting human rights?

 For additional ideas and activities, visit www.weliveourfaith.com.

Putting Faith to Work

Talk about what you have learned in this chapter:

 We understand that the Holy Spirit is present and active in God's plan of salvation.

 We trust the Holy Spirit to guide the life and teachings of the Church.

We rely on the help and guidance of the Holy Spirit.

Decide on ways to live out what you have learned.

✝ ENCOUNTERING GOD'S WORD

❝ Where the Spirit of the Lord is, there is freedom. ❞
(2 Corinthians 3:17)

➡ **READ** the quotation from Scripture.

➡ **REFLECT** on these questions:
Why is there freedom wherever the Holy Spirit is? What kind of freedom is it? What does this statement suggest about the kind of community that the Church should be?

➡ **SHARE** your reflections with a partner.

➡ **DECIDE** how you can show that you have received the Holy Spirit.

Circle the letter of the correct answer.

1. _____ is a Hebrew word that means "Anointed One."

   a. Holy Spirit   **b.** Pentecost   **c.** Messiah   **d.** Magisterium

2. The _____ spoke through the prophets, teaching the Israelites to remain faithful to God.

   a. Nicene Creed   **b.** Holy Spirit   **c.** Magisterium   **d.** Messiah

3. The Holy Spirit is and has always been _____.

   a. the life of the Church   **b.** the Anointed One   **c.** a strong, driving wind   **d.** a cloud of fire

4. The day on which the Holy Spirit came to Jesus' first disciples is called _____.

   a. Baptism   **b.** Pentecost   **c.** Easter   **d.** Exodus

Short Answers

5. Who, through the power of the Holy Spirit, taught, healed, and worked miracles, and also saved people from sin? _____

6. What is a prophet? _____

7. What did the Apostle Peter tell the crowds gathered on Pentecost? _____
_____

8. Name one way that the Holy Spirit was active in God's relationship with the Israelites, our ancestors in faith. _____

9–10. ESSAY: How is the Holy Spirit at work in the Church? Give four examples.

Chapter 6 Assessment

RESPONDING...

Sharing Faith with Your Family

Discuss the following with your family:

- The Holy Spirit is always present with the Father and the Son.
- The Holy Spirit is active in God's plan of salvation.
- The Holy Spirit came to the disciples at Pentecost.
- The Holy Spirit is always guiding the Church.

Play the following game with your family to help each of you to recognize your family's gifts, which come through the Holy Spirit. One family member should start the game by thinking of another family member. He or she should make three statements about the other person's talents or gifts. The entire family should then try to guess the identity of the person described. The one who guesses correctly takes the next turn and chooses a different family member to highlight. The game continues until each family member has had a turn.

The Worship Connection

Name prayers from Mass or the sacraments that mention the Holy Spirit. In these prayers, what do we ask of, or profess to believe about, the Holy Spirit?

More to Explore

The Holy Spirit is often called the *Advocate*. (See John 14:15–26 for Jesus' use of this word.) Look up *advocate* in the dictionary. How is it defined? Why is it a fitting name for the Holy Spirit?

Catholic Social Teaching ☑ Checklist

Theme of Catholic Social Teaching:
Dignity of Work and the Rights of Workers

How it relates to Chapter 6: The Holy Spirit helps us in our human efforts to continue Jesus' work in the world. As Catholics we believe in the value of work. We are called to respect workers and uphold their rights.

How can you do this?

☐ At home:

_____

☐ At school/work:

_____

☐ In the parish:

_____

☐ In the community:

_____

Check off each action after it has been completed.

Use these terms to complete the sentences. Add capitals if needed.

| Incarnation | grace | Blessed Trinity | Pentecost |
| Jesus Christ | faith | Divine Revelation | wisdom |

1. _____ is God making himself known to us.

2. The _____ is the three Divine Persons in one God: God the Father, God the Son, and God the Holy Spirit.

3. As Catholics, we believe that _____ is both truly divine and truly human.

4. _____ is a participation, or a sharing, in God's life or friendship.

5. The coming of the Holy Spirit on _____ marks the beginning of the Church.

6. _____ is a gift from God that enables us to believe in God, to accept all that he has revealed, and to respond with love for God and others.

Fill in the circle beside the correct answer.

7. The Gospels of Mark, Matthew, and Luke are known as the _____.
   ○ Old Testament   ○ synoptic Gospels   ○ epistles   ○ New Testament

8. The word *gospel* means "_____."
   ○ Savior   ○ good news   ○ Anointed One   ○ blessing

9. In the _____, we pray, "In the name of the Father, and of the Son, and of the Holy Spirit."
   ○ Hail Mary   ○ Lord's Prayer   ○ sign of peace   ○ Sign of the Cross

10. In the Bible, a solemn agreement between God and his people is called a _____.
    ○ blessing   ○ covenant   ○ Torah   ○ parable

11. The word *Messiah* comes from a Hebrew word that means "_____."
    ○ Jesus   ○ Savior   ○ Anointed One   ○ good news

12. God's plan for and protection of all creation is called _____.
    ○ worship   ○ providence   ○ humankind   ○ the book of Exodus

13. The Gospels are found in the _____.
    ○ New Testament   ○ Old Testament   ○ ecumenical movement   ○ Magisterium

Define the following.

14. epistles _____

_____

_____

15. Magisterium _____

_____

_____

16. deposit of faith _____

_____

_____

17. evangelization _____

_____

_____

18. Incarnation _____

_____

_____

Respond to the following.

19. Choose one of the "Big Questions" from this unit and answer it in an essay. (*How do I know God is present in my life?*; *In what ways can I find truth?*; *Why do relationships matter to me?*; *How do I know God loves me?*; *What is the good news for me?*; or *How do I find my way?*) Use at least three Faith Words from the unit in your essay.

_____

_____

_____

20. Use what you have learned in this unit to write an essay that argues *against* the following statement: *There is no way for human beings to know who God is.*

_____

_____

_____

_____

Imagine that you are an international journalist. In the space below, write a feature article to explain to the world who God is. Write a headline and include an appropriate image for your article.

Unit 2

Who Is Jesus?

7
The Promise of Salvation

"Our God is a God who saves."
(Psalm 68:21)

✚ **Leader:** Almighty God, you are always with us. Throughout our lives, we can call on you in times of need. And so we declare:

All: Our help is in the name of the Lord, who made heaven and earth.

Reader 1: "In you, LORD, I take refuge; let me never be put to shame. In your justice rescue and deliver me; listen to me and save me!"
(Psalm 71:1–2)

All: Our help is in the name of the Lord, who made heaven and earth.

Reader 2: "Be my rock and my refuge, my secure stronghold; for you are my rock and my fortress."
(Psalm 71:3)

All: Our help is in the name of the Lord, who made heaven and earth.

Leader: O Lord, we often receive your help in our lives through helping and being helped by others. And we are responsible for helping ourselves, too. May we always remember these things, as we continue to trust in you.

All: Our help is in the name of the Lord, who made heaven and earth.
Amen.

@✷ Visit www.weliveourfaith.com to find appropriate music and songs.

GATHERING...

The BiG Question:
Who or what helps me in difficult times?

Discover a signal for help. "SOS!" is known world-wide as a call for help. This is due in part to Samuel Morse, who developed Morse code in the 1800s. In Morse code, short electrical signals, or dots, and long electrical signals, or dashes, stand for letters and numbers. These signals were sent out to communicate messages. In Morse code, a message calling for help consisted of three dots, three dashes, and three dots (•••−−−•••), or the letters *SOS*. This signal could be broadcast very quickly, so it was used internationally.

With a partner, take turns writing an *S* or *O* in the grid below. Your goal is to get the letters *SOS* to appear in a row, horizontally or diagonally, during your turn. Each time you do this, score a point and take an additional turn. The person with the highest score wins!

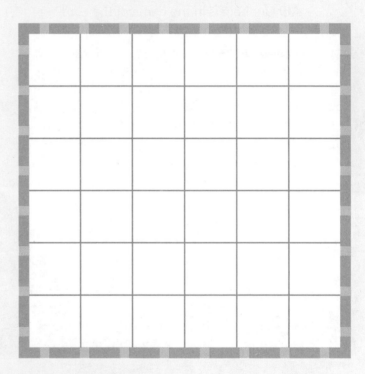

Discuss some real-life "SOS" situations around the world—situations in which people need help. Suggest actions that might be taken to help the people involved.

In this chapter we learn how original sin weakened our human nature and allowed ignorance, suffering, and death into the world, and how God promised help and salvation. Through this chapter, we hope

 to understand that throughout human history God has reached out to help his people

 to celebrate that God prom-ised salvation through his Son, Jesus Christ, the Messiah

 to respond to God's promise of salvation by helping and serving others.

"Hi. My name is Maura, and I'm an alcoholic. It has taken a lot for me to say that about myself. Getting through my first few meetings here was the hardest thing I've ever done. I remember thinking to myself: *I don't need this. These people are nothing like me!* But I needed someone to help me. I just couldn't stop drinking.

"So, I continued to come here and listen to your stories. Soon, I learned that your stories were a lot like my story. And all of you became the help I needed to get through the day. Now I have Maryann as my sponsor, and I'm really getting into the Twelve Steps. I actually admitted that I was powerless over alcohol. I am being honest with myself and others. I am also turning to God and to all of you to get me through this. So, I guess what I really want to say is this: Thank you for being here for me. I hope one day I can help another kid like me."

With these words, Maura, fifteen years old, looked gratefully at the other Alcoholics Anonymous members sitting around her. She couldn't believe that six months had already passed since her last drink.

The organization Alcoholics Anonymous began in 1935 with a friendship between two alcoholics, William Griffith Wilson and Dr. Robert Holbrook Smith. They met at a time when they were both struggling to stay sober. By sharing stories of their struggles and encouraging each other to depend on God, they helped each other to overcome their addiction one day at a time. Soon Wilson and Smith began meeting with other alcoholics to help them to get sober, too. Wilson and Smith shared their spiritual guidelines, which included: admitting that they were powerless over alcohol, turning to God for help, examining their past behavior, making amends, telling the truth, and serving others. Eventually, these spiritual guidelines developed into what is known as the "Twelve Steps," and their small gatherings grew into the larger organization known as Alcoholics Anonymous, or AA. Because AA protects its members' anonymity, Wilson and Smith were known for years as simply "Bill W." and "Dr. Bob."

The group that Bill W. and Dr. Bob began now has two million members worldwide. Members meet to pray together, share their stories and struggles, and work on following the Twelve Steps. Through their friendships, members help each other to cope with the difficulties of addiction. Several other organizations have grown out of AA to help people who have other kinds of addictions.

"You are never strong enough that you don't need help," said César Chávez (1927–1993), an American activist, a labor organizer, and the founder of the National Farm Workers Association.

Activity When has a friendship helped you through a difficult situation? List some ways that *you* might help your friends when they are having trouble in their lives.

God reaches out to help humankind.

From the very beginning of creation, God wanted the lives of all of his creatures to be filled with love, peace, happiness, and goodness. God created human beings to be at one with him, each other, and all of creation. And indeed the first human beings lived in this original state of holiness for which God had created them.

But why, you might ask, isn't life today always filled with love, peace, happiness, and goodness? Why do we need so much help at times? Well, God granted human beings the dignity of acting on their own and cooperating in his plan of loving goodness. God gave human beings the gift of **free will**, the freedom and ability to choose what to do. And it was of their own free will that the first humans chose to disobey God. The first humans chose not to respect God's warnings, nor to trust his words. They selfishly did what they wanted rather than what God commanded. They committed sin. **Sin** is a thought, word, deed, or omission against God's law that harms us and our relationship with God and others. Through sin, the first humans severely damaged their friendship with God.

We can read about this "fall" from God's friendship in Chapter 3 of the Book of Genesis. Here we find a story that uses many symbols to teach us important

truths about sin and suffering. We read of the sin of the first human beings, who are called Adam and Eve in the story. The first sin committed by the first human beings is known as **original sin**. It weakened all of human nature and allowed ignorance, suffering, and death into the world. Because of original sin, human nature needed to be restored to its original relationship with God. God promised to give human beings the help that they needed. With the very symbolic words, "He will strike at your head, while you strike at his heel" (Genesis 3:15), God promised that one day a descendant of the first humans would save humanity and crush the power of evil. Thus, God gave us the hope that sin and evil would one day be finally overcome. God gave us the hope of salvation.

Faith Words
free will
sin
original sin

Activity Write an uplifting motto that reminds people to have hope despite the sin and suffering in the world.

Evil and sin— why?

Sin is a terrible reality in human life. And, ultimately, the reason for the existence of evil is a mystery. Many saints and holy people in the Church have struggled to understand these truths. Here are some of their thoughts on the matter:

- Saint Augustine, a Christian philosopher in the early Church, wrote that he searched and searched for the reasons that evil existed, but found no solution. The only way to make

sense of evil and sin was to think of them as part of the mystery of God's plan for humankind.

- Saint Leo the Great, one of the Church's earliest popes, wrote that even though the first sin damaged humankind's original state of goodness and happiness, we are promised an even better life by Jesus Christ, who saves us from sin.

- Saint Thomas Aquinas, a theologian of the Middle Ages, wrote that even though sin is a terrible reality, there is nothing to prevent us from becoming better and holier people, even after sin.

- Saint Catherine of Siena, a Doctor of the Church, wrote that by seeking God's forgiveness for sin and turning back to him we can live a more virtuous life.

- Saint Paul, who spread Christianity to many lands, wrote that wherever there is sin, there is an even greater amount of grace from Jesus Christ.

With faith we can recognize that *"there is not a single aspect of the Christian message that is not in part an answer to the question of evil"* (CCC, 309).

What are your thoughts on the matter?

God offers his people the hope of salvation.

As the Book of Genesis continues, we learn about the terrible effects of original sin on humankind. In one story we even find out that Cain, one of the sons of Adam and Eve, killed his brother, Abel. Thus, murder, one of the worst effects of original sin, came into existence. But even after this, God did not turn away from humanity. God continued to watch over Cain, encouraging him to choose good over evil. And throughout the Old Testament, the same pattern emerges again and again—people struggle, even turn away from God, but God in his mercy always offers renewed hope.

We can see this pattern during the Exodus, when the Israelites wandered through the desert after leaving Egypt. They were hungry and thirsty. But when they cried out for help, God led them to food and drink. Eventually, with God's help, the people found Canaan, a land that God had promised to make their own.

> **"Through the prophets, God forms his people in the hope of salvation."**
> (CCC, 64)

When the Israelites settled into Canaan and became a nation, they had trouble keeping peace in their land and keeping the commandments. But when they cried out to God for help, God remembered his covenant and helped them. God sent judges, wise rulers who were often military leaders, to help them. The judges reminded the Israelites to keep their faith in God and restored peace to the land. Then, when the Israelites asked for a king to lead them and to protect them from their enemies, God helped them to choose their kings and to protect their land from invading nations.

But when the Israelite kings began to turn away from God, their nation was conquered and divided. People were scattered far from their promised land, suffered many injustices, and even lost faith. However, God encouraged them to keep their covenant with him. He did this through the words of the prophets whom he sent to speak in his name. They urged people to keep their faith in God and to trust that God would restore their nation. As we read in the *Catechism*, "Through the prophets, God forms his people in the hope of salvation" (64).

Activity Use what you have learned on this page to explain how God helped his people during each of the stages below.

During the Exodus . . .

When the Israelites settled into Canaan . . .

When the Israelites asked for a king . . .

When the Israelite kings began to turn away from God . . .

God promises a Messiah.

Who in your life calls you to live your faith?

As the Israelites struggled throughout their history, they listened to the prophets calling them to change their lives and to live by their covenant with God. These prophets reminded the people that God had promised to send the Messiah to bring them forgiveness and salvation.

The people expected the Messiah to be one who would bring victory over evil, injustice, and sin. In the Book of Isaiah, one of the great prophetic books of the Bible, we read of the Messiah as a mighty king. This king, it is said, would be a descendant of King David, one of the Israelites' greatest kings:

"His dominion is vast
and forever peaceful,
From David's throne, and over his kingdom"
(Isaiah 9:6).

Throughout Scripture, and often even within the same prophetic book, we find many other images in prophecies about the Messiah:

- a suffering servant who, "like a lamb led to the slaughter," was "harshly treated" but "opened not his mouth" (Isaiah 53:7)

- "a light for the nations" (Isaiah 42:6)

- the "Hope of Israel," a "savior in time of need" (Jeremiah 14:8)

- "a savior to defend and deliver" (Isaiah 19:20).

Yet every image led to the same hope: Through the Messiah, God would bring a reign of justice and peace. He would make a new covenant with his people and would be with them always, leading and guiding them to eternal happiness. So, though God's people were constantly struggling in a world damaged by sin and suffering, they continued to hope for the long-awaited salvation that God had promised—the coming of the Messiah.

Hebrew writings from a scroll of Isaiah found in a cave containing the scrolls of Qumran, near the Dead Sea

Activity Imagine you are asked to speak as God's prophet today. What would your hopeful message be? How would you deliver it?

The promise of a Messiah comes to fulfillment.

One of the prophecies about the Messiah from the Book of Isaiah stated, "Therefore the Lord himself will give you this sign: the virgin shall be with child, and bear a son, and shall name him Immanuel," which means "God is with us." (See Isaiah 7:14.) In time this prophecy of God's plan for salvation was fulfilled. To prepare Mary for her role in this plan, God blessed her in a special way. He made her free from original sin and from all sin since the very moment she was conceived. This truth about Mary's sinlessness is called the **Immaculate Conception**.

In Luke's Gospel we read that God sent an angel to tell Mary of her role in God's plan. An **angel** is a creature created by God as a pure spirit, without a physical body. Angels serve God as messengers, helping him to accomplish his mission of salvation. The angel who came to Mary said to her: "Behold, you

> **"The child to be born will be called holy, the Son of God."**
>
> (Luke 1:35)

will conceive in your womb and bear a son, and you shall name him Jesus. He will be great and will be called Son of the Most High . . . and of his kingdom there will be no end'" (Luke 1:31–33). The announcement to Mary that she would be the mother of the Son of God is called the **Annunciation**.

The name that Mary was to give to her child, *Jesus*, means "God saves" in Hebrew. And just as the prophecies had said, the child would be a descendant of King David, and would bring salvation to all people. But Mary, a young Jewish woman who was engaged to Joseph, a descendant of King David, did not understand how all of this could happen. She was not even married yet. So the angel explained, "The holy Spirit will come upon you, and the power of the Most High will overshadow you.

Faith Words

Immaculate Conception
angel
Annunciation

Therefore the child to be born will be called holy, the Son of God" (Luke 1:35). Mary, accepting God's plan, responded, "May it be done to me according to your word" (Luke 1:38).

The Old Testament prophecies about the Messiah were coming to fulfillment. The Messiah, Jesus Christ, our greatest hope, was coming to be among us and to save us from sin.

Activity Mary accepted God's plan of salvation. On a separate sheet of paper, write a prayer telling God that *you* accept the salvation that he offers.

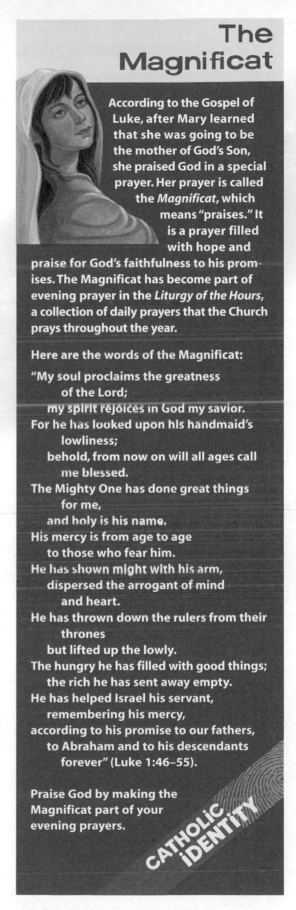

The Magnificat

According to the Gospel of Luke, after Mary learned that she was going to be the mother of God's Son, she praised God in a special prayer. Her prayer is called the *Magnificat*, which means "praises." It is a prayer filled with hope and praise for God's faithfulness to his promises. The Magnificat has become part of evening prayer in the *Liturgy of the Hours*, a collection of daily prayers that the Church prays throughout the year.

Here are the words of the Magnificat:

"My soul proclaims the greatness
    of the Lord;
    my spirit rejoices in God my savior.
For he has looked upon his handmaid's
    lowliness;
    behold, from now on will all ages call
    me blessed.
The Mighty One has done great things
    for me,
    and holy is his name.
His mercy is from age to age
    to those who fear him.
He has shown might with his arm,
    dispersed the arrogant of mind
    and heart.
He has thrown down the rulers from their
    thrones
    but lifted up the lowly.
The hungry he has filled with good things;
    the rich he has sent away empty.
He has helped Israel his servant,
    remembering his mercy,
according to his promise to our fathers,
    to Abraham and to his descendants
    forever" (Luke 1:46–55).

Praise God by making the Magnificat part of your evening prayers.

CATHOLIC IDENTITY

RESPONDING...

Recognizing Our Faith

Recall the question at the beginning of this chapter: *Who or what helps me in difficult times?* Answer this question from the perspective of:

• one of the Old Testament people mentioned in this chapter

_____

_____

• someone you know of who needs help getting through a difficult time

_____

_____

• yourself, now that you've completed this chapter.

_____

_____

Living Our Faith

In this chapter we learned how God helps his people and offers hope. This week make a decision to be an example of hope in your home, school, and neighborhood.

Venerable Matt Talbot

God can help us even when things seem hopeless. Matt Talbot was someone who knew this well. Born in 1856 in the slums of Dublin, Ireland, Matt was addicted to alcohol from the time he was twelve years old. When Matt began drinking, there were no alcoholic support groups and most people looked upon alcoholics as immoral. Matt faced his addiction shamefully and alone. Finally, when he was twenty-eight, Matt went to a priest for help. The priest advised Matt to make a pledge to stop drinking. He also told Matt to think about Christ and his suffering on the cross. Matt took this advice and began to live a simple life of prayer and fasting. He found happiness and peace in helping others who were in need.

Though Matt suffered physically and mentally in his efforts to stay sober, he kept his pledge. He continued to live a life of prayer, fasting, and generosity until his death in 1925. Matt's efforts to overcome his addiction with God's help is a powerful example for us.

Pray that God will give hope to all people who are facing problems.

 For additional ideas and activities, visit www.weliveourfaith.com.

Putting Faith to Work

Talk about what you have learned in this chapter:

 We understand that throughout human history God has reached out to help his people.

 We celebrate that God promised salvation through his Son, Jesus Christ, the Messiah.

We respond to God's promise of salvation by helping and serving others.

Decide on ways to live out what you have learned.

✝ ENCOUNTERING GOD'S WORD

❝ **Rejoice in hope, endure in affliction, perservere in prayer.** ❞

(Romans 12:12)

➡ **READ** the quotation from Scripture.

➡ **REFLECT** on these questions:
What does it mean to rejoice? to endure? to persevere? What are some examples of "affliction"—a condition of great suffering? What does this quote ask us to do when faced with it?

➡ **SHARE** your reflections with a partner.

➡ **DECIDE** on one person with whom you will share the hopeful message of this Scripture passage this week.

Write the letter that best defines each term.

1. _____ free will

2. _____ original sin

3. _____ angel

4. _____ Immaculate Conception

a. the announcement to Mary that she would be the mother of the Son of God

b. the freedom and ability to choose what to do

c. the first sin committed by the first human beings

d. a creature created by God as a pure spirit, without a physical body, who serves God and helps him to accomplish his mission of salvation

e. the truth that God made Mary free from original sin and from all sin since the very moment she was conceived

Short Answers

5. Throughout Scripture, we read of many images that were prophesied about the Messiah. What are two of them? _____

6. What does the name *Jesus* mean in Hebrew? _____

7. What story do we find in Chapter 3 of the Book of Genesis, and what important truths does it teach us?

_____

8. What hope does God give us? _____

9-10. ESSAY: What are examples of ways God has reached out to help his people?

Sharing Faith with Your Family

Discuss the following with your family:
- God reaches out to help humankind.
- God offers his people the hope of salvation.
- God promises a Messiah.
- The promise of a Messiah comes to fulfillment.

Write the name of each family member on a slip of paper. Have each family member draw a slip of paper from a bowl. Each day, do something for the person whose name you drew that will help to give him or her a greater sense of hope.

The Worship Connection

A prayer from the Liturgy of the Hours asks, "God, come to my assistance. Lord, make haste to help me." Pray these words when you need help.

More to Explore

In this chapter we learned that God helps his people and gives them hope. Use the Internet or a parish bulletin to research groups or organizations that offer help to those in need.

Catholic Social Teaching ☑ Checklist

Theme of Catholic Social Teaching:
Rights and Responsibilities of the Human Person

How it relates to Chapter 7: All people have a right to food, shelter, clothing, religious freedom, and life itself. Just as God helps us, we have a responsibility to help and protect one another.

How can you do this?

☐ At home:

_____

☐ At school/work:

_____

☐ In the parish:

_____

☐ In the community:

_____

Check off each action after it has been completed.

GATHERING...

"For today in the city of David a savior has been born for you who is Messiah and Lord."

(Luke 2:11)

✚ **Leader:** "Each year his parents went to Jerusalem for the feast of Passover, and when he was twelve years old, they went up according to festival custom." (Luke 2:41) So begins a Gospel story about Jesus as a boy going on a family journey. He was going to Jerusalem for Passover, the Jewish feast celebrating how God freed the people of Israel from slavery in Egypt. Let us close our eyes now and imagine meeting Jesus then, at twelve years old.

Imagine yourself journeying with your family to Jerusalem for Passover. Your family decides to stop for a rest. The caravan halts at the side of a dirt road outside the city, and you all pile out. A few other families also stop to rest. They get out and begin to share some refreshment and conversation. On the horizon, you can see the magnificent place of worship called the Temple of Jerusalem. It is glistening in the lowering sun.

You hear some young people laughing and talking. You walk over to see if you know anyone. Standing there is a boy around your age. He introduces himself as Jesus. He smiles, and you shake hands. You begin to talk. What kinds of things do you discuss? What does Jesus want to know about your life? What do you tell him? How does he respond? Before long you feel that he is your good friend.

Soon your parents are calling you. It's time to continue the journey into Jerusalem. As you and Jesus leave each other, you promise Jesus that you will always be friends. (silent reflection)

Now let us open our eyes and pray:

All: O God, help us to keep our promise and grow in our relationship with Jesus Christ, your Son. Amen.

 Visit www.weliveourfaith.com to find appropriate music and songs.

GATHERING...

The BiG Question:

Do I keep my promises?

Discover some famous promises. Can you match the person to the promise that he or she made? Check your answers below.

1 "After my death I will let fall a shower of roses."

2 "The English will have no more power over you."

3 "We choose to go to the moon.... And it will be done before the end of this decade."

4 "I promise to bring back gold, spices, and silks from the Far East, to spread Christianity, and to lead an expedition to China."

| Saint Thérèse of Lisieux | Christopher Columbus | Saint Joan of Arc | John F. Kennedy |

Answers:

1. Saint Thérèse of Lisieux. Some Catholics say that when they pray for Saint Thérèse's help, they see a rose just before their prayer is answered.
2. Saint Joan of Arc, speaking to the French people. Joan succeeded in helping France to drive back invading English troops and restore the French king. Joan died as a martyr in 1431.
3. President John F. Kennedy in 1962, promising that America would land on the moon by 1970. The first Americans landed on the moon in 1969.
4. Christopher Columbus, Italian navigator and explorer for Spain. Columbus could not keep his promise because he never reached the Far East, but he is celebrated for exploring the Bahamas, the Caribbean Islands, and the Americas.

What is a promise that needs to be kept in our world today?

In this chapter we consider how the Gospels reveal Jesus as the promised Messiah through details they give regarding his birth and early life. Through this chapter, we hope

 to learn how the coming of Jesus Christ fulfilled Israel's hopes for the promised Messiah

 to trust that Jesus Christ, true God and true man, continues to be with us and to share God's life with us in a special way

to evangelize by sharing the truth that Jesus Christ is the promised Messiah.

You might not know their names or much about them, but your ancestors, all the family members who came before you, have a special connection to your life today. In a very real way, you and your family are living witnesses of promises that your ancestors kept long ago. How so? Well, promises were the very foundations of your ancestors' lives. These promises included the promise of marriage, the promise to build a better life for themselves and their families, the promise to work hard to help one another, and the promise of living in freedom.

Through all of their comings and goings, all of their hard work and hope, your ancestors lived for the promise of a better life—not only for themselves but for their children and their children's children, and for their whole network of relations, including, in the end, *yourself*.

Activity What promises do people today need to make to future generations?

"Every civilization rests on a set of promises. . . . Hope and faith depend on the promises; if hope and faith go, everything goes," wrote Herbert Sebastian Agar (1897–1980), U.S. author, historian, and Pulitzer Prize winner.

Jesus Christ is the promised Messiah.

God had promised to remain with his people forever and to send the Messiah to lead and save them. The coming of Jesus Christ fulfilled this promise. Jesus was conceived within, carried by, and born from the womb of a mother, just as every human being is. And yet Jesus Christ was conceived by the power of the Holy Spirit. He is the son of Mary and the Son of God. The Son of God "worked with human hands, He thought with a human mind, acted by human choice, and loved with a human heart. Born of the Virgin Mary, He has truly been made one of us, like us in all things except sin" (*Pastoral Constitution on the Church in the Modern World*, 22).

The accounts of Jesus' birth and childhood found in the first two chapters of the Gospels of Matthew and Luke are called the **infancy narratives**. They include a *genealogy*, or family history, and various stories about the early life of Jesus. The infancy narratives emphasize who Jesus is: Emmanuel, in whom "God is with us" (Matthew 1:23)—the Son of God, descended from the family line of David, who was of the line of Abraham.

Faith Word
infancy narratives

The infancy narratives proclaim that Jesus Christ is the promised Savior. He will carry out God's plan of salvation. They show that the events surrounding Jesus' conception, birth, and early childhood fulfilled God's promises to his people, which can be found in the Old Testament. Here are some of the promises that Jesus' birth fulfilled:

OLD TESTAMENT PROMISES	FULFILLMENT FOUND IN INFANCY NARRATIVE
God promised Abraham, "In your descendants all the nations of the earth shall find blessing" (Genesis 22:18).	Jesus' ancestry is traced back to David and to Abraham. (See Matthew 1:1–17.)
"The Lord himself will give you this sign: the virgin shall be with child, and bear a son, and shall name him Immanuel." (Isaiah 7:14)	God calls the Virgin Mary to become the mother of God's only Son. (See Matthew 1:22–23.)
"For a child is born to us, a son is given to us; upon his shoulder dominion rests. They name him Wonder-Counselor, God-Hero, Father-Forever, Prince of Peace. His dominion is vast and forever peaceful, From David's throne, and over his kingdom, which he confirms and sustains By judgment and justice, both now and forever." (Isaiah 9:5–6)	The angel tells Mary that the child to be born "will be great and will be called Son of the Most High, and the Lord God will give him the throne of David . . . and of his kingdom there will be no end" (Luke 1:32–33).

Activity If the birth of Jesus Christ were being announced today in the media, what might this announcement say?

Jesus fulfills the hopes of Israel.

As we read in Scripture about Jesus' early life, we learn that Jesus' mother, Mary, and foster-father, Joseph, were devout Jews. They followed all the laws of Moses. These laws required that a first-born son be consecrated to the Lord after his birth. To **consecrate** is to make sacred for God. A mother was also required to offer a sacrifice to the Lord forty days after the birth of a son. The customary offering was a lamb and a turtledove, but those too poor to afford both could offer two turtledoves or pigeons.

So, after Jesus' birth, Joseph and Mary decided to travel to the Temple in Jerusalem to fulfill these requirements. The Temple was the sacred place where Jewish people gathered to worship God. Joseph and Mary brought the offering appointed for those who were poor. And while they were in the Temple, something remarkable happened. A man named Simeon, who was full of faith in the Lord, took the infant Jesus in his arms and praised God, saying:

"My eyes have seen your salvation,
    which you prepared in sight
        of all the peoples,
a light for revelation to the Gentiles,
    and glory for your people Israel" (Luke 2:30–32).

> **"God is with us."**
> (Matthew 1:23)

An elderly woman named Anna was also in the Temple. She was a holy woman with the gift of prophecy. She too "gave thanks to God and spoke about the child to all who were awaiting the redemption of Jerusalem" (Luke 2:38). In the words of Simeon and the response of Anna, we find the true expression of Israel's hope for the promised Messiah.

Faith Word

consecrate

Activity Imagine that you are in the Temple with Anna and Simeon, praising Jesus as the Messiah. What words of praise would you use?

The Temple in Jerusalem

The Temple in Jerusalem was first built by Israel's King Solomon around 966 B.C. It took eleven years to build this great stone structure, known as Solomon's Temple. It was said that the *ark of the covenant*, a wooden box that held the tablets of the Ten Commandments, was kept inside this Temple's holiest, innermost room. This room was called the *holy of holies*.

Solomon's Temple was destroyed when Jerusalem was attacked in 587 B.C. It was rebuilt, but with so few resources that the new structure was not nearly as grand or as elegant as Solomon's Temple. In 19 B.C., however, King Herod destroyed this structure in order to rebuild the Temple again. He vowed that the new Temple would be considered the greatest of all. It took more than 10,000 workers and nearly eight years of labor before the Temple was ready to be used by the public. This splendid Temple was where Mary and Joseph brought the baby Jesus to consecrate him to the Lord.

Although this Temple was also destroyed, many Jews continue to visit the site where it stood. They come to pray at the Western Wall, or Wailing Wall, considered to be a last remnant of the Temple.

Go online to find out more about the Western Wall today.

BELIEVING...

Jesus is the Son of God.

What are some important traditions in your family?

Though we know very little about Jesus' early life, we do know through Scripture that Jesus was a devout Jew and that he "grew and became strong, filled with wisdom; and the favor of God was upon him" (Luke 2:40). Nurtured by his family and his Jewish community, Jesus was raised in the rich traditions of the Jewish faith. He learned about the commandments, the prophecies, and other sacred writings. The following story from Luke's Gospel gives us a glimpse of what Jesus was like as a young person at about your age:

"Each year his parents went to Jerusalem for the feast of Passover, and when he was twelve years old, they went up according to festival custom. After they had completed its days, as they were returning, the boy Jesus remained behind in Jerusalem, but his parents did not know it. Thinking that he was in the caravan, they journeyed for a day and looked for him among their relatives and acquaintances, but not finding him, they returned to Jerusalem to look for him. After three days they found him in the temple, sitting in the midst of the teachers, listening to them and asking them questions, and all who heard him were astounded at his understanding and his answers. When his parents saw him, they were astonished, and his mother said to him, 'Son, why have you done this to us? Your father and I have been looking for you with great anxiety.' And he said to them, 'Why were you looking for me? Did you not know that I must be in my Father's house?' But they did not understand what he said to them. He went down with them and came to Nazareth, and was obedient to them; and his mother kept all these things in her heart. And Jesus advanced [in] wisdom and age and favor before God and man." (Luke 2:41–52)

This story is the last story of Luke's infancy narrative and the only story in the Gospels about Jesus as a youth. It portrays Jesus as a young man so interested in his faith that he stays behind in the Temple while his family journeys home after Passover.

And this story reflects the humanity and divinity of Jesus: Jesus knew that the Temple was his "Father's house," yet he was also a boy thought to be lost, with parents frantic to find him, and still with many more life experiences ahead of him.

Activity Jesus lived his Jewish faith. List some ways that *you* will live your faith this week.

Jesus is true God and true man.

Though it does not tell of the events of Jesus' birth and childhood, John's Gospel offers a summary of these events and of who Jesus is. John begins with a *prologue*, or introduction. This prologue is a great poetic hymn that summarizes the themes of John's Gospel. Its opening lines are:

"In the beginning was the Word,
    and the Word was with God,
    and the Word was God."
                    (John 1:1)

The words *In the beginning* also start off the Book of Genesis and its account of creation. John is using these words here to signal that a great new creation begins in Jesus Christ. In John's prologue we also read:

"And the Word became flesh
    and made his dwelling among us,
    and we saw his glory,
    the glory as of the Father's only Son,
    full of grace and truth."
                    (John 1:14)

So, the Word, Jesus Christ, who was with God and is God, took on our human nature and lived among us *as* a human being. Jesus was not "disguised" as a human being or "just pretending" to be human. Without losing his divine nature, the only Son of God, the Word, became truly human. With this prologue, John's Gospel, like Matthew's and Luke's Gospels, helps us to understand that in Jesus Christ "God is with us" and has become one of us. Jesus is true God and true man.

> **"We saw his glory,
> the glory as of the Father's only Son,
> full of grace and truth."**
>   (John 1:14)

Activity With a partner think of ways you could explain to a second grader that "God is with us."

The seven sacraments

Jesus, the fulfillment of God's promise, is present with us in a special way in the seven sacraments. Sacraments truly bring about what they represent. They are effective signs of God's love and presence and are the most important celebrations of the Church. They unite all Catholics with Jesus and with one another. By celebrating the sacraments, we are cooperating with God's plan of salvation because the grace that we receive in the sacraments strengthens us against sin and helps us to live as Jesus' disciples.

The sacraments of ...	are called ...	and all ...
Baptism Confirmation Eucharist	*Sacraments of Christian Initiation*	• offer glory to God and bring us together in praise and worship of God • make us holy • help to strengthen and unify the Church and make us a sign of God's love in the world.
Penance and Reconciliation Anointing of the Sick	*Sacraments of Healing*	
Holy Orders Matrimony	*Sacraments at the Service of Communion*	

Put a check mark next to each sacrament that you have received. Choose one of the sacraments that you have checked. Explain some details about this sacrament to another person and have that person try to guess which sacrament you are describing.

Recognizing Our Faith

Recall the question at the beginning of this chapter: *Do I keep my promises?* Just as God was faithful to his promises, we are called to be faithful to our promises. Make a display of images that show people keeping promises to make the world a better place. These images may consist of photos from magazines, newspapers, the Internet, or your group's own drawings.

Living Our Faith

Be an evangelizer. Tell one other person about the birth of Jesus and the ways it fulfilled God's promise of a Messiah.

Saint Joseph

Joseph, like Mary, had an important role to play in God's promise of salvation. According to Matthew's Gospel, an angel came to Joseph in a dream and explained that Mary's child, conceived by the Holy Spirit, would bring salvation to humankind. Joseph listened to the angel and married Mary.

Partners in FAITH

After Jesus' birth in Bethlehem in the land of Israel, an angel told Joseph to flee to Egypt with Mary and Jesus to protect Jesus from a massacre of infants ordered by the king. The family stayed in Egypt until the angel told Joseph it was safe to bring them home to Israel. They settled there in a town called Nazareth. Keeping the promise of marriage, Joseph looked after his family. He worked as a carpenter to provide for them and raised Jesus in the traditions of the Jewish faith. Joseph probably died before Jesus began his public ministry.

We celebrate two feast days in honor of Saint Joseph: March 19 and May 1.

How was Saint Joseph faithful to his promises? How can you be more faithful as a disciple of Jesus?

Putting Faith to Work

Talk about what you have learned in this chapter:

 We learn how the coming of Jesus Christ fulfilled Israel's hopes for the promised Messiah.

 We trust that Jesus Christ, true God and true man, continues to be with us and to share God's life with us in a special way.

 We evangelize by sharing the truth that Jesus Christ is the promised Messiah.

Decide on ways to live out what you have learned.

✝ ENCOUNTERING GOD'S WORD

"If you belong to Christ, then you are Abraham's descendant, heirs according to the promise."

(Galatians 3:29)

➡ **READ** the quotation from Scripture.

➡ **REFLECT** on these questions:
In what way do you "belong to Christ"? How are you a descendant of Abraham? If an *heir* is one who inherits something, what promise do you inherit as one who belongs to Christ?

➡ **SHARE** your reflections with a partner.

➡ **DECIDE** to be an example to others as one who belongs to Christ.

Complete the following.

1. The _____ are the accounts of Jesus' birth and childhood in the Gospels of Matthew and Luke.

2. One story about Jesus portrays him as a young man so interested in his faith that he stays behind in the Temple of Jerusalem after the feast of _____.

3. In the words of Simeon and the response of Anna, who saw the baby Jesus being consecrated in the Temple of Jerusalem, we find that Jesus fulfilled Israel's hopes for the promised _____.

4. _____, without losing his divine nature, took on our human nature and lived among us as a human being.

Write *True* or *False* next to the following sentences. On a separate sheet of paper, change the false sentences to make them true.

5. _____ The Temple was a sacred place where Jewish people gathered to worship God.

6. _____ Nurtured by his family and community, Jesus was raised in the rich traditions of the Christian faith.

7. _____ The Gospel writer John is true God and true man.

8. _____ To *consecrate* is to make sacred for God.

9–10. ESSAY: What is one of the promises from the Old Testament that Jesus' birth fulfilled? Explain your answer.

Sharing Faith with Your Family

Discuss the following with your family:

- Jesus Christ is the promised Messiah.
- Jesus fulfills the hopes of Israel.
- Jesus is the Son of God.
- Jesus is true God and true man.

Jesus grew up within a family. His time spent with his family was important for his growing in "wisdom and age and favor" (Luke 2:52). The same holds true for us. Plan a monthly event to strengthen your family ties, such as a special meal, an activity, or a service project that involves gathering with your family.

The Worship Connection

This chapter recalled the promise God made to Abraham. At Mass, Abraham is called "our father in faith." Think of a reason why this name is appropriate.

More to Explore

Find photos and information in travel brochures, online, or in magazine articles about the region where Jesus grew up, which is now a part of the Middle East known as Israel or Palestine. Share your findings.

Catholic Social Teaching ☑ Checklist

Theme of Catholic Social Teaching:
Solidarity of the Human Family

How it relates to Chapter 8: As Catholics we are called to love our neighbors, wherever they live. We are all part of one human family. We promise to stand by one another.

How can you do this?

☐ At home:

_____

☐ At school/work:

_____

☐ In the parish:

_____

☐ In the community:

_____

Check off each action after it has been completed.

9

The Coming of God's Kingdom

"I must proclaim the good news of the kingdom of God, because for this purpose I have been sent."

(Luke 4:43)

Leader: So many people in the world need to hear the good news that our Lord Jesus Christ proclaimed. We pray for these people now.

Reader 1: Lord, help all those who are poor and in need, especially (volunteers name specific people or groups). Bless and strengthen all people who share what they have with those who are poor.

All: "Blessed are the poor in spirit, for theirs is the kingdom of heaven."

(Matthew 5:3)

Reader 2: Lord, help all those who are grieving, sad, or suffering, especially (volunteers name specific people or groups). Bless and strengthen all people who give comfort to those who are hurting.

All: "Blessed are they who mourn, for they will be comforted."

(Matthew 5:4)

Reader 3: Lord, help all those who are being treated unjustly, especially (volunteers name specific people or groups). Bless and strengthen all people who work to make wrongs right.

All: "Blessed are they who hunger and thirst for righteousness for they will be satisfied."

(Matthew 5:6)

Reader 4: Lord, help all those whose homes, communities, or nations are places of conflict, especially (volunteers name specific people or groups). Bless and strengthen all people who work to establish peace.

All: "Blessed are the peacemakers, for they will be called children of God."

(Matthew 5:9)

Reader 5: Lord, help all those who are persecuted for religious reasons or for their efforts to establish justice, peace, and harmony, especially (volunteers name specific people or groups). Bless and strengthen all people who do what is right despite criticism, rejection, and persecution.

All: "Blessed are they who are persecuted for the sake of righteousness, for theirs is the kingdom of heaven."

(Matthew 5:10)

All: Amen.

 Visit www.weliveourfaith.com to find appropriate music and songs.

95

The BiG QuEStion:

How can I make a difference?

Discover some people who have made a difference. With a partner brainstorm some names of people who made a difference through their positive actions in our country or in the world. Then complete the "Hall of Fame" below.

Making a Difference
Hall of Fame

Name:	Name:	Name:
_____	_____	_____
Made a difference by:	**Made a difference by:**	**Made a difference by:**
_____	_____	_____
_____	_____	_____
_____	_____	_____
_____	_____	_____
_____	_____	_____
_____	_____	_____
_____	_____	_____

Thank God for the positive actions of these people, as well as for people who have made a difference in your own life.

In this chapter we learn that in Jesus God's Kingdom began. All people are called to spread this Kingdom. Through this chapter, we hope

 to understand that God's Kingdom is the power of God's love active in our lives and in our world

 to trust that, by living according to the Beatitudes, we will find true happiness as we spread God's Kingdom

 to proclaim God's Kingdom every day through what we say and what we do.

Carlo was the best swimmer on the swim team. His grandfather used to come to every swim meet to watch him race. But Carlo's grandfather was growing older. When he became weak and could not leave the senior citizens' home to attend all of Carlo's swim meets, Carlo wondered what he could do . . .

A doctor at the senior citizens' home told Carlo that water exercises might be a good way for Carlo's grandfather to grow stronger . . .

Carlo made an arrangement with the senior citizens' home to provide transportation for his grandfather to the local pool once a week. Carlo was there to help his grandfather do some of the water exercises that Carlo had learned at swim practice . . .

Carlo's grandfather began to regain some of his strength. He again made it to some of Carlo's swim meets . . .

How did Carlo make a difference?

“No act of kindness, no matter small, is ever wasted,” wrote Aesop, famous Greek fable writer from the sixth century B.C.

Soon a few other residents of the senior citizens' home began asking about the water exercises. They were interested in doing them, too . . .

So, Carlo approached the management of the pool about starting a weekly water exercise program for senior citizens. Before long he was teaching a weekly water exercise class for senior citizens . . .

More and more people began to join the water exercise program . . .

Activity You may not be able to start an exercise class, but there are many things that you can do to make a difference in people's lives. Write one thing that you can do to help someone today. Be sure to do it. Note the ways that your action can make a difference to the person you helped, to yourself, and perhaps to other people, too.

Today's date:

Action to help someone:

Difference this action can make:

Jesus prepares for his work as God's Son.

In the New Testament we read of a prophet sent by God to prepare the way for the Messiah. This prophet was John, Jesus' cousin. John called the people to repent—to be sorry for their sins, ask God for forgiveness, and decide not to sin anymore. John baptized his followers in the Jordan River as a sign of their desire to repent and to change their lives. But John, called John the Baptist, also told the people, "One mightier than I is coming after me. . . . I have baptized you with water; he will baptize you with the holy Spirit" (Mark 1:7–8).

When Jesus was about thirty years old, he left his hometown of Nazareth and traveled to the Jordan River to be baptized by John. John realized that Jesus did not need to be baptized. But Jesus asked John to allow it, so John baptized him. This baptism was a sign that Jesus was beginning his mission to bring salvation from sin. As Jesus came up from the water he saw the Holy Spirit, "like a dove, descending upon him. And a voice came from the heavens, 'You are my beloved Son; with you I am well pleased'" (Mark 1:10–11).

The Holy Spirit then led Jesus into the desert. For forty days, Jesus was alone there, praying and fasting. And there, three times the devil tempted Jesus to rebel against God's plan for salvation. But Jesus refused the temptation to use his power for his own benefit and instead accepted God's plan. Jesus said, "Get away, Satan! It is written:

'The Lord, your God, shall you worship
   and him alone shall you serve'" (Matthew 4:10).

This account of Jesus in the desert helps us to understand that, though divine, Jesus struggled with human weaknesses and temptations. Yet, because of his trust in God the Father, Jesus was able to resist sin and evil.

Activity Today young people are up against all sorts of temptations to give in to evil and sin. Think about what these temptations might be.

What strengthens us to resist temptation?

Jesus ushers in God's Kingdom.

Jesus, anointed by the Holy Spirit when he was baptized, and strengthened by the same Spirit during his temptation in the desert, was now ready to begin his ministry. So, Jesus went to the region of Galilee and began to preach, "This is the time of fulfillment. The kingdom of God is at hand. Repent, and believe in the gospel" (Mark 1:15).

The coming of God's Kingdom was a constant theme of Jesus' preaching. He understood and used the term *Kingdom of God* in the context of his Jewish faith and heritage. Yet Jesus broadened people's understanding of this term. He helped them to understand that God was promising salvation for all people, not just saving and restoring the earthly kingdom of Israel. Jesus showed by his life and his love that the Kingdom of God is not a place that can be found on a map. The **Kingdom of God** is the power of God's love active in our lives and in our world. With the coming of Jesus Christ, God's Kingdom came into the world. Yet the Kingdom of God will not be complete until Jesus returns in glory at the end of time.

Faith Word
Kingdom of God

In proclaiming the coming of God's Kingdom, Jesus was expressing God's desire for goodness and happiness for all people. He was calling people to help bring about these things by turning to God. Jesus was saying that:

- God's presence and reign can be found in him and in the things he said and did

- grace and freedom from sin are offered to everyone

- by living in God's presence, people spread God's Kingdom and can move toward life with God forever.

By all he said and did, Jesus was showing people the power of God's love active in their lives.

> "The kingdom of God is at hand."
> (Mark 1:15)

Activity Give three examples from recent news events showing ways that people spread the Kingdom of God in our world today.

1.

2.

3.

Stories of the Kingdom

Jesus told parables to help people to learn more about God's Kingdom. In these parables Jesus spoke about everyday things, such as planting seeds, harvesting crops, baking bread, and fishing. He did this to help people to look at their lives in a new way. Here are two examples of Jesus' parables about God's Kingdom:

The Parable of the Mustard Seed (Mark 4:30–32)
Jesus compared the Kingdom of God to a mustard seed that someone planted in a field. This small seed grew into "the largest of plants," and all "the birds of the sky can dwell in its shade" (Mark 4:32).

Message: The Kingdom of God spreads through God's grace working in us. We are all invited to dwell in this Kingdom, to be part of God's life and love.

The Parable of the Fishing Net (Matthew 13:47–50)
Jesus compared God's Kingdom to a fishing net that collects all kinds of fish from the sea. The fishermen sort the bad fish from the good. Jesus said, "Thus it will be at the end of the age. The angels will . . . separate the wicked from the righteous" (Matthew 13:49).

Message: We are all called to share in God's Kingdom. But we must accept God's invitation and live good lives if we want happiness with God forever at the end of time.

Read Matthew 13 to find more parables about the Kingdom of God.

BELIEVING...

Jesus teaches us to spread the Kingdom of God.

What are some things that people usually think will make them happy?

One day, a large crowd followed Jesus to a mountain. In his message that day, known as the Sermon on the Mount, Jesus taught his disciples about spreading God's Kingdom. He taught them about this by giving them the **Beatitudes**, teachings that describe the way to live as his disciples. The word *beatitude* means "blessed" or "happy." Jesus explained that by living according to the Beatitudes, we can help spread God's Kingdom, and, in turn, we can find true happiness.

The Beatitudes are a promise of God's blessings. They give us hope in the Kingdom of God, also called the kingdom of heaven. Jesus' message of hope for all who live the Beatitudes is: "Rejoice and be glad, for your reward will be great in heaven" (Matthew 5:12).

Faith Word
Beatitudes

THE BEATITUDES	MESSAGE
"Blessed are the poor in spirit, for theirs is the kingdom of heaven." (Matthew 5:3)	This beatitude tells us about our attitude toward the things we have; we should not be overly attached to possessions. Our confidence should be in God. We are called to share whatever we have with others.
"Blessed are they who mourn, for they will be comforted." (Matthew 5:4)	We are to be signs of hope despite the sadness, evil, and injustice we see in the world. As Jesus' disciples, we are to comfort those who suffer injustice and loss.
"Blessed are the meek, for they will inherit the land." (Matthew 5:5)	The meek are the humble—that is, those who realize that their talents and abilities come from God. We are to use our God-given talents and abilities to do what is good, showing love for God and others.
"Blessed are they who hunger and thirst for righteousness, for they will be satisfied." (Matthew 5:6)	The greatest desire of those who hunger and thirst for righteousness is for God's power and presence to be at work in the world. As Jesus' disciples we try to do God's will. We put our trust in God and carry out Christ's work of justice.
"Blessed are the merciful, for they will be shown mercy." (Matthew 5:7)	Those who show love and forgive others will themselves receive love and forgiveness in God's Kingdom. We are to show compassion to all people.
"Blessed are the clean of heart, for they will see God." (Matthew 5:8)	The clean of heart are those who are open to God and God's law. They are sincere in everything they do. We are to be faithful Christians and find Christ in others.
"Blessed are the peacemakers, for they will be called children of God." (Matthew 5:9)	God wants all people to love one another and to have the peace that comes from loving him and trusting in his will. We are called to be reconcilers in our homes, communities, and world. We are to bring people together.
"Blessed are they who are persecuted for the sake of righteousness, for theirs is the kingdom of heaven." (Matthew 5:10)	Prophets were often persecuted when they brought people God's message. We are to live out our Christian faith even when others do not understand our beliefs.

Activity Living out the Beatitudes can help us to make life different for ourselves and others. On a separate sheet of paper, make a third column that can be added to the Beatitudes chart. Title this column *Making a Difference*. Under this heading, list a practical way to live out each of the Beatitudes.

Jesus teaches us to pray for God's Kingdom.

During the Sermon on the Mount Jesus also taught his followers how to pray. In the Beatitudes Jesus had described the way that his disciples should live. Now he taught them how to ask for this "new life" in prayer. The prayer that Jesus taught them was the Lord's Prayer, a prayer to God the Father.

The Lord's Prayer, also called the Our Father, "is truly the summary of the whole gospel" (*CCC*, 2761). It sums up Jesus' whole message of trust in and love for the Father. Everything Jesus said and did reflected his awareness of his Father's presence in his life, and when we pray the Lord's Prayer we are asking our Father to act in our lives and in our world. We ask the Holy Spirit to help us to make the Kingdom come alive in people's hearts and lives. And we hope for the Lord's return at the end of time.

> "Rejoice and be glad, for your reward will be great in heaven."
>
> (Matthew 5:12)

The chart at the bottom of the page shows the words and message of the Lord's Prayer, which is based on Matthew 6:9–13.

Activity With your group, prepare a prayer service that includes the Lord's Prayer. Your prayer service might also include a song, a Scripture reading, a psalm, and prayers for those in need.

The Sacraments of Initiation

Three sacraments that lay the foundation for our lives as disciples of Christ are Baptism, Confirmation, and Eucharist. They are called the Sacraments of Christian Initiation. Through the reception of these sacraments we are initiated into the Church and receive the grace to spread God's Kingdom.

The Lord's Prayer is an important part of each of these sacraments. In Baptism and Confirmation, the handing on of the Lord's Prayer is a sign of our "new birth into the divine life" (*CCC*, 2769). And "in the *Eucharistic liturgy* the Lord's Prayer appears as the prayer of the whole Church" (*CCC*, 2770).

Thank God for the grace that he gives us in these sacraments.

CATHOLIC IDENTITY

The Lord's Prayer

WE PRAY	OUR WORDS MEAN
Our Father, who art in heaven, hallowed be thy name;	God is present to all who love him. We have become God's people and he is our God. We look forward to being with him forever.
thy kingdom come; thy will be done on earth as it is in heaven.	We ask God to unite us with the work of Christ and to bring about his Kingdom. We pray to God for the ability to do his will.
Give us this day our daily bread; and forgive us our trespasses as we forgive those who trespass against us;	We ask God for everything we need for ourselves and for the world. We use his gifts to work toward his plan of salvation. We ask God to heal us, and we ask for forgiveness from others when needed. We follow the example of Christ and forgive those who have hurt us.
and lead us not into temptation, but deliver us from evil. Amen.	We pray that God will protect us from all that could draw us away from his love. We ask him to guide us to choose good in our lives, and we ask him for the strength to follow his law.

RESPONDING...

Recognizing Our Faith

Recall the question at the beginning of this chapter: *How can I make a difference?* Imagine that you were asked to discuss this question with a group of fifth graders. How would you use the material presented in this chapter to teach them to spread the Kingdom of God and make a difference in the world?

Living Our Faith

Think for a moment: Which of your words and actions *yesterday* helped to spread the Kingdom of God? What can you do *today* to spread God's Kingdom?

Jean Donovan

"I pray that I will be an example of Christ's love and peace. I pray that people will always be more important to me than the job I do," said Jean Donovan, who truly lived what Jesus taught about God's Kingdom. Born in 1953, Donovan had a carefree outlook on life but also wanted to make a difference in others' lives. During college, she spent her junior year in Ireland, where she volunteered and heard missionaries talk about their experiences helping people in Peru.

After college, Donovan was still deeply affected by these experiences. She made a decision that changed her own and others' lives. She began youth ministry work with her local diocese. This led to an opportunity to serve in El Salvador, in Central America, with the priests and religious brothers and sisters of Maryknoll, a Catholic mission society. At that time, El Salvador was in the midst of a civil war. Donovan and her companions tried not to let violence and danger interfere with their work. But while driving back from an airport, Donovan and three religious sisters, Sisters Ita Ford, Maura Clarke, and Dorothy Kazel, were attacked and killed.

Take time to pray for missionaries who risk their lives to spread God's Kingdom.

 For additional ideas and activities, visit www.weliveourfaith.com.

Putting Faith to Work

Talk about what you have learned in this chapter:

We understand that God's Kingdom is the power of God's love active in our lives and in our world.

We trust that, by living according to the Beatitudes, we will find true happiness as we spread God's Kingdom.

We proclaim God's Kingdom every day through what we say and what we do.

Decide on ways to live out what you have learned.

✝ ENCOUNTERING GOD'S WORD

❝ The coming of the kingdom of God cannot be observed, and no one will announce, 'Look, here it is,' or, 'There it is.' For behold, the kingdom of God is among you.❞

(Luke 17:20–21)

➡ **READ** the quotation from Scripture.

➡ **REFLECT** on the following question:
When and how is the Kingdom of God "among you" as Jesus stated?

➡ **SHARE** your reflections with a partner.

➡ **DECIDE** to do one thing each day, among your friends and family, to help spread the Kingdom of God.

Circle the letter of the correct answer.

1. _____ baptized people in the Jordan River as a sign of their desire to repent and to change their lives.

   a. Jesus   **b.** Matthew   **c.** Mark   **d.** John

2. Jesus' whole message of trust in and love for God his Father is summarized in the _____.

   a. Kingdom of God   **b.** Beatitudes   **c.** Lord's Prayer   **d.** Sermon on the Mount

3. The Kingdom of God is the power of _____ active in our lives and in the world.

   a. God's love   **b.** God's desire   **c.** Jewish heritage   **d.** Jewish faith

4. Jesus taught his disciples about spreading God's Kingdom by giving them the _____, teachings that describe the way to live as his disciples.

   a. Jewish heritage   **b.** Beatitudes   **c.** Lord's Prayer   **d.** parables

Short Answers

5. What happened when Jesus was alone in the desert for forty days and nights? _____

   _____

6. What does the word *beatitude* mean? _____

7. What is another name for the Lord's Prayer? _____

8. What was a constant theme of Jesus' preaching? _____

9–10. ESSAY: What did Jesus help people to understand about the term *Kingdom of God*?

Sharing Faith with Your Family

Discuss the following with your family:

- Jesus prepares for his work as God's Son.
- Jesus ushers in God's Kingdom.
- Jesus teaches us to spread the Kingdom of God.
- Jesus teaches us to pray for God's Kingdom.

One way that we can proclaim the Kingdom of God is to acknowledge the good works of others. When your family is together this week, take a few minutes to recognize how each person makes a difference in the family, and thank him or her for it.

The Worship Connection

At Mass, the Lord's Prayer is followed by an ancient *doxology* (prayer of praise): "For the kingdom, the power, and the glory. . . . " Listen for this prayer at Mass.

More to Explore

People from all cultures are invited into God's Kingdom. Choose an unfamiliar country. Research it as if you were going to live there. How is God's love active among the people there?

Catholic Social Teaching ☑ Checklist

Theme of Catholic Social Teaching:
Call to Family, Community, and Participation

How it relates to Chapter 9: As Catholics we are called to make a difference in society through our participation in our families, our communities, the nation, and the world. In doing so we continue to spread the Kingdom of God through our words and actions.

How can you do this?

☐ At home:

_____

☐ At school/work:

_____

☐ In the parish:

_____

☐ In the community:

_____

Check off each action after it has been completed.

family with a new home

"He went around all of Galilee, teaching in their synagogues, proclaiming the gospel of the kingdom, and curing every disease and illness among the people."

(Matthew 4:23)

✝ **Leader:** Let us begin with a moment of reflection. Recall the last time you were home with an illness or injury.

As you recovered, you probably looked forward to returning to your normal routine, including seeing your friends at school, playing sports, and going outside. As you began to feel better, you gradually began to do these things again. Most likely, over time, your life was full of activity, and your illness or injury was nearly forgotten—a distant memory.

On a slip of paper, write a prayer for someone who is going through an illness, an injury, a hardship, or a crisis. Ask God to enable this person to live life fully again. Connect your slip of paper to those of your group, forming a prayer chain for healing. Display this prayer chain so that your group will remember to pray for people who need healing.

Leader: For all those who are suffering hardships or are hurting in any way, we pray:

All: Lord, have mercy.

@ Visit www.weliveourfaith.com to find appropriate music and songs.

The BiG QueStion:

How do I get beyond hardships and hurts?

 iscover whether you can forgive, forget, move on, get beyond it, let it go, and put it past you! Take the quiz below.

1 You run into someone who was not very nice to you in the past. You

   (a) greet him or her but avoid a conversation.

   (b) ignore him or her.

   (c) greet him or her and begin a conversation.

2 You and a friend make plans to go out. Your friend cancels at the last minute. You tell your friend

   (a) you are annoyed and will never make plans with him or her again.

   (b) you don't like breaking plans at the last minute, but you can reschedule.

   (c) not to worry about it, but you don't call him or her for a while.

3 You try out for a team at school, but, to your disappointment, you don't make the cut. Next year's tryouts are likely to find you

   (a) with a year's worth of practice under your belt, ready to give it another try.

   (b) trying out for another sport instead.

   (c) still grumbling about a certain coach who "plays favorites."

4 In the hallway at school, someone rushes past you and knocks your books to the ground. This event

   (a) irritates you for the moment, but you pick up your books and move on.

   (b) doesn't bother you.

   (c) makes you so angry that you promise to find who did it and get even.

Scoring:

Find the points values for your answers below. Add these numbers together to get your total score.

(1) a = 2; b =1; c = 3 (2) a = 1; b =3; c = 2
(3) a = 3; b =2; c = 1 (4) a = 2; b =3; c = 1

4–6: Keep in mind that dwelling on our hardships or hurts can prevent us from living our lives to the fullest. Jesus calls us to forgive others, and he wants us to have peace in our lives.

7–9: Continue to try to make more decisions to move on or to forgive someone. Respect your decisions and your feelings. Then you can let God take it from there.

10–12: You are open to forgiveness when you are hurt and you forge ahead when hardship strikes, but always remember that your own feelings and well-being are important.

How do you show that you have forgiven someone?

In this chapter we learn that Jesus demonstrated his power over sickness and sin. Jesus offers forgiveness of sin and healing to all. Through this chapter, we hope

 to understand that Jesus has the power to heal and to forgive and that during his ministry he called Apostles and disciples to share in his mission

to appreciate that Jesus calls us to have faith in his ability to heal us and forgive us

to reach out to others with Jesus' offer of healing, compassion, and forgiveness.

"The pain changed my destiny." Those were the words of Manuel Lozano Garrido, who got beyond painful hardships in his life as a Catholic journalist in Spain. Born in 1920, he actively lived his Catholic faith throughout his life. When Garrido was sixteen, a priest appointed him to secretly distribute Holy Communion to Catholics, who were being punished for openly practicing their faith during the civil war taking place in Spain. As an adult, Garrido began writing for the Catholic media and the Associated Press, a worldwide news service. But suddenly, when Garrido was in his early twenties, his body began to break down. He had *spondylitis*, a serious illness with no known cure. It affects the spine, causing pain, inflammation, and deformity. Soon Garrido was in a wheelchair, unable to write with either hand.

There was no physical healing in sight, but, with the help of his faith, Garrido looked beyond his physical hardships to find new meaning in his life. He did not stop working as a journalist. He began to dictate his writings into a tape recorder, writing nine books about spirituality and articles on various topics. He also founded and published *Sinai*, a magazine for those who were sick. And though visually impaired for the last ten years of his life, Garrido kept working as a journalist. He became the winner of the first Bravo! prize for journalism from the Spanish Catholic bishops in 1969. Since Garrido's death in 1971, journalists have written more than two hundred letters to the pope requesting his beatification.

Activity Manuel Lozano Garrido's illness never left him, but he got beyond it to continue his work as a Catholic journalist. Can you think of a person who goes beyond his or her own pain or suffering to do good work for others? What do you learn from this person's example? Write your answers below. Then, separately, design an e-card encouraging this person to continue his or her good work.

"Keep your face to the sunshine and you cannot see the shadow" are words often attributed to Helen Keller (1880–1968), who lost her sight and hearing as a child but became a well-known writer, lecturer, and advocate for disabled people.

Jesus offers freedom and life.

Following Jewish custom, Jesus observed the **Sabbath**, a day set apart to rest and honor God. And while in the synagogue in Nazareth one Sabbath day, Jesus stood up to read and was handed the scroll of the prophet Isaiah. Unrolling it, he found this passage:

"The Spirit of the Lord is upon me,
     because he has anointed me
          to bring glad tidings to the poor.
He has sent me to proclaim liberty
          to captives
     and recovery of sight to the blind,
          to let the oppressed go free,
and to proclaim a year acceptable to
          the Lord." (Luke 4:18–19)

After reading this passage, Jesus announced to all present, "Today this scripture passage is fulfilled in your hearing" (Luke 4:21). And indeed it was. Jesus was the Anointed One, who had come to fulfill those words of Isaiah—liberating people, setting them free from sickness, from hunger, from fear, from exclusion and injustice, and even from sin and death. What an extraordinary mission Jesus took on! He ushered in the Kingdom of God. He offered freedom from sin and the gift of God's life to everyone.

Faith Words
Sabbath
Apostles

From the beginning of his ministry, Jesus gathered a community of disciples. These disciples were men and women who traveled with Jesus, witnessed his healings and miracles, and heard his preaching. Twelve of Jesus' disciples shared his mission in a special way. These men were Jesus' **Apostles**. The first two whom Jesus called to be his Apostles were fishermen named Simon and Andrew, who were brothers. Amazingly, they immediately left everything and followed Jesus. Then Jesus called two more brothers who were fishermen— James and John, the sons of Zebedee. They too followed Jesus' call, as did "Philip and Bartholomew, Thomas and Matthew the tax collector; James, the son of Alphaeus, and Thaddeus; Simon the Cananean, and Judas Iscariot" (Matthew 10:3–4).

The Calling of the Apostles Peter and Andrew by Duccio di Buoninsegna (1255–1318)

The word *apostle* means "one who is sent." Jesus sent his Apostles out to share his message of God's love. And when it was time for Jesus to return to his Father, the Apostles would lead and serve the whole community of Jesus' disciples. They would heal and forgive people in Jesus' name and spread the Kingdom of God throughout the world.

Activity The Apostles' work continues in the Church today through bishops, who are the successors of the Apostles. With your group find out the name of the bishop of your diocese. In what ways does he carry on Jesus' mission of freedom and life? How is his office, or role, unique in the Church?

Grow where you're planted

The Church is "the seed and beginning" of God's Kingdom on earth (*CCC*, 567). Like a seed that is planted into the earth and grows, the Church has been planted into the world by Christ and helps the Kingdom of God to grow. We are the Church. As the seed of God's Kingdom, we are called to make the power of God's love active in our lives and in the world.

We are called to share the good news of Christ. And we are called to be healers and forgivers. To do this, we:

• help people in need
• forgive people who have hurt us
• show compassion for people who are hurting or sad
• treat the people in our lives with kindness
• find peaceful solutions to conflicts and encourage others to do the same
• pray for others as well as for ourselves
• and, when we sin, repair our friendship with God and those we have hurt, receiving the Sacrament of Penance and Reconciliation.

Think of another way that you can be a healer and forgiver.

Jesus heals and forgives.

During Jesus' ministry he forgave the sins of those who asked for God's forgiveness, and he healed those who were suffering from illnesses. Jesus' healing and forgiveness were special signs that he was not only human but divine. They were signs of the power of God's love active in the world. Through Jesus' miracles of healing and forgiveness, he shared the life and love of God with others. These miracles showed that God's Kingdom had begun.

There was no type of suffering that Jesus couldn't heal, because in Jesus the power of God was at work. Jesus healed people physically—restoring them from sickness, weakness, suffering, and disability. He also healed people spiritually and emotionally, too—forgiving their sins and removing their guilt, their hurt, their loneliness, and their anxiety. Here are two examples:

"Great crowds came to him, having with them the lame, the blind, the deformed, the mute, and many others. They placed them at his feet, and he cured them. The crowds were amazed when they saw the mute speaking, the deformed made whole, the lame walking, and the blind able to see, and they glorified the God of Israel." (Matthew 15:30–31)

"A large crowd met him. There was a man in the crowd who cried out, 'Teacher, I beg you, look at my son; he is my only child. For a spirit seizes him and he suddenly screams and it convulses him until he foams at the mouth; it releases him only with difficulty, wearing him out.' . . . Jesus rebuked the unclean spirit, healed the boy, and returned him to his father. And all were astonished by the majesty of God.'" (Luke 9:37–39, 42–43)

Jesus performed these miracles not to draw attention to himself but to bring people to faith and to enhance their lives.

Activity Imagine that you are living during Jesus' time. You see the hurts and hardships of the people. And you see Jesus responding to these hurts and hardships. Describe your thoughts and feelings about these events.

BELIEVING...

Jesus calls us to faith.

How does it feel to be healed? to be forgiven?

In the Gospels we find that Jesus healed those who trusted in him, those who had a sincere faith in his ability to help them. Often, as Jesus healed them, he said, "Your faith has saved you" (Mark 5:34). Jesus teaches us that when we seek his healing, whether from physical ills, from hurt, or from the suffering caused by sin, we must have faith:

"Bartimaeus, a blind man, the son of Timaeus, sat by the roadside begging. . . . He began to cry out and say, 'Jesus, son of David, have pity on me.' . . . Jesus said to him in reply, 'What do you want me to do for you?' The blind man replied to him, 'Master, I want to see.' Jesus told him, 'Go your way; your faith has saved you.' Immediately he received his sight and followed him on the way." (Mark 10:46, 47, 51–52)

During his ministry Jesus freed many people from their burdens to live their lives anew. And in healing them, Jesus often said to them, "Your sins are forgiven" (Luke 7:48). Jesus, as God's only Son, gave people a newfound freedom—taking away their burdens and, even more important, forgiving

their sins. And after they were healed and forgiven, they gained new life and strength:

"When Jesus returned to Capernaum after some days, it became known that he was at home. Many gathered together so that there was no longer room for them, not even around the door, and he preached the word to them. They came bringing to him a paralytic carried by four men. Unable to get near Jesus because of the crowd, they opened up the roof above him. After they had broken through, they let down the mat on which the paralytic was lying. When Jesus saw their faith, he said to the paralytic, 'Child, your sins are forgiven.' . . . [The paralytic] rose, picked up his mat at once, and went away in the sight of everyone." (Mark 2:1–5, 12)

Activity What message from these healing stories applies to your life today?

Jesus shows God's power and love.

In witnessing Jesus' miracles, the disciples saw Jesus' power to act in ways that went beyond the ordinary laws of nature. Here are two events that show the disciples experiencing Jesus' extraordinary power:

One day, when Jesus got into a boat, his disciples followed him. Suddenly, while Jesus slept, a violent storm began, and the boat was overtaken by waves. The disciples woke Jesus, saying, "Lord, save us! We are perishing!" (Matthew 8:25).

Jesus said, "Why are you terrified, O you of little faith?" (Matthew 8:26) and got up and calmed the storm.

Afterwards, his disciples said, "What sort of man is this, whom even the winds and the sea obey?" (Matthew 8:27).

Another time, Jesus' disciples were out in a boat while Jesus went alone to a mountain to pray. The wind was tossing the boat about, when suddenly Jesus came walking toward the disciples on the sea. The disciples were fearful, thinking it was a ghost. Jesus told them, "Take courage, it is I; do not be afraid" (Matthew 14:27).

Peter said, "Lord, if it is you, command me to come to you on the water" (Matthew 14:28). Jesus called Peter to come, and Peter began to walk on the water.

But the wind was strong, and Peter was afraid and began to sink. He cried to Jesus, "Lord, save me!" (Matthew 14:30). Though Peter had doubted Jesus, Jesus put out his hand and saved Peter.

Then they got into the boat, and the wind calmed down. And those in the boat said to Jesus, "Truly, you are the Son of God" (Matthew 14:33).

Jesus' disciples witnessed Jesus calming the winds and the sea, healing the sick, forgiving sinners, and even raising the dead to life. They witnessed his life of deep prayer and his extraordinary teachings. They also saw that Jesus was fully human. Jesus got hungry and tired as they did; he enjoyed what they enjoyed and feared what they feared; he was a person just like them. Yet there was more—in Jesus they could see and feel God's power and grace at work. When Jesus was with them, they had an overwhelming sense of God's presence. Jesus strengthened their belief in God's power and love.

> **"What sort of man is this, whom even the winds and the sea obey?"**
> (Matthew 8:27)

Activity On a separate sheet of paper, illustrate one way that Jesus is with us today—strengthening our belief in God's power and love.

The Sacraments of Healing

At times in our lives we experience suffering, illness, and sin. During these times we need to be strengthened and our life of grace needs to be restored. For these times the Church celebrates two special sacraments of healing and forgiveness: the Sacrament of Penance and Reconciliation, and the Sacrament of the Anointing of the Sick. In the Sacrament of Penance, our relationship with God and the Church is strengthened and restored. In the Sacrament of the Anointing of the Sick, God's grace and comfort are given to those who are seriously ill or suffering because of old age.

Through these sacraments the Church continues Jesus' healing ministry.

In what other ways does the Church continue Jesus' healing ministry?

CATHOLIC IDENTITY

Recognizing Our Faith

Recall the question at the beginning of this chapter: *How do I get beyond hardships and hurts?* In this chapter we learned that Jesus heals and forgives us. In the space here, write a short prayer that asks Jesus for healing, whether for yourself or for someone you know. Keeping your prayers anonymous, your group can compile these prayers into a book of prayers to pray regularly.

Living Our Faith

Think of a way to be an example of Jesus' healing, compassion, and forgiveness—and do it.

Blessed Francis Xavier Seelos

Partners in FAITH

Francis Xavier Seelos came to the United States from Germany during a time when many Europeans were immigrating to America in search of opportunity and freedom. Francis, wanting to serve these immigrants, was ordained a priest in 1844. Father Francis began his work in Pittsburgh, Pennsylvania.

Funny and kind, Father Francis brought comfort to troubled hearts. His presence and prayers were soon known for their healing effects on those who were sick or hurting. A source of sound advice, he had a special gift for bringing God's peace, comfort, and healing to those who waited for hours on long lines to confess their sins and receive absolution.

Beatified by Pope John Paul II in 2000, Blessed Francis Xavier Seelos reminds us of the peace and healing that come from Jesus Christ.

In what ways can you remind others of the healing power of Jesus Christ?

@ For additional ideas and activities, visit www.weliveourfaith.com.

Putting Faith to Work

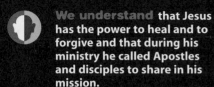

Talk about what you have learned in this chapter:

We understand that Jesus has the power to heal and to forgive and that during his ministry he called Apostles and disciples to share in his mission.

We appreciate that Jesus calls us to have faith in his ability to heal us and forgive us.

We reach out to others with Jesus' offer of healing, compassion, and forgiveness.

Decide on ways to live out what you have learned.

✝ ENCOUNTERING GOD'S WORD

"O Lord, my God, I cried out to you and you healed me."

(Psalm 30:3)

➡ **READ** the quotation from Scripture.

➡ **REFLECT** on these questions:
What situations might cause someone to want to "cry out" like the person in the quotation? How could healing be found in these situations?

➡ **SHARE** your reflections with a partner.

➡ **DECIDE** to turn to God for healing when you need it. How will you express your need to God?

Underline the correct answer.

1. Following Jewish custom, Jesus observed the **(Sabbath/synagogue/mission)**, a day set apart to rest and honor God.

2. The word **(community/apostle/Christian)** means "one who is sent."

3. Jesus' healing and forgiveness were special signs that he was not only human but **(divine/apostolic/suffering)**.

4. Jesus strengthened his disciples' belief in God's power and **(love/faith/mission)**.

Complete the following.

5. The _____ were twelve men with whom Jesus chose to share his mission in a special way.

6. Through Jesus' miracles of _____ and _____, he shared the life and love of God with others.

7. Jesus teaches us that when we seek his healing, we must have _____.

8. In Jesus' miracles, the disciples witnessed Jesus' power to act in ways that went beyond the ordinary _____.

9–10. ESSAY: Explain this statement: *Jesus healed people physically, emotionally, and spiritually.*

RESPONDING...

Sharing Faith with Your Family

Discuss the following with your family:

- Jesus offers freedom and life.
- Jesus heals and forgives.
- Jesus calls us to faith.
- Jesus shows God's power and love.

Gather with your family and name people you know who are sick, in the hospital, or going through a difficult time. Write each name on a slip of paper. Take turns drawing these slips of paper from a bowl. Pray for the person whose name you drew. You might also send an encouraging note or get-well wishes to this person.

The Worship Connection

At Mass, before going forward to receive the Eucharist, we pray:

"Lord, I am not worthy to receive you, but only say the word and I shall be healed." (Roman Missal)

More to Explore

Many Catholic groups work to help people throughout the world to get through various hardships. Research one group and find out how it continues the healing ministry of Jesus.

Catholic Social Teaching ☑ Checklist

Theme of Catholic Social Teaching:
Life and Dignity of the Human Person

How it relates to Chapter 10: As Catholics we are called to promote the well-being of all, from the moment of their conception through their natural death. All people deserve our help to get beyond their hardships and hurts.

How can you do this?

☐ At home:

_____

☐ At school/work:

_____

☐ In the parish:

_____

☐ In the community:

_____

Check off each action after it has been completed.

"I am the bread of life; whoever comes to me will never hunger, and whoever believes in me will never thirst."

(John 6:35)

✝ **Leader:** Jesus, because of your coming into the world, we need not hunger nor thirst for God's presence, mercy, justice, peace, life, truth, or love. You are the Son of God, the Bread of Life, who shares God's life with all. And so we pray:

Leader:	**All:**
Jesus, Bread of Life,	have mercy on us.
Jesus, Son of God,	have mercy on us.
Jesus, Splendor of the Father,	have mercy on us.
Jesus, Eternal Light,	have mercy on us.
Jesus, Sun of Justice,	have mercy on us.
Jesus, Son of the Virgin Mary,	have mercy on us.
Jesus, Our Way and Our Life,	have mercy on us.
Jesus, Prince of Peace,	have mercy on us.
Jesus, Eternal Truth,	have mercy on us.
Be merciful,	spare us, O Jesus.
Be merciful,	graciously hear us, O Jesus.
Lamb of God, who takes away the sins of the world,	spare us, O Jesus.
Lamb of God, who takes away the sins of the world,	graciously hear us, O Jesus.
Lamb of God, who takes away the sins of the world,	have mercy on us, O Jesus.
Jesus, hear us.	Jesus, graciously hear us.

Leader: Lord Jesus Christ, your presence never fails those who love you. In union with God the Father and the Holy Spirit, may you live and reign now and forever. Amen.

(based on the Litany of the Holy Name)

 Visit www.weliveourfaith.com to find appropriate music and songs.

The BiG QuEstion:

Will God always be there for me?

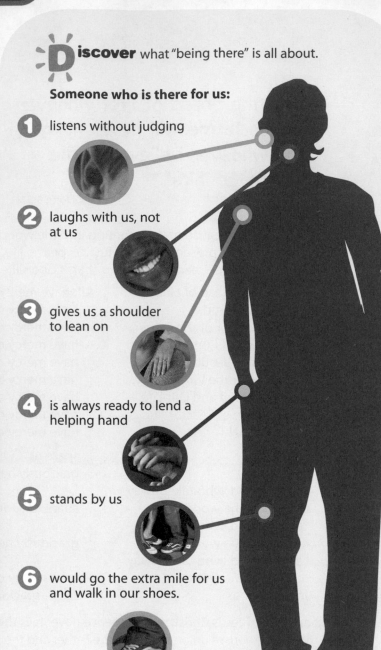

Discover what "being there" is all about.

Someone who is there for us:

1 listens without judging

2 laughs with us, not at us

3 gives us a shoulder to lean on

4 is always ready to lend a helping hand

5 stands by us

6 would go the extra mile for us and walk in our shoes.

Think about the ways you have been this kind of person for others.

In this chapter we discover that Jesus is the Bread of Life, is always present with his disciples, and accomplished God's plan of salvation. Through this chapter, we hope

 to realize that Jesus wants his disciples to have life with God forever

 to revere Jesus' giving of himself as the Bread of Life and as our Savior

 to proclaim the truth that God is always present with us through the person of Jesus Christ.

Think of all the beginnings and endings that you go through in life. Life is full of them. Beginnings include experiences such as starting a new school year, going on vacation, turning another year older, and belonging to a new team or afterschool club. Each time you start something new, you change, grow, and become stronger, more capable, and more knowledgeable.

But endings are a part of life, too. Every school year ends, every vacation comes to a close, your activities change, someone moves away, or sometimes you face even sadder endings, such as a death or a divorce in your family. But no matter how sad life's endings can be, with each ending you continue to change, to grow, and to become stronger, more capable, and more knowledgeable. And throughout all of these beginnings and endings, it helps to have friends who are always there for you.

Activity Think of someone who is always there for you, no matter what is happening in your life. Complete the certificate of appreciation for this person below.

In Appreciation of

_____

for

_____

_____

_____

Gratefully,

_____

(your signature)

66 **What the caterpillar calls the end, the butterfly calls the beginning.** 99
(Anonymous)

BELIEVING...

Jesus prepares his disciples for all that is to come.

One day, on the way to a region called Caesarea Philippi, Jesus questioned his disciples. He tried to find out what they were thinking about him. Jesus' disciples told him that some people said that he was "John the Baptist, others Elijah, still others Jeremiah or one of the prophets" (Matthew 16:14). Jesus asked them again, "But who do you say that I am?" (Matthew 16:15).

It was his Apostle Simon, also called Peter, who replied for all of the disciples. Peter said, "You are the Messiah, the Son of the living God" (Matthew 16:16). Jesus blessed Peter for recognizing this truth. But Jesus, knowing that his role as Messiah was not yet clear to the people, warned all of the disciples not to tell anyone about this for the time being.

Yet the disciples continued to witness Jesus' ability to help people to live full and holy lives. They saw him bring this "fullness of life" to those he spoke to, ate with, prayed with, forgave, and healed. They saw and heard Jesus invite all people to live faithfully the life that would bring them happiness with God. But Jesus knew that the future events of his life might not seem so "full of life" to his disciples. He knew that people would oppose him, question his teachings, and threaten his life. He knew that his mission of salvation would require him to suffer and die. His disciples would find all of these events difficult to understand. So, Jesus began to prepare them for all that was to come.

Jesus told his disciples that his suffering and death were coming. But he also told them that on the third day he would rise. He would fulfill the promise that had been made to God's people throughout the ages. Through his life, death, and rising from the dead, Jesus would save all people *from* sin and the power that sin has over humanity, and save them *for* fullness of life with God.

Jesus challenged his disciples to live their lives in complete commitment to his Gospel message. Jesus taught that a life lived in true discipleship leads to **eternal life**, a life of happiness with God forever.

Faith Word
eternal life

Activity Based on what you have learned about Jesus, how was he "always there" for his disciples?

Jesus tells his disciples he will always be with them.

Jesus focused his public ministry on enabling people to have life, both here and hereafter. Jesus spoke the following words to his disciples, telling them about the new life that only he, as God's divine Son, could give:

"I am the bread of life; whoever comes to me will never hunger, and whoever believes in me will never thirst." (John 6:35)	Jesus wanted his disciples to know that belief in him is needed in order to have life with God.
"I am the living bread that came down from heaven; whoever eats this bread will live forever; and the bread that I will give is my flesh for the life of the world." (John 6:51)	By calling himself the Bread of Life and the Living Bread, Jesus was telling his disciples that he was truly the Son of God sent to bring God's life to them.
"Whoever eats my flesh and drinks my blood has eternal life. . . . Just as the living Father sent me and I have life because of the Father, so also the one who feeds on me will have life because of me." (John 6:54, 57)	Jesus taught that his disciples would have life with God forever if they truly believed that he was the Son of God and if they lived as his disciples.

Only Jesus could satisfy people's hunger and thirst for God—he was all the food they needed for eternal life. But when Jesus spoke of himself as the Bread of Life and as food and drink, many people were troubled by his words. They asked themselves, "How can this man give us [his] flesh to eat?" (John 6:52). But at his last meal with his disciples on the night before he died, Jesus shed new light on the meaning of his words.

At that meal, known as the Last Supper, Jesus gave his disciples a special way to remember him and to be with him. Jesus "took the bread, said the blessing, broke it, and gave it to them, saying, 'This is my body, which will be given for you; do this in memory of me.' And likewise the cup after they had eaten, saying, 'This cup is the new covenant in my blood, which will be shed for you'" (Luke 22:19–20). Jesus' breaking of the bread and sharing of the cup was an offering of himself for our salvation. It was the Eucharist, Jesus' gift to all of his disciples.

Through the Eucharist Jesus could remain with his disciples forever because Jesus is wholly and completely present in the bread and wine that become his

> **" The bread that I will give is my flesh for the life of the world. "**
> (John 6:51)

Body and Blood. This true presence of Jesus Christ in the Eucharist is called the **Real Presence**. Through the Eucharist, the Son of God, the Bread of Life, joins the lives of those who receive him to the eternal life and presence of God—Father, Son, and Holy Spirit.

Activity Write and title a poem about Jesus, who is always present to us in the Eucharist.

Faith Word

Real Presence

Truly present

During Mass the priest does and says what Jesus did and said at the Last Supper. Through the priest's words and actions, and by the power of the Holy Spirit, the bread and wine are changed into the Body and Blood of Christ. Jesus truly becomes present to us in the Eucharist under the appearances of bread and wine. This change that the bread and wine undergo is called *transubstantiation*. *Trans* means "change"; *-substantia* means "substance"; *-tion* means "the act of." What the bread and wine really are—their substance—becomes the Body and Blood of Christ, yet what they look like and taste like—their appearances—remain the same.

Each time you receive Holy Communion, remember that Jesus is truly present in what looks like bread and wine, but is really his Body and Blood. You are receiving Jesus himself.

CATHOLIC IDENTITY

Pilate presents Jesus to the crowd. Based on the painting *Ecce Homo* (*Behold the Man*) by Antonio Ciseri (1821–1891).

Jesus suffers for the sins of humanity.

When do you pray? What do you pray for?

After Jesus shared the Last Supper with his disciples, he went alone to a garden to pray to his Father. Jesus had given himself to his disciples in the Eucharist and was now preparing to give his life for all of humanity. He prayed, "Father, if you are willing, take this cup away from me; still, not my will but yours be done" (Luke 22:42). Jesus trusted in God his Father and knew that God was with him in his suffering. As Jesus prayed he "was in such agony . . . that his sweat became like drops of blood falling on the ground" (Luke 22:44).

Later that night, Judas Iscariot, one of Jesus' own Apostles, betrayed Jesus in the garden by greeting him with a kiss. By this sign that he had arranged, Judas identified Jesus to those who had come to arrest him. These men took Jesus. They brought him before the Sanhedrin, the supreme religious court of the Jews, and before Caiaphas, the high priest. Caiaphas said to Jesus, "I order you to tell us under oath before the living God whether you are the Messiah, the Son of God" (Matthew 26:63).

Jesus said, "You have said so" (Matthew 26:64). The high priest said, "He has blasphemed!" (Matthew 26:65). Caiaphas was accusing Jesus of

blasphemy, of referring to God in a disrespectful or irreverent way. And the rest replied, "He deserves to die!" (Matthew 26:66). Jesus was then taken before the Roman governor, Pontius Pilate. When Judas heard of all this, he regretted what he had done. Judas was so overtaken with grief that he went off and took his own life.

At first Pontius Pilate wanted to release Jesus, but Pilate's enemies accused him of trying to stir up a rebellion against the emperor. So Pilate let the crowds decide Jesus' fate. They shouted out for Jesus' crucifixion. And thus Pilate handed Jesus over to them to be crucified.

Activity Why was Jesus suffering in the garden? How did Jesus find help when suffering?

How does knowing that God is with you help you?

Jesus fulfills God's plan of salvation.

In the Gospels we can find many details about the suffering that Jesus experienced before he died. We read that the Roman soldiers took Jesus and cruelly mistreated him. They mocked him, spat in his face, and placed a crown of thorns on his head. Then they forced Jesus to carry his cross to Golgotha, a hillside in Jerusalem whose name means "place of the skull." Today this place is called Calvary. There the soldiers laid Jesus on the cross, nailed his hands and feet to it, and hoisted the cross up onto the hill.

Jesus hung there in desperate suffering while his mother, Mary, and some of the women disciples stood helplessly at the foot of the cross. Bystanders insulted the dying Jesus. Some even mocked Jesus, saying, "He saved others; he cannot save himself" (Mark 15:31).

At about three o'clock in the afternoon, as Jesus took his last breath, within the Temple "the veil of the sanctuary was torn in two from top to bottom" (Mark 15:38). A Roman officer standing at the foot of the cross, having watched Jesus die, was heard to say, "Truly this man was the Son of God!" (Mark 15:39). Joseph of Arimathea, a Jewish

Sixteenth-century Byzantine icon of the crucifixion

❝Truly this man was the Son of God!❞
(Mark 15:39)

member of the council who had not agreed with the plan for Jesus' death, went to Pilate and requested the body of Jesus. Then, as the women disciples looked on, Joseph took Jesus' body, wrapped it for burial, laid it in an unused tomb, and had a huge stone rolled across the entrance. This all happened on Friday, the day before the Jewish Sabbath.

As Catholics, we recall this day as Good Friday because it was the day on which Jesus sacrificed his life on the cross. Jesus, our Redeemer, died to fulfill God's plan of salvation and to offer us eternal life with God. In Jesus' dying, the miracle of our salvation had just begun!

Activity The Church sings the words below on Good Friday. Pray them now with your group.

We worship you, Lord.
We venerate your cross,
we praise your resurrection.
Through the cross you brought joy to the world.

May God be gracious and bless us;
and let his face shed its light upon us.

We worship you, Lord.
We venerate your cross,
we praise your resurrection.
Through the cross you brought joy to the world.
(Roman Missal)

A holy city

Jesus' crucifixion took place in Jerusalem. This city, located in Israel, is a spiritual home for three of the world's major religions: Judaism, Islam, and Christianity.

Judaism's roots in Jerusalem were planted more than 3,000 years ago. At that time, according to biblical accounts, King David captured Jerusalem and made it a cultural and spiritual center for Judaism. The first Jewish Temple was built in Jerusalem. Over the next several hundred years, the city fell under siege by numerous groups, including the Persians and the Romans. More than once the city and the Temple were destroyed. The Jewish people were exiled only to return shortly thereafter. As the location of Jesus' crucifixion and Resurrection, Jerusalem also became important as the birthplace of Christianity. In 313 A.D., Emperor Constantine made Christianity the official religion of the Roman Empire, which included Jerusalem.

In 638 A.D., Jerusalem was captured by armies of Muslims. Muslims, whose religion is called Islam, believe that their prophet, Mohammed, rose to heaven from the city of Jerusalem.

Throughout the ages the city has experienced religious conflicts among the three groups who hold claim to the city and its spiritual significance: Jews, Muslims, and Christians. In news articles you will find stories about the tensions and conflicts in and around Jerusalem today. What are some ways that peace might be reached?

Recognizing Our Faith

Recall the question at the beginning of this chapter: *Will God always be there for me?* Jesus gave us his life so that we could have life with God forever. God is always there for us. Choose a creative way to present this truth to others. Write your plan here.

Living Our Faith

In this chapter we learned that God is with us always through the life and love of Jesus Christ. This week, remember and take comfort in knowing that God is always with you.

The Hospice Movement

A *hospice* is a facility or program that provides care and support for people who are dying from an illness. A hospice encourages family members to "be there" for a loved one who is afflicted with a terminal illness. The mission of a hospice is to enhance the quality of life for all persons affected by dying and grief. The word *hospice* comes from the Latin word *hospitium*, which means "guesthouse." Centuries ago, when travel was often difficult and dangerous, someone making a pilgrimage to a holy place could find refuge in a hospice kept by a local monastery or religious order.

In the late 1870s Sister Mary John Gaynor and the Sisters of Charity opened a home for the terminally ill in Dublin, Ireland, and the name *hospice* became associated with the care of those who were dying. Through the work of Doctor Cicely Saunders in the 1960s, the hospice movement grew. Saunders, a British physician, helped to incorporate the comforts of family and home care with the attention and support of doctors and professionals.

How can you show care and support for those who are afflicted with a terminal illness?

 For additional ideas and activities, visit www.weliveourfaith.com.

Putting Faith to Work

Talk about what you have learned in this chapter:

 We realize that Jesus wants his disciples to have life with God forever.

 We revere Jesus' giving of himself as the Bread of Life and as our Savior.

 We proclaim the truth that God is always present with us through the person of Jesus Christ.

Decide on ways to live out what you have learned.

✝ ENCOUNTERING GOD'S WORD

❝I am the living bread that came down from heaven; whoever eats this bread will live forever.❞

(John 6:51)

➡ **READ** the quotation from Scripture.

➡ **REFLECT** on the following:
Bread is a basic food on which many people depend for nourishment. Why do you think Jesus compared himself to bread? Some disciples who heard Jesus make this comparison did not believe what he said, and they walked away. (See John 6:60–71.) How would you react to Jesus' words?

➡ **SHARE** your reflections with a partner.

➡ **DECIDE** to thank Jesus for sharing himself with you as the Bread of Life.

Write *True* or *False* next to the following sentences. On a separate sheet of paper, change the false sentences to make them true.

1. _____ Eternal life is the true presence of Jesus Christ in the Eucharist.

2. _____ Jesus died to fulfill God's plan of salvation and to offer us eternal life with God forever.

3. _____ Jesus' Real Presence refers to a life of happiness with God forever.

4. _____ Through his life, death, and rising from the dead, Jesus saved all people from sin.

Short Answers

5. What do we, as Catholics, call the day that Jesus, our Redeemer, died? _____

_____

6. What was Peter's response on behalf of the disciples when Jesus asked them, "But who do you say that I am?" (Matthew 16:15)? _____

7. What gift did Jesus give to all of his disciples at the Last Supper? _____

_____

8. Which Apostle betrayed Jesus in the garden by greeting him with a kiss? _____

_____

9–10. ESSAY: Why did Jesus call himself the Bread of Life?

RESPONDING...

Sharing Faith with Your Family

Discuss the following with your family:

- Jesus prepares his disciples for all that is to come.
- Jesus tells his disciples he will always be with them.
- Jesus suffers for the sins of humanity.
- Jesus fulfills God's plan of salvation.

It is important to remember that God is always with us in our families. And it is important not only to "be there" for those still among us but to remember family members who have passed away. What are some ways to stay connected to these loved ones?

- Display favorite photos of these family members.
- _____
- _____

The Worship Connection

At Mass this Sunday, listen for the words *eternal life*. Praise and thank Jesus for this gift of unending life.

More to Explore

God is always present through the person of Jesus Christ. Use the Internet, periodicals, and reference books to find examples of art and music that communicate God's presence to you.

Catholic Social Teaching ☑ Checklist

Theme of Catholic Social Teaching:
Care for God's Creation

How it relates to Chapter 11: God is always there for us. In return, he asks us to take care of, or be stewards of, his creation. As Catholics we are called to protect our planet, living our faith in relationship with all of God's creation.

How can you do this?

☐ At home:

_____

☐ At school/work:

_____

☐ In the parish:

_____

☐ In the community:

_____

Check off each action after it has been completed.

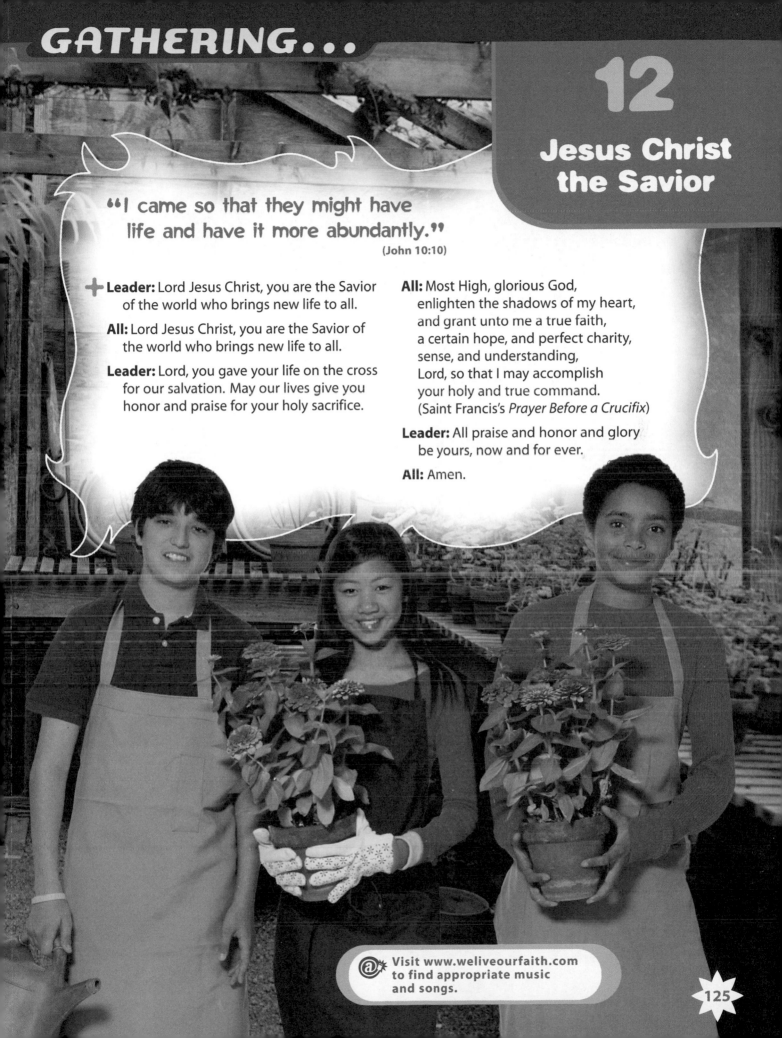

GATHERING...

12 Jesus Christ the Savior

> "I came so that they might have life and have it more abundantly."
> (John 10:10)

✛ **Leader:** Lord Jesus Christ, you are the Savior of the world who brings new life to all.

All: Lord Jesus Christ, you are the Savior of the world who brings new life to all.

Leader: Lord, you gave your life on the cross for our salvation. May our lives give you honor and praise for your holy sacrifice.

All: Most High, glorious God,
enlighten the shadows of my heart,
and grant unto me a true faith,
a certain hope, and perfect charity,
sense, and understanding,
Lord, so that I may accomplish
your holy and true command.
(Saint Francis's *Prayer Before a Crucifix*)

Leader: All praise and honor and glory be yours, now and for ever.

All: Amen.

@ Visit www.weliveourfaith.com to find appropriate music and songs.

125

The BiG QuEStion:

Why is life worth living?

Discover what is important to your life. Imagine yourself stranded on a desert island with only three of your possessions. If you could choose these three possessions, what would they be? List them below.

1

2

3

Results:

Review your list and think about what moved you to choose these items over everything else in your life.

Why are these things important to your life? What would you say makes life worth living?

In this chapter
we learn that Jesus Christ is the Savior; by his death and Resurrection he freed us from sin and opened for us the way to new life. Through this chapter, we hope

to know
that Jesus Christ, through the Paschal Mystery—his suffering, death, Resurrection, and Ascension—accomplished his work of salvation

to open our hearts
to Jesus' call to share our gifts as the Body of Christ in the world

to continue
Christ's work of salvation through what we say and what we do.

Long ago, there lived a young farmer named Simon. He enjoyed life on the farm, but he also dreamed of new adventures. One day, while out plowing the field, Simon found a treasure map. Seeing an opportunity to explore the world and become rich, Simon set out in search of the treasure.

> "Life is like a coin. You can spend it any way you wish, but you only spend it once," said Lillian Dickson (1901–1983), missionary.

The first part of his journey involved a long boat trip. On board were all kinds of interesting people, from explorers to hunters to wealthy thrill-seekers. Simon had a wonderful time meeting all the people and asking them about their lives. When he was alone, he kept looking at his map and dreaming of riches and treasure. He couldn't wait!

However, Simon never reached his intended destination. One day, the boat encountered a terrible storm. Simon was knocked overboard, lost his map in the sea, and was washed up on the shores of a small town. Simon was taken in and cared for by the family of the town blacksmith. The family took a liking to Simon. The blacksmith taught Simon how to make horseshoes, furniture, and other metal crafts. Simon worked for the blacksmith and eventually earned enough to be able to live on his own.

Simon also fell in love with the blacksmith's eldest daughter. They were married and had a son.

Simon eventually took over the blacksmith's business, and his family grew. Simon lived a long and happy life. And though no one ever heard him mention a map, from time to time he could be heard to call his children and grandchildren "my treasure."

Activity Discuss the following:

- **How might Simon answer the question "Why is life worth living?"**

- **If Simon had reached his intended destination and located the treasure, how might his answer be different?**

- **What do you think the lesson of this story is? Can you relate it to your own life in any way?**

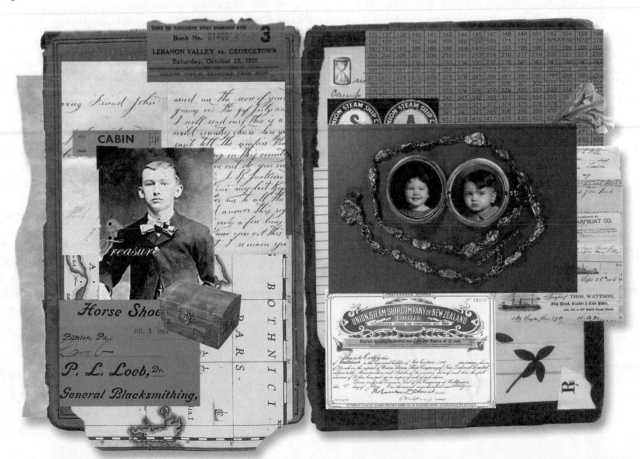

Jesus Christ is risen from the dead.

Early on the third day after Jesus' death on the cross, some of Jesus' disciples went to his tomb and found the stone rolled away and the tomb empty. In his Gospel, Mark identifies these as the women disciples Mary Magdalene, Mary, the mother of James, and Salome. A young man in a white robe was at the tomb and told them, "Do not be amazed! You seek Jesus of Nazareth, the crucified. He has been raised . . . Go and tell his disciples and Peter, 'He is going before you to Galilee; there you will see him, as he told you'" (Mark 16:6–7). The young man referred to here was really an angel.

At first all of this was unbelievable to Jesus' disciples. Then the risen Christ appeared to Mary Magdalene and to some of the other disciples, showing them his wounds and even eating with the disciples. What an extraordinary experience it must have been to see the risen Christ alive and full of glory! But still some who heard about these appearances could not believe that Jesus was risen.

Then, as the eleven Apostles were gathered for a meal, the risen Christ appeared to them all together. He urged those who were weak in faith to now believe in him and in his Resurrection. He then said to his Apostles, "Go into the whole world and proclaim the gospel to every creature. Whoever believes and is baptized will be saved; whoever does not believe will be condemned" (Mark 16:15–16).

The risen Christ also told the Apostles that they would be able to do many things in his name, including driving out demons, speaking new languages, and healing the sick. He *commissioned* them, or sent them out, to carry on the work of salvation and liberation that he had begun. Armed with the Gospel of Christ, they were to evangelize all people.

Activity The risen Christ commissions you to do his work, too. How can you be an evangelizer, proclaiming the Gospel of Christ? To whom would you make your first proclamation?

Life without end

In rising from the dead, Jesus Christ overcame death and promised new life. By our Baptism into Christ, we are bonded to his dying and rising. This can give us such a sense of hope! Though we may worry about death, our faith in the risen Christ can help us to face it with less fear. We know that all those who have responded to God's grace and have remained in his friendship will have eternal life when they die. And because of our belief in Jesus' death and rising, we can have the hope of eternal life and of our own resurrection at the end of time.

At death those who have lived lives of holiness on earth will immediately share the joy of heaven and eternal life. Those whose hearts need to be made perfectly pure will prepare for heaven in purgatory. There they will grow in the holiness necessary to enjoy the happiness of heaven. Unfortunately, those who have chosen to turn from God's mercy and have refused his forgiveness will remain forever separated from God and will not share in eternal life. This eternal separation from God is called hell.

God always wants us to choose the kind of life that will lead to the joy of heaven. Pray that all of your family and friends will share in eternal life with God.

CATHOLIC IDENTITY

Christ's work of salvation is accomplished.

Jesus once told his disciples that a time would come when he would leave them and return to his Father in heaven. Now this time had come. The risen Christ led the disciples "as far as Bethany, raised his hands, and blessed them. As he blessed them he parted from them and was taken up to heaven" (Luke 24:50–51). This event, which we read about in Luke's Gospel, is known as the **Ascension**. It marks Jesus' return in all his glory to his Father in heaven.

> "By his death, Christ liberates us from sin; by his Resurrection, he opens for us the way to a new life."
>
> (CCC, 654)

Luke also wrote about the Ascension in the Acts of the Apostles. In this book of the Bible we discover that the risen Christ remained with his Apostles for forty days before he ascended to heaven. He spoke to them about the power of the Holy Spirit. He taught them about the Kingdom of God. And he prepared them to carry on his mission.

Empowered by the courage, strength, and wisdom that they had received from Jesus, the Apostles began to tell everyone about his suffering, death, Resurrection, and Ascension. The suffering, death, Resurrection, and Ascension of Jesus Christ are known as the **Paschal Mystery**. It was through the Paschal Mystery that Jesus Christ accomplished his work of salvation. As the *Catechism* reminds us, "The Paschal mystery has two aspects: by his death, Christ liberates us from sin; by his Resurrection, he opens for us the way to a new life" (654).

In the Acts of the Apostles we can also read that, after Jesus' Ascension, two men dressed in white garments stood beside the Apostles, saying, "Men of Galilee, why are you standing there looking at the sky? This Jesus who has been taken up from you into heaven will return in the same way as you have seen him going into heaven" (Acts of the Apostles 1:11). These men, who were really angels, God's messengers, were telling the Apostles that Jesus would come back to them again. Indeed Jesus had already promised this to his disciples. At the Last Supper, Jesus had said, "And if I go and prepare a place for you, I will come back again and take you to myself, so that where I am you also may be" (John 14:3). With these words, Jesus was speaking to his disciples of his second coming at the end of time. And, as disciples of Jesus, we too wait in joyful hope for Jesus' return at his second coming at the end of time.

Faith Words

Ascension

Paschal Mystery

Activity A *triptych* is a set of three side-by-side panels showing images that relate to a central theme. Design a triptych showing three images that relate to the Paschal Mystery.

Jesus is with us

In Matthew's Gospel, Jesus' words remind us that when we gather in his name, he is with us. Indeed, when members of the Church are gathered to learn and reflect, and to pray and celebrate, Jesus is there. No matter where in the world the Mass is taking place, in this celebration of the Sacrament of the Eucharist, Jesus is truly present in the community gathered, in the word of God proclaimed, in the priest, and in the reception of Jesus' Body and Blood in Holy Communion. When the priest consecrates the bread and wine, he always prays the words that Jesus said at the Last Supper. And it is Jesus Christ, acting through the priest and by the power of the Holy Spirit, who transforms the bread and wine into his Body and Blood.

When we receive the Body and Blood of Christ at Mass, Jesus lives in us, and we in him. Jesus nourishes us with his word and joins us together as the Body of Christ, the Church. The grace that we first received in Baptism grows in us. And we are strengthened to love and serve others, especially those who are poor or in need.

How can you show that Jesus' presence in your life makes life worth living?

Christ's life and mission continue in the Church.

What gives you strength in your life?

Empowered by the Holy Spirit's coming at Pentecost, the Apostles and the whole community of disciples took up the task of carrying on the mission of Jesus. This was the beginning of the Church. All the believers were confident that the Spirit would guide them; remember, the tongues of fire "came to rest on each one . . . . And they were all filled with the holy Spirit" (Acts of the Apostles 2:3–4).

The Apostles established many communities of Christians, who all met regularly to celebrate the Eucharist. Nourished by the Eucharist, they were able to live what Jesus preached, serve and heal others, and share the good news of salvation, leading more and more people to Christ. "They devoted themselves to the teaching of the apostles and to the communal life, to the breaking of the bread and to the prayers. Awe came upon everyone, and many wonders and signs were done through the apostles. All who believed were together and had all things in common; they would sell their property and possessions and divide them among all according to each one's need. Every day they devoted themselves to meeting together in the temple area and to breaking bread in their homes. They ate their meals with exultation and sincerity of heart, praising God and enjoying favor with all the people. And every day the Lord added to their number those who were being saved." (Acts of the Apostles 2:42–47)

The Eucharist, known at that time as the breaking of the bread, was at the center of the life of the early Church. And it continues to be the center of the Church's life today. Saint Augustine once said, "The Eucharist is our daily bread . . . . Gathered into his Body and made members of him, we may become what we receive"—the Body of Christ. The presence of Christ in us helps us to live as Jesus did, serving others and inviting them to hear the good news of salvation. Thus the life and mission of Jesus continue through each one of us, his disciples.

Activity

Use the code to reveal words of Jesus taken from the Gospel of Matthew.

A	D	E	G	H	I	M	N	O	R	T	W	Y
1	2	3	4	5	6	7	8	9	10	11	12	13

"__ __ __ __ __   __ __ __   __ __ __ __ __ __   __ __ __
 12 5 3 10 3   11 12 9   9 10 11 5 10 3 3   1 10 3

__ __ __ __ __ __ __ __   __ __ __ __ __ __ __   __ __
 4 1 11 5 3 10 3 2   11 9 4 3 11 5 3 10 6 8

__ __   __ __ __ __ ,   __ __ __ __ __   __ __   __ ."
 7 13   8 1 7 3   11 5 3 10 3   1 7   6

(See Matthew 18:20.)

The Church is the Body of Christ.

Baptism gives each member of the Christian community the responsibility to participate in the mission of Jesus. From the very beginning, Peter told the members of the Christian community that they were now "a chosen race, a royal priesthood, a holy nation, a people of his own" (1 Peter 2:9). And Peter instructed, "As each one has received a gift, use it to serve one another" (1 Peter 4:10).

> **"We, though many, are one body in Christ."**
> (Romans 12:5)

Then, as now, all of the Church's ministries and efforts were directed toward sharing God's love and spreading God's Kingdom. Baptism calls each person to participate fully in Jesus' saving and liberating mission. Realizing this makes life worth living.

Every member has something to contribute to the work of the faith community. Every one of us has gifts for building up the Body of Christ—the Church united together in Christ: "We, though many, are one body in Christ and individually parts of one another" (Romans 12:5), and Christ is the "head of the body, the church" (Colossians 1:18). Joined as the Body of Christ in the world, together we can continue Christ's work of salvation by:

- leading others to believe in Jesus Christ as Savior of the world

- bringing Jesus' healing and forgiveness to others

- living a life of prayer, holiness, and good works

- working to establish peace, reconciliation, and justice where they are needed

- reaching out to those who are poor, sick, lonely, oppressed, and rejected

- proclaiming, by all we say and do, the good news of salvation.

The Church, the Body of Christ, is a sign to the world of the salvation, forgiveness, freedom, and new life that Christ offers. You too can participate in this saving work. In what ways do you contribute?

Activity Design an eye-catching advertisement to display on a cab, bus, or train that shows that being a disciple of Christ makes life worth living.

RESPONDING...

Recognizing Our Faith

Recall the question at the beginning of this chapter: *Why is life worth living*? How has your response to the question changed after reading this chapter? Choose a favorite song or tune, and write new words for it that express your response to this question.

Living Our Faith

In this chapter we learned that Jesus Christ gave the Church, the Body of Christ, the responsibility to carry on his mission. Decide on one way you can live out this responsibility.

Saint Mary Magdalene

Saint Mary Magdalene was a faithful disciple of Jesus. She accompanied Jesus and his Apostles as they traveled to many towns and villages to preach the good news of the Kingdom of God. She was witness to Christ's life and teachings. She was present at Jesus' crucifixion and stood at the cross when others had fled. At Jesus' death she mourned, and she wept as he was laid in the tomb. In Scripture we read that when she and other women returned to the tomb to anoint Jesus with spices, they discovered the tomb empty and learned that Jesus had risen from the dead. We then read that Mary Magdalene was one of the first people to see the risen Christ as the women made their way back to Galilee to tell Peter and the other Apostles the news about Jesus. Because of her faithfulness as a disciple and her role as a witness to Jesus' Resurrection, Saint Mary Magdalene became known in early Christian writings as "the apostle to the Apostles." The Church celebrates and remembers Saint Mary Magdalene on July 22.

Saint Mary Magdalene was a witness to Christ's life and teaching. What are some things you can do to be a witness to Christ?

 For additional ideas and activities, visit www.weliveourfaith.com.

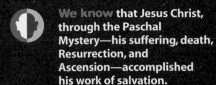

Putting Faith to Work

Talk about what you have learned in this chapter:

We know that Jesus Christ, through the Paschal Mystery—his suffering, death, Resurrection, and Ascension—accomplished his work of salvation.

We open our hearts to Jesus' call to share our gifts as the Body of Christ in the world.

We continue Christ's work of salvation through what we say and what we do.

Decide on ways to live out what you have learned.

✝ ENCOUNTERING GOD'S WORD

"I am with you always, until the end of the age."
(Matthew 28:20)

➡ **READ** the quotation from Scripture.

➡ **REFLECT** on these questions:
How does it feel to know that Jesus is with you always? Have you ever stopped to think that Jesus is really with you through day-to-day events? How does his presence change your life? How does it make life worth living?

➡ **SHARE** your reflections with a partner.

➡ **DECIDE** to be more aware that Jesus is always with you.

Underline the correct answer.

1. On the (**first/second/third**) day after Jesus' death on the cross, some of Jesus' disciples went to his tomb and found the stone rolled away and the tomb empty.

2. As disciples of Jesus we wait in joyful hope for Jesus' return in his (**first/second/third**) coming at the end of time.

3. The (**Apostles/angels/Ascension**) established many communities of Christians who all met regularly to celebrate the Eucharist.

4. (**Baptism/Paschal Mystery/Resurrection**) gives each member of the Christian community the responsibility to participate in the mission of Jesus.

Complete the following.

5. The Church united together in Christ is called the _____.

6. Jesus' return, in all his glory, to his Father in heaven forty days after his Resurrection is known as the

_____

7. Jesus Christ's suffering, death, Resurrection, and Ascension, through which he accomplished his work of salvation, are known as the _____.

8. The Eucharist, which at that time was known as _____, was at the center of the life of the early Church.

9–10. ESSAY: What are some ways that we, the Body of Christ, can continue Christ's work of salvation?

Sharing Faith with Your Family

Discuss the following with your family:

- Jesus Christ is risen from the dead.
- Christ's work of salvation is accomplished.
- Christ's life and mission continue in the Church.
- The Church is the Body of Christ.

Invite your family to discuss ways that being Christ's disciples and belonging to the Church makes life worth living. Encourage each family member to share his or her ideas and opinions.

The Worship Connection

This week at Mass notice the ways that we celebrate Christ's presence and love in our lives.

More to Explore

What services does your parish or community provide to help make life more worthwhile for people? Make a list of a few services to which you and your friends could donate your time.

Catholic Social Teaching ☑ Checklist

Theme of Catholic Social Teaching:
Dignity of Work and the Rights of Workers

How it relates to Chapter 12: Employers should provide a safe working environment, just wages, and fair working hours. As Catholics, we support the things that improve quality of life and make life worth living for workers throughout the world.

How can you do this?

☐ At home:

_____

☐ At school/work:

_____

☐ In the parish:

_____

☐ In the community:

_____

Check off each action after it has been completed.

Write the letter of the answer that best defines each term.

1. _____ consecrate

2. _____ Kingdom of God

3. _____ free will

4. _____ Apostles

5. _____ Ascension

6. _____ eternal life

7. _____ sin

8. _____ Real Presence

a. the creatures created by God as pure spirits, without physical bodies

b. a thought, word, deed, or omission against God's law that harms us and our relationship with God and others

c. to make sacred for God

d. the power of God's love active in our lives and in our world

e. God's gift to human beings of the freedom and ability to choose what to do

f. twelve men chosen by Jesus to share his mission in a special way

g. the true presence of Jesus Christ in the Eucharist

h. Jesus' return in all his glory to his Father in heaven

i. Jesus' teachings that describe the way to live as his disciples

j. a life of happiness with God forever

Write *True* or *False* next to the following sentences. Then, on the lines provided, change the false sentences to make them true.

9. _____ Jesus accomplished his work of salvation through the Paschal Mystery, or teachings that describe how to live as Jesus' disciples.

_____

_____

10. _____ Through Jesus' miracles of healing and forgiveness, he shared the life and love of God with others.

_____

_____

11. _____ At the Jordan River, Jesus gave his disciples a special way to remember him and to be with him: the Eucharist.

_____

_____

12. _____ The Church is the Body of Christ.

_____

_____

13. _____ God promised his people a Messiah, giving all of us the hope of salvation.

_____

_____

Complete the following.

14. Throughout the Old Testament the same pattern emerges again and again—people struggle, even turn away from God, _____

_____.

15. God made Mary free from original sin and all sin from the very moment she was conceived; this truth is called the _____.

16. The _____ is a summary of the entire Gospel.

17. As Catholics, we recall _____ as the day that Jesus, our Redeemer, sacrificed his life on the cross to fulfill God's plan of salvation and to offer us eternal life with God.

18. Empowered by the _____ at Pentecost, the Apostles and the whole community of disciples took up the task of carrying on the mission of Jesus.

Respond to the following.

19. Explain the following statement: *Jesus healed people physically, spiritually, and emotionally.*

_____

_____

_____

_____

20. In the Old Testament Book of Isaiah, we find many images of prophecies about the Messiah. Explain how Jesus fulfilled the following prophecy: a suffering servant who, "like a lamb led to the slaughter," was "harshly treated" but "opened not his mouth" (Isaiah 53:7).

_____

_____

_____

_____

ALTERNATIVE ASSESSMENT

The Gospels reveal to us the story of Jesus' early life and his ministry. Based on what you have learned, write a skit about an event in Jesus' ministry. Include characters' lines and stage directions.

Perform the skit for your class or group.

Choose six Faith Words from the box and write the definition for each.

Tradition	Blessed Trinity	faith	Messiah	evangelization
Incarnation	Magisterium	covenant	grace	Gospels

1. _____

_____

2. _____

_____

3. _____

_____

4. _____

_____

5. _____

_____

6. _____

_____

Fill in the circle beside the correct answer.

7. The suffering, death, Resurrection, and Ascension of Jesus Christ are known as

the _____.

○ Immaculate   ○ infancy   ○ Paschal   ○ Sabbath
Conception   narratives   Mystery

8. The _____, the power of God's love active in our lives and in our world, came
into the world with the coming of Jesus Christ.

○ Kingdom   ○ Immaculate   ○ Body of Christ   ○ Beatitudes
of God   Conception

9. God reveals the truth, his Divine Revelation, through _____ and Tradition.

○ The Beatitudes   ○ angels   ○ Scripture   ○ parables

10. Jesus taught that a life lived in true discipleship leads to _____, a life of
happiness with God forever.

○ free will   ○ Real Presence   ○ original sin   ○ eternal life

11. _____ is a thought, word, deed, or omission against God's law that harms us and
our relationship with God and others.

○ Temptation   ○ Sin   ○ Free will   ○ Salvation

12. Through the _____, the teachings that describe the way to live as Jesus' disciples, Jesus taught his disciples about spreading God's Kingdom.

    ○ Eucharist   ○ Beatitudes   ○ Last Supper   ○ infancy narratives

13. Following Jewish custom, Jesus observed the _____, a day set apart to rest and honor God.

    ○ Sabbath   ○ synagogue   ○ Sanhedrin   ○ Passover

Complete the following.

14. All of our beliefs as Catholics revolve around the mystery of the _____ _____ because it is the mystery of *who God is.*

15. We evangelize when we _____.

16. Jesus' whole message of trust in and love for God his Father is summarized in the _____.

17. Empowered by the _____ coming at Pentecost, the Apostles and the whole community of disciples took up the task of carrying on the mission of Jesus.

18. The words _____, _____, and _____ express the relationship among the three Divine Persons of God.

Respond to the following.

19. Using the information presented in Unit 1, answer the question: *Who is God?*

_____

_____

_____

_____

20. Choose one of these chapters in Unit 2: *Jesus, the Promised Messiah*; *Jesus the Healer*; *Jesus, the Bread of Life*; or *Jesus Christ the Savior*. Summarize what it teaches you about Jesus.

_____

_____

_____

_____

Unit 3

How Is Jesus Christ Alive in the Church Today?

"*Do I not fill
both heaven and earth?
says the Lord.*"

(Jeremiah 23:24)

✚ **Leader:** Lord God, you are always here. You surround us, you call us, and you want us to know you.

Group 1: "The Lord is my shepherd;
there is nothing I lack.
In green pastures you let me graze;
to safe waters you lead me;
you restore my strength."

(Psalm 23:1–3)

Group 2: "You guide me along the right path
for the sake of your name.
Even when I walk through a
dark valley,
I fear no harm for you are at
my side."

(Psalm 23:3–4)

Group 3: "Only goodness and love will
pursue me
all the days of my life;
I will dwell in the house of the Lord
for years to come."

(Psalm 23:6)

All: O God,
open our eyes to your presence,
open our ears to your voice,
open our minds to your word,
open our hands to service of others,
and open our hearts to faith.
Help us not only to recognize you,
but to respond to you in joy and love.
Amen.

Ⓐ Visit www.weliveourfaith.com
to find appropriate music
and songs.

The BiG QuEstion:

How can I recognize God in my life?

Discover whether you can recognize and identify the ordinary objects in the photographs below. Hint: Each ordinary thing is shown *very* close up.

1

2

3

4

Answers:
1. needle and thread 2. moth's eye 3. leaf 4. human hair and skin

Did you recognize each of these ordinary things for what they were? Extraordinary, isn't it, to see ordinary things in a new way? Have you ever had experiences such as that before? Discuss with your group.

In this chapter
we learn about the sacraments. Through these effective signs, God reaches out to us in Jesus Christ. Through this chapter, we hope

 to understand
that, through the sacraments, God shares his life and love with us

 to appreciate
the gift of the sacraments and their importance for us as members of the Body of Christ, the Church

 to respond
to the gift of the sacraments by participating in them with faith and living what we celebrate.

There's a funny story about some people who went on a camping trip. After a meal by the campfire, they settled down for the night and went to sleep. Some hours later, one of the campers awoke and nudged another, saying, "Hey, look up at the sky and tell me what you see."

The other camper replied, "I see millions and millions of stars."

The first camper asked, "And what does that tell you?"

The other camper replied, "Astronomically, it tells me that there are millions of galaxies and potentially billions of planets. Theologically, it tells me that God is great and that we are small. Meteorologically, it tells me that we will have a beautiful day tomorrow. What does it tell you?"

The first camper said, "It tells me that somebody stole our tent!"

It is often easy to miss the things in life that are the most obvious. Even when we have big questions about life and the world, we may not need to search very far to begin to recognize some answers.

Activity Where do you think you can begin to look in order to recognize *God* in your life? In your answer include one obvious response and one not-so-obvious response. Then compare your responses with those of your group.

> **"People see God every day; they just don't recognize him,"** said Pearl Bailey (1918–1990), an actress and a singer.

A new view

In 1874 a group of artists shocked people when they unveiled their paintings in an exhibit in Paris, France. These artists, known as Impressionists, had broken free from the established rules of style and color followed by artists at the time. The Impressionists painted the world in a way that people had never seen. Rather than trying to paint realistic, conventional scenes, the Impressionists tried to paint modern life—and in a way that people would recognize as meaningful. They painted in a creative style, using lots of color, light, and texture to express the mood and emotions of each scene they depicted. Their paintings presented a revolutionary new view of art and life.

Although Impressionist paintings are not shocking to us now, they were considered scandalous at the time. Impressionist art was unpopular with critics and the public in the mid-1800s, and it was not chosen for display in major art exhibitions. However, Impressionist artists remained true to their style of painting despite the unpopularity of their works. Today Impressionist works are worth millions of dollars and are displayed in the most famous museums in the world.

What are some positive and valuable points of view that artists today, including musical artists and filmmakers, can show us through their works?

Les Tuileries (The Tuileries Gardens) by Claude Monet (1840–1926)

143

Through the sacraments we share in God's life and love.

Everything in creation exists by God's power and reflects God's goodness. But whether we recognize this or not depends on our faith in God and in all of his blessings. Take a beautiful sunset, for example. We may know the scientific explanation for it, but as people of faith we also recognize in it the wonder of God's presence in our world. So, through God's great gift of faith, we recognize God's outreach to us—God reaching out, inviting us to share in his life and love, and helping us to see him in all things.

Jesus Christ is the high point of God's outreach to us, for in Jesus Christ, God is with us. And God's Kingdom, the power of God's love active in our lives and in the world, is present and among us through the life and love of Jesus. Jesus' first disciples experienced this presence of God's love because they could actually *see* Jesus. He was part of their lives. After he died and rose from the dead, Jesus appeared to his disciples and promised them, "I am with you always, until the end of the age" (Matthew 28:20). And even after Jesus ascended to his Father, this promise to the disciples assured them that God would always be with them. Through the Holy Spirit, Jesus' presence would continue in their lives.

As Jesus' disciples and members of the Church, we have received this same promise. And, gradually, over a long period of time, the Catholic Church recognized certain symbolic actions, or *rituals*, as powerful signs of the risen Christ made present in the community through the power of the Holy Spirit. The Church also recognized these rituals as sources of special help for living as a community of disciples. Eventually the Church named seven special signs it had received from Christ as the seven sacraments that we celebrate in the Church today.

Faith Word
sacrament

Each of the sacraments is a sign of God present in our lives. But the sacraments are different from all other signs. A **sacrament** is an effective sign given to us by Jesus Christ through which we share in God's life. So, in the Sacrament of Baptism, we not only celebrate being children of God, we actually *become* children of God. And in the Sacrament of Penance, we not only celebrate that God forgives, we actually *receive* God's forgiveness. Sacraments truly bring about, or *effect*, what they represent, and thus they are the most important celebrations of the Church.

Activity List the sacraments you have received. How have they helped you to experience God in your life?

The grace of the sacraments enables us to respond to God's love.

In each sacrament we can recognize particular ways that Jesus' life reveals God's presence and the power of God's love. And in each sacrament Jesus, through the Holy Spirit, shares God's life with us and effects change in our lives. We need only to respond to God's grace.

> "The seven sacraments are the signs and instruments by which the Holy Spirit spreads the grace of Christ the head throughout the Church which is his Body."
>
> (CCC, 774)

Jesus welcomed all those who wanted to follow him.	In the Sacrament of Baptism, we are welcomed into the Church, becoming children of God.	
Jesus sent the Holy Spirit to his disciples.	In the Sacrament of Confirmation, we are sealed with the Gift of the Holy Spirit.	
Jesus nourished people's bodies and souls.	In the Sacrament of the Eucharist, we receive Jesus Christ, the Bread of Life.	
Jesus had compassion for sinners and assured them of God's mercy.	In the Sacrament of Penance, we turn to God with sorrow for sin and receive his love and forgiveness.	
Jesus had special concern for the sick and the suffering, and healed them.	In the Sacrament of Anointing of the Sick, people who are sick and suffering are helped and comforted.	
Jesus chose the Apostles as leaders and empowered them to serve the whole Church.	In the Sacrament of Holy Orders, baptized men are ordained to lead and serve the Church.	
Jesus loved his family and learned from their faithful love for one another.	In the Sacrament of Matrimony, a baptized man and woman are strengthened for family life and service by their faithful love.	

Through the power of the Holy Spirit, each sacrament gives us grace. The grace that we receive in the sacraments is called **sanctifying grace**. Sanctifying grace enables us to love God, to love ourselves as God loves us, to love others as we love ourselves, and to live as God calls us to live. As the *Catechism* states, "The seven sacraments are the signs and instruments by which the Holy Spirit spreads the grace of Christ the head throughout the Church which is his Body" (774).

Faith Word
sanctifying grace

The seven sacraments enable us to respond to God's saving grace in the everyday events of life. The Holy Spirit works through the sacraments to empower us to live as faithful disciples of Christ. The sacraments reflect the values and ministry of Jesus. We are called to live out those values and continue Jesus' work of salvation, sharing with others the good news that God is with us always.

Activity Inside each square in the chart, design a logo to represent the sacrament described.

As the Church we are united in Christ and celebrate his Paschal Mystery.

What are some things that you celebrate?

As Catholics we know that, because of Jesus' Paschal Mystery, we can see the world in a whole new way. It is through this mystery that Jesus brought salvation to the world. For each of us, discovering and living out the meaning of Christ's Paschal Mystery is the work of a lifetime. We take our first step in living it out through the **liturgy**, the official public prayer of the Church, by praying together and showing what we believe. The liturgy includes the celebration of the Eucharist, also called the Mass, and the other sacraments. It also includes the Liturgy of the Hours. To every celebration of the liturgy, we bring our own selves and our relationship with God, and we join together as Jesus' own friends and disciples, just as Jesus' first followers did. We proclaim the good news of Jesus Christ and celebrate the Paschal Mystery.

Faith Word

liturgy

Whenever the liturgy is celebrated, it is the whole Church who celebrates. Thus, the whole Church celebrates each sacrament. By the sacraments we are joined together in Christ, not only with those who are celebrating the sacraments with us, but with the whole Church throughout the world. The sacraments join Catholics all over the world with Jesus and with one another. They unite us as the Body of Christ, the entire Church united together in Christ.

It is within the life of the Church that we encounter and celebrate the great gift of God's grace that we receive through the seven sacraments. Through this grace, we are able to respond to the presence of God in our lives. Though God's grace prepares us to respond to him through the sacraments, we must be open, or properly *disposed*, to receive this grace. The *Catechism* states that the sacraments "bear fruit in those who receive them with the required dispositions" (1131). And one of these required dispositions is a commitment to live according to the grace of each sacrament.

The Holy Spirit helps us to live this way, with awareness of God working in our lives. Through the power of the Holy Spirit, we follow Jesus' example and his commandment to love one another. In this way we can live as disciples of Jesus. And, looking at life through the lens of faith, we become aware of God's presence in our lives—of God reaching out to us each day in love.

Activity Who in your life would you consider to be an example of someone who is aware of God's presence and lives as a disciple of Jesus? Explain your choice. Reflect on the reason for your choice. What might you learn from this person's example?

The sacraments sanctify us and build up the Body of Christ.

In the *Catechism* we read, "The purpose of the sacraments is to sanctify men, to build up the Body of Christ and, finally, to give worship to God" (1123). Thus, as acts of liturgy celebrated by the Church through the power of the Holy Spirit, the sacraments have a threefold purpose:

> **"The purpose of the sacraments is to sanctify men, to build up the Body of Christ and, finally, to give worship to God."**
>
> *(CCC, 1123)*

- to **sanctify** us, or make us holy, giving us the grace we need to live as disciples of Jesus and members of the Church

- to build up the Church as the Body of Christ, making the Church an effective sign of God's Kingdom in the world

- to offer worship to God, bringing us to God with thanks and praise and returning to us the grace we need to live as God's people.

The sacraments can be grouped into three categories. These categories reflect three important stages of Christian life: (1) birth and growth, (2) healing, and (3) mission. The Sacraments of Baptism, Confirmation, and Eucharist are called the *Sacraments of Christian Initiation*. Through them we are born into the Church, strengthened, and nourished. The Sacraments of Penance (also called Reconciliation) and Anointing of the Sick are known as the *Sacraments of Healing*. Through them we experience God's forgiveness, peace, and healing. The Sacraments of Holy Orders and Matrimony are called *Sacraments at the Service of Communion*. Through them we are strengthened to serve God and the Church through service to others.

As Catholics we celebrate all of the sacraments as a community. With the help and support of one another, we grow in *holiness*—sharing in God's goodness and responding to his love by the way we live. All of the sacraments call us to live with love for God and in service to others. Through the Sacraments of Christian Initiation we are all called to a common vocation of holiness and to the mission

Faith Word

sanctify

of evangelizing the world. In the Sacraments of Healing we are strengthened to face and overcome the power of sin and sickness and are called to restore our relationship with God and the Church. And in the Sacraments at the Service of Communion, certain members of the Church are called by God to serve the Church through the particular vocations of marriage and ordained ministry. Yet in all the seven sacraments, the Holy Spirit works through the Church to communicate the graces of Jesus Christ and to carry on his saving work.

Activity With a partner write and present a speech about the sacraments' threefold purpose or about the three stages of life they reflect.

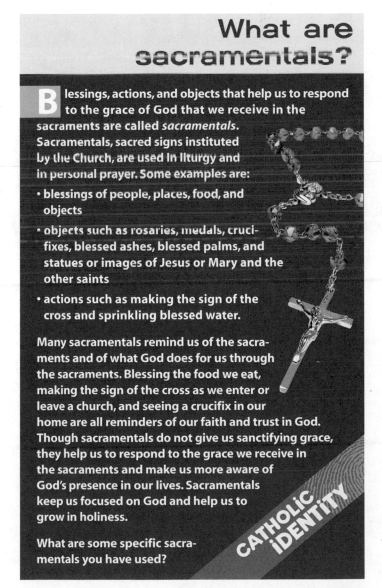

What are sacramentals?

Blessings, actions, and objects that help us to respond to the grace of God that we receive in the sacraments are called *sacramentals*. Sacramentals, sacred signs instituted by the Church, are used in liturgy and in personal prayer. Some examples are:

- blessings of people, places, food, and objects

- objects such as rosaries, medals, crucifixes, blessed ashes, blessed palms, and statues or images of Jesus or Mary and the other saints

- actions such as making the sign of the cross and sprinkling blessed water.

Many sacramentals remind us of the sacraments and of what God does for us through the sacraments. Blessing the food we eat, making the sign of the cross as we enter or leave a church, and seeing a crucifix in our home are all reminders of our faith and trust in God. Though sacramentals do not give us sanctifying grace, they help us to respond to the grace we receive in the sacraments and make us more aware of God's presence in our lives. Sacramentals keep us focused on God and help us to grow in holiness.

What are some specific sacramentals you have used?

CATHOLIC IDENTITY

Recognizing Our Faith

Recall the question at the beginning of this chapter: *How can I recognize God in my life?* Respond to this question by making a mural representing God's presence throughout different stages of your life and membership in the Church. Sketch your ideas for your mural here.

Living Our Faith

One of the purposes of the sacraments is to build up the Body of Christ. In what ways does your parish respond to this purpose? What can you do to participate?

Olivier Messiaen

Partners in FAITH

As a child, Olivier Messiaen was awed by the songs of birds and heard music in the sounds of nature. His fascination with the music in the world around him motivated him to compose his own music. When he was eleven, his parents enrolled him in the Paris Conservatory to study music. After completing his studies, he became an organist for a cathedral in Paris.

When World War II began, Messiaen was drafted into the French army. While fighting the German forces, he was captured and sent to a prison camp in Poland. Yet he continued to compose music arising from a fascination with nature and a love for God. Using paper borrowed from a sympathetic German guard, he composed *Quartet for the End of Time*, one of his most celebrated works. The German guards allowed him to perform this music for his fellow prisoners. After the war, Messiaen returned to Paris and became a professor at the Paris Conservatory. Until his death in 1992, he continued to compose the music that he loved.

Olivier Messiaen saw the extraordinary in ordinary life. He recognized the presence of God. In your own life, how can you try to do the same?

 For additional ideas and activities, visit www.weliveourfaith.com.

Putting Faith to Work

Talk about what you have learned in this chapter:

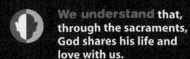 **We understand** that, through the sacraments, God shares his life and love with us.

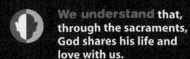 **We appreciate** the gift of the sacraments and their importance for us as members of the Body of Christ, the Church.

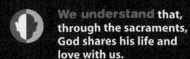 **We respond** to the gift of the sacraments by participating in them with faith and living what we celebrate.

Decide on ways to live out what you have learned.

✝ ENCOUNTERING GOD'S WORD

"I praise you, so wonderfully you made me;
wonderful are your works!"

(Psalm 139:14)

➡ **READ** the quotation from Scripture.

➡ **REFLECT** on the following question:
What "wonderful works" remind you of God? Think of examples from nature and your everyday life.

➡ **SHARE** your reflections with a partner.

➡ **DECIDE** on one way to praise God for his wonderful works each day this week.

Write the letter of the answer that best defines each term.

1. _____ liturgy

2. _____ sanctifying grace

3. _____ sacrament

4. _____ sanctify

a. the grace we receive, through the power of the Holy Spirit, in the sacraments

b. a symbolic action

c. the official public prayer of the Church

d. to make holy

e. an effective sign given to us by Jesus Christ through which we share in God's life

Complete the following.

5. The sacraments reflect three important stages of Christian life:

(1) _____,

(2) _____, and

(3) _____.

6. The Sacraments of Healing are _____.

7. The Sacraments of Christian Initiation are _____.

8. The Sacraments at the Service of Communion are _____.

9–10. **ESSAY:** What does it mean to say that the sacraments are *effective* signs? Give one specific example.

RESPONDING...

Sharing Faith with Your Family

Discuss the following with your family:

- Through the sacraments we share in God's life and love.
- The grace of the sacraments enables us to respond to God's love.
- As the Church we are united in Christ and celebrate his Paschal Mystery.
- The sacraments sanctify us and build up the Body of Christ.

The gateway to all the sacraments is Baptism. Find out the dates on which you and others in your family were baptized. Have a special family meal to commemorate each Baptism and your new life as children of God.

The Worship Connection

Check your parish bulletin to learn when a sacrament such as Anointing of the Sick or Matrimony will be celebrated. If possible, plan to attend with your family.

More to Explore

Research how one of the seven sacraments is celebrated in an Eastern Catholic Church. Share your findings with your group.

Catholic Social Teaching ☑ Checklist

Theme of Catholic Social Teaching:
Care for God's Creation

How it relates to Chapter 13: In this chapter we learned that everything in creation exists by God's power and reflects God's presence. We are called to protect and care for all of God's creation.

How can you do this?

☐ At home:

_____

☐ At school/work:

_____

☐ In the parish:

_____

☐ In the community:

_____

Check off each action after it has been completed.

"For in one Spirit we were all baptized into one body."
(1 Corinthians 12:13)

✛ **Leader:** At Baptism, we were born again. Let us thank Jesus for this great gift of new life.

All: "No one can enter the kingdom of God without being born of water and Spirit." (John 3:5)

Reader 1: Father, through sacramental signs, you give us grace and reveal the wonders of your power.

Reader 2: You have given us the gift of water and have made it a powerful sign of the grace that you give us in Baptism.

All: "No one can enter the kingdom of God without being born of water and Spirit." (John 3:5)

Reader 3: Your Spirit breathed upon the waters at the very beginning of creation and made them holy.

Reader 4: You made the waters of the great flood a sign of the waters of Baptism, washing away sin and bringing a new beginning of goodness.

All: "No one can enter the kingdom of God without being born of water and Spirit."(John 3:5)

Reader 5: You led your people, the Israelites, out of slavery through the waters of the Red Sea. This is a sign of the freedom that you give us, your holy people, through the waters of Baptism.

Reader 6: In the waters of the Jordan River, your Son, Jesus Christ, was baptized by John and was anointed with the Spirit.

All: "No one can enter the kingdom of God without being born of water and Spirit." (John 3:5)

Reader 7: And as your Son hung on the cross, water and blood flowed from his side.

Reader 8: After he was risen, your Son sent his disciples forth to proclaim the good news to all nations and to baptize them in the name of the Father, and of the Son, and of the Holy Spirit.

All: "No one can enter the kingdom of God without being born of water and Spirit." (John 3:5) Amen.

@ ✦ Visit www.weliveourfaith.com to find appropriate music and songs.

The BiG QuEstion:

Why do I long to belong?

Discover the names of the groups to which these animals belong. See if you can match each group of animals below to the name by which we commonly know it.

a group of chicks	**band**
a group of baboons	**bed**
a group of fish	**army**
a group of dogs	**pit**
a group of elephants	**brood**
a group of frogs	**fold**
a group of geese	**gaggle**
a group of gorillas	**herd**
a group of snakes	**pride**
a group of oysters	**pack**
a group of lions	**school**
a group of sheep	**tribe**

Scoring:

Give yourself one point for each correct answer. The correct answers are as follows: chicks—brood; baboons—tribe; fish—school; dogs—pack; elephants—herd; frogs—army; geese—gaggle; gorillas—band; snakes—pit; oysters—bed; lions—pride; sheep—fold.

6 or more points: Wow! You may want to compete on a television game show one day.

4–5 points: Great! You'll impress your friends the next time you go to the zoo.

1–3 points: Good work. You may want to investigate some nature programs.

What are some groups that people belong to?

In this chapter we learn that, in Baptism, we are freed from sin and born into the family of God through Jesus Christ. Through this chapter, we hope

 to recognize that, in Baptism, we become members of the Church and are offered salvation from sin

 to appreciate that, through Baptism, we belong forever to Christ

 to respond to the grace of Baptism by reaching out with love to others.

Would it surprise you to know that a human baby is one of the most helpless beings on earth? A baby calf can stand on its own within an hour or so of its birth. Kittens learn to hunt for their own food within weeks of being born. Black bear cubs are expected to strike out on their own about seventeen months after they are born. But a human baby totally depends on its family and other caregivers for many years, during a long period of infancy and childhood. In fact, as humans we usually do not become totally independent for at least eighteen years.

Scientists call the bond between an infant and its family or caregivers "attachment." The potential for attachment is inborn in each human being. Scientists have found that, of all the pictures and objects shown to infants, the ones they are most

"What do we live for, if it is not to make life less difficult to each other?" wrote Mary Ann Evans (1819–1880), the English novelist best known as George Eliot.

attracted to are those that resemble, in some way, the outline of a human face. No wonder we form such strong bonds with other human beings!

Our attachment to our family is foremost, but as we grow we also form bonds with others in our lives—extended family (grandparents, cousins, aunts, uncles), and then friends, classmates, club members, co-workers, and other people who come into our lives. So, while we were born as individuals, we were also born for companionship with others.

Activity A family tree traces the roots of your family. Design a relationship tree representing all the people in your life, including family members.

In Baptism we receive new life in Christ.

In the liturgy, especially during the Easter season, we celebrate the Resurrection, Christ's rising from death to new life. We celebrate that Jesus' victory over sin and death makes possible our salvation—the forgiveness of sins and the restoration of humanity's friendship with God. We rejoice that all creation is made new and that we are given the hope of happiness in God's Kingdom both now and forever. Yet, as Jesus told Nicodemus, a member of the Sanhedrin, "No one can see the kingdom of God without being born from above. . . . of water and Spirit" (John 3:3, 5).

The Sacrament of Baptism is our rebirth in water and the Spirit. Baptism, like faith, is necessary for salvation. It is in Baptism that sin, both original sin and personal sin, is taken away. In Baptism, the immersion into, or plunging into, water symbolizes that we die to sin and rise to new life in Christ. We are purified and renewed. Belonging to Christ, we are called "Christian," and God gives us his grace, his own life and love.

God sent his Son, Jesus Christ, to bring the good news of his love to the whole world. As Jesus journeyed to preach the good news, he invited people to join him. Jesus wanted everyone to know God and to share his life and love. Jesus reached out to all people, including those who were discriminated against and isolated—Samaritans, lepers, tax collectors, women, and all those who were in need of healing, whether of body, mind, or spirit. Those who followed Jesus became part of his community of disciples. Jesus showed that everyone is to be invited into this community. After his death and Resurrection, before he returned to his Father in heaven, Jesus gave his Apostles the power to continue his mission. Jesus asked the Apostles to make new disciples, saying to them, "Go into the whole world and proclaim the gospel to every creature. Whoever believes and is baptized will be saved" (Mark 16:15–16). Through the Apostles, the good news of salvation was offered to anyone who believed in Jesus and was baptized.

In the Church today, through the Sacrament of Baptism, Jesus, by the power of the Holy Spirit, continues to include and welcome all those who believe in him. Through the Sacrament of Baptism, we are made members of Jesus' community of believers, the Church, and given the hope of eternal life. As Saint Paul wrote, "For just as in Adam all die, so too in Christ shall all be brought to life" (1 Corinthians 15:22). In Baptism we are freed from sin and born into the family of God, joined to Jesus Christ, and filled with the Holy Spirit. We become part of the Body of Christ and are united with all those who have been baptized in Christ. And through Baptism, we too are called to the mission of sharing the good news of Christ and spreading the Kingdom of God.

Activity As part of your parish's evangelization effort, brainstorm ways you can help your parish invite people to become disciples of Jesus.

Extraordinary circumstances

A bishop, priest, or deacon is the ordinary minister of Baptism. However, in emergencies, such as the immediate danger of death, anyone can baptize. In such cases, a person baptizes by pouring water over the head of the person to be baptized and saying, "I baptize you in the name of the Father, and of the Son, and of the Holy Spirit."

But what happens if infants or children die without being baptized? Though "the Lord himself affirms that Baptism is necessary for salvation" (CCC, 1257), God himself is free to do what he thinks best in every situation. Jesus' own words—"Let the children come to me; do not prevent them" (Mark 10:14)—give us hope that through God's mercy there is a way of salvation for these children.

The Church also recognizes that those who give their lives in witness to the faith without having received the Sacrament of Baptism are "baptized by their death for and with Christ" (CCC, 1258). This is the *Baptism of blood.* And the Church recognizes the *desire for Baptism,* which happens when someone "seeks the truth and does the will of God in accordance with his understanding of it" (CCC, 1260). Each of these "brings about the fruits of Baptism without being a sacrament" (CCC, 1258).

Would you know how to baptize someone in an emergency?

We are washed and anointed.

In Jewish ritual, water was a powerful symbol of salvation and purification from sin. During the time of Jesus, Jewish people practiced a ritual of washing in water to prepare for sacred times or events. John the Baptist encouraged people to participate in this ritual washing, baptizing them in the waters of the Jordan River and urging them to prepare themselves for the coming of God's Kingdom.

> **"Whoever believes and is baptized will be saved."**
> (Mark 16:16)

When some of the Jewish authorities asked John who he was and why he was baptizing, he acknowledged that he was not the Messiah. And he said, "I baptize with water; but there is one among you whom you do not recognize, the one who is coming after me, whose sandal strap I am not worthy to untie" (John 1:26–27). The next day, when Jesus came toward him at the Jordan River, John made it known that Jesus was the one of whom he had spoken. John said, "Behold, the Lamb of God, who takes away the sin of the world" (John 1:29). And John added, "I did not know him, but the reason why I came baptizing with water was that he might be made known to Israel" (John 1:31).

Baptism of Jesus, Byzantine (mid-1600s)

After Jesus' baptism by John, John also said, "I saw the Spirit come down like a dove from the sky and remain upon him . . . The one who sent me to baptize with water told me, 'On whomever you see the Spirit come down and remain, he is the one who will baptize with the holy Spirit.' Now I have seen and testified that he is the Son of God" (John 1:32–34). Thus, this baptismal anointing by the Spirit made public that Jesus Christ is the Messiah, the Anointed One. Jesus' relationship with God his Father was revealed, and God the Holy Spirit came upon Jesus, anointing him and establishing him as priest, prophet, and king.

In the Sacrament of Baptism, we too are anointed, blessed with holy oil. As baptized members of the Church, Jesus calls all of us to share in his priesthood. This priesthood is not the ordained priesthood but the *priesthood of the faithful*, in which we can all participate—in the liturgy, especially the Eucharist, in prayer, and in the offering of our lives to God. Jesus also calls us as prophets to proclaim the good news and give witness to his truth. And Jesus, who exercised his kingship by drawing all of humanity to himself, calls us to kingship, asking us to respond to God's love and to care for others, especially those who are poor and suffering.

At Baptism we are sealed, or marked forever, as belonging to Christ. This spiritual mark, or character, can never be erased. Once we have received the Sacrament of Baptism, no matter what may happen, we belong to Christ and the Church. Thus, Baptism is a sacrament that is never repeated. Once we have been baptized, we are permanently marked with the sign of faith and have the hope of living in God's love forever.

Activity If the spiritual mark of Baptism could be represented visually, what do you think it would look like? Draw your idea here.

At Baptism we are welcomed into the Church.

How can you make someone feel welcomed?

We are welcomed as members of the Church through Baptism. Baptism is "the basis of the whole Christian life, the gateway to life in the Spirit . . . and the door which gives access to the other sacraments" (*CCC*, 1213). Baptism is the very first sacrament that we celebrate, and it leads us to the other two Sacraments of Christian Initiation, Confirmation and Eucharist. But not everyone begins or completes Christian initiation at the same time. Many people are baptized as infants or young children. Others are baptized as older children, adolescents, or adults. No one is ever too old or too young to begin a new life in Christ.

From the beginning, the Church has initiated adults. In fact, whole families have been baptized and welcomed into the Church. Today adults and children of catechetical age are baptized in a way very similar to that practiced by the early Church. After a period of inquiry, they are welcomed to prepare for and celebrate the Sacraments of Initiation in a process of formation called the **catechumenate**. This includes prayer and liturgy, religious instruction based on Scripture and Tradition, and service to others. Those who enter the catechumenate are called **catechumens**. These adults and older children participate in the Rite of Christian Initiation of Adults (RCIA). They participate in prayer celebrations that introduce them to the meaning of the sacraments and the life of the Church. They usually join the assembly for the Liturgy of the Word during the Sunday celebration of the Eucharist. And they receive the three Sacraments of Initiation in one celebration, usually at the Easter Vigil. The entire parish takes part in the formation of catechumens—some members serve as sponsors and godparents, others teach the catechumens about the Catholic faith, others pray for them, and all are to act as examples of discipleship to Jesus.

Infants or very young children can also be baptized into the faith of the Church. As we can read in the *Catechism*, "The practice of infant Baptism is an immemorial tradition of the Church" (1252). When infants and young children are baptized, the parents choose a godmother and godfather for the child. The godparents are to be examples of Christian discipleship and promise to support the child as he or she grows in faith. The parents, godparents, and the entire parish community agree to help the children grow in faith. Since Baptism is a sacrament that gives witness to the faith of the Church, it is celebrated within the community of believers. The participants in the sacrament include the child being baptized, the parents of the child, the godparents, the rest of the child's family, the parish community, and the celebrant. The **celebrant** is the bishop, priest, or deacon who celebrates the sacrament for and with the community.

> **Faith Words**
> catechumenate
> catechumens
> celebrant

Activity The Church community shares responsibility for the faith of those to be baptized. Write a note to someone preparing for Baptism, assuring that person of your prayers.

The catechumenate

How does an adult become a Catholic? Usually the person begins by contacting a parish. After deciding to take formal steps toward becoming a Catholic, the person is accepted into the catechumenate and becomes a catechumen.

The word *catechumen* comes from a Greek word meaning "to echo." In ancient times, students "echoed," or memorized and recited, what the teacher said. Catechumens grow in their understanding of the Christian life in important ways:

• *instruction:* They are invited to ponder the impact of Catholic beliefs on their lives.

• *moral conversion:* They are invited to turn toward God and change their way of life.

• *worship:* They usually participate in Sunday Mass but are dismissed after the homily to reflect together on the word of God. Until they are baptized, they do not participate in the Liturgy of the Eucharist.

• *ministry:* They learn to serve by assisting parish groups with outreach to those in need.

How does your own discipleship reflect these four parts of the catechumenate?

We celebrate the Sacrament of Baptism.

The Rite of Baptism for Several Children, as celebrated outside the Mass, is outlined below. Symbols shown in italics in the left column are defined in the right column.

RECEPTION OF THE CHILDREN

The celebrant asks the name of the child and what the parents seek from the Church for the child. The parents respond, "Baptism." The celebrant reminds the parents and godparents of their duty to teach the child about the Christian faith. The celebrant welcomes the child on behalf of the Church community. Then, with the words "I claim you for Christ our Savior by the sign of the cross," the celebrant traces the *sign of the cross* on the child's forehead with his thumb. The parents and godparents are invited to do the same.

Sign of the new life Christ has won for us

LITURGY OF THE WORD

The celebrant reads from Scripture. Others also read, and a psalm or song follows. The celebrant then gives the homily. The prayer of the faithful is said; the community prays for the child about to be baptized, for the whole Church, and for the world.

The celebrant leads the community in a litany asking the saints for their help. The celebrant prays for the child to be baptized, asking God to free the child from original sin and to send the Holy Spirit to be with the child.

Then the celebrant anoints the child with the *oil of catechumens*. The celebrant also lays his hand on the child in silence. The participants move to the baptismal font or pool.

Holy oil that represents a strengthening against evil and a cleansing from sin

THE CELEBRATION OF THE SACRAMENT

The celebrant blesses the *baptismal water*. If this water was already blessed at the Easter Vigil, the celebrant may say another kind of blessing.

The celebrant asks the parents and godparents a series of questions, such as, "Do you reject sin so as to live in the freedom of God's children?" and "Do you believe in God, the Father almighty, creator of heaven and earth?" By responding "I do" to each question, the parents and godparents renew their baptismal promises and affirm the faith of the Church.

The celebrant baptizes the child in the water of the baptismal font or pool by immersing or pouring water over the child three times while saying, "I baptize you in the name of the Father, and of the Son, and of the Holy Spirit."

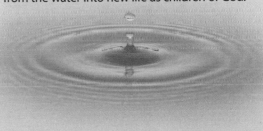

Blessed water in a baptismal font or pool. Those being baptized die to sin and rise up from the water into new life as children of God.

EXPLANATORY RITES

The celebrant anoints the child with *chrism*.

The celebrant gives the newly baptized a *white garment* and says, "See in this white garment the outward sign of your Christian dignity."

The celebrant takes the Easter candle, saying, "Receive the light of Christ." A parent or godparent lights the child's *candle* from the Easter candle. The celebrant says, "These children of yours have been enlightened by Christ. . . . May they keep the flame of faith alive in their hearts." The celebrant may pray a special prayer over the child's ears and mouth.

Perfumed oil that has been blessed by the bishop and is a sign of the Gift of the Holy Spirit. The anointing signifies that the newly baptized person shares in the mission of Christ.

An outward sign of the baptized person's new life in Christ and the universal call to holiness and purity. White symbolizes the purity of Christ.

A sign of the light and goodness of Christ and the light of faith shining in the newly baptized

CONCLUSION OF THE RITE

The celebrant gathers with the family near the altar to pray the Lord's Prayer and then offers a final blessing. The celebrant dismisses the whole community, saying, "Go in peace." All respond, "Thanks be to God."

> **"I claim you for Christ our Savior by the sign of the cross."**
> (Rite of Baptism for Several Children)

Activity With a partner highlight or underline each symbol and action of Baptism. Discuss what each signifies.

Recognizing Our Faith

Recall the question at the beginning of this chapter: *Why do I long to belong?* Plan a prayer service about belonging to Christ through Baptism. Use the chart below as an outline. Try to incorporate some symbols from the celebration of Baptism.

Scripture Readings	Prayers	Music/Songs	Symbols and Actions

Living Our Faith

In our daily lives what are some ways that we show we belong to Christ and his Church? Choose one of these to act on today.

Partners in FAITH

Marla Ruzicka

Marla Ruzicka was born on December 31, 1979. At an early age, she was already responding to the grace of Baptism by working for justice. She campaigned for equal athletic opportunities for girls in her hometown of Lakeport, California. She also raised awareness about the unfair working conditions of factory workers. Eager to learn about different cultures, she studied abroad in Cuba and Jerusalem.

Ruzicka was always ready to make a difference in the lives of others. She continued to travel to help people—hurricane victims in Honduras, AIDS victims in Africa, and people affected by war in Afghanistan and Iraq. At the age of twenty-six, she founded the Campaign for Innocent Victims in Conflict (CIVIC). This organization worked to give a voice to innocent victims of war.

Ruzicka was a Catholic who lived her baptismal promises and acted as a disciple of Christ in the world. On April 16, 2005, she was killed by a car bomb while working with CIVIC.

How did Marla Ruzicka live out her baptismal promises? How can you live out yours now?

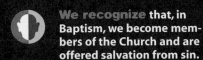

Putting Faith to Work

Talk about what you have learned in this chapter:

We recognize that, in Baptism, we become members of the Church and are offered salvation from sin.

We appreciate that, through Baptism, we belong forever to Christ.

We respond to the grace of Baptism by reaching out with love to others.

Decide on ways to live out what you have learned.

✝ ENCOUNTERING GOD'S WORD

"If you knew the gift of God . . . you would have asked . . . and he [Jesus] would have given you living water."

(John 4:10)

➡ **READ** the quotation from Scripture.

➡ **REFLECT** on the following question:
What does it mean to call Jesus the living water?

➡ **SHARE** your reflections with a partner.

➡ **DECIDE** to do something this week to share your faith in Jesus with someone else.

Circle the letter of the correct answer.

1. The _____ is the bishop, priest, or deacon who celebrates a sacrament for and with the community.
   a. celebrant   **b.** catechumen   **c.** catechumenate   **d.** godparent

2. In the Sacrament of Baptism we are sealed, or marked forever, as belonging to _____.
   a. the RCIA   **b.** the Sanhedrin   **c.** Jesus Christ   **d.** John the Baptist

3. At the Jordan River the baptismal anointing by the Spirit made public that _____ is the Messiah.
   a. Jesus Christ   **b.** John   **c.** Paul   **d.** Nicodemus

4. Baptism, like _____, is necessary for salvation.
   a. friendship   **b.** faith   **c.** community   **d.** catechumenate

Short Answers

5. What does God do for us in the Sacrament of Baptism? _____

6. What do the white garment and the lighted candle signify in Baptism? Explain. _____

7. What is required of the godparents of a child who is baptized? _____

8. What is the catechumenate? _____

9–10. ESSAY: Use what you have learned in this chapter to explain the following statement: *No one is ever too old or too young to begin a new life in Christ.*

RESPONDING...

Sharing Faith with Your Family

Discuss the following with your family:
- In Baptism we receive new life in Christ.
- We are washed and anointed.
- At Baptism we are welcomed into the Church.
- We celebrate the Sacrament of Baptism.

Share memories and stories of Baptisms in your family. You might look through family photos, videos, or mementos. Discuss how you can help each other to live your baptismal promises.

The Worship Connection

As you bless yourself with holy water at the entrace to the church this Sunday, make a point of thanking God for your Baptism.

More to Explore

Visit the place where Baptisms are celebrated in your parish. Note the placement of the baptismal font and any symbols.

Catholic Social Teaching ☑ Checklist

Theme of Catholic Social Teaching:
Call to Family, Community, and Participation

How it relates to Chapter 14: We are all created as social beings, needing to be with others and to be involved in family life and our community. As baptized Catholics, we are called to live as children of God and as responsible members of the Church and society.

How can you do this?

☐ At home:

_____

☐ At school/work:

_____

☐ In the parish:

_____

☐ In the community:

_____

Check off each action after it has been completed.

GATHERING...

Confirmation

❝If we live in the Spirit, let us also
follow the Spirit.❞

(Galatians 5:25)

✝ **Leader:** When we were baptized and given
new life as members of the Body of
Christ, we were baptized in the name of
the Father, and of the Son, and of the
Holy Spirit.

God our Father
made you his children by water
    and the Holy Spirit:
may he bless you
and watch over you with his fatherly love.

All: Amen.

Leader: Jesus Christ the Son of God
promised that the Spirit of truth
would be with his Church for ever:
may he bless you and give you courage
in professing the true faith.

All: Amen.

Leader: The Holy Spirit
came down upon the disciples
and set their hearts on fire with love:
may he bless you,
keep you one in faith and love,
and bring you to the joy of God's kingdom.

All: Amen.

(Rite of Confirmation)

Visit www.weliveourfaith.com
to find appropriate music
and songs.

The BiG QuEStion:
What good qualities do I have?

Discover how love is a gift. See if you can change the word *gift* to the word *love* by playing the "letter swap" game. Start with the word *gift* and swap one of its letters with one of the letters in the word *love* to form a new word. This word must be a real word. Write it in the second row. Then repeat the process (with a different letter from the word *love*) two more times. Write each new word in the appropriate row. The word *love* is formed in the fifth row when you are finished playing the "letter swap" game.

G	I	F	T
L	O	V	E

Answers:
second row: LIFT
third row: LIFE
fourth row: LIVE

Which of your good qualities, or gifts, make you a more loving person?

In this chapter we learn about the Sacrament of Confirmation and its role in strengthening us to live as disciples of Jesus Christ. Through this chapter, we hope

 to understand that the Sacrament of Confirmation completes Baptism and seals us with the Gift of the Holy Spirit

 to desire to respond to the Holy Spirit by using our gifts to serve others

 to respond to the guidance of the Holy Spirit through a life of faith and witness.

Lion: What you say makes sense, Little Mouse. I am a great hunter, but I will allow my compassion and mercy to overrule my hunting instinct, just for now. Go on your way, and give my best to your family!

Narrator: The mouse went on his way. Some days later, on another trip to find food, the mouse heard a loud moaning coming from a hole in the ground. Looking down, he was shocked to see King Lion bound by thick ropes and stuck in a deep pit.

Mouse: King Lion, it is your friend, Little Mouse. What happened to you?

Lion: Oh, Little Mouse, I am done for! They have caught me! They will take me away from the beautiful African plains! They will put me in a cage, and who knows what will happen to me after that? I cannot get free, and no one can help me!

Mouse: I can help you, King Lion. I have very sharp teeth. These ropes are strong, but with cleverness and patience, I can chew through them and set you free. Hold still, now. Let me get to work!

Narrator: The mouse began to chew. He chewed all night, rope by rope, knot by knot, until the trap simply fell apart. The mighty lion leapt to his feet, jumped out of the pit, and stood before Little Mouse.

Lion: Thank you, Little Mouse, for using your gifts of patience and cleverness to help me. I will never forget your kindness!

Narrator: Once upon a time, a majestic lion, the King of Beasts, lived on the beautiful plains of Africa. He was known far and wide as a mighty hunter who never failed to provide food for his family. Waking from a nap one day, he noticed a mouse scampering at his feet.

Lion: Aha, Little Mouse! What are you doing, and where are you going?

Mouse: Good afternoon, King Lion. I am carrying grains home to my family.

Lion: Well, it so happens that I am in the mood for a snack. I will whack you with my great paw and eat you up!

Mouse: Oh, please, King Lion! Don't do that! My family is very hungry and they have waited a long time for this good grain that I have here. I know you are a mighty hunter. You could catch something much bigger than I if you tried. Please let me go!

Mouse: And thank you, King Lion, for sparing my life. You used your gifts of mercy and compassion, and so I was still alive to help you today. I will never forget your kindness!

Activity What does this tale teach about using one's good qualities? Design a card for your wallet that lists your good qualities. Keep it with you as a reminder of the gifts that you have at your disposal for helping others.

66In the arena of human life, the honors and rewards fall to those who show their good qualities in action,99 wrote Aristotle (384–322 B.C.), Greek philosopher.

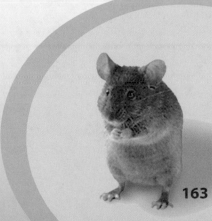

The disciples receive the Holy Spirit.

Jesus wanted all of his disciples to be his witnesses. He called them to continue his mission of sharing God's love and spreading God's Kingdom. Yet they would not be alone in this work, for Jesus promised to send the Holy Spirit to guide and help them. The presence of the Holy Spirit was one of the ways that God had always expressed his love for humanity. But in Jesus Christ, the Spirit's presence truly became known. As we read in the *Catechism*, Jesus "was conceived of the Holy Spirit; his whole life and his whole mission are carried out in total communion with the Holy Spirit whom the Father gives him 'without measure'" (1286).

One day Jesus spoke to his disciples, saying, "Whoever believes in me, as scripture says:
> 'Rivers of living water will flow from within him'" (John 7:38).

Jesus was referring to the Gift of the Holy Spirit. Like living water, the Holy Spirit would come to the disciples if they believed in Jesus. After Jesus' Ascension, Peter and the disciples were gathered in Jerusalem for the Jewish feast of Pentecost. The word *Pentecost* comes from a Greek word meaning "fiftieth." On the fiftieth day after Passover the Jews celebrated a harvest festival. They thanked God for all their blessings, especially the fruits of the earth. It was during this feast that the outpouring of the Holy Spirit that Jesus had promised took place.

After he had received the Gift of the Spirit, Peter got up to address the large crowd that had gathered. He proclaimed the words of the prophet Joel, "'It will come to pass . . . ,' God says,
> 'that I will pour out a portion of my spirit
>   upon all flesh . . . . and it shall be that
>   everyone shall be saved
>   who calls on the name of the Lord'"

(Acts of the Apostles 2:17, 21).

Peter also told the crowd of people that God the Father had indeed raised Jesus and that what had just taken place had been the outpouring of the Holy Spirit. The people were amazed and asked Peter and the others what they should do. Peter told them to repent and to be baptized in Jesus' name and receive the Gift of the Holy Spirit. About three thousand people believed and became disciples that day.

Each year on Pentecost Sunday—fifty days after Easter—we celebrate the outpouring of the Holy Spirit upon the Apostles and upon all Christ's disciples. It is a time for us to thank God for the Gift of the Holy Spirit. We gather to celebrate that through the Apostles and their successors, all those who believe in Jesus Christ can receive this same outpouring of the Holy Spirit.

Activity Imagine you are a reporter at the time of Pentecost. What two questions would you ask Peter? How do you think he would respond? Role-play your interview.

The laying on of hands and anointing are signs of the Holy Spirit's presence.

Strengthened and guided by the Holy Spirit, the Apostles baptized many who came to believe in Jesus. The newly baptized received the strengthening power of the Holy Spirit, too, when the Apostles placed their hands on them. These early Church members understood the importance of this laying on of hands. This ancient action was a powerful sign of God's blessing, and by it authority and grace were given in God's name. "The apostles, in fulfillment of Christ's will, imparted to the newly baptized by the laying on of hands the gift of the Spirit that completes the grace of Baptism." (*CCC*, 1288) So, from the very beginning of the Church, there was a connection between Baptism and the laying on of hands by the Apostles. This laying on of hands is recognized as the beginning of the Sacrament of Confirmation, which "perpetuates the grace of Pentecost in the Church" (*CCC*, 1288).

> Confirmation "perpetuates the grace of Pentecost in the Church" (*CCC*, 1288).

In the early days of the Church, an anointing was joined to the laying on of hands. This anointing with **chrism**, perfumed oil consecrated, or blessed, by a bishop, "highlights the name 'Christian,' which means 'anointed' and derives from that of Christ himself whom God 'anointed with the Holy Spirit'" (*CCC*, 1289). In time the anointing became the essential sign of the Gift of the Holy Spirit. And since Baptism and Confirmation were usually celebrated together, the baptized person received a double anointing with chrism. The first anointing after Baptism was given by the priest and was completed through a second anointing by the bishop.

As the Church grew, the territory covered by a **diocese**, a local area of the Church led by a bishop, greatly expanded. When the dioceses grew, the bishops were not always able to be present at all baptismal celebrations. The Church in the East continued to celebrate Confirmation and Baptism at the same time. A priest could confer both sacraments, but, for the anointings after Baptism, he needed to use chrism, or myron, that had been blessed by the bishop.

The Church in the West, however, to emphasize the unity of Catholics with their bishop, reserved the celebration of Confirmation to the bishop himself. Thus, the separation between the celebration of Baptism and that of Confirmation began. The original minister of Confirmation is the bishop, who may, if there is a need, grant that a priest confer this sacrament.

Whether the Sacraments of Baptism and Confirmation are celebrated at the same time or at different times, the Sacrament of Confirmation "confirms baptism and strengthens baptismal grace" (*CCC*, 1289).

Activity Who is the bishop of your diocese? As a sign of your unity with him, pray for him.

East and West

In the earliest days of the Church, there was no official "Eastern" or "Western" (Roman) Church. There was simply the Church. The Churches that we now know as the Eastern Churches originated in the eastern half of the Roman Empire. Many of them were founded by the Apostles. Gradually, differences created tensions between the Churches of the East and the Church in Rome. In 1054, a tragic split, or *schism*, came about within the Church. This schism has lasted to this day. The Eastern Churches that split from the Catholic Church are now called, collectively, the Eastern Orthodox Church. The Eastern Churches that chose to remain in union with or were later reunited with the Church of Rome and its pope and bishops are called the Eastern Catholic Churches. They are *Churches* because each Church follows its own ancient tradition, retaining its own bishops, language, and liturgical customs.

The Catholic Church today consists of twenty-two Churches: The Roman Catholic Church and twenty-one Eastern Catholic Churches. Research them!

Faith Words

chrism

diocese

The Sacrament of Confirmation completes Baptism.

What things in life require preparation?

Preparation for the Sacrament of Confirmation is very important. One must be in a *state of grace* in order to be fully open to its effects. Receiving the Sacrament of Penance readies one for the celebration of Confirmation. Those preparing for Confirmation are called **candidates**. Candidates prepare by praying and reflecting on the life of Jesus Christ, the mission of the Church, and the Gift of the Holy Spirit. They discover what it means to be anointed with chrism and are led to see how this anointing will change their lives. They learn how Confirmation will complete their Baptism. Each candidate's relationship with Christ, begun at Baptism, is strengthened through this preparation for Confirmation.

During this preparation candidates choose a name, usually that of a saint, whose example they can follow. Although they can choose the name of any saint, candidates are encouraged to take their baptismal names. This highlights the link between the Sacraments of Baptism and Confirmation. When candidates prepare for Confirmation, they also choose a **sponsor**, someone who can be involved in their preparation for Confirmation and who will help them to grow in faith. A sponsor needs to be a Catholic who is at least 16 years of age and who has received the Sacraments of Initiation, is respected and trusted by the candidate, and is an example of Christian living. To emphasize the link between Baptism and Confirmation, candidates are encouraged to select one of their godparents as a sponsor. However, candidates may choose a friend, someone from the parish, or a relative other than a parent. Sponsors play an important role in the celebration of Confirmation since they present the candidates to the bishop for anointing.

As in all of the sacraments, the entire parish community participates in the preparation of the candidates for Confirmation. Some members are part of the direct preparation of the candidates. They teach them more about the Catholic faith and the sacrament they are about to receive. They help the candidates to prepare themselves for the outpouring of the Holy Spirit by encouraging them to do good works. The whole parish community prays with and for the candidates. Some people in the parish may meet with candidates to talk about their faith, and some may help the candidates to find meaningful ways to serve other people in the parish, in the local community, and in the world. All of the people in the parish are called on to be examples of Christian discipleship and openness to the Holy Spirit.

Faith Words
candidates
sponsor

Activity Design an e-card for a Confirmation candidate. Include an appropriate message, poem, or prayer of support.

We are sealed with the Gift of the Holy Spirit in Confirmation.

Because Confirmation leads us to the Eucharist and full initiation into the Church, it is usually celebrated within Mass. After the Scripture readings, the pastor or a parish leader presents the candidates to be confirmed to the bishop. The bishop then gives the homily, reflecting on the readings and on the Sacrament of Confirmation. The bishop may ask the candidates about their faith and their understanding of Confirmation. The candidates then stand and renew their baptismal promises, reaffirming the faith that was professed at Baptism. Then the bishop invites all the people to pray for the outpouring of the Holy Spirit on the candidates. All pray in silence. The bishop and the priests celebrating with him then lay hands upon the candidates by extending their hands over them. The bishop prays that the Holy Spirit will come upon the candidates and that they will receive the gifts of the Holy Spirit. Each candidate, presented by a sponsor, approaches the bishop for anointing. The sponsor places his or her right hand on the candidate's shoulder as a sign of support and guidance. The bishop confirms each candidate by laying his hand on the candidate's head, tracing the sign of the cross on the candidate's forehead with chrism, and calling the candidate by name, saying, "Be sealed with the Gift of the Holy Spirit" (Rite of Confirmation). The person confirmed responds, "Amen." This anointing confirms and completes the baptismal anointing. Like the character or mark of Baptism, the seal of Confirmation is with us always. Because of this we receive Confirmation only once.

The bishop then shares a sign of peace with the newly confirmed. This action reminds us of the union of the whole Church with the bishop. The assembly then prays the prayer of the faithful, and all assembled continue to worship God in the Liturgy of the Eucharist.

When our Baptism is completed through the Sacrament of Confirmation, we receive a special outpouring of the Holy Spirit. Like the Apostles on Pentecost, we are given the strength to spread and defend the faith by our words and actions. Confirmation not only unites us more closely to Christ and the Church, it also strengthens the gifts of the Holy Spirit within us. When we respond to the Holy Spirit and use the gifts we have received, the results, or fruits of the Holy Spirit, are evident in our lives. The fruits of the Holy Spirit are: "charity, joy, peace, patience, kindness, goodness, generosity, gentleness, faithfulness, modesty, self-control, chastity" (*CCC*, 1832).

Activity Think about one fruit of the Holy Spirit that you can live out today.

> **"Be sealed with the Gift of the Holy Spirit."**
> (Rite of Confirmation)

The gifts of the Holy Spirit

In Baptism the Holy Spirit shares seven spiritual gifts with us. These gifts help us to follow Christ's teachings and to give witness to our faith. The gifts of the Spirit are:

- **wisdom**, the knowledge and ability to recognize and follow God's will in our lives
- **understanding**, the ability to love others as Jesus calls us to
- **counsel** (right judgment), the ability to make good choices
- **fortitude** (courage), the strength to give witness to our faith in Jesus Christ
- **knowledge**, the ability to learn more about God and his plan, leading us to wisdom and understanding
- **piety** (reverence), a love and respect for all that God has created
- **fear of the Lord** (wonder and awe), a recognition that God's presence and love fills all creation.

In the Sacrament of Confirmation, these seven gifts of the Holy Spirit are increased in us. And when we are filled with the gifts of the Spirit, others see in us the joy of God's Kingdom.

What are some ways the world would be changed if everyone were filled with the gifts of the Holy Spirit?

CATHOLIC IDENTITY

RESPONDING...

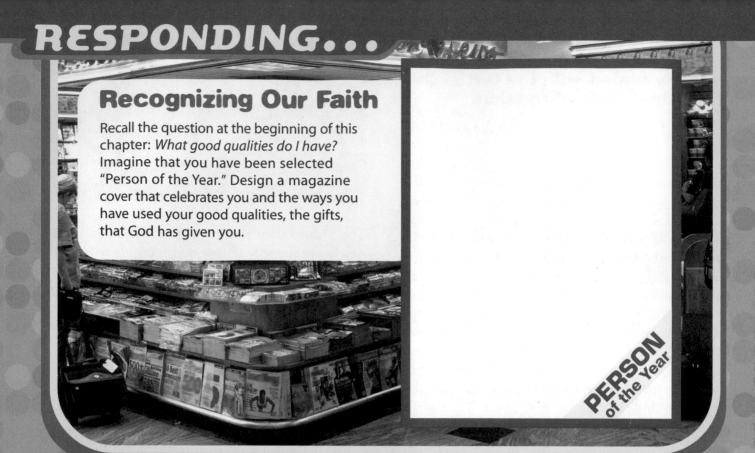

Recognizing Our Faith

Recall the question at the beginning of this chapter: *What good qualities do I have?* Imagine that you have been selected "Person of the Year." Design a magazine cover that celebrates you and the ways you have used your good qualities, the gifts, that God has given you.

PERSON of the Year

Living Our Faith

In this chapter we learned that Confirmation helps us to live as faithful witnesses to Christ. What can you do this week to be a faithful witness?

Blessed Miguel Pro

Miguel Pro was born in Mexico in 1891. His two sisters, who dedicated their lives to serving God, were a positive example for him. In 1911, during a time in Mexican history when Catholics, especially priests and members of religious communities, were being persecuted by the government, Miguel entered the Society of Jesus. In order to continue their studies, Miguel and other seminarians had to flee Mexico. In 1925 Miguel was ordained a priest in Belgium. He returned to Mexico in 1926, even though he risked torture, arrest, and even execution for following his vocation. But he thought of ways to serve God despite the watchful eyes of the government. He disguised himself to be unrecognizable as a priest in order to celebrate the sacraments. In 1927 Father Pro was falsely accused of a bombing attempt and sentenced to death. As he faced the firing squad he forgave his executioners and died shouting, "*¡Viva Cristo Rey!*"—meaning "Long live Christ the King!" The Church remembers Blessed Miguel Pro on November 23.

Reflect on the courage of Father Pro and the Mexican people in living their faith. Where is this gift of the Holy Spirit needed today?

Putting Faith to Work

Talk about what you have learned in this chapter:

We understand that the Sacrament of Confirmation completes Baptism and seals us with the Gift of the Holy Spirit.

We desire to respond to the Holy Spirit by using our gifts to serve others.

We respond to the guidance of the Holy Spirit through a life of faith and witness.

Decide on ways to live out what you have learned.

✝ ENCOUNTERING GOD'S WORD

❝There are different kinds of spiritual gifts but the same Spirit; there are different forms of service but the same Lord.❞

(1 Corinthians 12:4–5)

➡ **READ** the quotation from Scripture.

➡ **REFLECT** on the following:
Saint Paul wrote these words to the first Christians in Corinth, Greece. He was reminding these Christians that all the gifts that we receive from the Holy Spirit have the same value and are meant to be shared to serve others. What gifts of the Holy Spirit can you use to serve others?

➡ **SHARE** your reflections with a partner.

➡ **DECIDE** on a way to use your gifts and serve others this week.

Write the letter of the answer that best defines each term.

1. _____ candidate

2. _____ chrism

3. _____ sponsor

4. _____ diocese

a. local area of the Church led by a bishop

b. someone involved in a candidate's preparation for Confirmation who will help the candidate to grow in faith

c. someone preparing for the Sacrament of Confirmation

d. perfumed oil blessed by a bishop

e. Greek word meaning "fiftieth"

Complete the following.

5. In Confirmation, the _____ and _____ are signs of the Holy Spirit's presence.

6. Through preparation for Confirmation each candidate's relationship with Christ, begun at _____, is strengthened.

7. We are sealed with the _____ of the _____ in Confirmation.

8. The presence of the _____ was one of the ways that God had always expressed his love for humanity.

9–10. **ESSAY:** How does a candidate prepare for Confirmation?

RESPONDING...

Sharing Faith with Your Family

Discuss the following with your family:

- The disciples receive the Holy Spirit.
- The laying on of hands and anointing are signs of the Holy Spirit's presence.
- The Sacrament of Confirmation completes Baptism.
- We are sealed with the Gift of the Holy Spirit in Confirmation.

Write each of the twelve fruits of the Holy Spirit on a separate slip of paper. Place the slips in a large bowl in your family's prayer space. Invite each member of the family to take one slip each day and think about that particular fruit of the Holy Spirit. Have them reflect on ways that it is evident or missing in their lives and the lives of others. At the end of the week, as a family, discuss your experiences and observations.

The Worship Connection

At every Eucharist, we pray that the Holy Spirit will gather us together in unity. Listen for this petition. Each time we pray it, make a decision to contribute to unity and harmony in your family, school, parish, neighborhood and diocese.

More to Explore

Use the Internet, your diocesan newspaper, and parish/diocesan Web sites to find out about the celebration of the Sacrament of Confirmation in your diocese.

Catholic Social Teaching ☑ Checklist

Theme of Catholic Social Teaching:
Rights and Responsibilities of the Human Person

How it relates to Chapter 15: We can respond to the Gift of the Holy Spirit by accepting our responsibility to protect the rights of others and by working for justice and quality of life wherever they are lacking.

How can you do this?

☐ At home:
_____

☐ At school/work:
_____

☐ In the parish:
_____

☐ In the community:
_____

Check off each action after it has been completed.

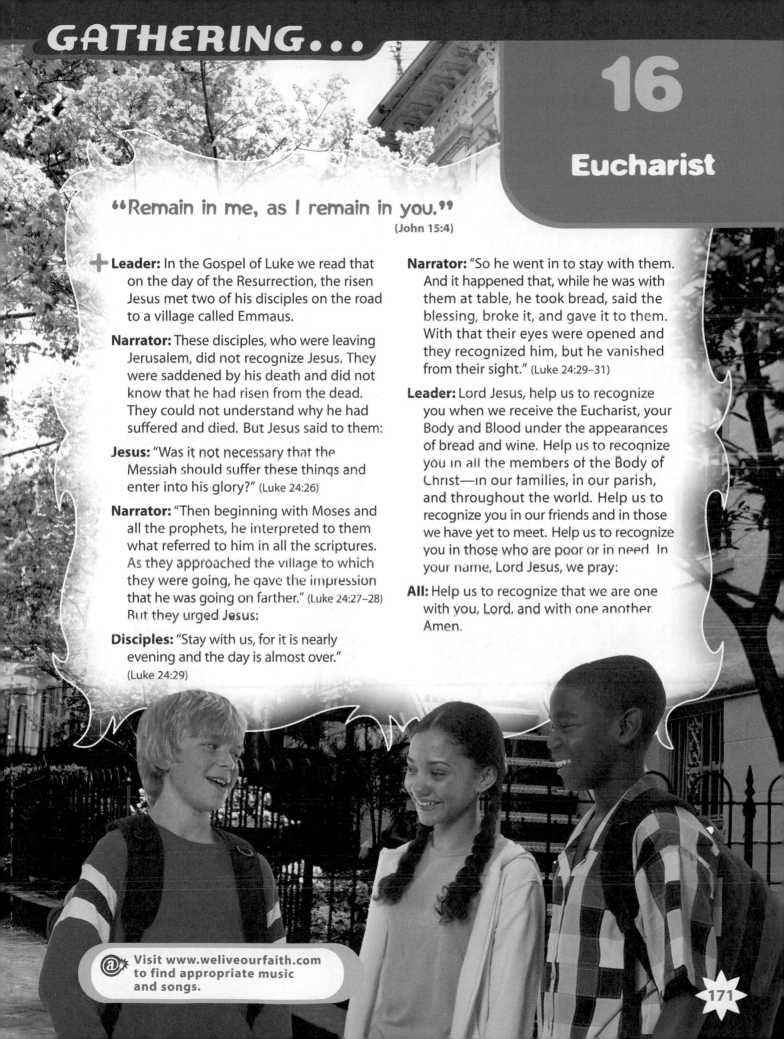

"Remain in me, as I remain in you."
(John 15:4)

✝ **Leader:** In the Gospel of Luke we read that on the day of the Resurrection, the risen Jesus met two of his disciples on the road to a village called Emmaus.

Narrator: These disciples, who were leaving Jerusalem, did not recognize Jesus. They were saddened by his death and did not know that he had risen from the dead. They could not understand why he had suffered and died. But Jesus said to them:

Jesus: "Was it not necessary that the Messiah should suffer these things and enter into his glory?" (Luke 24:26)

Narrator: "Then beginning with Moses and all the prophets, he interpreted to them what referred to him in all the scriptures. As they approached the village to which they were going, he gave the impression that he was going on farther." (Luke 24:27–28) But they urged Jesus:

Disciples: "Stay with us, for it is nearly evening and the day is almost over."
(Luke 24:29)

Narrator: "So he went in to stay with them. And it happened that, while he was with them at table, he took bread, said the blessing, broke it, and gave it to them. With that their eyes were opened and they recognized him, but he vanished from their sight." (Luke 24:29–31)

Leader: Lord Jesus, help us to recognize you when we receive the Eucharist, your Body and Blood under the appearances of bread and wine. Help us to recognize you in all the members of the Body of Christ—in our families, in our parish, and throughout the world. Help us to recognize you in our friends and in those we have yet to meet. Help us to recognize you in those who are poor or in need. In your name, Lord Jesus, we pray:

All: Help us to recognize that we are one with you, Lord, and with one another. Amen.

@ **Visit www.weliveourfaith.com to find appropriate music and songs.**

The BiG QuEStion:

How does unity with others strengthen me?

iscover the value of unity in life. Read this humorous tale.

There is a story about four people. Their names are **Everybody**, **Somebody**, **Anybody**, and **Nobody**. The story goes that there was a very important job that needed to be done. **Everybody** was supposed to do this job. Now **Anybody** could have done this job, but **Nobody** was willing to do it. Then **Somebody** got angry about this because it was **Everybody**'s job to do. Well, **Everybody** thought that **Anybody** could have done it!

But **Nobody** realized that **Everybody** blamed **Somebody** for not doing the job. Still **Nobody** did it. The arguing got worse, and finally **Nobody** would talk to **Anybody** and **Everybody** blamed **Somebody**. What a shame that **Anybody** could have done the job, and **Everybody** could have helped **Somebody**, but who ended up doing the job? **Nobody**!

Nobody

Everybody

Somebody

Anybody

How does this story relate to the need for unity? In what ways does unity help us to accomplish things and do the work that we are called to do?

In this chapter
we learn that, in the Eucharist, we are made one with Christ and one with the entire Church. Through this chapter, we hope

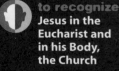 **to recognize** Jesus in the Eucharist and in his Body, the Church

 to be thankful for Jesus' gift of himself in the Eucharist

 to share the strength and love of Jesus with others.

American hockey team at Olympic award ceremony, Lake Placid, New York, 1980

During the 1980 Winter Olympics, on the day before the hockey match between the U.S. and Soviet Union teams, an article in *The New York Times* declared that the Soviet team would certainly win the Olympic gold medal unless the ice melted, or unless the U.S. team performed a miracle. The U.S. team was made up of amateur and college hockey players, while the Soviet team consisted of highly skilled, professional players. Everyone thought that the odds of the U.S. hockey team winning this match were slim to none.

Yet, defying all expectations, the U.S. hockey team defeated the Soviet team. Did the ice melt, or was it a miracle? Neither! The U.S. hockey players—though from all different parts of the country, with varying levels of hockey experience—banded together and worked hard to win the game. But it didn't stop there. With one united effort and with their hearts set on a common goal of victory, they beat the Finnish team in the final game for the gold medal! Their gold-medal win is considered by many to be the greatest American sports achievement of the twentieth century. It is also a powerful example of how people can come together as one to achieve a common goal.

Activity What role has unity played in your life? Write a story about a positive experience of working together with others to meet a common goal. The story can be based on your own life or on other events. Then write a slogan to summarize this experience, or choose one of the slogans on this page. Share your slogan and story with your group.

"Coming together is a beginning, keeping together is progress, and working together is success."
(attributed to Henry Ford, American inventor and businessman)

"I am because we are."
(African proverb)

"United we stand, divided we fall."
(Aesop, famous ancient fable-writer)

"Few burdens are heavy when everyone lifts."
(Anonymous)

"Many of us are more capable than some of us . . . but none of us is as capable as all of us!"
(Tom Wilson, author of the comic strip *Ziggy*)

"No road is long with good company."
(Turkish proverb)

BELIEVING...

We are nourished by the Body and Blood of Christ.

Throughout the history of salvation, bread and wine were a source of life for God's people. During Jesus' public ministry, when he miraculously fed a crowd of people assembled to hear his words and see his works, Jesus showed the importance of sustaining life, of feeding the hungry. He "took the loaves, gave thanks, and distributed them" (John 6:11). Jesus also shared the importance of sustaining God's life within us. He taught, "For my flesh is true food, and my blood is true drink. Whoever eats my flesh and drinks my blood remains in me and I in him . . . Whoever eats this bread will live forever" (John 6:55–56, 58).

Through the Sacrament of the Eucharist we receive everlasting nourishment—the bread and wine that by the power of the Holy Spirit become the Body and Blood of Christ. And as we become one with Christ, sharing in his Body and Blood in the Sacrament of the Eucharist, we complete our initiation into Christ and his Church. Like the first Apostles and disciples we gather as a community to share the life of Jesus, to become one with him and with one another. Through our unity in the Eucharist we are the Body of Christ in the world. We are his living presence, sharing God's life with others, recognizing needs in the world just as Jesus did, and reaching out to meet the needs of others in his name. Nourished by the Body and Blood of Christ

we commit ourselves to living as Christ lived and to working for true justice and peace. We too try to feed those who are hungry, reach out to comfort those who are sorrowful, and seek ways to heal those who are ill. Through our unity with Jesus Christ, really present in the Eucharist, we are able to live the fullness of God's life in us—with the Spirit strengthening and preparing us to "proclaim the Paschal mystery of Jesus 'until he comes'" at the end of time (*CCC*, 1344).

Activity Our unity with Jesus Christ in the Eucharist calls us to be Christ for others and to work for justice and peace as he did. There are many injustices in the world today. What are some things we can do to work for justice as Jesus did? Complete the chart below, naming some injustices and ways that, nourished by Christ, you can work to overcome them.

INJUSTICE	OVERCOMING INJUSTICE

174

Jesus gives his disciples a new covenant.

On the night that we, as Catholics, now celebrate as Holy Thursday, Jesus and his disciples were in Jerusalem. They gathered in the upper room of a house to celebrate the Passover. On this Jewish feast they remembered the way God had delivered their people from slavery and death in Egypt. They recalled the night on which God had told the Hebrews in Egypt to sacrifice a lamb and mark their doorways with its blood. On that night, a plague swept through Egypt, killing all of the Egyptians' firstborn sons. But it *passed over* the homes marked with blood, thus sparing the Hebrews. The Egyptians, in their fear, allowed the Hebrews to leave Egypt, and so the Hebrews began their journey, or *exodus,* to freedom.

> **"Whoever eats this bread will live forever."**
> (John 6:58)

Paschal means "of or relating to the Passover." At the Passover meal that Jesus and his disciples ate, everything—the unleavened bread, the wine, the lamb, the bitter herbs—had special meaning in light of the Exodus from Egypt. And for Jesus and his disciples, this Paschal meal was a reminder, as it still is for Jews today, of God's covenant with his people.

This Paschal meal was the last meal that Jesus would share with his disciples before his death. Jesus "took the bread, said the blessing, broke it, and gave it to them, saying, 'This is my body, which will be given for you; do this in memory of me.' And likewise the cup after they had eaten, saying, 'This cup is the new covenant in my blood, which will be shed for you'" (Luke 22:19–20). As it is explained in the *Catechism,* "The Eucharist that Christ institutes at that moment will be the memorial of his sacrifice" (611), for, as the priest of the new covenant, Jesus offered himself as the Paschal lamb and sacrificed himself in the breaking of the Paschal bread, his Body. And through the suffering and death on the cross that Jesus endured, the new covenant between God and his people was sealed with Jesus' Blood.

God brought freedom to the people of Israel, and then, through Christ, freed us from the slavery of sin. We can again share in God's love and friendship. Jesus Christ is given as our deliverance, not just at a point in time, but for all time in the Eucharistic sacrifice. In the Sacrament of the Eucharist, all who share the Body and Blood of Christ come to the fulfillment of hope—to new freedom and new life.

Faith Word
Paschal

The Last Supper from the movie *King of Kings* (1961)

Activity Write a prayer to Jesus that you can say after you receive him in the Eucharist.

Sacrament of redemption

The *Catechism* calls the Eucharist "the sacrament of redemption" (1846). In the Eucharist we receive the Body and Blood of Jesus Christ, which he offers for our redemption and the forgiveness of our sins. As Jesus said, "This is my body, which will be given for you . . . . my blood, which will be shed for you" (Luke 22:19, 20).

Through the celebration of the Eucharist, we receive forgiveness for our *venial sins,* our less serious sins. The Eucharist also strengthens our love for God, our neighbor, and ourselves and helps us to live united to God. However, we cannot be united to God unless we freely choose to love him. So, if we *seriously* sin against him, we commit a *mortal sin* and cannot receive Holy Communion before first being absolved in the Sacrament of Penance. Only then will we be restored to God's friendship and ready to receive Christ in the Eucharist. Children who are preparing for First Holy Communion also must first receive the Sacrament of Penance.

Give thanks for the forgiveness you receive through the Eucharist.

BELIEVING...

We are one with Jesus Christ.

How can we share Christ's presence with others?

After the Resurrection, as some of Jesus' disciples were walking to the village of Emmaus, the risen Jesus walked with them, though they did not know it was he. At supper Jesus "took bread, said the blessing, broke it, and gave it to them. With that their eyes were opened and they recognized him" (Luke 24:30–31).

After Christ's Ascension, his disciples would be enlightened by the Holy Spirit, enabled to understand Christ's words and actions more completely. Filled with the Spirit, the disciples would recognize the Eucharist as the reality of Christ's presence in the breaking of the bread.

The making of altar breads

Altar breads, or unconsecrated hosts, are the small round wafers of bread that are later consecrated at Mass, becoming the Body of Christ. Altar breads are often made by religious communities dedicated to a life of prayer. These communities bake and sell altar breads as a way to support themselves in their way of life. The Benedictine Sisters of Perpetual Adoration, for example, bake two million altar breads each week at their monastery in Clyde, Missouri. They send these altar breads to parishes in the United States, Haiti, Mexico, Nicaragua, Canada, Ireland, Russia, New Zealand, Australia, and Japan—and even to ships at sea.

Altar breads are made of wheat flour and water. Because Jesus used unleavened Passover bread at the Last Supper, the dough for the Eucharist bread is also unleavened—in other words, baked without yeast so that it does not rise.

Do you know who makes the altar breads that your parish uses? Try to find out. Say a special prayer in thanksgiving for these people the next time you receive the Eucharist.

We read in the Acts of the Apostles that in the small Christian community, the early Church, the Eucharist continued to be celebrated, through the power of the Holy Spirit, in the breaking of the bread. As members of the Church, we too gather in community for the Eucharist. We gather on Sunday or Saturday evening for **Mass**, the celebration of the Eucharist. At this celebration Christ is present in the person of the priest, in the assembly, in God's word, and most especially under the appearances of bread and wine. We hear the stories about God, and, just as the disciples on the road to Emmaus, we recognize in the breaking of the bread the true presence of Christ—his Body and Blood under the appearances of bread and wine. We partake of Christ's Body as he commanded us and drink the cup of his Blood, sharing in his life.

> **Faith Word**
>
> Mass

Through the Real Presence of Christ, Body and Blood, which we receive in the Eucharist, we are nourished to live as Jesus' disciples and carry on his mission. In the Eucharist Christ's presence becomes a reality in our lives. And through this "Sacrament of sacraments" (*CCC*, 1211), we are enabled to share the reality of Christ's presence with one another.

Activity Design a concept for a video game that has a main character whose mission is to share the ways Christ is present in the world. Include obstacles or challenges this character has to overcome, plus good works or actions the character has to perform. On a separate sheet of paper, list your ideas or draw some scenes from your game, and share with a partner. Don't forget to name your video game and character(s).

We celebrate the Eucharist.

We gather as an assembly in the name of the Blessed Trinity, the Triune God, to celebrate the Eucharist. And "all who eat the one broken bread, Christ, enter into communion with him and form but one body in him" (*CCC*, 1329). In assembly with the priest we are the Body of Christ. Together at Mass we worship and pray.

THE MASS: THE CELEBRATION OF THE EUCHARIST	
Introductory Rites *Entrance Chant* *Gloria* *Greeting* *Collect* *Act of Penitence*	Together we enter into prayer. We confess our unworthiness, seeking to be made holy to participate in the sacrifice of Christ that will be made present for us.
Liturgy of the Word *First Reading* *Gospel* *Responsorial Psalm* *Homily* *Second Reading* *Profession of Faith* *Alleluia or Gospel Acclamation* *Prayer of the Faithful*	We glorify God and listen to the stories of God's covenant with his people. We rise at the reading of the Gospel, the good news of Jesus' presence with us. In the words of the homily the priest or deacon explains more fully what the Scripture readings mean for us today. We affirm our belief in God and the history of salvation. We pray, as the Body of Christ, for our community, the whole Church community, and all God's people.
Liturgy of the Eucharist *Preparation of the Gifts* *Prayer over the Offerings* *Eucharistic Prayer* *Communion Rite* *Lord's Prayer* *Rite of Peace* *Breaking of the Bread* *Holy Communion*	Prepared by healing, listening, sharing, and prayer, we offer the gifts, bread and wine, as Christ did, and we join ourselves to him. We praise the greatness and wonder of God. By the power of the Holy Spirit, through the words and actions of the priest, the bread and wine become the Body and Blood of Christ. We acclaim the life, death, and Resurrection of Jesus. He is present on the altar for the glory of God, and we shout out in joy. We beg the Father's strength and support in the words Jesus gave us and we share a sign of peace. We receive Christ in Holy Communion. Sanctified by his Body and Blood, we become one with and in Christ. Together we reflect on our oneness with Jesus.
Concluding Rites *Greeting* *Blessing* *Dismissal*	The priest blesses us in the name of the Father, the Son, and the Holy Spirit and the priest or deacon dismisses us to go in peace, do good works, and praise and bless the Lord. Salvation history is fulfilled in the eucharistic celebration of Jesus, and we are commissioned to share this fulfillment with those community members who could not be with us. We also share it with the whole world—through what we do in Jesus' name.

Note: Also see page 309 for a description of each of these individual parts.

> **"**All who eat the one broken bread, Christ, enter into communion with him and form but one body in him.**"**
> (*CCC*, 1329)

Activity How can you fulfill the commission which is given to you during the Concluding Rites?

RESPONDING...

Recognizing Our Faith

Recall the question at the beginning of this chapter: *How does unity with others strengthen me?* In this chapter we learned that through the Eucharist we are united to Christ and to one another. How does this unity strengthen us? Design a flier or an insert for your parish's weekly bulletin that answers this question.

Living Our Faith

This week decide on one way you can share Christ's presence with another person.

Partners in FAITH

Catholic Relief Services

Catholic Relief Services (CRS) is a nonprofit organization that was founded in 1943 to help poor, homeless, and disadvantaged people living outside the United States. CRS first began by helping people who became refugees as a result of World War II (1939–1945). *Refugees* are people who must leave their own countries due to war, famine, or oppression. The organization helped refugees settle in the United States and in other free countries.

Today CRS continues its good works around the world by helping people who are poor or hungry, working to remove the causes of poverty, and giving aid to people in need, no matter where they live. CRS has helped people affected by religious persecution, civil wars, and natural disasters such as earthquakes and tsunamis. Through these actions, CRS promotes justice and peace around the world.

The Eucharist calls us to work for justice and peace. Decide on one thing you will do this week to promote justice and peace.

 For additional ideas and activities, visit www.weliveourfaith.com.

Putting Faith to Work

Talk about what you have learned in this chapter:

We recognize Jesus in the Eucharist and in his Body, the Church.

We are thankful for Jesus' gift of himself in the Eucharist.

We share the strength and love of Jesus with others.

Decide on ways to live out what you have learned.

✝ ENCOUNTERING GOD'S WORD

At the Last Supper, after Jesus washed the feet of the disciples, he said,

" If I, therefore, the master and teacher, have washed your feet, you ought to wash one another's feet. I have given you a model to follow, so that as I have done for you, you should also do "

(John 13:14–15).

➡ **READ** the quotation from Scripture.

➡ **REFLECT** on the following:
During the Holy Thursday liturgy, the Church follows Jesus' command to do as he did by performing the ritual action of the washing of the feet. But how do we, the Church, carry out Jesus' command in everyday life?

➡ **SHARE** your reflections with a partner.

➡ **DECIDE** on one way to truly serve others this week, and make it happen!

Short Answers

1. What is another name for the celebration of the Eucharist? _____

2. What does the word *Paschal* mean? _____

3. How does Jesus nourish us? _____

4. How was the new covenant between God and his people sealed? _____
_____

Complete the following.

5. The Liturgy of the Word consists of the following parts: _____
_____

6. The Liturgy of the Eucharist consists of the following parts: _____
_____

7. In the Sacrament of the Eucharist, by the power of the _____, through the words and actions of the priest, the bread and wine become the Body and Blood of Christ.

8. At the end of Mass, the priest blesses us in the name of the Father, the Son, and the Holy Spirit and the priest or deacon dismisses us to _____.

9–10. **ESSAY:** How does the Eucharist unite us to Christ and to one another?

Chapter 16 Assessment

179

RESPONDING...

Sharing Faith with Your Family

Discuss the following with your family:

- We are nourished by the Body and Blood of Christ.
- Jesus gives his disciples a new covenant.
- We are one with Jesus Christ.
- We celebrate the Eucharist.

Think of a way to help your family become more aware of the Sunday celebration of the Eucharist as a special time to strengthen your unity with Christ and one another. You might want to find a simple family activity that could become an "after-Mass" custom. What could that be for your family?

The Worship Connection

At every Mass, we pray the Lord's Prayer, asking for our "daily bread," a reminder of the Eucharist we are soon to receive, and asking for forgiveness "as we forgive." We are then ready to become one with Christ and one another in Holy Communion.

More to Explore

Research the way cultures affect the celebration of the Eucharist in this country and around the world.

Catholic Social Teaching ☑ Checklist

Theme of Catholic Social Teaching:
Option for the Poor and Vulnerable

How it relates to Chapter 16: For Jesus, helping people who were poor, weak, disadvantaged, and in need was always a top priority. As his Church, the Body of Christ, we have an obligation to continue his work.

How can you do this?

☐ At home:

_____

☐ At school/work:

_____

☐ In the parish:

_____

☐ In the community:

_____

Check off each action after it has been completed.

GATHERING...

17

Penance and Anointing of the Sick

"Come to me, all you who labor and are burdened, and I will give you rest."

(Matthew 11:28)

Leader: Confident that Jesus loves each person, let us pray for those in need of his care.

All: Lord Jesus, you invite all who are burdened to come to you.
Allow your healing hand to heal them.
Touch our souls with your compassion for others;
touch our hearts with your courage and infinite love for all;
touch our minds with your wisdom, and may we always proclaim your praise.

Teach us to reach out to you in all our needs, and help us to lead others to
you by our example.
(based on a prayer by the Sacred Heart Monastery in Hales Corners, Wisconsin)

Leader: Lord Jesus, you care for us. You share your healing power with us in the Sacraments of Penance and the Anointing of the Sick. May our hearts be healed through forgiveness, and may all who are ill be strengthened through prayer and anointing. We ask this with faith in you.

All: Amen.

 Visit www.weliveourfaith.com to find appropriate music and songs.

181

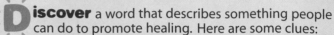

The BiG Question:

Who helps to heal me when I am suffering?

Discover a word that describes something people can do to promote healing. Here are some clues:

- The word is seven letters long.

- The first letter of the word can be found in the word *raffle* but not in the word *laughter*.

- The second letter can be found in *roman* but not in *manner*.

- The third letter can be found in *mentor* but not in *memento*.

- The fourth letter can be found in *elegant* but not in *elephant*.

- The fifth letter can be found in *interest* but not in *restaurant*.

- The sixth letter can be found in *vain* but not in *animal*.

- The seventh letter can be found in *pace* but not in *captor*.

The word is:

_____

Answer:
forgive

Discuss why it is important to forgive. How does forgiving someone promote healing?

In this chapter
we learn about the peace, healing, and forgiveness that are available to us in the Sacraments of Penance and Anointing of the Sick. Through this chapter, we hope

to know
that Jesus Christ offers God's forgiveness and healing for all our sins and sufferings

to appreciate
the healing power of Jesus Christ that we receive in the Sacraments of Healing through the Church

to promote
healing, forgiveness, and reconciliation in the world around us.

"I am a New York City Police Officer. On July 12, 1986, I was on patrol in Central Park and stopped to question three teenagers. While I was questioning them, the oldest, Shavod Jones, a fifteen-year-old, took out a gun and shot me in the head and neck.

"Thanks to the quick action of my fellow police officers, I was rushed to a hospital. Once it became clear I was going to survive, the surgeon came into my room and told my wife, Patti Ann, and me that I would be paralyzed from the neck down for the rest of my life. I was married just eight months, and my wife, twenty-three years old, was three months pregnant.

"Our faith suddenly became very important to us: the Catholic Mass, prayers, our need for God. It was God's love that put me back together. I spent the next eighteen months in the hospital. While I was there, my wife gave birth to our son, Connor. At his baptism, I told everyone I forgave the young teen who shot me.

"The only thing worse than a bullet in my spine would have been to nurture revenge in my heart. Such an attitude would have extended my tragic injury into my soul, hurting my wife, son, and others even more. It is bad enough that the physical effects are permanent, but at least I can choose to prevent spiritual injury.

"People often ask if I forgave Shavod right away, or if it took time. It has evolved over fourteen years. I think about it almost every day. I was angry at him but I was also puzzled, because I found I couldn't hate him. More often than not I felt sorry for him. I wanted him to find peace and purpose in his life. I wanted him to turn his life to helping and not hurting people. That's why I forgave him. It was also a way of moving on, a way of putting the terrible incident behind me." (excerpts from "Why I Forgave My Assailant," a speech by Detective Steven McDonald)

Detective Steven McDonald, confined to a wheelchair and a breathing machine, hopes his story will have an impact on all who need peace and reconciliation. He speaks to young people at school assemblies in the New York metropolitan area and has traveled to Northern Ireland and Israel to promote peacemaking.

Activity List some of the reasons that people forgive one another.

"The message that God forgives has a prior condition: that we forgive those who have injured us," wrote Corrie ten Boom (1892–1983), who found healing even though she and her family were sent to Nazi concentration camps during World War II.

God is loving and forgiving.

Throughout the ages the prophets called people to live out their covenant with God. They called people to repentance and conversion. **Conversion** is turning back to God with all one's heart. Jesus too wanted people to turn away from sin and grow closer to God. And by the way that Jesus lived, he helped people to turn to God his Father. He showed them how to follow God's law. He also taught that God loves and values all of us, even when we sin.

Every sin weakens our friendship with God. Less serious sin, **venial sin**, does not turn us completely away from God. But very serious sin, **mortal sin**, does completely turn us from God because it is a choice that we freely make to do something that we know is seriously wrong. Even if we commit serious sin, however, God never stops loving us, and he will always forgive us if we are truly sorry. Jesus used the following parable to teach us about this truth:

"A man had two sons, and the younger son said to his father, 'Father, give me the share of your estate that should come to me.' So the father divided the property between them. After a few days, the younger son collected all his belongings and set off to a distant country where he squandered his inheritance on a life of dissipation. When he had freely spent everything, a severe famine struck that country, and he found himself in dire need. So he hired himself out to one of the local citizens who sent him to his farm to tend the swine. And he longed to eat his fill of the pods on which the swine fed, but nobody gave him any. Coming to his senses he thought, 'How many of my father's hired workers have more than enough food to eat, but here am I, dying from hunger. I shall get up and go to my father and I shall say to him, "Father, I have sinned against heaven and against you. I no longer deserve to be called your son; treat me as you would treat one of your hired workers."' So he got up and went back to his father. While he was still a long way off, his father caught sight of him, and was filled with compassion. He ran to his son, embraced him and kissed him. His son said to him, 'Father, I have sinned against heaven and against you; I no longer deserve to be called your son.' But his father ordered his servants, 'Quickly bring the finest robe and put it on him; put a ring on his finger and sandals on his feet. Take the fattened calf and slaughter it. Then let us celebrate with a feast, because this son of mine was dead, and has come to life again; he was lost, and has been found.' Then the celebration began" (Luke 15:11–24).

Just as the younger son in this parable turned from his father, we sometimes turn from God our Father. Through this story Jesus taught us what we need to do to receive God's forgiveness in the Sacrament of Penance. Like the younger son in the parable, we must have sorrow, or *contrition*, for turning away from God and must tell God that we are sorry, or make a *confession*. By our words and actions we must also show that we are sorry, or do *penance*, and resolve to avoid sin in the future. Then, through the person of the priest, God grants us *absolution*—forgives us, and welcomes us back.

> **Faith Words**
> conversion
> venial sin
> mortal sin

Activity Reread the parable, thinking of the father as representing God. How would you describe God, based on this parable? Share your response.

We celebrate the Sacrament of Penance and Reconciliation.

Jesus not only spoke about God's mercy toward sinners; Jesus put God's mercy into action. As the Son of God, Jesus granted forgiveness to sinners as only God could do. Yet Jesus, also being human, like us in all ways but sin, knew our humanity. He knew that we had a need for continued spiritual healing and reconciliation. So, after his death and Resurrection, Jesus Christ appeared to his Apostles and shared with them his authority to forgive sin:

> Jesus said, **"Peace be with you"** (John 20:21).

"[Jesus] said to them . . . , 'Peace be with you. As the Father has sent me, so I send you.' And when he had said this, he breathed on them and said to them, 'Receive the holy Spirit. Whose sins you forgive are forgiven them, and whose sins you retain are retained'" (John 20:21–23).

Jesus wanted all people to hear his call to conversion and to receive God's forgiveness. From the beginning of the Church, the Apostles continued Jesus' call to conversion. Through Baptism they granted God's forgiveness to those who believed.

Baptism frees us from original sin and any sins that we may have committed. Baptism begins our life anew. Yet, after Baptism, we sometimes make choices that do not show love for God, ourselves, and others. We do not follow our conscience. Our **conscience** is our ability to know the difference between good and evil, right and wrong. We sometimes turn from God and are again in need of his forgiveness. And just as he did more than two thousand years ago, Jesus continues to forgive those who are truly sorry. Jesus does this through the Church in the Sacrament of Penance and Reconciliation. Priests are empowered to forgive sins by the authority Christ bestows on them in the Sacrament of Holy Orders. And, in the Sacrament of Penance, the priest, in the name of Christ and the Church, and through the power of the Holy Spirit, grants the forgiveness of our sins.

In this sacrament our relationship with God and the Church is strengthened and restored.

The Sacrament of Penance is usually celebrated in one of two ways: an individual meets with a priest for the celebration (Rite of Reconciliation of Individual Penitents), or a group gathers to celebrate the sacrament with one or more priests (Rite of Reconciliation of Several Penitents with Individual Confession and Absolution). Personal confession of sins and individual absolution are always part of each of these rites. And "the sacrament of Penance is always, by its very nature, a liturgical action, and therefore an ecclesial and public action" (*CCC*, 1482). Through this Sacrament of Healing, we proclaim our faith in God's mercy, give thanks for the gift of forgiveness, and resolve to live more faithfully as Christ's disciples.

Faith Word
conscience

Activity How will you show that, as Christ's disciple, you share in his mission of reconciliation?

God gives us peace

The Sacrament of Penance and Reconciliation has been called the sacrament of conversion, of Penance, of confession, of forgiveness, and of Reconciliation. This sacrament has four main parts:

- *contrition*, a heartfelt sorrow for sins, with a desire to sin no more
- *confession*, the act of telling our sins to the priest, thus acknowledging our responsibility for our actions and expressing our desire for God's forgiveness. The priest is bound by the *seal of confession* to never reveal what is confessed.
- *penance*, specific prayer or acts of service that the priest will tell us to do in order to show that we are sorry
- *absolution*, which takes place when, through the person of the priest, God forgives us our sins, or *absolves* us.

Through this powerful Sacrament of Healing, God gives us his peace, and we are reconciled to God and the Church.

CATHOLIC IDENTITY

Jesus comforts all who are in need.

How can we cope with suffering and sickness?

Jesus' healing power was a sign that in him God's Kingdom had begun. And since Jesus wanted all people to experience God's power and presence in their lives, he shared his ministry with his Apostles. Jesus sent them out to share the message of the Kingdom of God. They traveled throughout the land, teaching and healing in Jesus' name. "They anointed with oil many who were sick and cured them." (Mark 6:13) After Jesus' death and Resurrection, Jesus told the Apostles that one of the signs that would "accompany those who believe" was that they would "lay hands on the sick, and they will recover" (Mark 16:17, 18).

While all of the sacraments bring us closer to God and one another, the Sacrament of the Anointing of the Sick celebrates in a special way Jesus' work of healing. And from the time of the Apostles, faithful believers have turned to the Church for this healing and comfort. In fact, in Saint James's writing to one of the early Christian communities about the need for healing, we can see the beginnings of the Sacrament of the Anointing of the Sick. James said that anyone who is suffering should pray. Anyone who is sick should call on the priests of the Church, "and they should pray over him and anoint [him] with oil in the name of the Lord, and the prayer of faith will save the sick person, and the Lord will raise him up" (James 5:14–15).

As all sacraments, the Anointing of the Sick is a celebration of the whole Church community. Recalling that Jesus saves us by his suffering, death, and Resurrection, the community asks God, in this Sacrament of Healing, to save those who are suffering. The priest who administers the sacrament and those gathered represent the whole Church, offering comfort and support to those who are sick and encouraging them. This message of hope and support is also for people who care for those who are sick, especially for their families and friends.

The Church encourages its members to welcome the grace of this sacrament. Thus, in times of serious sickness, children, adults, and the elderly are all invited to be strengthened by God's grace in the Anointing of the Sick. This sacrament is meant to help people in living their faith during times of suffering and so can be celebrated more than once—as determined by each person's needs.

Many parishes offer a communal celebration of the Anointing of the Sick at Mass. However, this sacrament is often celebrated in hospitals, in homes, at the site of an accident, or wherever someone is in need of it. Whenever possible, friends and family members should be present for the celebration, supporting those who are ill and continuing Jesus' saving work of healing.

Activity With your group list some people in your family or community who are suffering from a serious illness. Together pray for these people. Then design get-well cards to send to them.

We celebrate the Sacrament of the Anointing of the Sick.

In the Sacrament of the Anointing of the Sick, God's grace and comfort are given to those seriously ill or suffering because of their old age. They receive strength, peace, and courage to face the difficulties that come from serious illness or old age. The grace of the Sacrament of the Anointing of the Sick may even restore to physical health those who are ill. But for all those who receive this sacrament, it:

> **"And the prayer of faith will save the sick person."**
>
> (James 5:15)

- renews their trust and faith in God
- unites them to Christ and to his suffering
- prepares them, when necessary, for death and the hope of life forever with God.

Since the Anointing of the Sick often takes place outside the celebration of the Mass, the sacrament usually begins with the Liturgy of the Word and is followed by Holy Communion. In this way those being anointed are further strengthened and nourished by the word of God and by the Body and Blood of Christ. Holy Communion also joins them to their parish community with whom they are unable to celebrate the Eucharist.

THE MAIN PARTS OF THE ANOINTING OF THE SICK

The Prayer of Faith: The whole Church is represented by the priest, family, friends, and other parish members gathered to pray. Trusting in God's mercy, they ask for help for those who are sick. Several intentions are offered. After each one, those present answer, "Lord, have mercy." (Rite of Anointing of the Sick)

The Laying On of Hands: In silence the priest lays his hands on the person who is sick. The priest's laying on of hands is a sign of blessing and a calling of the Holy Spirit upon the person.

The Anointing with Oil: Using the oil of the sick, the priest anoints the person's forehead first, saying, "Through this holy anointing may the Lord in his love and mercy help you with the grace of the Holy Spirit." Response: "Amen." (Rite of Anointing of the Sick)

Then the priest anoints the person's hands, saying, "May the Lord who frees you from sin save you and raise you up." Response: "Amen." (Rite of Anointing of the Sick)

As those who are very ill approach the hour of death, they are given the Body of Christ in the Eucharist as *viaticum*, or "food for the journey." Viaticum strengthens those who are dying as they prepare for death and the hope of eternal life. Receiving the Body of Christ, they can be encouraged, for Jesus said, "Whoever eats my flesh and drinks my blood has eternal life, and I will raise him on the last day" (John 6:54).

When the Sacraments of Penance, Anointing of the Sick, and the Eucharist as viaticum are celebrated together, they are called the "last sacraments." Through these sacraments, Jesus helps us to recognize that suffering and death are only temporary experiences on the path toward eternal happiness with God.

Activity Enlarge this Venn diagram: in the larger outside section of the circles, fill in what is specific to that sacrament; in the overlapping sections what each set of sacraments has in common; in the center what all three have in common. Some possible entries: grace, healing, forgiveness, nourishment.

Holy oils

Each year at the Chrism Mass, a special Mass held before Easter, the bishop of each diocese blesses oil that will be used for anointing in sacraments in the diocese. The Chrism Mass is usually held in the diocesan cathedral. Three types of oils are blessed:

- the oil of catechumens, which is used to anoint people in preparation for Baptism
- the oil of the sick, which is used to anoint people in the Anointing of the Sick
- the chrism oil, which is a fragrant oil used to anoint in Baptism, Confirmation, and Holy Orders. Each parish will receive a supply of these oils following the Mass.

Describe how the anointing that takes place in the Anointing of the Sick is similar to or different from the anointing that you learned about in Chapter 14, "Baptism," and Chapter 15, "Confirmation."

RESPONDING...

Recognizing Our Faith

Recall the question at the beginning of this chapter: *Who helps to heal me when I am suffering?* What was your answer? Now turn the question around: *Whom do I help to heal when they are suffering?* Reflect for a few moments on the ways you may have promoted, and can continue to promote, the healing of others.

Living Our Faith

Frequent confession strengthens our relationship with Christ and the Church. Make an effort to receive the Sacrament of Penance on a regular basis.

Partners in FAITH

Saint Peregrine

As a young man in Italy in the thirteenth century, Peregrine Laziosi belonged to a political group that was against the Church and the pope. During one political rally he angrily struck the face of a priest who belonged to an order known as the Servites. This priest, now known as Saint Philip Benizi, prayed for Peregrine instead of striking back at him. This merciful act changed Peregrine's outlook on life. He sought forgiveness and also eventually became a Catholic. In an attempt to do penance for his old ways, he vowed to "stand up" and serve God and the Church as a Servite. During his years of service he experienced the healing of a cancerous condition in his leg, a recovery for which he was grateful to God.

Saint Peregrine is the patron saint of cancer patients. His feast day is May 1. The Servites continue the work of Saint Peregrine. One way they serve is by working to help seriously ill people and their caregivers to find healing, support, peace, and God in their daily lives.

In what way can you offer support to someone in need of healing?

@ For additional ideas and activities, visit www.weliveourfaith.com.

Putting Faith to Work

Talk about what you have learned in this chapter:

We know that Jesus Christ offers God's forgiveness and healing for all our sins and sufferings.

We appreciate the healing power of Jesus Christ that we receive in the Sacraments of Healing through the Church.

We promote healing, forgiveness, and reconciliation in the world around us.

Decide on ways to live out what you have learned.

✝ ENCOUNTERING GOD'S WORD

"Gracious is the LORD and just;
yes, our God is merciful.
I shall walk before the Lord
in the land of the living."

(Psalm 116:5, 9)

➡ **READ** the quotation from Scripture.

➡ **REFLECT** on the following question:
Can you recall a time when God was merciful to you?

➡ **SHARE** your reflections with a partner.

➡ **DECIDE** to thank God for his mercy now and always. You might wish to pray the first two lines of the Scripture quotation as a prayer of thanksgiving.

Complete the following paragraph.

Jesus taught us what we need to do to receive God's forgiveness in the Sacrament of Penance. We must have sorrow, or _____ (1), for turning away from God and must tell God that we are sorry, or make a _____ (2). By our words and actions we must also show that we are sorry, or do _____ (3), and resolve to avoid sin in the future. Then, through the person of the priest, God grants us _____ (4)—forgives us, and welcomes us back.

Short Answers

5. What are the main parts of the Anointing of the Sick? _____

6. What is viaticum? _____

7. Which sacraments, when celebrated together, are called the "last sacraments"? _____

8. Explain what conversion is. _____

9–10. ESSAY: How are the Sacraments of Penance and Anointing of the Sick related?

RESPONDING...

Sharing Faith with Your Family

Discuss the following with your family:
- God is loving and forgiving.
- We celebrate the Sacrament of Penance and Reconciliation.
- Jesus comforts all who are in need.
- We celebrate the Sacrament of the Anointing of the Sick.

This week, before sharing a meal together, ask each member of your family to think of something for which you need forgiveness or of someone you need to forgive. Then think of all those in the community and world who need God's healing. Pray together that God's forgiveness and healing touch all those who are in need of it, including your family.

The Worship Connection

At every Mass we pray for people in the Church community who are sick or who have died. Remember in silent prayer people in your own life who are sick or whose lives on earth have come to an end.

More to Explore

Many parishes hold communal celebrations of the Anointing of the Sick. Find out when one of these is to be held in yours or a nearby parish. How can your group help with the celebration?

Catholic Social Teaching ☑ Checklist

Theme of Catholic Social Teaching:
Life and Dignity of the Human Person

How it relates to Chapter 17: All human beings have human dignity because they are created in God's image and redeemed by Jesus Christ. All people have the right to life, healing, and compassion. As Catholics we respect and promote this right.

How can you do this?

☐ At home:

_____

☐ At school/work:

_____

☐ In the parish:

_____

☐ In the community:

_____

Check off each action after it has been completed.

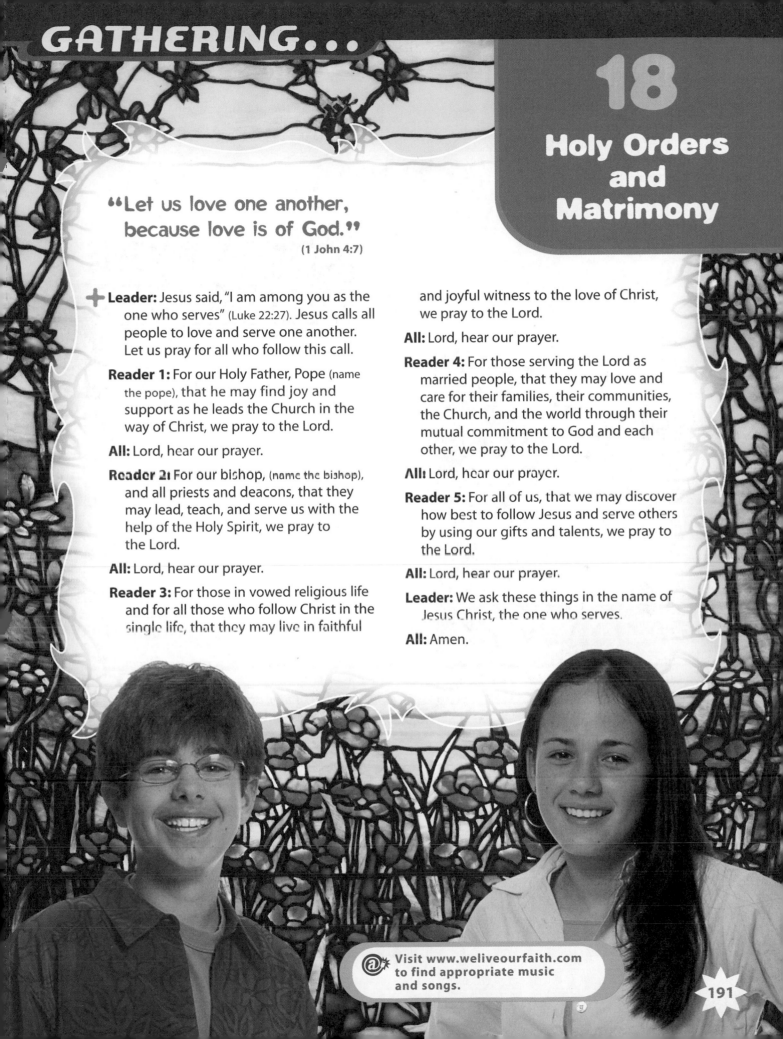

GATHERING...

18
Holy Orders and Matrimony

"Let us love one another, because love is of God."

(1 John 4:7)

✛ **Leader:** Jesus said, "I am among you as the one who serves" (Luke 22:27). Jesus calls all people to love and serve one another. Let us pray for all who follow this call.

Reader 1: For our Holy Father, Pope (name the pope), that he may find joy and support as he leads the Church in the way of Christ, we pray to the Lord.

All: Lord, hear our prayer.

Reader 2: For our bishop, (name the bishop), and all priests and deacons, that they may lead, teach, and serve us with the help of the Holy Spirit, we pray to the Lord.

All: Lord, hear our prayer.

Reader 3: For those in vowed religious life and for all those who follow Christ in the single life, that they may live in faithful and joyful witness to the love of Christ, we pray to the Lord.

All: Lord, hear our prayer.

Reader 4: For those serving the Lord as married people, that they may love and care for their families, their communities, the Church, and the world through their mutual commitment to God and each other, we pray to the Lord.

All: Lord, hear our prayer.

Reader 5: For all of us, that we may discover how best to follow Jesus and serve others by using our gifts and talents, we pray to the Lord.

All: Lord, hear our prayer.

Leader: We ask these things in the name of Jesus Christ, the one who serves.

All: Amen.

@✲ Visit www.weliveourfaith.com to find appropriate music and songs.

191

The BiG QuEstion:
What does God call me to do with my life?

Discover the person you will become. What do you think your life will be like when you are twenty-five years old?

Name:

Age: 25

All about my life

In what ways, if any, does your future self reflect the person you are right now?

In this chapter we learn about the Sacraments at the Service of Communion: Matrimony and Holy Orders. Through this chapter, we hope

 to understand that those who receive Matrimony and Holy Orders are called to love and serve Christ and the Church in a particular way

 to respect the sacredness of the sacramental commitments involved in marriage and ordained ministry

 to serve others as God calls us, right here, right now.

God calls people to serve him in various ways. Below, a couple preparing to serve God in married life and a man preparing to serve God in ordained ministry share answers to some questions you might have about these sacramental commitments.

Interview with a couple preparing for marriage

1. Have you always felt called to be married? Yes. Not everyone's experience is the same, but, for us personally, growing up in large, supportive families gave us the hope of one day meeting the right person, getting married, starting families, and sharing God's love with each other.

2. How did you meet each other? What helped you to discern your call to marriage? We met when a mutual friend arranged a blind date between us. What helped us to discern our call was probably our great love for each other. We felt the need to spend the rest of our lives together.

3. Matrimony is one of the Sacraments at the Service of Communion. In what ways do you expect service to be a part of your marriage commitment? We expect service to have an important role in our marriage. Together we'll be there for our family and friends, and we'll take care of each other and help each other with our everyday needs. And, since we hope to start a family, we expect to take care of the children we hope to have.

4. What do you think the greatest challenge of married life will be? What do you think the greatest gift of married life will be? It will be a challenge to get accustomed to each other's daily habits and routines. The greatest gift of our marriage, we hope, will be one day seeing what a beautiful life and family we have.

5. What qualities do you think are important for married people to have? Faith in God, trust, respect, loyalty, motivation, and compassion. We'll need to constantly remind ourselves of the importance of these qualities, which can help to keep a great marriage going.

6. Overall, what experiences do you think your future as a married couple will hold? We think our future will hold lots of love. We look forward to supporting each other in our daily lives and, hopefully, having a family of our own.

Interview with a man preparing for the priesthood

1. Have you always felt called to the priesthood? No. As a young person I was not sure in what direction God would lead me.

2. What helped you to discern your call to the priesthood? During college, I was inspired by a pastor at a parish off campus. He was what I thought a priest should be, kind and able to help others to be the best they can be. I began to volunteer in the parish, and, through serving others, I felt called to the priesthood. It was a gradual process.

3. Holy Orders is one of the Sacraments at the Service of Communion. In what ways do you expect service to be a part of your life as a priest? I want to be a true pastor. I am looking forward to serving God and the people of my future parish.

4. What do you think the greatest challenge of the priesthood will be? What do you think the greatest gift of the priesthood will be? I think the greatest challenge will be scheduling my time so that I can be available to as many people as possible. The greatest gift will be sharing Christ with others in the sacraments and through my service.

5. What qualities do you think are important for priests to have? The ability to listen is one quality a priest must have. A priest must also be compassionate and an example to the parish community of trying to live as Jesus did.

6. Overall, what experiences do you think your future as a priest will hold? I hope my future will hold many experiences of serving the Church by being a true shepherd to my parish.

Activity What new insights do these interviews give you about Matrimony and Holy Orders? Share your ideas.

"Whatever you are, be a good one" is a quotation widely attributed to the sixteenth U.S. president, Abraham Lincoln (1809–1865).

Matrimony is a Sacrament at the Service of Communion.

Through the Sacraments of Christian Initiation we become disciples of Christ and members of the Catholic Church. We are all called to holiness. We are called to share God's love and spread God's Kingdom in this life, preparing for eternal life and the fulfillment of the Kingdom. Yet there are two sacraments, Holy Orders and Matrimony, in which Church members are called to a specific mission of service to others. Thus, Holy Orders and Matrimony are called the Sacraments at the Service of Communion.

Through the Sacrament of Matrimony, a baptized man and woman enter a lifelong commitment to live as faithful and loving partners. They also promise to lovingly accept children as a gift from God. Being made in God's image, men and women share the same human dignity, and God gives them a part in his plan for continuing the human family. In the Old Testament we read that God blesses the love of man and woman for one another, saying, "Be fertile and multiply" (Genesis 1:28). He tells them that "a man leaves his father and mother and clings to his wife, and the two of them become one body" (Genesis 2:24).

So, from the beginning, God called men and women to commit to one another in a life-giving love, one that imitates God's covenant of faithfulness and commitment to them. Their love is a sign of God's love for all his people. And their marriage covenant is modeled on Christ's love for the Church, sometimes called the Bride of Christ. Christ's love for the Church is permanent and unconditional. Thus, a married couple's love for each other is also to be permanent and unconditional.

The married couple becomes one in their service for others. The love that they share for God and for each other is shown in the fruits of their lives together—openness to others, lifelong sacrifice, and **charity**, or love, which is a gift from God that enables us to love him and to love our neighbor. The married couple's expression of their love includes

Faith Word
charity

the procreation of new life and the moral and spiritual education of their children. "In this sense the fundamental task of marriage and family is to be at the service of life." (*CCC*, 1653)

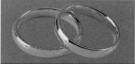 **Did you realize that Matrimony is a sacrament of service to Christ and the Church? Explain your answer.**

The Rite of Marriage

The celebration of the Sacrament of Matrimony, or the Rite of Marriage, often takes place within the Mass. The Scripture readings proclaimed during the Liturgy of the Word may be selected in advance by the couple themselves. After the reading of the Gospel, the Rite of Marriage begins as the deacon or priest asks the couple three important questions: Are they free to give themselves in marriage? Will they love and honor each other for the rest of their lives? Will they lovingly accept children from God and raise them in the faith? After answering these questions, the bride and groom exchange vows of love and *fidelity*, or faithfulness.

The deacon or priest asks God to strengthen their union. The rings are then blessed, and the couple exchanges them as a sign of their love and fidelity. The whole assembly prays the prayer of the faithful, and, if Mass is being celebrated, the Liturgy of the Eucharist follows. After the Lord's Prayer, the priest faces the couple and prays a special prayer, the nuptial blessing, which asks for God's blessing upon the marriage. As a sign of their union with Jesus, the source of their love, the bride and the groom, if they are Catholic, each receive Holy Communion.

What can you do in your life now to show your union with Jesus?

In Matrimony, couples receive grace for lifelong love and service.

Throughout his public ministry, Jesus' words and actions upheld the importance and the sanctity of marriage. He said, "What God has joined together, no human being must separate" (Matthew 19:6). And in John's Gospel we find that Jesus even performed the first miracle of his public ministry at a wedding feast. In doing so, he confirmed the goodness of marriage, upheld it as a covenant not to be broken, and forever established it as a sacrament.

In all the other sacraments, Jesus offers God's grace through an ordained minister who celebrates the sacrament. But in the Sacrament of Matrimony, the bride and groom confer the sacrament on each other, and Jesus acts through them and through their promise to always love and be true to each other. The priest or deacon, however, is the official witness of the sacrament on behalf of the Church. He blesses the union of the couple whom God has joined together. The whole Church celebrates that Jesus' love is made present through the love of the newly married couple and that their love is blessed and strengthened by the grace of this sacrament.

Being human, all married couples can encounter difficulties in their relationship. Yet, as the *Catechism*, quoting the *Pastoral Constitution on the Church in the Modern World,* states, "Christian spouses are fortified and, as it were, *consecrated* for the duties and dignity of their state by a special sacrament" (1535). In the Sacrament of Matrimony, Jesus Christ remains with the couple in their lives as they live

> **"The fundamental task of marriage and family is to be at the service of life."**
>
> (CCC, 1653)

and work. He shares his love with them so that they can love and forgive each other. And he supports and strengthens them to live as loyal and trustworthy partners. The grace that they receive through this sacrament strengthens them, helping them to overcome their difficulties.

Through all of life's problems and challenges, God continues to offer the couple his healing if they call upon him. They can also turn to their family and parish community for prayer and support. And they should frequently celebrate the Sacraments of Eucharist and Penance, asking for the help of the Holy Spirit in making decisions that both honor and protect their marriage and their families, and strengthen them to remain loyal to their marriage promises and to each other.

When married couples share the goodness of their love with others, their own love for each other and for Christ grows. They are strengthened to serve God and the Church—the People of God. Not only as faithful Christians but also as faithful spouses, they are to share the good news of Christ and give witness to their faith. Living by the vows that they make in the Sacrament of Matrimony, couples can do this every day. At home, at work, and in their local community, couples can live out their fidelity to God and each other. With God's help, they can live out the commitment that they made in this sacrament of service.

Activity Think of one married couple you know of who, with God's help, shares the good news of Christ and gives witness to their faith. How do they do this?

Jesus called his Apostles to continue his work.

In what ways do you share the work of Jesus?

Throughout his public ministry, Jesus Christ taught his followers that they too could share in God's love and spread God's Kingdom. And many people followed Jesus as disciples. Once Jesus went to a mountain where he spent all night praying to his Father. "When day came, he called his disciples to himself, and from them he chose Twelve, whom he also named apostles." (Luke 6:13) Jesus shared his ministry with the Twelve Apostles in a special way, speaking to them about God his Father, teaching them about the Kingdom of God, and showing them ways to bring God's love to all people. He then sent the Apostles out to "proclaim the kingdom of God and to heal [the sick]" (Luke 9:2).

After his death and Resurrection, the risen Jesus returned to his Apostles and gave them the authority to continue his work. He commissioned them, saying, "'Peace be with you. As the Father has sent me, so I send you.' And when he had said this, he breathed on them and said to them, 'Receive the holy Spirit'" (John 20:21–22). Through these words and actions Jesus entrusted the Apostles with his own work. They would minister to his community, lead them in worship, and baptize, heal, and forgive in his name. And the Holy Spirit guided them to continue this mission, inviting people to share in God's Kingdom.

Everywhere they went, the Apostles gathered believers into local Church communities. With the help of each local Church, they chose leaders and ministers for the community. The Apostles laid hands on those chosen and commissioned them. In this way the Apostles handed on what Christ had given them: the Gift of the Holy Spirit and the authority to carry out the mission of Jesus Christ.

These local leaders served their communities in various ways. They were responsible for the worship within the community, assisted in caring for those who were sick or in need, and led the community by preaching the good news of Jesus Christ and sharing the teachings of the Apostles. These leaders, eventually known as bishops, continued the Apostles' work in their local communities and acted on behalf of the Apostles. Other local leaders who worked with the bishops became known as presbyters, or priests. And those who assisted in the worship and service of the community were called deacons.

Guided by the Holy Spirit, the bishops, the successors of the Apostles, also shared Jesus' authority by commissioning others to continue the ministry of the Apostles. This was done by the laying on of hands and by a special prayer to the Holy Spirit. The Church still does this today in the Sacrament of Holy Orders. In this sacrament, through the laying on of hands and the prayer of consecration, those receiving Holy Orders are "*consecrated* in Christ's name 'to feed the Church by the word and the grace of God'" (*CCC*, 1535). So, the leadership of the Church throughout history can be traced back to the Apostles, and thus to Jesus Christ!

Activity How do bishops, priests, and deacons work together to continue the ministry of the Apostles? How can you help to support their ministries?

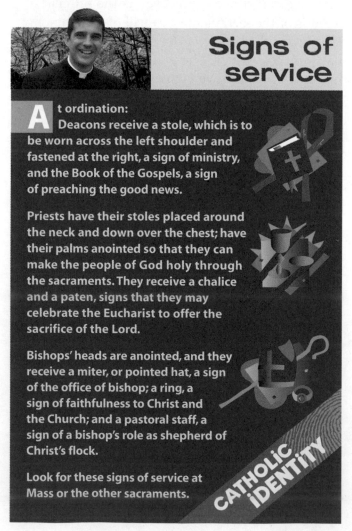

Signs of service

At ordination: Deacons receive a stole, which is to be worn across the left shoulder and fastened at the right, a sign of ministry, and the Book of the Gospels, a sign of preaching the good news.

Priests have their stoles placed around the neck and down over the chest; have their palms anointed so that they can make the people of God holy through the sacraments. They receive a chalice and a paten, signs that they may celebrate the Eucharist to offer the sacrifice of the Lord.

Bishops' heads are anointed, and they receive a miter, or pointed hat, a sign of the office of bishop; a ring, a sign of faithfulness to Christ and the Church; and a pastoral staff, a sign of a bishop's role as shepherd of Christ's flock.

Look for these signs of service at Mass or the other sacraments.

CATHOLIC IDENTITY

Those called to Holy Orders are consecrated to the service of others.

Through Baptism and Confirmation we are consecrated to the common priesthood of the faithful. Yet there is a distinct *ministerial priesthood.* Through the Sacrament of Holy Orders, men who are called by the Church are ordained: Ordained priests and bishops form the ministerial priesthood, and men who are ordained as deacons become part of the ministry of service to the Church.

Baptized men who have been accepted as candidates for Holy Orders spend several years at a seminary, a place where they pray, study, and prepare for their particular ministry. As in Baptism and Confirmation, those who receive Holy Orders are forever sealed with a sacramental character. This configures them to Christ and marks them as forever in the service of Christ and the Church. Thus, the Sacrament of Holy Orders cannot be repeated.

> In the Sacrament of Holy Orders men are **"***consecrated in Christ's name***"** (CCC, 1535).

Through Holy Orders, a **deacon** shares in Christ's mission by assisting bishops and priests in the service of the Church. Some men, single or married, become permanent deacons, remaining deacons for life. Other men remain unmarried and become deacons as a step toward the priesthood. Having been ordained into the *diaconate* as deacons, they continue on to be ordained into the *presbyterate,* becoming priests. A **priest** is ordained to preach the Gospel and serve the faithful, especially celebrating the Eucharist and the other sacraments. A priest who becomes a bishop is ordained into the *episcopate.* To become a bishop, a priest must be chosen for episcopal consecration by the pope, with the advice of other bishops and Church members. A **bishop** receives the fullness of the Sacrament of Holy Orders and continues the Apostles' mission of leadership and service.

Thus, in the sacramental act called ordination, bishops, priests, and deacons receive one or more of the three degrees of orders: *episcopate, presbyterate,* and *diaconate.* A bishop always ordains a newly chosen bishop, or bishop-elect, as well as candidates for the priesthood and diaconate. The celebration of Holy Orders always takes place during the Mass. The Liturgy of the Word includes readings about ministry and service. After the Gospel reading, those to be ordained are presented to the bishop celebrant. He speaks to the people about the roles these men will have in the Church, about their responsibilities to teach, to lead, and to worship. He also speaks directly to those being ordained, questioning them to make sure that they understand and accept their responsibilities to lead and serve in Jesus' name.

The bishop celebrant invites the whole assembly to pray that God will bless those to be ordained. Then, in complete silence, he lays his hands over the head of those to be ordained. At the ordination of a priest, other priests present also lay their hands upon the candidate as a sign of their unity and service to the diocese. At the ordination of a bishop-elect, other bishops present lay their hands upon him as a sign of their unity in service to the Church. Then the bishop celebrant prays the prayer of consecration, which is different for each of the degrees of orders, and extends his hands over each man. By the power of the Holy Spirit, each man is ordained to continue Jesus' ministry in a particular service in the Church.

> **Faith Words**
> deacon
> priest
> bishop

Activity In many parishes in your diocese there are permanent deacons. Find out what they do in their ministry of service.

RESPONDING...

Recognizing Our Faith

Recall the question at the beginning of this chapter: *What does God call me to do with my life*? Name three things in this chapter that you learned about Matrimony and Holy Orders.

1.

2.

3.

Would these things encourage you to serve God and others through one of these sacraments?

Living Our Faith

Become more aware and appreciative of clergy and married couples who are truly living lives of service to the Church.

Pope Benedict XVI

On April 19, 2005, Cardinal Joseph Ratzinger was elected pope—the visible head of the Catholic Church and the bishop of Rome. For his name as pope, he chose Benedict XVI, honoring Saint Benedict of Nursia and Pope Benedict XV, both of whom displayed courage and a commitment to peace.

Partners in FAITH

Pope Benedict XVI experienced the need for courage and peace early in his life. Born in 1927, he grew up during the rise of the Nazi political party in his native Germany. In the face of this turbulent atmosphere, Pope Benedict XVI focused on his faith. He was ordained a priest in 1951 and appointed Archbishop of Munich in 1977. Three months later he became a cardinal.

As a cardinal he was Pope John Paul II's chief theological adviser for twenty years. With his faithfulness to Church teachings, Pope Benedict XVI brings to the papacy a strong commitment to his role to teach, govern, and sanctify the Church.

Find out more about Pope Benedict XVI. How can you support him in his service to the whole Church?

 For additional ideas and activities, visit www.weliveourfaith.com.

Putting Faith to Work

Talk about what you have learned in this chapter:

 We understand that those who receive Matrimony and Holy Orders are called to love and serve Christ and the Church in a particular way.

We respect the sacredness of the sacramental commitments involved in marriage and ordained ministry.

 We serve others as God calls us, right here, right now.

Decide on ways to live out what you have learned.

✛ ENCOUNTERING GOD'S WORD

"Put on then, as God's chosen ones, holy and beloved, heartfelt compassion, kindness, humility, gentleness, and patience, bearing with one another and forgiving one another. . . . And over all these put on love."

(Colossians 3:12–14)

➡ **READ** the quotation from Scripture.

➡ **REFLECT** on the following:
In these words from Saint Paul, compassion, kindness, humility, and other qualities are written about as things we can "put on" as we do clothing. And, we are told, over all of these, we must put on love. How does this quotation help you to understand your call to love God and others?

➡ **SHARE** your reflections with a partner.

➡ **DECIDE** to share this love that Saint Paul talks about with all those in your life.

Underline the correct answer.

1. Through the Sacrament of (**Christian Initiation/Matrimony/Holy Orders**) a baptized man and woman enter a lifelong commitment to live as faithful and loving partners.

2. A (**bishop/priest/deacon**) receives the fullness of the Sacrament of Holy Orders and continues the Apostles' mission of leadership and service.

3. Through Holy Orders, a (**couple preparing for marriage/presbyter/deacon**) shares in Christ's mission by assisting bishops and priests in the service of the Church.

4. A (**bishop/priest/deacon**) is consecrated to preach the Gospel and serve the faithful, especially through the Eucharist and other sacraments.

Complete the following.

5. In the Sacrament of Matrimony the _____ and _____ confer the sacrament on each other.

6. During the celebration of the Sacrament of Holy Orders, in the sacramental act called _____, bishops, priests, and deacons receive one or more of the three degrees of orders.

7. The three degrees of orders in the Sacrament of Holy Orders are _____, _____, and _____.

8. The marriage covenant is modeled on Christ's love for the _____, the Bride of Christ.

9–10. ESSAY: Why are Holy Orders and Matrimony called the Sacraments at the Service of Communion?

Chapter 18 Assessment

RESPONDING...

Sharing Faith with Your Family

Discuss the following with your family:

- Matrimony is a Sacrament at the Service of Communion.
- In Matrimony, couples receive grace for lifelong love and service.
- Jesus called his Apostles to continue his work.
- Those called to Holy Orders are consecrated to the service of others.

Everyone is called to love and service. Together make a checklist of ways that each person or group of persons in a family can love and serve in a parish, in a diocese, and in the Church. Live out your love and service this week.

The Worship Connection

At Mass this week, notice the actions of the priest and deacon in the liturgy. Think about what each of their responsibilities and functions are in helping the community with prayer and worship.

More to Explore

Explore the Internet for Catholic missions that include as missionaries both priests and married couples.

Catholic Social Teaching ☑ Checklist

Theme of Catholic Social Teaching:
Solidarity of the Human Family

How it relates to Chapter 18: Just as married couples love, serve, and nurture their families, all Catholics are called to love, serve, and build up the *human family*—all people throughout the world from all racial, cultural, and religious backgrounds, who share our human dignity.

How can you do this?

☐ At home:

_____

☐ At school/work:

_____

☐ In the parish:

_____

☐ In the community:

_____

Check off each action after it has been completed.

Define the following.

1. celebrant _____

_____

2. diocese _____

_____

3. sacrament _____

_____

4. conscience _____

_____

5. sanctify _____

_____

6. liturgy _____

_____

7. Mass _____

_____

Fill in the circle beside the correct answer.

8. In the Sacrament of _____, the laying on of hands and anointing with chrism are signs of the Holy Spirit's presence.

○ Baptism ○ Confirmation ○ Matrimony ○ Eucharist

9. In the Sacrament of _____, we are welcomed into the Church, becoming children of God.

○ Baptism ○ Confirmation ○ Matrimony ○ Eucharist

10. In the Sacrament of _____, we receive Jesus Christ, the Bread of Life.

○ Baptism ○ Confirmation ○ Matrimony ○ Eucharist

11. _____ are Sacraments of Healing.

○ Matrimony and Holy Orders ○ Penance and Anointing of the Sick

○ Baptism and Confirmation ○ Anointing of the Sick and Eucharist

12. In the Sacrament of _____, a baptized man and woman are strengthened for family life and service by their faithful love.

○ Baptism ○ Confirmation ○ Matrimony ○ Eucharist

13. Through the power of the Holy Spirit, we receive _____ in the sacraments, which enables us to love God, to love ourselves as God loves us, to love others as we love ourselves, and to live as God calls us to live.

○ charity   ○ conscience   ○ chrism   ○ sanctifying grace

14. _____ is turning back to God with all one's heart.

○ Mortal sin   ○ Venial sin   ○ Conversion   ○ Confession

Complete the following.

15. The four main parts of the Mass are _____

_____.

16. The four main parts of the Sacrament of Penance are _____

_____.

17. The three degrees of orders in the Sacrament of Holy Orders are _____

_____.

18. People can receive the Sacrament of the Anointing of the Sick when they are

_____.

Respond to the following.

19. Use what you have learned in this unit to answer the question: *How is Jesus Christ alive in the Church today?*

_____

_____

_____

_____

20. List the seven sacraments. Choose two sacraments and list what is common to both sacraments and what is unique about each.

_____

_____

_____

_____

ALTERNATIVE ASSESSMENT

Design a Web site to inspire Catholics to participate in the celebration of the seven sacraments. First, design a home page introducing the three categories of sacraments. Make sure that visitors to your site understand why the sacraments are categorized this way. Then design and write linking Web pages that describe each individual sacrament. Sketch your ideas here. Then make a formal presentation of your completed Web site.

Unit 4

How Does the Church Live As the Body of Christ?

GATHERING...

19

We Live Out Our Vocation

"Thus says the LORD, . . . I have called you by name: you are mine."

(Isaiah 43:1)

✝ **Leader:** Lord God, you call all of us, as members of the Church, to lives of service. And you call each of us, as individuals, to serve in a particular way. In the Old Testament we find the words of the prophet Jeremiah as he describes his call to become a prophet.

Reader: A reading from the book of the prophet Jeremiah

"The word of the LORD came to me thus:

Before I formed you in the womb I knew you,
    before you were born I dedicated you,
    a prophet to the nations I appointed you.

'Ah, Lord GOD!' I said,
    'I know not how to speak; I am too young.'

But the LORD answered me,

Say not, 'I am too young.'
    To whomever I send you, you shall go;
    whatever I command you, you shall speak.
Have no fear before them,
    because I am with you to deliver you,
    says the LORD." (Jeremiah 1:4–8)

The word of the Lord.

All: Thanks be to God.

Leader: Lord God, may we too receive the strength and courage to serve as you call us. And may we discover this call through prayer, serving others, reflecting on who we are, listening to your word, and being aware of your guiding presence in our lives. We pray:

All: May we be witnesses of your love to the world
and strive with courage for good things which alone last for ever.
(Prayer After Communion, Mass for Religious Vocations)
Amen.

Visit www.weliveourfaith.com to find appropriate music and songs.

205

The BiG Question:

How am I preparing for my future?

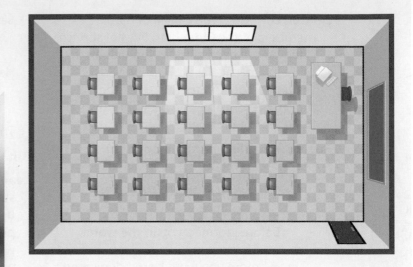

Discover more about who you are; this can help you to prepare for your future. Complete the following exercise to find out what your choice of a seat in class reveals about who you are.

It's the first day of class. Look at the outline of a classroom here. Mark an **X** on the seat where you would normally choose to sit in class. Then check your results below.

Results:

If the seat you chose was: .... *then maybe you:*

in the front .... want to be near the teacher, like being seen, are outgoing, like to be up front where the action is, or want to be sure you hear everything the teacher says.

in the back .... like to see everything that's happening in the room, dislike attention but like having everyone turn around when you talk, or feel secure near the back wall (or maybe even like to sleep in class!).

by the window .... like to daydream in class, like the outdoors, or like the idea of a wide-open space next to you.

by the door .... like having a quick way out of a situation or are often in a rush to do things.

What else do you think your choice of a seat says about who you are? How can knowing who you are today help you to plan for the rest of your life?

In this chapter we learn that all members of the Church share a common vocation, a call to holiness and evangelization. But we are also called as individuals to serve in a particular way. Through this chapter, we hope

 to understand the particular call to service lived out by those in the laity, the consecrated life, and the ordained ministry

 to contemplate these particular vocations and their possibilities for our own lives

 to serve God and the Church now by spreading the good news of Jesus Christ.

Do the potential responsibilities in your future—maintaining a job, perhaps supporting a family—seem overwhelming or exciting? It might help you to learn about someone who was able to manage great responsibilities even when faced with adversity.

Mary Anne Madden was born in 1820 in County Cavan, Ireland. Having immigrated to Canada following the death of her father, she began writing poems and articles for a Montreal magazine. In 1846 she married James Sadlier of D&J Sadlier, a Catholic publishing company based in New York City. Mary wrote articles and stories for the *Tablet*, a journal that published educational stories for Catholic immigrants. Mary also translated French spiritual and catechetical texts, compiled a book on purgatory, developed a Bible-based religious education instruction book, and wrote more than sixty inspirational novels, including "teaching novels" and readers for Catholic schoolchildren.

In addition to her writing career—which in itself was unusual at the time for a woman—Mary was the mother of six children. After her husband died in 1869, leaving Mary to run the Catholic publishing business and support her family, Mary still found time for good works. She founded homes for orphans, young women, and the elderly. In 1895

the University of Notre Dame awarded Mary the Lactare Medal for her contributions to the humanitarian efforts of the Church. In 1902 Pope Leo XIII gave her a special blessing for her "illustrious service to the Catholic Church."

Mary Sadlier was a Catholic who successfully balanced her personal responsibilities as a mother with charitable acts of public service and a creative career. Think of someone you know right now who handles a variety of obligations well. Ask that person for advice, or just observe how he or she accomplishes his or her goals. Think about ways you can apply these methods to your own life.

Activity Mary Sadlier was a woman who continued to grow in her abilities and achievements while sharing God's love with others. Discuss how you can do the same.

> **"The vocation of every man and woman is to serve other people,"** said Leo Tolstoy (1828–1910), one of Russia's greatest authors.

BELIEVING...

God calls each of us to a particular vocation.

By faith in Christ and by Baptism, we become members of the Church, the People of God. We share in the priesthood of the faithful and have a common vocation. A **vocation** is a call to a way of life. Our **common vocation** is our call from God to holiness and to evangelization. But God also calls each of us to live out our common vocation in one of the following particular vocations:

Laity: The laity are also called laypeople or the Christian faithful. They are members of the Church who share in the mission to bring the good news of Christ to the world. All Catholics begin their lives as members of the laity. Many remain members of the laity for their entire lives, following God's call either in the single life or in marriage. If they marry, receiving the Sacrament of Matrimony, they make a vow of fidelity to their spouse, in the name of Christ and the Church.

Consecrated life: Catholics who follow God's call to the consecrated life are often called "religious" and are said to be living the "religious life." In the consecrated life, men and women profess, or promise God that they will practice, poverty, chastity through celibacy, and obedience to the Church and to their religious communities. Poverty, chastity, and obedience are called the **evangelical counsels**.

Ordained ministry: Some baptized Catholic men follow God's call to this particular vocation. Through the Sacrament of Holy Orders, they are consecrated to the ministerial priesthood as priests and bishops, or to the permanent diaconate. They are given the grace to serve God's people and have various responsibilities of ministry, worship, and leadership within the Church.

Faith Words

vocation
common vocation
evangelical counsels

It takes many years for most people to discover their particular vocation. You might not realize it, but the lessons you learn now are preparing you for your future vocation. Right now, the ways that you are responding to God and other people in your life are paving the way to your future life. So, listen to your heart and pray that God's call to a particular vocation will become clear to you. As you listen, remember that "in the Church, there is diversity of service but unity of purpose" (*Decree on the Apostolate of the Laity*, 2).

Activity Write a list of interview questions about the particular vocations of the laity, the consecrated life, and the ordained priesthood or diaconate. Use them to interview someone in each of these vocations.

208

The evangelical counsels

Vows are deliberate, free promises that are made to God in the Church. To follow vows of poverty, chastity, and obedience, known as the evangelical counsels, may seem to be a great and difficult challenge in today's world. However, the evangelical counsels can be understood as characteristics of Jesus' own life. By his life and teachings, Jesus was calling people to dedicate themselves to God with all their hearts. He spoke of the need for people to avoid being overly distracted by the concerns of life. He wanted people to seek God, to serve others, and to treasure God's Kingdom. He taught, "If you wish to be perfect, go, sell what you have and give to [the] poor, and you will have treasure in heaven. Then come, follow me" (Matthew 19:21).

So, religious men and women, who vow to give up their personal possessions, to remain single and celibate, and to be obedient to God and their religious communities, are making an effort to focus on the life of service that they have chosen. They are inviting others to see in them an example of Jesus Christ. In this way the evangelical counsels are practices through which religious men and women can *evangelize* the world.

Think of one practical thing that you can do to evangelize others by your words and actions.

CATHOLIC IDENTITY

Some are called to live as laypeople.

God calls each of us to love and serve him and the Church. Single people and married people serve God and the Church in many ways, sharing God's love in their families and parishes. A husband and wife share God's love in a special way with each other and form a new Christian family. Though much of their time and energy is focused on loving and caring for their families, husbands and wives can also serve others in their neighborhoods, parishes, and communities in many ways.

Single people often devote themselves to sharing their gifts and talents with others through their work. Sometimes they care for their brothers or sisters or take on the extra responsibility of caring for their parents. They may also dedicate more of their time to their parishes and local communities. In these ways they work to make the world a better, safer, and more holy place.

Members of the laity, single or married, live their faith as citizens, voters, and workers. They have a responsibility to bring the good news of Christ to their workplaces and local communities, treating others equally, fairly, and justly. Laypeople can also serve the Church by becoming involved in city, state, and national governments. In these situations they can often take on leadership positions and make many decisions, utilizing the teachings of Jesus and their knowledge of the Catholic faith.

> **"In the Church, there is diversity of service but unity of purpose."**
> *(Decree on the Apostolate of the Laity, 2)*

The Christian faithful are also called to be active in their parishes, taking part in the parish community. They can:

- participate in the celebration of the sacraments and parish programs

- serve on the pastoral council, as school principals, as teachers, as *catechists*, or religious education instructors, as directors of religious education, or in music, liturgy, and youth ministry

- assist at Mass as ushers and greeters or as altar servers, musicians, readers, and extraordinary ministers of Holy Communion. The laity serve in their dioceses, too. They may work in or hold offices in such ministries as education, worship, youth, and social ministries.

Right now you are a member of the laity, the Christian faithful. You are called by Christ to live as one of his disciples. So, take part in your parish celebrations and activities. Be an example of Christian living. And follow what God calls you to do right now—sharing the good news of Jesus Christ at home, in school, and in your neighborhood.

Activity You can follow your present vocation as a member of the laity. You can stand up for what is right and just, helping others to see Christ's love for them and his presence in the world. With a partner choose one specific way your group can do this today.

BELIEVING...

Some are called to the consecrated life.

What are your hopes for your future?

Canon law is the name that we give to the body of laws that govern the Church. Canons, or laws, provide for good order in *ecclesial*, or Church, governance. The *Catechism* often refers to canons contained in the *Code of Canon Law*. One of these canons refers to the types of particular vocations and clarifies that men and women come to the consecrated life from both the hierarchy or the laity.

The men and women who are called by God to the consecrated life profess the evangelical counsels of poverty, chastity, and obedience. "It is the *profession* of these counsels, within a permanent state of life recognized by the Church, that characterizes the life consecrated to God." (*CCC*, 915) Profession of the evangelical counsels is expressed by making **vows**, deliberate and free promises made to God, to practice:

Poverty. Those taking this vow promise to live simply as Jesus did. They agree to share their belongings and to own no personal property. This helps them focus their hearts and minds on God without being distracted by material things.

Chastity. Those taking this vow choose to live a life of loving service to God, the Church and their community. They live a life of **celibacy**, remaining single, and promising to devote themselves to the work of God and the Church for the sake of the Kingdom.

Obedience. Those taking this vow promise to listen carefully to God's direction in their lives by obeying the leaders of the Church and of their communities. They serve wherever their community and the Church need them. They try to live the way Christ did and follow God's will.

These vows that men and women in the consecrated life make show that, by devoting their lives to the work of their communities, they try to follow Jesus' example of sharing God's love with all people each day.

> **Faith Words**
> canon law
> celibacy
> vows

Activity In groups, discuss ways you can support the work of religious priests, brothers, and sisters.

Many good works

Many religious work to spread the good news of Christ by living in one community, praying together, sharing their meals, and working with other members of their community. Some religious live away from their community and work where they are needed. Yet they are still members of their community. Some religious communities are set apart from society, usually living in monasteries or convents. These religious devote their lives to praying for the world. They provide for their needs through their prayer and through their work. Whatever their work, it is always offered as another form of prayer. Other communities combine prayer with a life of service in the many different parish ministries. They may also be teachers, doctors, nurses, or social workers. Some religious serve as missionaries. Missionaries may spend weeks, months, or even years living with the people they serve and sharing God's love with them. They learn the culture and traditions of the people they serve, even learning a new language so that they can teach about Jesus Christ and the Catholic faith.

All of us can work as missionaries in our parishes, our communities, and the world. Whether we are laypeople, those in religious life, or ordained ministers, we can all serve those who are poor, suffering, elderly, or in need.

What are some of the different ways that you can help and serve others in your life today?

Some men are ordained as priests and permanent deacons.

God calls some baptized men to serve him through the vocation of the priesthood. Receiving the Sacrament of Holy Orders, these men are ordained to serve the Church through teaching, worship, and leadership. In the sacraments, priests act in the name and the person of Jesus Christ to help us encounter Christ personally and communally.

There are two different types of priests: diocesan priests and religious priests. Diocesan priests are called to serve in a particular diocese. They help the bishop of that diocese by ministering in parishes. They also may assist in schools, hospitals, and prisons, depending on the local needs. Diocesan priests promise to lead a celibate life. They also promise to respect and obey their bishop.

Religious priests are called to a specific religious order or congregation, such as the Franciscans, Dominicans, or Jesuits. These priests follow the religious rule, or plan of life, adopted by their founder.

God also calls some men to serve him as deacons—men who receive the Sacrament of Holy Orders, but are ordained to assist the bishops and priests and to serve the whole Church. Deacons can preach, baptize, witness marriages, preside at burials, and assist the priest at Mass by reading the Gospel, preparing the altar, and distributing Holy Communion. Deacons are not ministers of the Sacraments of Confirmation, Penance, Anointing of the Sick, and Holy Orders. Permanent deacons are often married and have an occupation or a career to support themselves. A deacon's life is a sign of the service to which all Christians are called.

Together, the laity, those in the consecrated life, and ordained ministers make up the Church. And all have a part in the mission of the Church. No one group is more important or special than another. As Saint Paul wrote, "There are different forms of service but the same Lord" (1 Corinthians 12:5). The Church needs all members to be able to continue Jesus' work. Each of us has a role in evangelization—spreading the good news and sharing God's great love with others. For all Catholics, whether single, married, priests, bishops, deacons, or members of a religious community or congregation, there are many challenges along the way to a particular vocation. But all along the way our prayers, words, and actions must tell others about Jesus Christ.

> **"There are different forms of service but the same Lord."**
> (1 Corinthians 12:5)

Activity By Baptism you share in the mission of evangelization. How will you evangelize? To whom will you go? With whom will you speak? Explain below.

Recognizing Our Faith

Recall the question at the beginning of this chapter: *How am I preparing for my future?* What vocation are you interested in? What three things can you do to add to your knowledge about this vocation?

1.

2.

3.

Living Our Faith

Decide this week to become more aware of the vocations of those you meet. Pray that each person will be strengthened to live out his or her vocation.

Partners in FAITH

Blessed Laura Montoya

Laura Montoya was born in 1874 in Colombia, South America. Her father died when she was two years old. As Laura grew older, it was necessary for her to help support her family. Although Laura received little education while growing up, she studied and eventually became a teacher. Later, she became involved in missionary work among poor communities. She began to teach and evangelize the native peoples who lived in the rainforests of Columbia. To better serve the native peoples, she founded the Congregation of the Missionary Sisters of Mary Immaculate and St. Catherine of Siena. Laura, known as the "Teacher of the Indians," continued serving and evangelizing until her death in 1949.

On April 25, 2004, Pope John Paul II beatified Laura Montoya. Today, the Missionary Sisters of Mary Immaculate and St. Catherine of Siena teach and evangelize in nineteen countries.

Teaching is one way to evangelize. What are some other ways to spread the good news of Christ?

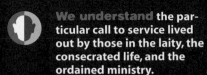

Putting Faith to Work

Talk about what you have learned in this chapter:

We understand the particular call to service lived out by those in the laity, the consecrated life, and the ordained ministry.

We contemplate these particular vocations and their possibilities for our own lives.

We serve God and the Church now by spreading the good news of Jesus Christ.

Decide on ways to live out what you have learned.

✝ ENCOUNTERING GOD'S WORD

Jesus said:

❝I am the vine, you are the branches. Whoever remains in me and I in him will bear much fruit, because without me you can do nothing❞

(John 15:5).

➡ **READ** the quotation from Scripture.

➡ **REFLECT** on the following:
By comparing himself to a vine and his disciples to the branches, Jesus teaches us that we are to be united to him. Jesus' words can remind us that whatever particular vocation we choose, we are all Jesus' disciples, called to continue the work that he began. How can Jesus' words help you to feel empowered to live out a particular vocation?

➡ **SHARE** your reflections with a partner.

➡ **DECIDE** on a way to strengthen your unity with Jesus Christ as you try to discover your particular vocation.

Write *True* or *False* next to the following sentences. On a separate sheet of paper, change the false sentences to make them true.

1. _____ A vocation is a call to a way of life.

2. _____ By faith in Christ and by Baptism, we become members of the Church.

3. _____ God calls each member of the Church to a particular vocation: the laity, the consecrated life, or the Christian faithful.

4. _____ Men and women who are called by God to the consecrated life profess the evangelical counsels of poverty, chastity, and service.

Circle the letter of the correct answer.

5. _____ is the name of the body of laws that govern the Church.

   a. Ecclesial   **b.** Laity   **c.** Religious life   **d.** Canon law

6. All members of the Church have a _____, our call from God to holiness and evangelization.

   a. common vocation   **b.** ministerial priesthood   **c.** religious order   **d.** consecrated life

7. There are two different types of priests: _____.

   a. bishop and laity   **b.** diaconate and diocesan   **c.** diocesan and religious   **d.** Jesuit and Franciscan

8. All Catholics begin their lives as members of the _____.

   a. laity   **b.** consecrated life   **c.** ordained ministry   **d.** permanent diaconate

9–10. ESSAY: You are called to live as Christ's disciple. What are some ways you can respond to this call?

Sharing Faith with Your Family

Discuss the following with your family:

- God calls each of us to a particular vocation.
- Some are called to live as laypeople.
- Some are called to the consecrated life.
- Some men are ordained as priests and permanent deacons.

With your family think of ways that you can live out your common vocation—your call to holiness and to evangelization.

The Worship Connection

Our first vocation is to become like Jesus Christ. At every Mass the priest prays that we might share in Christ's divinity as he came "to share in our humanity" (Roman Missal). Listen for this moment at Mass.

More to Explore

Various religious communities and dioceses have missionary programs for which laypeople volunteer. Find out what opportunities might be available to you.

Catholic Social Teaching ☑ Checklist

Theme of Catholic Social Teaching:
Care for God's Creation

How it relates to Chapter 19: God calls all people, no matter what their particular vocation, to care for all that he has created.

How can you do this?

☐ At home:

_____

☐ At school/work:

_____

☐ In the parish:

_____

☐ In the community:

_____

Check off each action after it has been completed.

GATHERING...

We Gather As Christ's Disciples

"Where two or three are gathered together in my name, there am I in the midst of them."

(Matthew 18:20)

✛ **Leader:** In the Church we are gathered together as Christ's disciples. Let us now profess our faith as members of the Church.

All: We believe in one God,
　　the Father, the Almighty,
　　maker of heaven and earth,
　　of all that is seen and unseen.

We believe in one Lord, Jesus Christ,
　　the only Son of God,
　　eternally begotten of the Father,
　　God from God, Light from Light,
　　true God from true God,
　　begotten, not made, one in Being
　　　with the Father.
　　Through him all things were made.
　　For us men and for our salvation
　　　he came down from heaven:
　　by the power of the Holy Spirit
　　　he was born of the Virgin Mary,
　　　and became man.

　　For our sake he was crucified
　　　under Pontius Pilate;
　　he suffered, died, and was buried.

On the third day he rose again
　　in fulfillment of the Scriptures;
he ascended into heaven
　　and is seated at the right hand
　　of the Father.
He will come again in glory to judge
　　the living and the dead,
　　and his kingdom will have no end.

We believe in the Holy Spirit, the Lord,
　　the giver of life,
　　who proceeds from the Father and
　　　the Son.
　　With the Father and the Son he is
　　　worshiped and glorified.
　　He has spoken through the Prophets.

We believe in one holy catholic
　　and apostolic Church.
　　We acknowledge one baptism for the
　　　forgiveness of sins.
　　We look for the resurrection of the dead,
　　　and the life of the world to come.

　　Amen.

@ Visit www.weliveourfaith.com to find appropriate music and songs.

GATHERING...

The BiG QuEstioN:

In what ways can I help to change the world?

Discover some things that can help you to change the world little by little. Below are some things that can remind you of what needs to be done.

toothpick: to remind me to pick out the good qualities in others. What are some qualities that you seek in others?

_____

rubber band: to remind me to be flexible. Think about a time that you needed to be flexible. What did you do?

_____

bandage: to remind me to heal hurt feelings—mine or someone else's. Think about who it is that you need to forgive.

_____

pencil: to remind me to list my blessings every day. Make a list of your blessings.

_____

eraser: to remind me that everyone makes mistakes. Think about a mistake that you made. What did you learn?

_____

roll of tape: to remind me to stick with it; I can accomplish anything. What goal would you like to achieve?

_____

piece of peppermint: to remind me that I am worth a "mint." What are some things that only you can do?

_____

chocolate: to remind me that everyone needs love. Who is someone that you love?

_____

What are some other items that might remind you of ways to help change the world?

In this chapter
we explore the virtues of faith, hope, and love and the ways that we, as members of the Church, can live by these virtues. We also learn that the Church is one, holy, catholic, and apostolic. Through this chapter, we hope

 to understand that the virtues of faith, hope, and love unite us to God

 to love, to hope, and to have faith as we follow Jesus Christ together as the Church

 to live in a way that proclaims the marks of the Church: one, holy, catholic, and apostolic.

The following poem was seen posted in Mother Teresa's office in Calcutta, India.

People are often unreasonable, illogical and self-centered;
Forgive them anyway.
If you are kind, people may accuse you of selfish, ulterior motives;
Be kind anyway.
If you are successful, you will win some false friends and some true enemies;
Succeed anyway.
If you are honest and frank, people may cheat you;
Be honest anyway.
If you find serenity and happiness, they may be jealous;
Be happy anyway.
The good you do today, people will often forget tomorrow;
Do good anyway.
Give the world the best you have, and it may never be enough;
Give the world the best you've got anyway.
You see, in the final analysis it is between you and God;
It was never between you and them anyway

(Based on the words of Kent M. Keith)

Activity With your group choose one of the lines of the poem to role-play for the group. Then choose one line that you will live out this week.

"You must be the change you want to see in the world," said Mohandas K. Gandhi (1869–1948), peace activist and civil rights leader from India.

BELIEVING...

God gives us many gifts.

Every day we have the opportunity to live as Jesus' disciples. We may not even realize that the choices that we make each day reveal a lot about our discipleship. Our choices in life can become habits, whether for good or for bad. A good habit that helps us to act according to God's love for us is called a **virtue**.

The **theological virtues** of faith, hope, and charity have God as their source, God as their motive, and God as their object. They are called theological because *theo* in Greek means "god." These virtues bring us closer to God and increase our desire to be with God forever. They make it possible for us to have a relationship with God—the Father, the Son, and the Holy Spirit. Faith, hope, and charity are the foundation of our lives as Christians.

The virtue of *faith* enables us to believe in God and all that the Church teaches us. Faith helps us to believe all that God has told us about himself and all that he has done. The gift of faith helps us to believe that God is with us and is acting in our lives. And though God makes faith possible for us, faith still has to be a choice that we make. Jesus once said to his disciples, "Blessed are those who have not seen and have believed" (John 20:29). Jesus also asks us, as his disciples, to choose to respond to God's gift of faith—to believe, even at those times when we cannot see or understand.

The virtue of *hope* enables us to trust in God's promise to share his life with us forever. Hope makes us confident in God's love and care for us, keeping us from becoming discouraged or giving up when times are difficult. As we read in Saint Paul's letter to the Romans, "Hope does not disappoint, because the love of God has been poured out into our hearts through the holy Spirit that has been given to us" (Romans 5:5).

Faith Words
virtue
theological virtues

Thus, hope helps us to trust in Christ and to rely on the strength of the Holy Spirit. Hope is a gift that helps us to work to spread the Kingdom of God here on earth and to look forward to eternal happiness in the Kingdom in heaven.

The virtue of *charity* enables us to love God and to love our neighbor as ourselves. Charity, or love, is the greatest of all virtues, for love "bears all things, believes all things, hopes all things, endures all things. Love never fails" (1 Corinthians 13:7–8). All the other virtues come from love and lead back to it. Love is the goal of our lives as Christians. And love is possible because God loves us first, with a never-ending love. In our lives God's love is always there for us and can especially be experienced through the community of believers, the Church.

Activity How do your words and actions at school and at home show that you have faith, hope, and love?

The cardinal virtues

The theological virtues are the foundation of the human virtues. The human virtues are habits that come about by our own efforts, prompted by God's grace. They lead us to live a good life. They result from our making the decision, over and over again, to live by God's law. These human virtues guide the way we think, feel, and behave. There are four human virtues that are pivotal—all other virtues are grouped around them. Since the Latin word *cardo* means "pivot," we call them the cardinal virtues. They are: prudence, justice, fortitude, and temperance.

Prudence helps us to make sound judgments and directs our actions toward what is good. *Justice* is respecting the rights of others and giving them what is rightfully theirs. *Fortitude* enables us to act bravely in the face of troubles and fears. *Temperance* helps us to keep our desires under control and to balance our use of material goods.

Think of life situations in which you might be able to practice these virtues.

CATHOLIC IDENTITY

218

As members of the Church, we come together in faith, hope, and love.

During his ministry Jesus taught about many things. He talked about the meaning of the Ten Commandments and gave his disciples the Beatitudes as a model for living and working toward future happiness. Jesus taught his disciples that God's law is a law of love and then showed them the way to live it.

Guided by the Holy Spirit, we can live as Jesus' disciples, following Jesus' example of loving God and one another. And, as his disciples and members of the Church, we have the hope of living according to his command to love one another as he loved us. As the *Catechism*, states, "The Church 'is the visible plan of God's love for humanity,' because God desires 'that the whole human race may become one People of God, form one Body of Christ, and be built up into one temple of the Holy Spirit'" (776).

> **"The Church 'is the visible plan of God's love for humanity.'"**
> (CCC, 776)

Jesus is our example of faith, hope, and unconditional love. He showed us how to love as no one else could. He kept his promises, lived by the virtues, took care of his family and friends, and treated all people with respect. He listened to people and cared for their needs, even when he was tired. He stood up for the rights of others and helped them to find peace and comfort. He continued to love his disciples even when they were too afraid to return that love, and he gave people a reason to hope in God's mercy. Jesus brought people God's forgiveness and healing, giving them the hope of peace and of everlasting life with God. And Jesus does this for all of us, his disciples and members of his Body, the Church.

As Jesus Christ's disciples who have come together as his Church, we are called to bring his message everywhere, living as he lived and showing forth his presence. It is through this community of the Church that we, as disciples, come to believe and to learn what it means to believe. Our faith in Christ is guided and strengthened by the Church; in fact, our faith is the faith of the Church. And as members of the Body of Christ, the Church, we must answer Christ's call to discipleship by believing and hoping in God and by loving God and others as Jesus Christ did.

Activity How is your parish a visible sign of God's love for humanity? Plan a one-minute announcement that presents what your parish does.

Christ shares his holiness with us today through the Church, where we are first made holy in Baptism. Then, throughout our lives, we are called to holiness by God and the Church—a holiness that stems from the gift of grace that we receive in the sacraments, from the gifts of the Holy Spirit, and from the practice of the virtues. And our holiness grows as we respond to God's love in our lives, living as Christ's disciples.

The Church is one and holy.

Why is it important for a community to be one?

In the seven sacraments that Jesus gave us, we receive God's grace to live as Jesus' followers. We are united by our belief in Christ and celebrate our faith as a community. In the sacraments we profess our faith. In the celebration of the Eucharist, we do this especially when we pray the Nicene Creed. A **creed** is a statement of belief. In the Nicene Creed we state that "we believe in one holy catholic and apostolic Church." The Church is one, holy, catholic, and apostolic. These four characteristics are the **marks of the Church**.

The first mark of the Church is *one*. The Church is one because all its members believe in the one Lord, Jesus Christ. The Church is one because we all share the same Baptism and together are the one Body of Christ. As we read in the New Testament, there is "one body and one Spirit . . . one Lord, one faith, one baptism; one God and Father of all" (Ephesians 4:4, 5–6). And the Church is one because we are guided and united by the Holy Spirit under the leadership of the pope and bishops; we are one in the sacraments we celebrate and in the laws that help us to live as disciples of Christ and faithful members of the Church.

The second mark of the Church is *holy*. God alone is good and holy. But God shared his holiness with all people by sending his Son to us. And

Through our Baptism God calls all members of the Church to holiness. The Christian faithful, religious sisters and brothers, and ordained ministers live out this call in different ways. Yet these differences make the Church an amazing sign of God's goodness and holiness.

> **Faith Words**
> creed
> marks of the Church

Activity On this page, find and highlight or underline the ways the Church is one and holy.

The precepts of the Church

The precepts of the Church are found on page 306. They are laws of the Church that remind us that we are called to grow in holiness and serve the Church. They help us to see that loving God and others is connected to a life of prayer, worship, and service. They guide our behavior and teach us how we should act as members of the Catholic Church.

The precepts of the Church help us to know and fulfill our responsibilities as members of the Church. They help to unite us as followers of Jesus Christ. They make all Church members more aware that the Church is one, holy, catholic, and apostolic.

Read the precepts of the Church together and discuss why each is important.

The Church is catholic and apostolic.

The third mark of the Church is *catholic*. The word *catholic* means "universal"—worldwide and open to all people everywhere. The Church has been universal since the beginning. Jesus commissioned his Apostles, saying, "Go, therefore, and make disciples of all nations, baptizing them in the name of the Father, and of the Son, and of the holy Spirit" (Matthew 28:19). Thus, the Apostles traveled wherever they could to preach the Gospel message. They baptized believers and established local Church communities. The Church continued to grow, and today there are Catholics all across the world.

Pope Benedict XVI meets with bishops from Southern Africa (2005)

Truly catholic, or universal, the Church is made up of people from all over the world. Thus, Catholics have different ways of living, dressing, and celebrating. These different customs and practices are part of the Church's life. They add beauty and wonder to the Church. Yet with all of our diversity, we are still one. We are united by our faith in Jesus and by our membership in the Church. We are joined by the celebration of the seven sacraments and by the leadership of our Holy Father, the pope, and all the bishops. We are the Body of Christ and the People of God.

We experience the Church as worldwide in our parish communities, too. Together, we grow and celebrate our faith, learning what it means to be Catholic. In this family of faith we are joined with Catholics who may be very different from us. We come together from different countries, speaking different languages and having different customs. But we are united by our love for Christ and by our common call to holiness. We are strengthened to love as Jesus loved and to continue his work for justice and peace, welcoming all people as Jesus Christ did and telling everyone about his saving love and about the Church.

The fourth mark of the Church is *apostolic*, or built on the faith of the Apostles. Jesus chose the Apostles to care for and lead the community of believers. He gave them the mission of spreading the good news and baptizing new members of the Church. We read about the ministry of the Apostles and their work in the early Church in the New Testament. The faith we profess and practice is based on some of the earliest creeds. The Apostles' Creed tells us about Jesus, his teachings, and the teachings of the Apostles. We still pray the Apostles' Creed today.

The Church is apostolic today because the life and leadership of the Church is based on that of the Apostles. The pope, the bishop of Rome, and the bishops, the successors of the Apostles, continue this ministry of the Apostles today. The pope and the bishops carry out the Apostles' mission, given to them by Jesus. As baptized Catholics, disciples of Jesus, and members of the Church, we too are encouraged to share in this work of spreading the good news of Jesus Christ and the Kingdom of God.

> "Go, therefore, and make disciples of all nations."
> (Matthew 28:19)

Activity On this page, find and highlight or underline the ways the Church is catholic and apostolic.

221

RESPONDING...

Recognizing Our Faith

Recall the question at the beginning of this chapter: *In what ways can I help to change the world?* If you were to make a kit of things that would remind others of this question, what would it include? Why?

Living Our Faith

Decide how you can be a visible sign of God's love today.

Saints Raphael, Gabriel, and Michael, Archangels

The Church often prays for the assistance of the angels and all the saints for help in living as disciples of Jesus. The word *angel* comes from the Greek word *ángelos*, meaning "messenger." In the Bible, we learn that God sent angels as messengers to his people. We read about the angel Raphael in the book of Tobit.

Partners in FAITH

Raphael is a Hebrew name meaning "My healer is God." In the books of Daniel and Luke, we read about the angel Gabriel. *Gabriel* is a Hebrew name that means "My strength is God." In the books of Daniel, Jude, and Revelation, we read about the angel Michael. In Hebrew the name *Michael* means "Who can compare with God?"

Raphael, Gabriel, and Michael have a special ranking as angels; they are known as archangels. The early Church declared them to be saints in recognition of their holiness. The angels, and all the saints, can be our guides in living out the virtues of faith, hope, and charity. The Church remembers and celebrates Saints Michael, Gabriel, and Raphael, Archangels, on their feast day, September 29.

What message do you think God would like delivered to the world today?

@ For additional ideas and activities, visit www.weliveourfaith.com.

Putting Faith to Work

Talk about what you have learned in this chapter:

 We understand that the virtues of faith, hope, and love unite us to God.

 We love, we hope, and we have faith as we follow Jesus Christ together as the Church.

 We live in a way that proclaims the marks of the Church: one, holy, catholic, and apostolic.

Decide on ways to live out what you have learned.

✝ ENCOUNTERING GOD'S WORD

Jesus said:

❝ **I am the good shepherd, and I know mine and mine know me** ❞
(John 10:14).

➡ **READ** the quotation from Scripture.

➡ **REFLECT** on this question:
How can knowing that Jesus is our good shepherd help strengthen us to change the world?

➡ **SHARE** your reflections with a partner.

➡ **DECIDE** on one way that you can help to "shepherd" others to change the world by their example.

Complete the following.

1. A virtue is a good habit that helps us to _____
_____.

2. The virtue of faith enables us to _____
_____.

3. The virtue of hope enables us to _____
_____.

4. The virtue of charity enables us to _____
_____.

Short Answers

5. What are the marks of the Church? _____

6. What is a creed? _____

7. What does the Apostles' Creed tell us about? _____
_____

8. What does the word *catholic* mean? _____

9–10. ESSAY: Explain the ways the Church lives out this statement: *We believe in one holy catholic and apostolic Church.*

Chapter 20 Assessment

RESPONDING...

Sharing Faith with Your Family

Discuss the following with your family:

- God gives us many gifts.
- As members of the Church, we come together in faith, hope, and love.
- The Church is one and holy.
- The Church is catholic and apostolic.

As a family choose an uplifting movie to watch together, and identify ways the virtues of faith, hope, and charity are being portrayed in this movie.

The Worship Connection

During the Rite of Peace at Mass, we share a sign of peace with one another. It is the risen Christ, present in each member of the community, that we share. This is one way that we express our oneness with Christ and with one another as members of the Church.

More to Explore

Research to find examples in the world today of the Church living as one, holy, catholic, and apostolic.

Catholic Social Teaching ☑ Checklist

Theme of Catholic Social Teaching:
Rights and Responsibilities of the Human Person

How it relates to Chapter 20: As members of the Church we are responsible for caring for others and ensuring that their basic rights are upheld. These include the right to life and to those things necessary for a decent life.

How can you do this?

☐ At home:

_____

☐ At school/work:

_____

☐ In the parish:

_____

☐ In the community:

_____

Check off each action after it has been completed.

GATHERING...

**"Blessed are the merciful,
for they will be shown mercy."**

(Matthew 5:7)

✚ **Leader:** Let us pray to God who cares for all.

All: Have mercy on your people, Lord.

Reader 1: Guard the Church.
Watch over (name the pope),
our Pope.
Protect and bless (name the bishop),
our bishop.

All: Have mercy on your people, Lord.

Reader 2: Save your people.
Preserve peace among the
nations.
Bring an end to strife and hatred.
Guide the rulers of nations.

All: Have mercy on your people, Lord.

Reader 3: Guide parents in the fulfillment
of their responsibilities.
Nourish children by your
loving care.
Support and give solace to
the aged.

All: Have mercy on your people, Lord.

Reader 4: Be a helper to the poor.
Comfort those who are troubled.
Grant deliverance to captives.
Bring exiles back to their
homeland.

All: Have mercy on your people, Lord.

Reader 5: Grant health to the sick.
Be present to those who are
dying.
Admit those who have died into
the company of the saints.

(Liturgy of the Hours)

All: Have mercy on your people, Lord.

Leader: Jesus, you taught us to be
compassionate as your Father is
compassionate. Grant us your mercy,
and help us to show it to others.

All: God, our loving Father, we ask this in
the name of your Son, Jesus Christ,
through the Holy Spirit. Amen.

HELP THE HOMELESS

Visit www.weliveourfaith.com
to find appropriate music
and songs.

Saint Anthony's FOOD DRIVE

The BiG QuEstion:

What am I responsible for?

iscover your attitudes about responsibility. Take the following quiz.

1 It is important to admit my mistakes.
○ agree   ○ disagree   ○ neutral

2 I have the responsibility to help out at home.
○ agree   ○ disagree   ○ neutral

3 I must try to do my best, even in difficult times.
○ agree   ○ disagree   ○ neutral

4 I have the responsibility to speak out when I know that something is untrue, unethical, or immoral.
○ agree   ○ disagree   ○ neutral

5 I have the responsibility to stand up for others when they're being treated unfairly.
○ agree   ○ disagree   ○ neutral

6 It is important to show respect for others' feelings, even during a disagreement.
○ agree   ○ disagree   ○ neutral

7 I must follow through on my commitments.
○ agree   ○ disagree   ○ neutral

Results:

After taking this quiz, share your results together as a group. Tally the responses and figure out the percentage of your group that chose each response.

Brainstorm together about ways to act more responsibly in your lives.

In this chapter
we learn that Jesus entrusts us with the responsibility of caring for our neighbor. One way we fulfill this responsibility is by performing the Works of Mercy. Through this chapter, we hope

 to understand
that Jesus calls his disciples to show mercy and compassion to those who are in need in body, mind, heart, or soul

 to choose
discipleship and eternal life by showing mercy and compassion through the Works of Mercy

 to practice
the Works of Mercy.

134 million

number of children between the ages of seven and eighteen who do not attend school
(CARE)

3.5 million

number of people who are homeless in the United States
(Urban Institute)

21

number of children who die every minute from malnutrition and preventable disease
(CARE)

35.9 million

number of people in the United States living at the federal poverty level
(U.S. Census Bureau)

1

number of dollars that 1.2 billion people throughout the world get by on per day
(Bread for the World)

860 million

number of adults who cannot read
(OXFAM)

45 million

number of people in the United States without health insurance
(U.S. Census Bureau)

30,000

number of people who die each day in the world from extreme poverty
(OXFAM)

"Life is moral responsibility," wrote Elizabeth Stuart Phelps (1844–1911), U.S. novelist and short-story writer.

Activity Which of these statistics especially concerned or alarmed you? What responsibility do you think people have with regard to these issues?

As Jesus' disciples we are called to follow his example.

At the Last Supper, Jesus washed his disciples' feet and then said to them, "I have given you a model to follow, so that as I have done for you, you should also do" (John 13:15). Thus, as disciples of Jesus and as members of the Catholic Church, we have a great goal: to be like Jesus Christ. We are to live as his followers and to become like him, doing for others the things that he would do.

In each of us, through the work of the Holy Spirit, Jesus' New Law, the Law of the Gospel, is lived out as the law of charity. And Jesus made charity, or love, the New Commandment, asking us to love as he does—to love even our enemies and to treat everyone as our neighbor. This call to love seems clear in the following parable that Jesus taught us.

"A man fell victim to robbers as he went down from Jerusalem to Jericho. They stripped and beat him and went off leaving him half-dead. A priest happened to be going down that road, but when he saw him, he passed by on the opposite side. Likewise a Levite came to the place, and when he saw him, he passed by on the opposite side. But a Samaritan traveler who came upon him was moved with compassion at the sight. He approached the victim, poured oil and wine over his wounds and bandaged them. Then he lifted him up on his own animal, took him to an inn and cared for him." (Luke 10:30–34)

Samaritans were from a territory between Judea and Galilee that was called Samaria, and the Jews considered them to be enemies. Yet the Samaritan in this parable showed mercy to a stranger who had been victimized and was suffering. This Samaritan treated the robbers' victim as a neighbor.

> **"Do to others whatever you would have them do to you."**
> (Matthew 7:12)

The Good Samaritan (after Delacroix), by Vincent Van Gogh (1853–1890) from the Collection Kröller-Müller Museum Otterlo, The Netherlands

This parable emphasizes the mercy and compassion that Jesus has and the mercy and compassion that he calls us to have, too. The parable helps us to remember that everyone is our neighbor and that Jesus calls us to treat others with the love and compassion with which he would treat them. We must all take to heart Jesus' words, referring to the Samaritan's actions: "Go and do likewise" (Luke 10:37).

Activity On a separate sheet of paper, write a modern-day version of the parable about the Good Samaritan.

As Jesus' disciples we have a responsibility to care for others.

In the Old Testament, when God asked Cain where his brother Abel was, Cain asked God, "Am I my brother's keeper?" (Genesis 4:9). Today our question might be, "To what extent am I responsible for loving and caring for others?" In the Gospels we find many examples of the ways Jesus cared for others, especially those who were neglected, poor, or oppressed. Following Jesus' example, we are also responsible for loving and caring for others. In fact, Jesus, who reminds us to love our neighbor as we love ourselves, calls us to look upon others as an extension of ourselves. Thus, we have the responsibility to treat others the way we would want to be treated—with love and compassion, and with the same respect and care that we would like to receive from them. Jesus asks us to "do to others whatever you would have them do to you" (Matthew 7:12). This is known as the *Golden Rule*, and it sums up the Law of the Gospel.

One way that we accept our responsibility to care for others is by performing the Works of Mercy. Mercy is one of the fruits of charity. It enables us to show love and compassion to those who are suffering in any way—whether in body, mind, heart, or soul. So, the **Works of Mercy** are acts of love by which we care for the bodily and spiritual needs of others. Mercy is a theme that is referred to in both the Old and New Testaments. The prophet Isaiah, for example, spoke of mercy in these words:

> "Sharing your bread with the hungry,
>   sheltering the oppressed and the homeless;
> Clothing the naked when you see them,
>   and not turning your back on your own"
> (Isaiah 58:7).

Golden Rule (1961) by Norman Rockwell (1884–1978)

Faith Word

Works of Mercy

But Jesus gave his disciples a whole new understanding of mercy. Jesus not only challenged his disciples to act mercifully, but he also identified himself with those whom his disciples would love and care for, saying, "Whatever you did for one of these least brothers of mine, you did for me" (Matthew 25:40).

The risen Christ is always present in our lives and in the world. And Christ asks us to see him in every person we meet, especially in those who are suffering or in need. He asks us to care for each person in a spirit of loving service, knowing that we are really loving and caring for Christ, who, through the Holy Spirit, lives in each person.

Activity How would your life change if you saw Christ in everyone? Share your thoughts with a partner.

The Works of Mercy

The ways that we, as Catholics, can live as disciples of Jesus and members of the Church include the Works of Mercy.

The *Corporal Works of Mercy* are acts of love that help us to care for the physical and material needs of others:
Feed the hungry.
Give drink to the thirsty.
Clothe the naked.
Visit the imprisoned.
Shelter the homeless.
Visit the sick.
Bury the dead.

The *Spiritual Works of Mercy* are acts of love that help us to care for the needs of people's hearts, minds, and souls:
Admonish the sinner.
Instruct the ignorant.
Counsel the doubtful.
Comfort the sorrowful.
Bear wrongs patiently.
Forgive all injuries.
Pray for the living and the dead.

Do you know people who are in need in body, mind, heart, or soul?

We can perform the Works of Mercy.

What can you do to live out the Works of Mercy?

All of the Works of Mercy are practical ways to live our faith by using whatever talents we have and by contributing whatever gifts we can to care for others and alleviate their suffering. For example, by contributing to a food pantry and to a clothing drive, we can live out the Works of Mercy that call us to "feed the hungry" and "clothe the naked." And though we might not be able to perform all the Works of Mercy at our present age—for example, ministering to people who are literally in prison— we can work with our families and friends to do the things that we can, such as helping those "imprisoned" by illness, poverty, fear, and hardship.

Our capacity to live out the Works of Mercy will also change and grow as we mature. However, at almost any age, we can give correction to those who need it, find ways to share helpful knowledge and give good advice, console people and be patient instead of losing our tempers, forgive people, and, of course, pray for people.

By performing even one of the Works of Mercy, we have the power to change lives. Those of us who are not afraid to love as Jesus called us to love have real power: our kindness and our forgiveness, our thoughtfulness and our understanding, our compassion and our friendliness, our joy and our love are powerful ways to help those who are sad, afraid, lonely, or suffering in any way. And since the power of our mercy is from God, who is all-merciful, it can last forever!

Activity Choose one of the Works of Mercy listed on page 229. List some ways you can live this out.

Look at your list. How can these actions change people's lives?

By caring for others we choose discipleship and eternal life.

Jesus calls us to perform the Works of Mercy and "invites us to recognize his own presence in the poor" (*CCC*, 2449). And Jesus especially asks us to give alms. **Almsgiving** is the sharing of our resources or time to help those who are poor or in need. Jesus said, "Give alms, and behold, everything will be clean for you" (Luke 11:41). With these words Jesus teaches that by caring for others we walk a path of true discipleship toward eternal life. Jesus made this especially clear to his disciples when he said to them:

"When the Son of Man comes in his glory, and all the angels with him, he will sit upon his glorious throne, and all the nations will be assembled before him. And he will separate them one from another. . . . Then the king will say . . . , 'Come, you who are blessed by my Father. Inherit the kingdom prepared for you from the foundation of the world. For I was hungry and you gave me food, I was

> Jesus "invites us to recognize his own presence in the poor" (*CCC*, 2449).

thirsty and you gave me drink, a stranger and you welcomed me, naked and you clothed me, ill and you cared for me, in prison and you visited me.' Then the righteous will answer him and say, 'Lord, when did we see you hungry and feed you, or thirsty and give you drink? When did we see you a stranger and welcome you, or naked and clothe you? When did we see you ill or in prison, and visit you?' And the king will say to them in reply,

'Amen, I say to you, whatever you did for one of these least brothers of mine, you did for me'" (Matthew 25:31–32, 34–40).

In this passage from the Gospel of Matthew, Jesus is speaking of the **last judgment**, Jesus Christ's coming at the end of time to judge all people. And Jesus tells us that at the last judgment we will be judged according to how well we have treated those who are poor or in need. We will be judged on how merciful we have been. Knowing this helps us to realize that each Work of Mercy that we perform now is preparing us for that day of final judgment. If we have been merciful, God will show us mercy—bringing us into the happiness of his love in his Kingdom forever.

Faith Words
almsgiving
last judgment

Activity Name some charitable groups that you can give alms to. How does their work reflect Jesus' mission of helping those who are poor and in need?

Time, talent, and treasure

God has given each of us unique and various gifts. He calls each of us to be a Christian steward, "one who receives God's gifts gratefully, cherishes and tends them in a responsible and accountable manner, shares them in justice and love with others, and returns them with increase to the Lord" (*Stewardship: A Disciple's Response*, Introduction). The Church uses the expression *time, talent,* and *treasure* to

sum up the gifts that we, as stewards, are meant to share:

• Do we use our *time* wisely and responsibly? Each of us has the exact same number of hours in a day. One simple but important way to be a good steward of God's gift of time is to attend Mass regularly and to pray.

• Do we use our *talents* while crediting God for making us talented? We need not excel to use our talents; we need only volunteer whatever gifts we have in order to serve others.

• Are we cheerfully generous with our *treasure,* or our money and possessions? By knowing the difference between our needs and our wants and trusting God with our lives we can become freer to follow the teachings of Jesus.

How will you be a steward of your time, talent, and treasure this week?

RESPONDING...

Recognizing Our Faith

Recall the question at the beginning of this chapter: *What am I responsible for?* Think back to the answer you gave at the beginning of this chapter. How has learning more about Jesus' teaching on the Works of Mercy affected the answer that you would give now?

Living Our Faith

Where in your community are the Works of Mercy being lived out? What can you do to participate in one of these efforts?

Sean Devereux

Sean Devereux was someone who lived out the Works of Mercy. Born in 1964, Devereux grew up in England. He was active in sports and volunteer work. His desire to help others led to a career as a teacher and eventually as a lay missionary in Africa.

Partners in FAITH

In 1989 he began to teach in Liberia, Africa, as a lay missionary. In 1990 civil wars broke out in Liberia, and the school where he taught was forced to close. But he remained in Africa and volunteered as a relief worker with the United Nations. One of his duties was distributing food to the hungry. He was beaten and imprisoned for protecting the food to make sure it was not stolen or sold for profit. The situation in Liberia grew even more dangerous: In 1992 all relief workers were ordered to leave. Not one to give up, he went to Somalia, Africa, to help with relief efforts there. He helped to organize aid for starving children who were victims of famine and violence. Though his work made him a target for violence, he remained in Somalia, devoted to helping others. He was assassinated in 1993 at the age of twenty-eight.

In what ways can you take on your responsibility to help others?

Putting Faith to Work

Talk about what you have learned in this chapter:

 We understand that Jesus calls his disciples to show mercy and compassion to those who are in need in body, mind, heart, or soul.

 We choose discipleship and eternal life by showing mercy and compassion through the Works of Mercy.

We practice the Works of Mercy.

Decide on ways to live out what you have learned.

✝ ENCOUNTERING GOD'S WORD

" **What good is it, my brothers, if someone says he has faith but does not have works? Can that faith save him?** "

(James 2:14)

 READ the quotation from Scripture.

 REFLECT on the following:
In this quotation, *works* means the good works summarized by the Works of Mercy. Why do you think these works are so important? How would you answer the question posed by James in his letter? (You can read James's answer in the Bible in James 2:15–17.)

 SHARE your reflections with a partner.

 DECIDE to look for ways to carry out the Works of Mercy in your everyday life.

Write the letter of the answer that best defines each term.

1. _____ almsgiving

2. _____ Works of Mercy

3. _____ last judgment

4. _____ Golden Rule

a. acts of love by which we care for the needs of others

b. Jesus Christ's coming at the end of time to judge all people

c. a turning to God with all one's heart

d. "Do to others whatever you would have them do to you." (Matthew 7:12)

e. the sharing of our resources or time to help those who are poor or in need

Short Answers

5. What is Jesus' message in the parable of the Good Samaritan? _____
_____

6. How does performing Works of Mercy prepare us for eternal life? _____
_____

7. What is our great goal as disciples of Jesus and as members of the Catholic Church? _____
_____

8. Name one practical way to live out the Works of Mercy. _____
_____

9–10. ESSAY: How do the Works of Mercy help us to live Jesus' New Law, the Law of the Gospel?

RESPONDING...

Sharing Faith with Your Family

Discuss the following with your family:
- As Jesus' disciples we are called to follow his example.
- As Jesus' disciples we have a responsibility to care for others.
- We can perform the Works of Mercy.
- By caring for others we choose discipleship and eternal life.

In the liturgical year, every day is dedicated to the honor of a particular saint. Together, find out which saints are celebrated on each of your birthdays or other days that are special to you, or discover the saints for whom you were named. Each person then chooses a saint and researches the ways this saint lived out the Works of Mercy.

The Worship Connection

At the Sunday Eucharist, listen carefully to the prayer of the faithful. What needs of the world do we pray for? Add one silent petition of your own.

More to Explore

Look for stories in the news that show how the Works of Mercy are being lived out today.

Catholic Social Teaching ☑ Checklist

Theme of Catholic Social Teaching:
Option for the Poor and Vulnerable

How it relates to Chapter 21: As Catholics we can join together to help and support those among us who are less fortunate or disadvantaged in any way.

How can you do this?

☐ At home:

_____

☐ At school/work:

_____

☐ In the parish:

_____

☐ In the community:

_____

Check off each action after it has been completed.

GATHERING...

22

We Work for Justice and Peace

"**Seek peace and pursue it.**"
(Psalm 34:15)

✛ **Leader:** On December 12, the Church celebrates Mary as patron of the Americas: Our Lady of Guadalupe. With confidence in her care for us, we now pray:

Reader 1: God of power and mercy,
you blessed the Americas at Tepeyac
with the presence of the Virgin Mary of Guadalupe.

Reader 2: May her prayers help all men and women
to accept each other as brothers and sisters.

Reader 3: Through your justice present in our hearts
may your peace reign in the world.

All: Grant this through Christ our Lord. Amen.
(Catholic Household Blessings and Prayers)

@ **Visit www.weliveourfaith.com to find appropriate music and songs.**

235

The BiG QuEStion:

Do I feel respected by others?

 iscover whether or not you show respect for others. Circle your response to each statement.

1 I treat other people the way I want to be treated.
True   False

2 I am considerate of other people.
True   False

3 I accept the personal differences of others.
True   False

4 I never intentionally ridicule, embarrass, or hurt other people.
True   False

5 I listen to what other people have to say.
True   False

6 I consider the feelings of all who will be affected by my actions and decisions.
True   False

7 I believe all people are equal.
True   False

8 I am tolerant of others' views.
True   False

Results:

Look over your responses. Circling *false* just once means that you have some work to do. Nobody is perfect, but remember that you are called to respect and care for everyone that God has created. Showing respect to others is often the first step to others respecting you.

Reflect silently on some of the improvements you might make in the way you treat other people.

In this chapter we learn that God calls us to practice social justice, to honor the human dignity of each human being, and to live lives of justice and peace. Through this chapter, we hope

 to understand that justice is the way to peace

 to accept our responsibility to work for the common good

to follow Catholic social teachings in our own lives.

Meredith and her friend Amy noticed a flyer announcing their school's participation in Catholic Relief Services. ⌘⌘ They volunteered to help raise money for efforts that would fight world hunger in union with the Catholic Relief Services/Foods Resource Bank development program. They and some friends held bake sales, car washes, and raffles. ⌘⌘⌘ Meredith and Amy forwarded the money raised to CRS/FRB. It joined community contributions, profits from crops donated by local farmers, and government grants to provide necessities such as seeds, farming tools, and other essentials to help farming communities in Africa, Asia, and Latin America. ⌘⌘⌘⌘ Some farming tools paid for by the money raised by Meredith and Amy were put on Lila's family truck in Kenya. Now her family members could farm their land to feed her entire family.

Activity Meredith and Amy were part of a chain of events whose consequences went beyond their school or neighborhood. What could you do today that might spark another such chain of events?

"Kindness is the golden chain by which society is bound together" is a quote widely attributed to German poet, novelist, and dramatist Johann Wolfgang von Goethe (1749–1832).

We are called to justice.

God calls us to practice **social justice**—opposing every form of injustice in society and working to promote justice for all people. Justice is based on the simple fact that all people have **human dignity**, the value and worth that we share because God created us in his image and likeness.

God made it known that anyone who hopes for salvation must act justly—respecting the rights of others, giving people the things that are rightfully theirs, and working to make life better for everyone. Jesus' example of making sure that no one in society was neglected or ignored gives us our best understanding of God the Father's call to justice.

As Jesus' disciples, we follow his example of faith in God the Father and a life of justice. And, as members of the Church, together we take on the serious responsibility of continuing Jesus' work of social justice. We uphold humanity's most basic human right, the right to life. We work to treat all people fairly and equally and to protect the rights of all people in our society—including children, those without a home, those who are new to our country, those who are disadvantaged, those who are different from us, and those who are in need in any way.

Recognizing that all people possess the same human rights, we work to be sure that they have the right to: practice faith and have a family; receive an education and work; experience equal treatment and safety; receive housing and health care.

Our Catholic understanding of justice reaches far beyond what is usual in our society. God calls us to a justice that exceeds the boundaries of what most people are willing to give—especially to those who are poor, oppressed, neglected, or in need in any way.

When we strive for this justice we are seeking **righteousness**, or conduct in conformity with God's will. Jesus told us:

"Blessed are they who hunger and thirst for righteousness,
    for they will be satisfied" (Matthew 5:6).

So, by striving for justice and seeking righteousness we work to attain the happiness of knowing that God's power and presence are at work in this world, as well as in the next!

Faith Words

social justice
human dignity
righteousness

Stewards of creation

God created the world to share his love and goodness and to show his glory and power. Creation is a marvelous gift for which we praise God. We also praise God for asking us to be *stewards of creation*—to care for his creation and to make sure that all people share in the goodness of creation.

Justice is sharing the resources that come from God's creation with those who do not have them. Justice is using the resources we have in a responsible way. We cannot use so much food, water, and energy that there is not enough for others. The world is not only God's gift to us. It is also his gift to the generations of people to come. We must work together to protect our environment and the good of all God's creation.

How can you be a good steward of God's creation?

Activity Today in the Church and in our world people's words and actions remind us that justice, peace, and love of neighbor are still part of our way of life. Work with your group to think of people in all walks of life who work for justice in our world.

We are called to peace.

God lovingly wills that all people live in peace. In Scripture we find that God's peace, which is more than just the absence of war and violence, is realized when everyone lives in true harmony with one another and with God's creation. We also find that peace and justice are very closely connected. They are like two sides of the same coin, and both are central to the coming of God's Kingdom.

"Justice will bring about peace;
  right will produce calm and security."
(Isaiah 32:17)

As disciples of Jesus, carrying out the mission of sharing God's love and spreading God's Kingdom, we must commit to justice and become peacemakers in every context of our lives. Yet in our society there are many types of violence—all of which contradict peace and are against God's loving will for us. One tragic form of violence is domestic violence. It takes place in many homes today and is particularly condemnable because it violates people where they should be safest—in their own family. At your age, you may not be able to prevent domestic violence, but you should know that it is an assault against human dignity. And if you have witnessed it, you must consciously work never to repeat or allow this type of violence in your life.

As Catholics, we recognize that some forms of violence are always wrong:

abortion The direct termination of the life of an unborn baby is always wrong. The Supreme Court of the United States has legalized abortion, but we must remember that what is legal is not always morally right. We should work to change laws in society that allow abortion.

euthanasia, or mercy killing We can never deliberately kill someone, even in cases of great suffering. Our faith requires us to take ordinary measures to preserve life. A dying patient, however, may refuse "'over-zealous' treatment" (*CCC*, 2278).

murder The deliberate taking of someone's life

suicide The taking of one's own life is an offense against God, who gave each of us the gift of life.

terrorism and related violence that intentionally targets innocent civilians Misusing our political views and personal beliefs to intimidate or attack innocent people is never acceptable.

There are many other forms of violence. Catholic teaching should shape our decisions on these:

war We should always try to use nonviolent means to resolve conflicts. War should be a last resort when other means fail to protect the innocent against fundamental injustice. Our American Catholic bishops have declared, "We do not perceive any situation in which the deliberate initiation of nuclear warfare . . . can be morally justified" (*The Challenge of Peace*, 1983, 150).

the death penalty The *Catechism* states, "The cases in which the execution of the offender is an absolute necessity 'are very rare, if not practically non-existent'" (2267).

environmental waste and pollution This is the destruction of those things in creation that God gave us to support life. To pollute the environment is to poison ourselves and to take away the possibilities of life for the generations that will come after us.

scandal "An attitude or behavior which leads another to do evil" (*CCC*, 2284). It is wrong when individuals or groups use their power and influence to tempt others to disrespect life in any way.

Though we realize that we will only experience the fullness of God's Kingdom in eternity, by doing God's will—living in justice and peace—we show that good can triumph over evil, hope over despair, love over hate. In Jesus Christ, through the Holy Spirit, God's grace is active in us, empowering us to live as disciples, doing God's will "on earth, as it is in heaven" (the Lord's Prayer). It is then that we show the world that God's Kingdom is among us!

Activity Discuss five concrete ways that people your age can work for justice in society, and five ways that people your age can be peacemakers.

"Justice will bring about peace."
(Isaiah 32:17)

BELIEVING...

We are called to work together for justice and peace.

How can you show that you believe in justice and peace?

Jesus worked for justice. He tried to make sure that people had what they needed. He healed the sick and fed the hungry. He listened to people when they told him about their needs. Jesus stood up for people who were neglected or ignored by society. And he spoke out against leaders who did not take care of people.

As disciples of Jesus, we cannot allow unjust conditions to exist without taking a stand against them.

> **"It is the *duty of citizens* to contribute . . . to the good of society."**
> (CCC, 2239)

The *Catechism* reminds us that "we have a responsibility for the sins committed by others when *we cooperate in them*: by participating directly and voluntarily in them; by ordering, advising, praising, or approving them; by not disclosing or not hindering them when we have an obligation to do so; by protecting evildoers" (1868).

Catholic social teaching is the teaching of the Church that calls all members to work for justice and peace as Jesus did. Jesus' life and teaching are the foundations of Catholic social teaching. And the whole Church is called to live by this social teaching—to put the good news of Christ into action. Thus, the Church encourages individuals and groups to bring the good news of Jesus Christ into society and to work for change in policies and laws so that the dignity and freedom of every person may be respected.

The social teachings of the Catholic Church teach us to build a "civilization of love"—for "love is the only force that can lead to personal and social perfection" (*Compendium of the Social Doctrine of the Church*, d:580). Catholic social teachings call all members to work for the common good. The **common good** is the well-being of every individual person and of the whole society to which everyone belongs. When we witness situations that serve the good of some but not the good of all, such as discrimination or poverty, we are called to oppose them. The *Catechism* reminds us that "it is the *duty of citizens* to contribute along with the civil authorities to the good of society" (2239). Thus, following the social teachings of our Church is one way that we, as Jesus' disciples, accept our responsibility to care for others.

Faith Words

Catholic social teaching
common good

Activity Discuss some ways that your parish and your diocese work for the common good of all people.

Social responsibility

The pope and our bishops remind us to respect the rights of all people. They teach us about the need to protect human life, to care for those who are poor, and to work for peace and justice. Their teaching can often take the form of an *encyclical*, a pastoral letter written by the pope and sent to the whole Church and even the whole world. These letters from the popes give us words of wisdom for our times. Here are two examples: "Everyone who has joined the ranks of Christ must be a glowing point of light in the world, a nucleus of love." (Pope John XXIII, *Peace on Earth*, 164)

"The goal of peace . . . will certainly be achieved through the putting into effect of social and international justice, but also through the practice of the virtues which favor togetherness, and which teach us to live in unity." (Pope John Paul II, *On the Social Concern of the Church*, 39)

Go to www.vatican.va to find other encyclicals that teach us about justice and peace.

CATHOLIC IDENTITY

Through Catholic social teaching we live out our discipleship.

As the Church, the People of God, we know that no one who professes to be a Christian can separate love for God from love for neighbor. Thus, being mindful of and living according to the following themes of Catholic social teaching help us to show our love of God through love for our neighbor—our brothers and sisters around the world.

THEMES OF CATHOLIC SOCIAL TEACHING	QUESTIONS
Life and Dignity of the Human Person Human life is sacred because it is a gift from God. We are all God's children, and share the same human dignity from the moment of conception to natural death. Our dignity—our worth and value—comes from being made in the image and likeness of God. This dignity makes us equal. As Christians we respect all people, even those we do not know.	What are some ways the dignity of students or teachers is not respected during class? Why do you think this happens? What are some conflicts in your school that have been resolved in a way that recognizes the dignity of those involved?
Call to Family, Community, and Participation As Christians we are involved in our family life and community. We are called to be active participants in social, economic, and political life, using the values of our faith to shape our decisions and actions.	What are some virtues that individuals practice? that families practice? that neighbors practice? How does the practice of these virtues influence society as a whole?
Rights and Responsibilities of the Human Person Every person has a fundamental right to life. This includes the things we need to have a decent life: faith and family, work and education, health care and housing. We also have a responsibility to others and to society. We work to make sure the rights of all people are being protected.	What is the difference between needing and wanting something?
Option for the Poor and Vulnerable We have a special obligation to help those who are poor and in need. This includes those who cannot protect themselves because of their age or their health. At different times in our lives we are all poor in some way and in need of assistance.	What are some ways people might be poor? What are some ways people are vulnerable?
Dignity of Work and the Rights of Workers Our work is a sign of our participation in God's work. People have the right to decent work, just wages, safe working conditions, and to participate in decisions about their work. There is value in all work. Our work in school and at home is a way to participate in God's work of creation. It is a way to use our talents and abilities to thank God for his gifts.	How might different kinds of work make people feel? How can we make people feel respected and valued for whatever work they do?
Solidarity of the Human Family Solidarity is a feeling of unity. It binds members of a group together. Each of us is a member of the one human family, equal by our common human dignity. The human family includes people of all racial, cultural, and religious backgrounds. We all suffer when one part of the human family suffers, whether they live near us or far away from us.	What are some problems or challenges that we face in our country? How are they similar to those of other countries? How are they different?
Care for God's Creation God created us to be stewards, or caretakers, of his creation. We must care for and respect the environment. We have to protect it for future generations. When we care for creation, we show respect for God, the creator.	What are some examples of society not protecting the environment? How can these situations be changed?

 **Read the chart and discuss the questions given for each theme.**

RESPONDING...

Recognizing Our Faith

Recall the question at the beginning of this chapter: *Do I feel respected by others*? How do the Church's teachings presented in this chapter guide people to respect one another?

Living Our Faith

Choose one of the themes of Catholic social teaching, and decide on a practical way to live it out this week.

Jesuit Volunteer Corps

The Jesuit Volunteer Corps (JVC) has become the largest Catholic lay volunteer program in the United States. JVC offers men and women the opportunity to work full-time for justice and peace. Volunteers serve the homeless, the unemployed, refugees, people with AIDS, the elderly, street youth, abused women and children, the mentally ill, and the developmentally disabled. Jesuit volunteers draw inspiration and direction from the traditions of the Society of Jesus, known as the Jesuits. Ignatius of Loyola, the founder of the Jesuits, sought to integrate a life of prayer with active work to build up the Kingdom of God. Members of the JVC are called to go where God will best be served and where people will best be helped. Working and serving in the JVC is one way to participate in the Church's mission to teach that all people have equal dignity and deserve to fulfill their potential in life.

How can you more fully practice social justice in your life?

 For additional ideas and activities, visit www.weliveourfaith.com.

Putting Faith to Work

Talk about what you have learned in this chapter:

 We understand that justice is the way to peace.

 We accept our responsibility to work for the common good.

 We follow Catholic social teachings in our own lives.

Decide on ways to live out what you have learned.

✝ ENCOUNTERING GOD'S WORD

"For family and friends I say, 'May peace be yours.' For the house of the LORD, our God, I pray, 'May blessings be yours.'"
(Psalm 122:8–9)

➡ **READ** the quotation from Scripture.

➡ **REFLECT** on these questions:
Do you pray for peace for your family and friends? How can your prayer also extend to those unknown to you, all the people in the world, the poor and those in need, and even your enemies, as Jesus taught?

➡ **SHARE** your reflections with a partner.

➡ **DECIDE** to put your prayer into action, at home, in your parish, and in the world.

Define.

1. human dignity _____

2. social justice _____

3. common good _____

4. Catholic social teaching _____

Complete the following.

5. Living according to the Church's social teaching helps us to show our love of God through _____ _____.

6. As members of the Church, together we take on the serious responsibility of continuing Jesus' work of social justice by _____.

7. As Catholics, we recognize that some forms of violence are always wrong: abortion, _____, _____, _____, and _____.

8. As disciples of Jesus, we cannot allow _____ to exist without taking a stand against them.

9–10. ESSAY: Summarize each theme of Catholic social teaching. (See page 241.)

Sharing Faith with Your Family

Discuss the following with your family:

- We are called to justice.
- We are called to peace.
- We are called to work together for justice and peace.
- Through Catholic social teaching we live out our discipleship.

Encourage your family to be aware of the "brothers and sisters" around the world who need comfort and aid. Urge your family to help others by doing an act of kindness each day this week. At the end of the week, share your experiences and discuss the ways that you have lived out the themes of Catholic social teaching.

The Worship Connection

At the Sunday Eucharist there may be a second collection to help those in need. Set aside some of your money this week to give at this collection.

More to Explore

Use the Internet to research Catholic organizations that promote peace and justice in our world today.

Catholic Social Teaching ☑ Checklist

Theme of Catholic Social Teaching: Choose a theme found in this chapter. _____

How it relates to Chapter 22: List the ways this theme relates to Chapter 22. _____
_____

How can you live out this theme?

☐ At home:
_____

☐ At school/work:
_____

☐ In the parish:
_____

☐ In the community:
_____

Check off each action after it has been completed.

23

We Are a Communion of Saints

❝If we walk in the light as he is in the light, then we have fellowship with one another.❞

(1 John 1:7)

Leader: During the third week of January, the Church prays for Christian unity. Let us now ask God to make all Christians one in his Son, Jesus.

Reader 1: Gracious Father,
we pray to you for your holy
  catholic Church.
Fill it with your truth.
Keep it in your peace.

Reader 2: Where it is corrupt, reform it.
Where it is in error, correct it.
Where it is right, defend it.
Where it is in want, provide for it.

Reader 3: Where it is divided, reunite it;
for the sake of your Son, our
  Savior Jesus Christ.

All: Amen.

(prayer for Christian unity, William Laud)

Leader: For all Christians everywhere—Catholic, Orthodox, Protestant—may our mutual love for Christ bring us joy and understanding. Let us pray to the Lord.

All: Lord, hear our prayer.

Leader: Almighty and eternal God,
you gather the scattered sheep
and watch over those you have
  gathered.

Look kindly on all who follow Jesus,
  your Son.
You have marked them with the seal
  of one baptism,
now make them one in the fullness
  of faith
and unite them in the bond of love.

We ask this through Christ our Lord.

All: Amen.

(prayer for Christian unity, *Catholic Household Blessings and Prayers*)

 Visit www.weliveourfaith.com to find appropriate music and songs.

The BiG QueStion:

Who are my role models?

Discover more about role models in the world today. Complete the trading card below for someone considered to be a role model today. Be sure to include an image of this person. Share the information with your group.

Name/Title: _____

Best-known saying: _____

_____

Insider info: _____

_____

What makes him or her a role model:

_____

_____

_____

_____

_____

What qualities do the role models chosen by your group have?

In this chapter we learn about ecumenism, the communion of saints, and the role of Mary, Mother of God, in the Church. Through this chapter, we hope

 to respect the faiths of others and to rejoice in what we share with people of other Christian faith communities

 to encourage one another as members of the Church, the Body of Christ, joined in the communion of saints

 to honor Mary as the Church's greatest saint and the mother of all who believe in Jesus Christ.

he dictionary defines a *role model* as a person whose behavior in a particular role is imitated by others. What kinds of behavior make someone a good role model? What qualities does a good role model need to have?

Generosity
Faith
Athletic Ability
Thoughtfulness

Wealth

"A good example has twice the value of good advice." (Anonymous)

Fashion Sense   Good Looks

Helpfulness   Persistence

Kindness   Fame   Friendliness

Popularity

Self-Worth   Ambition   Prestige

Activity With your group examine each of the qualities or types of behavior named above and discuss whether each is what you would look for in a good role model.

Jesus calls all to be one.

At the Last Supper Jesus prayed to his Father for his disciples, saying, "I pray not only for them, but also for those who will believe in me through their word, so that they may all be one, as you, Father, are in me and I in you" (John 17:20–21). Jesus wanted his disciples, both then and now, to be one, united in God. And we can be united by belief in the one faith passed on to us through the Apostles. We can be united in worshiping God together and in celebrating the sacraments.

Governed by the successors of Peter and the Apostles, Jesus wanted us, his Church, to continue to grow and to work together on earth so that we could join him in heaven. But "in this one and only Church of God from its very beginnings there arose certain rifts . . . and large communities became separated from full communion with the Catholic Church" (*CCC*, 817). These rifts, or divisions, took place over the centuries because of the sins of humanity. These sins include **heresy**, a denial after Baptism of a truth of the faith; **apostasy**, a total abandonment of one's faith; and **schism**, the refusal to submit to the leadership of Peter's successor, the pope, or a lack of unity with the members of the Church.

Because of these rifts, Christians were no longer one. There were Catholics, Orthodox Christians, and Episcopalians. There were Lutherans, Methodists, Presbyterians, Baptists, and many others.

Despite the differences that have arisen among Christians, there are important beliefs that all Christians have in common. These include Baptism, belief in both the humanity and the divinity of Jesus, belief that Jesus died and rose to save us from sin, and belief that the Bible is the inspired word of God. Yet the differences among Christians are still serious; and, because the separation has gone on for centuries, achieving Christian unity will take time. But the Catholic Church is committed to the work of **ecumenism**, the work to promote the unity of all Christians. The Church respects all Christians, sees the goodness in other Christian communities, and works with other Christian communities to bring about the unity of the Church.

Faith Words
heresy
apostasy
schism
ecumenism

As Catholics we pray for Christian unity at every Mass. And each year in January we celebrate a week of prayer for Christian unity. Prayer services and discussion groups are held. Together, we ask God that we may be one, as Christ called us to be.

Activity With a partner discuss what you know about the beliefs of Christians who are not Catholic. Then discuss the beliefs that we all share.

An ecumenical community

In France there is an international community of religious brothers known as Taizé. They are committed to ecumenism and unity. Since 1940 more than a hundred brothers—members of the Catholic Church and of other Christian churches who come from more than twenty-five nations—have lived at Taizé peacefully together. Roger Schutz, their founder, who died in 2005, was a religious brother known to most people as simply "Brother Roger."

Taizé's members work and pray for reconciliation, trust, and peace among all the peoples on earth. Their church, known as the Church of Reconciliation, brings together leaders and laypeople from Christian churches worldwide to pray and give praise to God. Since the 1950s thousands of young people from around the world have found their way to Taizé to participate in weekly prayer and reflection. Taizé has also become known for producing beautiful music and for coordinating meetings with people of other nations to encourage harmony and unity.

What is one way that your group can encourage harmony and unity?

As the Body of Christ, the Church, we help each other to live as disciples.

When we live as disciples of Jesus and faithful members of the Church, we live as the image of God that we were created to be, giving witness to God's presence in the world. We become living examples of God's love to everyone we meet. But to live as Jesus' disciples, we always need the help and support of other disciples. We need their example, their solidarity with us, and their encouragement to carry us along. All of this comes through the Church community. In the Church as baptized witnesses and believers, we pray for and encourage one another to live the faith that we all profess.

As Saint Thomas Aquinas said, "Since all the faithful form one body, the good of each is communicated to the others. . . . But the most important member is Christ, since he is the head. . . . Therefore, the riches of Christ are communicated to all the members, through the sacraments" (*CCC*, 947). Through our Baptism, and in all the other sacraments, especially the Eucharist, this unity, this communion in holy things and among holy people, binds us to Jesus Christ and to one another.

The Church, from the beginning, has honored martyrs, who died heroically for their faith in Jesus Christ, and all other saints who lived lives of holiness on earth and now share in the joy of eternal life with God. Because the saints are closely united to Christ, they pray for us, constantly helping the Church to grow in holiness. Their love for the Church is great. Other holy men and women were also friends and servants of God. The lives of all these people are examples for us. Together we are all joined in the *communion of saints*, all praying for one another. The **communion of saints** is the union of all the baptized members of the Church:

- *on earth*—These members respond to God's grace by living a good moral life, remaining in God's friendship, and becoming role models for one another.

- *in heaven*—These members lived lives of holiness on earth and now share in the joy of eternal life with God.

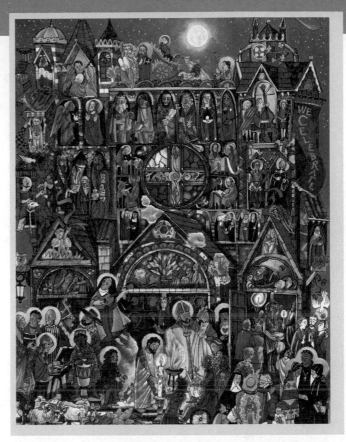

A Celebration of Saints by Brother Michael O'Neill McGrath

- *in purgatory*—These members are preparing for heaven, growing in the holiness necessary to enjoy the happiness of heaven.

Everything that each member does affects every other member. We on earth are strengthened by the example of the saints. The writings that they have left us and the prayers that they pray for us support us. We on earth also pray for one another, both for members of the Church on earth and for those in purgatory, that we may enter into eternal life with God just as the saints have done. Within the communion of saints, there is a treasury of prayers and good works, helping us to spread God's Kingdom here on earth and helping us to look forward to the fullness of the Kingdom in heaven.

> **"Since all the faithful form one body, the good of each is communicated to the others."**
> (CCC, 947)

Faith Word
communion of saints

Activity On a separate sheet of paper write a prayer expressing our unity within the communion of saints. Share these with your group.

Marian shrines

Many countries have shrines dedicated to Mary. Shrines are special places of prayer and devotion visited by millions of people on pilgrimages.

The national shrine of Our Lady of Czestochowa is in Poland. It contains an icon of Mary known as "The Black Madonna." Over the centuries the people of Poland have often turned to her in prayer, asking for her help and protection from invading armies.

A shrine dedicated to Our Lady of La Vang is in Vietnam. It honors Mary for her help and intercession during a time in Vietnam when the king had ordered the destruction of all the Catholic churches in the country.

There is a beautiful shrine called Our Lady of Africa, Mother of All Graces, in Abidjan in Africa. It reminds people of the hope and love that Jesus brings to us. Inside the shrine, a statue carved of wood shows Mary standing with the child Jesus in her arms.

There are many more shrines to Mary. Some more well-known ones include those in Fatima, Portugal and Lourdes, France. Learn about the shrines to Mary that exist in the world.

Our Lady of Czestochowa (Black Madonna), Byzantine icon

CATHOLIC IDENTITY

Mary is the perfect example of discipleship.

How are you encouraged by the example of the saints?

Ever since Jesus first preached his message of love, people have followed him. From the very beginning of the Church, Christ's disciples have given witness to their faith in him. Some of these disciples were inspired by the Holy Spirit to record their stories in the New Testament. These stories tell us of many disciples who came to believe in Jesus and follow him. But among all of Jesus' disciples, Mary, his mother, is the perfect example of discipleship. She is also Jesus' first and most faithful disciple, believing in him from the moment that God asked her to be the mother of his Son.

What we know about Mary comes from the Gospels. We first learn about her at the Annunciation, as she is told that God has chosen her to be the mother of his Son. Even then, Mary's words "Behold, I am the handmaid of the Lord. May it be done to me according to your word" (Luke 1:38) show her faithfulness to God and her openness to his loving and saving plan. Throughout her life Mary continues in her faithfulness to God, loving and caring for Jesus as a child and as a young man, and supporting Jesus throughout his ministry. Mary even stood with her son as he died on the cross, her faith never weakening even during this time of the greatest suffering and loss for her as a mother. After Jesus' death and Resurrection, Mary waited in prayer and with hope for the coming of the Holy Spirit.

From the moment of her conception, God blessed Mary. Never stained by sin, Mary had a pure heart and lived a life of holiness. She made possible the salvation that God had planned for all of humanity by physically bringing Jesus into our midst. And at the end of her earthly work, God blessed Mary in an extraordinary way. He brought her body and soul to live forever with the risen Jesus. This event is known as Mary's **Assumption**. It is celebrated as a special feast and often is marked as a holy day of obligation by the Church. As it is stated in the *Catechism,* "The Assumption of the Blessed Virgin is a singular participation in her Son's Resurrection and an anticipation of the resurrection of other Christians" (966).

As members of the communion of saints, looking forward to the glory that we will someday share with God—the Father, Son, and Holy Spirit—we look to Mary for our example of faithful discipleship. Like Mary we are called to live in openness to God's loving and saving plan for us. Along with Mary and all the other holy men and women in the Church who have answered Jesus' call to discipleship, we await the day on which we will rise to life everlasting.

Faith Word
Assumption

Activity Write a cinquain about Mary.

Mary is the Church's greatest saint.

The Church honors Mary as the greatest of all the saints and shows love for Mary through special devotions to her under her many titles. Yet these devotions differ "essentially from the . . . adoration which is offered to the Incarnate Word, as well as to the Father and Holy Spirit" (*Dogmatic Constitution on the Church*, 66). In our prayer to Mary, while we express our love for her, we pray to her to ask her to pray to God for us: to intercede for us and speak to God on our behalf.

Mary's titles, like the titles of the mysteries of the rosary, help us to understand her role in our lives and in the life of the Church.

Blessed Virgin
We learn from the Annunciation account that Mary was not yet married when the angel visited her. She was a virgin. Her son was conceived by the power of the Holy Spirit. Mary was truly blessed by God with the gift of his Son. Because Mary remained a virgin throughout her life, we often call her the Blessed Virgin, the Blessed Virgin Mary, and the Blessed Mother.

Mother of God
As the mother of Jesus, Mary went through the joys of being pregnant and having a baby. She cared for her son, loved him, prayed with him, and was an example of love and obedience to God. However, her son, truly divine as well as truly human, is the Son of God, the second Person of the Blessed Trinity who became man. Mary, therefore, is the Mother of God.

Mother of the Church
Mary is Jesus' mother. As Jesus was dying on the cross, he saw his mother and his disciple John at his feet. Jesus said to Mary, "Woman, behold, your son" (John 19:26). He said to John, "Behold, your mother" (John 19:27). Mary is the mother of all those who believe in and follow Jesus Christ. Thus, Mary is the Mother of the Church and our mother, too.

In its prayer and liturgy, and especially in the Eucharist, the Church remembers and celebrates special times in Mary's life as the mother of the Son of God. Here are some of the feast days on which the Church celebrates Mary:

January 1—The Blessed Virgin Mary, the Mother of God

February 11—Our Lady of Lourdes

March 25—The Annunciation of the Lord

May 31—The Visitation of the Blessed Virgin Mary

July 16—Our Lady of Mount Carmel

August 15—The Assumption of the Blessed Virgin Mary

August 22—The Queenship of the Blessed Virgin Mary

September 8—The Nativity of the Blessed Virgin Mary

September 15—Our Lady of Sorrows

December 8—Immaculate Conception of the Blessed Virgin Mary

December 12—Our Lady of Guadalupe

There are many more feasts and titles for Mary. We hear some of these titles when we pray a litany of Mary. The word *litany* comes from the Greek word for "prayer." Litanies of Mary are made up of a list of Mary's titles, each followed by a short request for her help. Litanies of Mary give praise to God for making a humble young woman the mother of his Son and of the Church.

> **"Behold, your mother."**
> (John 19:27)

Along with the litany and the rosary, there are many other popular devotions to Mary, including novenas, cultural celebrations, and pilgrimages. In all these ways we can celebrate Mary, for she is our mother, too.

Activity Use Mary's titles to complete this litany of Mary.

Leader:	All:
Holy Mary,	pray for us.
Holy Mother of God,	pray for us.
_____,	pray for us.
_____,	pray for us.
_____,	pray for us.
_____,	pray for us.
Pray for us, O glorious Mother of the Lord,	that we may become worthy of the promises of Christ.

RESPONDING...

Recognizing Our Faith

Recall the question at the beginning of this chapter: *Who are my role models?* Having learned all that you have in this chapter, make another trading card highlighting someone you would now choose as a role model. How will you follow this person's example?

Name/Title: _____

Best-known saying: _____

_____

Insider info: _____

_____

What makes him or her a role model:

_____

_____

_____

_____

Living Our Faith

Every day this week, pray the prayer you wrote on page 249, expressing the unity of the communion of saints.

Venerable Catherine McAuley

Catherine McAuley was born in 1778 in Dublin, Ireland. Orphaned at an early age, Catherine and her siblings went to live with Protestant relatives. This arrangement was difficult at times due to Catherine's strong Catholic faith, a faith for which her father had been a great role model. She began working for a wealthy family and devoted her spare time to helping others. The wealthy family acknowledged Catherine's good works and they left her a generous inheritance. This allowed her to educate and provide protection to children and women in need of social services.

In 1827, on the feast of Our Lady of Mercy, Catherine opened the "House of Mercy" in Dublin. It eventually evolved into a religious order known as the Sisters of Mercy. The Sisters of Mercy committed their lives to educating disadvantaged girls, giving shelter and assistance to women in peril, and helping people in need. Catherine's work influenced many people. She was a prayerful person committed to serving God. She died on November 11, 1841. Today, the Sisters of Mercy continue her good works.

In what ways is Catherine McAuley a good role model?

 For additional ideas and activities, visit www.weliveourfaith.com.

Putting Faith to Work

Talk about what you have learned in this chapter:

 We respect the faiths of others and rejoice in what we share with people of other Christian faith communities.

 We encourage one another as members of the Church, the Body of Christ, joined in the communion of saints.

 We honor Mary as the Church's greatest saint and the mother of all who believe in Jesus Christ.

Decide on ways to live out what you have learned.

✝ ENCOUNTERING GOD'S WORD

At a wedding in Cana, Mary saw that the wine had run out. After speaking with Jesus, Mary told the servers:

"Do whatever he tells you"
(John 2:5).

➡ **READ** the quotation from Scripture.

➡ **REFLECT** on the following:
Jesus did not tell Mary what he was going to do. Why do you think she was so confident that he would do something to help? Do you remember what happened next? You can read John 2:1–12 for the full story.

➡ **SHARE** your reflections with a partner.

➡ **DECIDE** to ask Mary to speak with Jesus for you the next time you are in need.

Write *True* or *False* next to the following sentences. On a separate sheet of paper, change the false sentences to make them true.

1. _____ Mary was Jesus' first and most faithful disciple.

2. _____ The communion of saints is the union of all the baptized members of the Church on earth.

3. _____ The Catholic Church is committed to the work of ecumenism, the work to promote the unity of all Christians.

4. _____ The word *litany* comes from the Greek word for "title."

Short Answers

1. What beliefs do all Christians share? _____
_____

2. What is the role of saints in the Church? _____
_____

3. Explain the event known as the Assumption of Mary. _____
_____

4. The Church honors Mary as the greatest of all saints and shows devotion to her through many titles.
Name three titles for Mary. _____

9–10. ESSAY: Use what you have learned in this chapter to explain this statement: *Jesus calls all to be one.*

Sharing Faith with Your Family

Discuss the following with your family:

- Jesus calls all to be one.
- As the Body of Christ, the Church, we help each other to live as disciples.
- Mary is the perfect example of discipleship.
- Mary is the Church's greatest saint.

Together, name the saints, holy people, or your own loved ones who have died whose examples have great meaning for you. Make a spiritual "family tree" using the people you've named. Together, compose a prayer asking for their help and intercession.

The Worship Connection

In every Eucharist we pray for the entire Church, on earth and in heaven. We pray, "In mercy and love unite all your children wherever they may be" (Eucharistic Prayer III). Listen for these words this Sunday at Mass.

More to Explore

Research pilgrimages and shrines dedicated to saints around the world. Share your findings.

Catholic Social Teaching ☑ Checklist

Theme of Catholic Social Teaching:
Solidarity of the Human Family

How it relates to Chapter 23: As Catholics, we believe that all people form one human family. To show solidarity we can pray for everyone in the world.

How can you do this?

☐ At home:

_____

☐ At school/work:

_____

☐ In the parish:

_____

☐ In the community:

_____

Check off each action after it has been completed.

GATHERING...

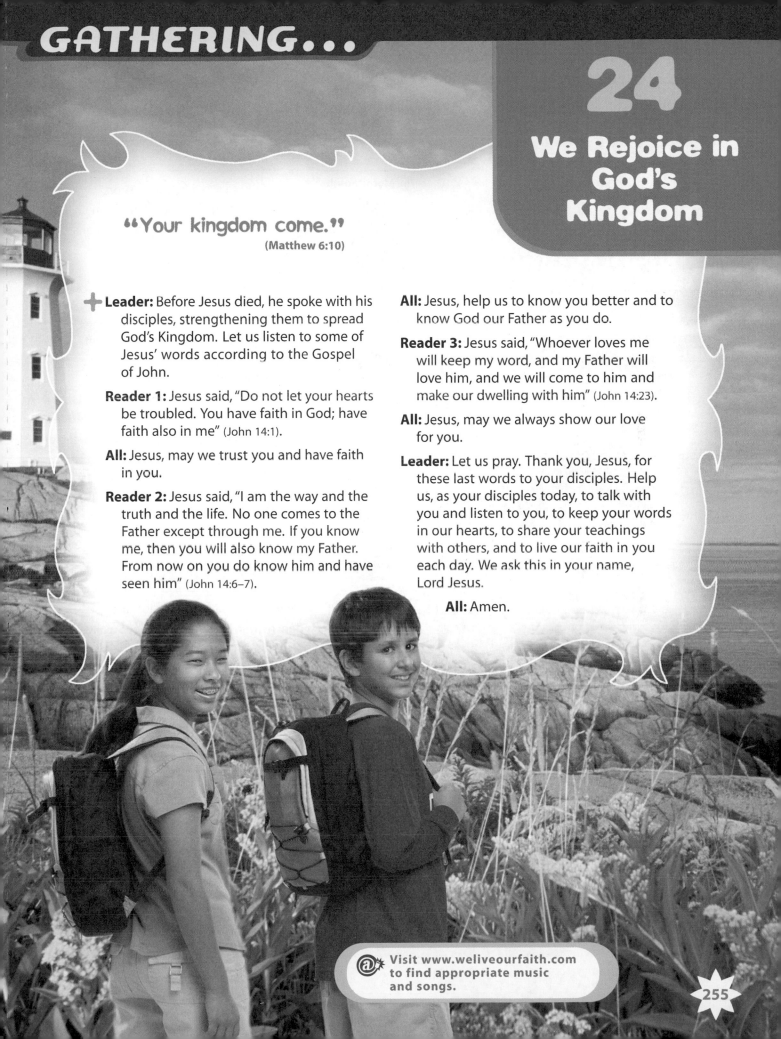

24
We Rejoice in God's Kingdom

"Your kingdom come."
(Matthew 6:10)

✚ **Leader:** Before Jesus died, he spoke with his disciples, strengthening them to spread God's Kingdom. Let us listen to some of Jesus' words according to the Gospel of John.

Reader 1: Jesus said, "Do not let your hearts be troubled. You have faith in God; have faith also in me" (John 14:1).

All: Jesus, may we trust you and have faith in you.

Reader 2: Jesus said, "I am the way and the truth and the life. No one comes to the Father except through me. If you know me, then you will also know my Father. From now on you do know him and have seen him" (John 14:6–7).

All: Jesus, help us to know you better and to know God our Father as you do.

Reader 3: Jesus said, "Whoever loves me will keep my word, and my Father will love him, and we will come to him and make our dwelling with him" (John 14:23).

All: Jesus, may we always show our love for you.

Leader: Let us pray. Thank you, Jesus, for these last words to your disciples. Help us, as your disciples today, to talk with you and listen to you, to keep your words in our hearts, to share your teachings with others, and to live our faith in you each day. We ask this in your name, Lord Jesus.

All: Amen.

@ **Visit www.weliveourfaith.com to find appropriate music and songs.**

255

The BiG Question:

Whom do I confide in?

 Discover four different styles of communicating. The way we communicate may influence whether or not others confide in us.

The Motormouth

- views talking as an "extreme sport"
- enjoys being the center of attention
- never holds back any feelings, opinions, or wants
- talks regardless of whether others are listening
- is not very good at keeping secrets

The Silent One

- views facial expressions as "the secret to all communication"
- shies away from the spotlight
- withholds feelings, opinions, and wants
- spends a lot of time listening and observing
- rarely disagrees with others or reveals secrets

The Interrupter

- views arguments as a "favorite pastime"
- likes to look smarter than the next guy
- states feelings, opinions, and wants in a bold way
- rarely lets others complete a sentence
- always wants the last word

The Assertive One

- views conversations as a "lost art"
- doesn't mind the spotlight, but really just wants to be heard and understood by others
- openly states feelings, opinions, and wants, but in a respectful way
- listens considerately to others' ideas
- can disagree in a tactful way

Discuss each type of communicator above. Which do you most identify with? What does each tell you about the importance of listening and talking?

In this chapter we learn that prayer opens our minds and hearts to God and strengthens us to share God's love and God's Kingdom with others. Through this chapter, we hope

 to explore the many forms of prayer through which human beings have expressed their faith and trust in God over the centuries

 to reflect prayerfully on the ways God has acted in our own lives

 to share God's love and our rich tradition of faithful prayer with others.

Do you usually feel better after confiding your troubles to a trusted friend? The need to confide in others seems to be a natural part of who we are as human beings. In fact, medical studies have shown that people with cancer who participate in group therapy have higher rates of recovery.

Having supportive companionship and people we can talk to can have even more benefits. It may lower our blood pressure, heart rate, and cholesterol. And confiding in a friend can help counteract or lessen the anxiety we experience on a daily basis—whether due to issues at school, family matters, or worldwide dilemmas such as poverty and war.

In any case, the simple act of releasing our thoughts and worries to a friend is enough to ease stress and make us feel better. And when that friend can provide valuable feedback to us, confiding in someone becomes all the more worthwhile.

Activity How do you know whom to confide in? Make a list of five qualities that a trustworthy friend should have.

"Put more trust in nobility of character than in an oath," said Solon, a Greek statesman who lived before the time of Christ.

BELIEVING...

We open our hearts to God.

As members of the Church, we not only believe in and celebrate the mystery of our faith, but we live it "in a vital and personal relationship with the living and true God. This relationship is prayer" (*CCC*, 2558). Through prayer, both public and private, we can draw everything in our lives into Christ's love.

Prayer is the raising of our minds and hearts to God. It is like a conversation: God calls to us in prayer, and we respond. Our prayer is a response to God's constant love for us. We listen to what God has to say to us, and we trust in him. We share our thoughts, dreams, and needs with God. We tell God what is happening in our lives, and we know that he is listening.

We can pray in the silence of our hearts, or we can pray aloud. We can pray alone or with others. We can even sing our prayer. Sometimes we do not use words to pray, but sit quietly, trying to focus only on God. But however we pray, we turn to God with hope and faith in his love for us. We rely on him for guidance and direction. We ask God to help us to follow his will. And we trust that he will help us to know his will for us.

Humility, the virtue that enables us to acknowledge that God is the source of all good, is the foundation of prayer. Humility is the "poverty of spirit" that Jesus calls us to in the Beatitudes. Through humility we are able to recognize God's will for us in the depths of our own hearts and souls. Thus, humility enables us to live in a way that brings about the best of everything for everyone. As Jesus tells us, the Kingdom already belongs to those who are "poor in spirit" (Matthew 5:3).

In prayer we open our minds and hearts to God. "According to Scripture, it is the *heart* that prays. If our heart is far from God, the words of prayer are in vain . . . . The heart is our hidden center . . . . The heart is the place of decision . . . . It is the place of truth . . . . It is the place of encounter, because as image of God we live in relation: it is the place of covenant" (*CCC*, 2562–2563).

> **"According to Scripture, it is the *heart* that prays."**
> (*CCC*, 2562)

So, prayer is our covenant with God in Christ through the Holy Spirit; prayer makes possible our union with Christ and with the Church. And this covenant helps us to live as Jesus did, serving others and inviting them to hear the good news of salvation. Thus, the life and mission of Jesus continue through each one of us—through Jesus' disciples who share God's love and spread God's Kingdom until he comes again in glory at the end of time.

Faith Words
prayer
humility

Activity What was the first prayer that you learned and from whom did you learn it? Is this person an influence on how and when you pray today? Why or why not?

God has always called people to prayer.

Throughout humanity's history, from creation to our present day, God has continued to reveal himself to us and call us to "that mysterious encounter known as prayer. In prayer, God's initiative of love always comes first; our own first step is always a response. As God gradually reveals himself and reveals man to himself, prayer appears as a reciprocal call" (CCC, 2567).

In Jesus Christ, the Son of God, we receive the full revelation of prayer. The prayer that the Father had expected from humankind is prayed by Christ for all of us, and the working of the Holy Spirit is revealed throughout Christ's ministry. Jesus' whole life is a prayer to his Father, and Jesus' prayer is evident to us through Scripture at many significant moments throughout his lifetime: times of blessing, decision, happiness, sorrow, healing and comfort, forgiveness, and thanksgiving and praise.

Jesus also prayed before two very significant events at which his Father gave witness to him: his baptism and his Transfiguration. By his baptism Jesus accepted his Father's will and consented to all that the salvation of humanity would mean for him. In great delight at his Son's acceptance of this mission of salvation, God the Father responded, letting all those present know, "This is my beloved Son, with whom I am well pleased" (Matthew 3:17). And the Spirit came upon Jesus, letting it be known that the Spirit is ever present in the Son of God.

Then, at his Transfiguration, for a brief moment Jesus' divine glory was seen by Peter, James, and John, and the Blessed Trinity was revealed, giving the three Apostles a preview of the Kingdom.

Each day the risen Jesus continues to be with us through prayer, and God continues to be active in our lives as Father, Son, and Holy Spirit. In our prayer and in the liturgy—especially in the Mass—we can rejoice continually in God's Kingdom, which is present now and will come in fullness at the end of time.

Activity How does prayer fit into your life now? What do you consider to be your "favorite" prayer? Discuss your responses.

Three ways of praying

"The Christian tradition comprises three major expressions of the life of prayer: vocal prayer, meditation, and contemplative prayer." (CCC, 2721)

Vocal prayer is prayer we pray aloud, often with others. The rosary is an example of vocal prayer. The prayers we pray at Mass and during the Liturgy of the Hours are vocal prayer. If we think about what we are saying, vocal prayer penetrates our minds and hearts so that we pray what we mean and mean what we pray. If we pray with sincerity, vocal prayer can lead to *meditation* and *contemplation*.

Meditation involves "thought, imagination, emotion, and desire" (CCC, 2723). Usually it begins with a reading from Scripture or a spiritual book. When we meditate, we can pray certain words or verses over and over until our very thoughts become a prayer. Or we can reflect on the reading for insights into our own situation. The reading can help us to find God's way amid the choices we face each day. Meditation, too, can lead to contemplation.

Contemplation is "a gaze of faith fixed on Jesus, an attentiveness to the Word of God, a silent love" (CCC, 2724). Contemplation is wordless prayer. It is an awareness of God's presence that can last half a minute, half an hour, half a day, or a whole lifetime. It is a gift from God that can come to anyone who seeks God and is open to God's love. A great contemplative, Saint Teresa of Ávila, used to urge her Carmelite sisters to seek God everywhere; even "among the pots and pans."

How do you seek God? Where do you find him?

BELIEVING...

We pray in many ways.

Do I take the time to pray each day?

Jesus taught us to pray with patience and with complete trust in God. He taught us to pray by showing us how he prayed. Jesus prayed in many circumstances and in many ways. Jesus praised God and thanked him for his blessings. Jesus asked God to be with him and to act on his behalf. Jesus prayed for the needs of others. Jesus forgave sinners in the name of his Father. Even as he was dying, Jesus prayed, "Father, forgive them, they know not what they do" (Luke 23:34).

So, from the example and words of Jesus, and most especially from the Lord's Prayer, we learn to pray. Whenever we pray, we show God our love—through our thoughts, our words, our actions, and even our feelings and senses. Urged by the Holy Spirit, we pray these basic forms of prayer: *blessing, petition, intercession, thanksgiving,* and *praise.*

BLESSING

"The grace of the Lord Jesus Christ and the love of God and the fellowship of the holy Spirit be with all of you." (2 Corinthians 13:13)

To **bless** is to dedicate someone or something to God or to make something holy in God's name. God continually blesses us with many gifts. Because God first blessed us, we can pray for his blessings on people and things.

PETITION

"O God, be merciful to me a sinner." (Luke 18:13)

Prayers of **petition** are prayers in which we ask something of God. Asking for forgiveness is the most important type of petition.

INTERCESSION

"And this is my prayer: that your love may increase ever more and more in knowledge." (Philippians 1:9)

Intercession is a type of petition. When we pray a prayer of **intercession**, we are asking for something on behalf of another person or a group of people.

THANKSGIVING

"Father, I thank you for hearing me." (John 11:41)

Prayers of **thanksgiving** show our gratitude to God for all he has given us. We show our gratitude most especially for the life, death, and Resurrection of Jesus. We do this when we pray the greatest prayer of the Church, the Eucharist.

PRAISE

"I shall praise the LORD all my life,
sing praise to my God while I live." (Psalm 146:2)

Prayers of **praise** give glory to God for being God. Prayers of praise do not involve our needs or our gratitude. We praise God simply because he is God.

Faith Words

bless
petition
intercession
thanksgiving
praise

Activity In groups, on separate sheets of paper, write five prayers, one in each form of prayer explained above.

We pray always.

Saint Paul wrote to the early Christian communities, "Pray without ceasing" (1 Thessalonians 5:17). We do this, too, calling on God constantly, through personal prayer and communal prayer. We can develop the habit of daily prayer, setting aside special times for prayer, when each morning we offer our entire day to God; before and after meals we thank God for his many gifts; and at night we reflect on the ways we have shown love for God and others. Each day we can also pray prayers of the Church, such as the Our Father and the Hail Mary, use our own words to pray, or reflect in silence on God's love and presence in our lives.

The habit of daily prayer also grows as we join in prayer with other members of the Church. We do this when we gather with the People of God for the celebration of the Mass. But we also can do this by praying the Liturgy of the Hours. The **Liturgy of the Hours** is the official public prayer of the Church made up of psalms, other readings from Scripture and Church teaching, prayers, and hymns. It is celebrated at various times during the day and helps us to praise God throughout the entire day, thereby reminding us that God is always active and present in our lives.

Over and over again, through all of our prayer, we can make the commitment to be disciples of Jesus and to live for God's Kingdom. This is a lifelong commitment because we are never "finished" growing in holiness in this life. To sustain us in this commitment, God gives us his grace. And as members of the Church, through God the Father, Son, and Holy Spirit, we strive to share God's love and spread his Kingdom together until the end of time.

Faith Word
Liturgy of the Hours

Activity In a booklet combine the prayers you wrote for the activity on page 260. Pray them throughout the year.

> "Father, I thank you for hearing me."
> (John 11:41)

Constant prayer

At every moment of every day, the Church is at prayer. In addition to the daily Eucharist in thousands of churches all over the world, Catholics gather for other forms of community prayer, one of which is the Liturgy of the Hours. It is the prayer of the entire Church, even when prayed by one person.

Catholics also gather for Eucharistic adoration. Though this takes place outside the celebration of the Mass, Jesus' presence in the Eucharist continues to be honored. After Holy Communion the remaining consecrated Hosts—the Most Blessed Sacrament—are placed, or reserved, in the tabernacle. The Most Blessed Sacrament, or the Eucharist, can be brought to those who are sick and unable to participate in the Mass. But we can also show Jesus our love and continue the thanksgiving that was begun at Mass by visiting and praying to him present in the Most Blessed Sacrament.

Many parishes have an Exposition of the Most Blessed Sacrament. In this ceremony the Most Blessed Sacrament is placed in a special holder called a *monstrance* and presented for all to see. In a devotion called *Benediction*, the community gathers to pray and to worship Jesus in the Most Blessed Sacrament. All who are gathered are blessed by the Real Presence of Christ in the Eucharist.

Though not part of the liturgy of the Church, *popular devotions* express ways that people of many different cultures and traditions may pray. They are a rich and diverse tradition and have been handed down to us through the centuries. These devotions include the stations of the cross, pilgrimages (journeys to shrines and other holy places), and processions in honor of Mary or the saints. These devotions draw us into the mystery of Christ among us.

Make your plan to pray constantly!

CATHOLIC IDENTITY

261

Recognizing Our Faith

Recall the question at the beginning of this chapter: *Whom do I confide in?* In what way does what you have learned in this chapter help you to confide in God more fully? What would you say to encourage a friend to confide in God through prayer?

Living Our Faith

Choose a specific time each day to pray.

Saint Teresa de Los Andes

The life of Saint Teresa de Los Andes (Teresa of the Andes) shows how powerful prayer can be. Born in 1900 in Santiago, Chile, and named Juanita, she was one of five children. She enjoyed many vacations at a family estate during her youth and wrote about her experiences. Encouraged by her brother, who taught her to pray the rosary, Juanita began to pray the rosary daily. She continued to strengthen her faith by praying, going to Mass, and trying to live a simpler way of life. She taught local children about Catholicism and organized help for the needy, and she even started a choir.

In 1919 Juanita decided to become a religious sister. She entered Carmel of the Andes, a Carmelite convent, and took the name Teresa de Jesús (Teresa of Jesus). She wrote in her diary that she wanted to devote her whole life to prayer and penance. At the age of nineteen, she faced a fatal illness with courage and trust in God. When she died in 1920, she had influenced so many people with her prayerful life that they flooded the convent chapel for her funeral. She was canonized in 1993—the first saint of Chile.

What are some ways you can encourage others to pray?

 For additional ideas and activities, visit www.weliveourfaith.com.

Putting Faith to Work

Talk about what you have learned in this chapter:

 We explore the many forms of prayer through which human beings have expressed their faith and trust in God over the centuries.

 We reflect prayerfully on the ways God has acted in our own lives.

We share God's love and our rich tradition of faithful prayer with others.

Decide on ways to live out what you have learned.

✝ ENCOUNTERING GOD'S WORD

❝ Then he [Jesus] told them a parable about the necessity for them to pray always without becoming weary. ❞

(Luke 18:1)

➡ **READ** the quotation from Scripture.

➡ **REFLECT** on these questions:
Why would "becoming weary" be a problem in prayer? How can we approach prayer with more faith and perseverance?

➡ **SHARE** your reflections with a partner.

➡ **DECIDE** to read Jesus' parable in Luke 18:1–8 and to pray as this parable teaches.

Circle the letter of the correct answer.

1. Which virtue is the foundation of prayer?

   a. hope   **b.** humility   **c.** faith   **d.** chastity

2. Prayers of _____ give glory to God for being God and do not involve our needs or our gratitude.

   a. praise   **b.** intercession   **c.** blessing   **d.** petition

3. Prayers of _____ are a type of petition in which we ask for something on behalf of another person or group of people.

   a. praise   **b.** intercession   **c.** thanksgiving   **d.** blessing

4. Prayers of _____ show our gratitude to God for all he has given us, most especially for the life, death, and Resurrection of Jesus.

   a. praise   **b.** intercession   **c.** thanksgiving   **d.** petition

Complete the following.

5. _____ is the raising of our hearts and minds to God.

6. From the example and words of Jesus, and most especially from the _____, we learn to pray.

7. Jesus prayed before two very significant events at which his Father gave witness to him—his _____ and his _____.

8. Prayers of _____ are prayers in which we ask something of God.

9–10. ESSAY: Why is it important to develop the habit of daily prayer?

Chapter 24 Assessment

263

Sharing Faith with Your Family

Discuss the following with your family:
- We open our hearts to God.
- God has always called people to prayer.
- We pray in many ways.
- We pray always.

Look at the prayers you wrote in this chapter. Each week, pray one of them together as a family. You may even want to write some prayers together and compile them in a Family Prayer Book. Then pray them together often!

The Worship Connection

The next time you participate in the Eucharist, sincerely pray each petition of the Lord's Prayer, the prayer that Jesus taught us.

More to Explore

Using the Internet, research prayer sites that offer tips and opportunities for prayer, and sites sponsored by religious orders devoted to prayer.

Catholic Social Teaching ☑ Checklist

Theme of Catholic Social Teaching:
Life and Dignity of the Human Person

How it relates to Chapter 24: God loves all of his children and gave us basic worth and dignity. Through prayer we deepen our relationship with God and show our respect for all people.

How can you do this?

☐ At home:

_____

☐ At school/work:

_____

☐ In the parish:

_____

☐ In the community:

_____

Check off each action after it has been completed.

Write the letter of the answer that best defines each term.

1. _____ marks of the Church

2. _____ prayer

3. _____ human dignity

4. _____ vows

5. _____ almsgiving

6. _____ ecumenism

7. _____ bless

8. _____ common good

9. _____ virtue

10. _____ common vocation

a. the sharing of our resources or time to help those who are poor or in need

b. to dedicate someone or something to God or to make something holy in God's name

c. opposing every form of injustice in society and working to promote justice for all people

d. the teaching of the Church that calls all members to work for justice and peace as Jesus did

e. the raising of our minds and hearts to God

f. the well-being of every individual person and of the whole society to which everyone belongs

g. a good habit that helps us to act according to God's love for us

h. deliberate and free promises made to God

i. the work to promote the unity of all Christians

j. the four characteristics of the Church: one, holy, catholic, and apostolic

k. the value and worth that we share because God created us in his image and likeness

l. our call from God to holiness and to evangelization

Write *True* or *False* next to the following sentences. Then, on the lines provided, change the false sentences to make them true.

11. _____ The Works of Mercy are acts of love by which we care for the bodily and spiritual needs of others.

_____

_____

12. _____ As disciples of Jesus, we cannot allow unjust conditions to exist without taking a stand against them.

_____

_____

13. _____ In the event known as the Annunciation, God blessed Mary by bringing her body and soul to live forever with the risen Jesus.

_____

_____

14. _____ The New Law is the name that we give to the body of laws that govern the Church.

_____

_____

Complete the following.

15. The communion of saints is the union of all the baptized members of the Church on _____, in _____, and in _____.

16. The basic forms of prayer are _____,

_____, _____,

_____, and _____.

17. God calls each of us to live out our common vocation in one of the particular vocations: _____, _____,

or _____.

18. The theological virtues of _____,

_____, and _____ have God

as their source, motive, and object.

Respond to the following.

19. Explain the message that Jesus emphasizes in the parable of the Good Samaritan, and suggest some ways that we can live out this message today.

_____

_____

_____

_____

20. Use what you have learned in this unit to answer the question: *How does the Church live as the Body of Christ?*

_____

_____

_____

_____

ALTERNATIVE ASSESSMENT

Write a pledge stating ways that you will live as a disciple of Jesus Christ and member of the Church. Remember to sign and date your pledge.

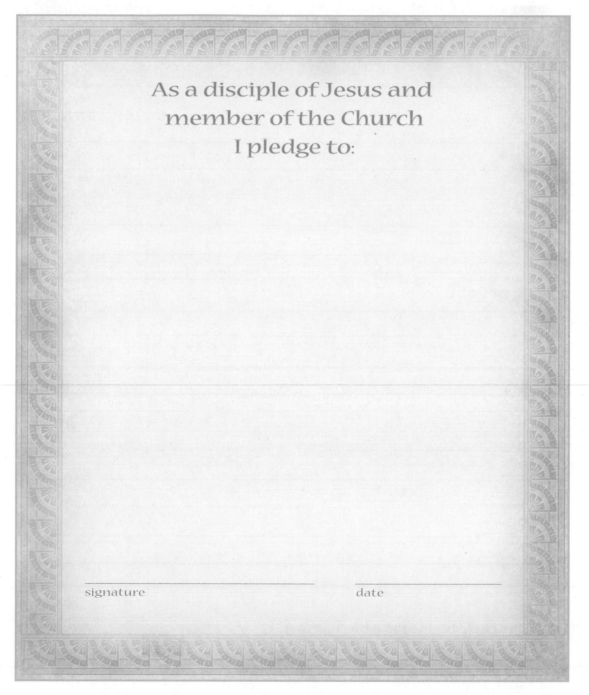

As a disciple of Jesus and
member of the Church
I pledge to:

_____   _____
signature   date

From time to time, look back at your pledge to remind yourself of the ways you have decided to live out your commitment to be a disciple of Christ and member of the Church.

Choose ten Faith Words from the box and write the definition for each.

epistles	Liturgy of the Hours	vocation	Real Presence
Kingdom of God	chrism	sanctifying grace	sacrament
ecumenism	human dignity	communion of saints	virtue
liturgy	Catholic social teaching	mortal sin	catechumenate

1. _____

_____

2. _____

_____

3. _____

_____

4. _____

_____

5. _____

_____

6. _____

_____

7. _____

_____

8. _____

_____

9. _____

_____

10. _____

_____

Fill in the circle beside the correct answer.

11. A major theme of _____ Gospel is that Jesus Christ is the *Word of God* who became a human being and lived among us.

    ○ Matthew's   ○ Mark's   ○ Luke's   ○ John's

12. _____ is the gift from God that enables us to believe in God, to accept all that he has revealed, and to respond with love for God and others.

    ○ Faith   ○ Humility   ○ Hope   ○ Chastity

13. The word *Messiah* comes from a Hebrew word that means "_____."

○ Anointed One   ○ happy   ○ thanksgiving   ○ One Who is Sent

14. Poverty, chastity, and obedience are called the _____.

○ evangelical counsels   ○ marks of the Church

○ theological virtues   ○ themes of Catholic social teaching

15. The accounts of Jesus' birth and childhood found in the first two chapters of the

Gospels of Matthew and Luke are called the _____.

○ synoptic   ○ infancy   ○ epistles   ○ Beatitudes
  Gospels   narratives

16. The _____ is the truth that the Son of God, the second Person of the Blessed
Trinity, became man and lived among us.

○ Pentecost   ○ Incarnation   ○ Resurrection   ○ transubstantiation

17. Faith, hope, and charity are known as the _____.

○ theological   ○ sacramentals   ○ cardinal   ○ fruits of the
  virtues   virtues   Holy Spirit

18. Feeding the hungry, visiting the sick, and sheltering the homeless are examples of

performing the _____.

○ Spiritual Works of Mercy   ○ marks of the Church

○ Corporal Works of Mercy   ○ evangelical counsels

19. The suffering, death, Resurrection, and Ascension of Jesus Christ are known as

the _____.

○ Last Supper   ○ Paschal Mystery   ○ Blessed Trinity   ○ Divine Revelation

20. _____ is God's plan for and protection of all creation.

○ Reverence   ○ Providence   ○ Covenant   ○ Blasphemy

Complete the following.

21. The main parts of the Anointing of the Sick are _____,

_____, and _____.

22. The Sacraments at the Service of Communion are _____

and _____.

23. The gifts of the Holy Spirit are _____,

_____, _____,

_____, _____,

_____, and _____.

24. As Catholics we believe in the Blessed Trinity: _____,

_____, and _____.

25. God reveals the truth, his Divine Revelation, through _____

and _____.

26. _____, _____, and

_____ are the Sacraments of Christian Initiation.

Respond to the following.

27. Choose a person from the New Testament whom you learned about this year and explain his or her role in Jesus' life.

_____

_____

_____

_____

28. Use what you have learned this year to explain the statement: *The Holy Spirit is active in God's plan for salvation.*

_____

_____

_____

_____

29. Explain the twofold message of the Great Commandment and ways to live it out.

_____

_____

_____

_____

30. To evangelize, we must know our faith and the teachings of the Church. What have you learned this year that will help you to be able to carry on the Church's mission of evangelization?

_____

_____

_____

_____

Contents

In the liturgical year, the date of Easter Sunday, the celebration of our Lord's Resurrection, depends each year on the spring equinox and the rising of the full moon. Easter Sunday follows the full moon after the spring equinox. The spring equinox is the day on which the sun crosses the equator, making day and night of equal length everywhere. Thus, the timing of Easter Sunday reminds us that our Lord's Resurrection brings light to our darkness.

Astronomers can calculate the date of the spring equinox. Looking at their calculations we find that Easter Sunday is always between March 22 and April 25. Using the date for Easter Sunday, each year's unique liturgical calendar can be determined.

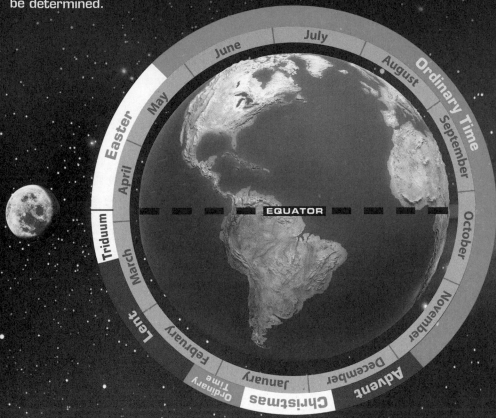

Activity As you complete each "Seasons and Celebrations" lesson, record below the dates when the Church celebrates each liturgical season this year. Then record what your group did to celebrate the season.

Advent   When: _____

What we did to celebrate: _____

_____

Christmas   When: _____

What we did to celebrate: _____

_____

Lent   When: _____

What we did to celebrate: _____

_____

Triduum   When: _____

What we did to celebrate: _____

_____

Easter   When: _____

What we did to celebrate: _____

_____

Ordinary Time When: _____

What we did to celebrate: _____

_____

"Behold, now is a very acceptable time; behold, now is the day of salvation."

(2 Corinthians 6:2)

♪ **This Is the Day**

This is the day, this is the day
that the Lord has made,
that the Lord has made;
we will rejoice, we will rejoice
and be glad in it,
and be glad in it.

This is the day that the Lord has made;
we will rejoice and be glad in it.
This is the day, this is the day
that the Lord has made.

The Liturgical Year

Some people spend a lot of time waiting for future events to make them happy. They believe that they can be happy only when they get certain things that they want, or travel to certain places, or make friends with certain people, or achieve certain other goals in their lives. But is this the way to happiness?

Activity To *rejoice* is to feel great happiness or delight over something. Recall times in your life when you have rejoiced about something on your own, with your family, or with your friends. What caused you to rejoice?

Now is the time to rejoice.

Every moment of our lives can be a time for happiness, a time to rejoice. Why? Because life itself is a gift from God, and God loves us more than we can imagine. Out of great love for us, God gave us his only Son, Jesus Christ. Jesus Christ suffered, died, rose from the dead, and ascended into heaven to save us from sin and to give us new life.

As Catholics we rejoice in the gift of God's Son every time we celebrate the liturgy. The *liturgy* is the official public prayer of the Church. The liturgy includes the celebration of the Eucharist, or Mass. The liturgy also includes the other sacraments, as well as the Liturgy of the Hours, a public prayer of the Church that is celebrated at various times during the day and night.

The Church rejoices in God's love and presence in the liturgy throughout the year. The Church year is called the liturgical year. The *liturgical year* is a sequence of specific seasons and feasts that are celebrated in the liturgy during a year's time. Examples of these seasons and feasts include Christmas, Lent, Easter, and Pentecost Sunday.

In every liturgical year we celebrate the whole life of Jesus Christ, from his Incarnation to his Resurrection, Ascension, and sending of the Holy Spirit. We celebrate his birth, his youth, his public ministry, and his Paschal Mystery—his suffering, death, Resurrection, and Ascension, through which he accomplished the work of salvation. In the liturgy and through the liturgical year, we remember and rejoice that Jesus Christ won salvation for us by his Paschal Mystery. But we do not merely remember how Jesus Christ saved us. Rather, in every liturgy, the Holy Spirit actually makes the salvation of Jesus Christ present and active in our lives.

The liturgical year is a reminder that *all* time is holy and important. By celebrating the feasts and seasons of the liturgical year, we can rejoice in the gift of all time—past, present, and future. Every moment in time is an opportunity to praise God and to give glory to God. We can praise God for his love and celebrate the life that he has given to us. We can give glory to God by trying to be aware of his loving presence at all times and by living in a way that reflects our faith in him.

Activity Identify something that you can rejoice about this day. Then write a prayer thanking God for this reason to rejoice.

We rejoice in Jesus Christ throughout the liturgical year.

The following seasons are included in the liturgical year. For each season, a specific color of vestments and decorations is used.

Advent The liturgical year begins in late November or early December with the season of Advent. Advent is the time to prepare for the celebration of Jesus' birth. Every day we can celebrate that Jesus comes into our lives. But during Advent we await Christmas, the celebration of the coming of the Son of God, Jesus Christ, and we look forward to his second coming at the end of time. The color for Advent is purple, a sign of expectation.

Christmas The Christmas season begins on Christmas Day with the celebration of the birth of the Son of God. During this entire season we celebrate that God is with us always. The color for Christmas is white, a sign of joy.

Lent The season of Lent begins on Ash Wednesday. During Lent we remember that Jesus suffered, died, and rose to new life to save us from our sins and to give us new life in the Kingdom of God. During Lent we work to grow closer to Jesus and to one another through prayer, fasting, and almsgiving. We pray for and support all who are preparing for the Sacraments of Initiation. We prepare for the Easter Triduum. The color for Lent is purple, for penance.

Triduum The Easter Triduum is the Church's greatest and most important celebration. The word *triduum* means "three days." During the three days of the Easter Triduum—from Holy Thursday evening, through Good Friday and Holy Saturday, until Easter Sunday evening—we remember and celebrate in the liturgy, with many special traditions and rituals, the suffering, death, and Resurrection of Jesus Christ. The color for Good Friday is red, for Jesus' suffering. The color for the other days of the Triduum is white.

Easter The season of Easter begins on Easter Sunday evening and continues until Pentecost Sunday. During this season we rejoice in Jesus' Resurrection and in the new life we have in Jesus Christ. We also celebrate Christ's Ascension into heaven. The color for the Easter season is white, while Pentecost's color is red and signifies the descent of the Holy Spirit upon the Apostles.

Ordinary Time The season of Ordinary Time is celebrated in two parts. The first part is between Christmas and Lent, and the second part is between Easter and Advent. During this time we celebrate the life and teachings of Jesus Christ and learn what it means to live as his disciples. The color for Ordinary Time is green, a sign of life and hope.

Each Sunday of the liturgical year is a great celebration of the Church, or a solemnity. Beyond each Sunday, there are other solemnities in the liturgical year on which we are obliged to attend Mass to give special honor to Jesus Christ for the salvation he has given to us. These are called holy days of obligation. The following are the holy days of obligation in the United States:

Solemnity of Mary, Mother of God (January 1)
Ascension (when celebrated on Thursday during the Easter Season)*
Assumption of Mary (August 15)
All Saints' Day (November 1)
Immaculate Conception (December 8)
Christmas (December 25)

*(Some dioceses celebrate the Ascension on the following Sunday.)

Activity Design a slogan that highlights the meaning of a season or celebration discussed in this lesson.

RESPONDING...

✠ **Leader:** During the liturgical year we honor Jesus Christ, who delivers us from the darkness of sin and death and brings us into the light of his life. Let us rejoice as we listen to this reading from Scripture.

Reader 1: A reading from the Book of Ecclesiastes

Reader 2: "There is an appointed time for everything,
and a time for every affair under the heavens."

Reader 3: "A time to be born, and a time to die;
a time to plant, and a time to uproot the plant."

Reader 4: "A time to weep, and a time to laugh;
a time to mourn, and a time to dance."

Reader 5: "A time to scatter stones, and a time to gather them;
a time to embrace, and a time to be far from embraces."

Reader 6: "A time to seek, and a time to lose;
a time to keep, and a time to cast away."

Reader 7: "A time to rend, and a time to sew;
a time to be silent, and a time to speak."

Reader 8: "A time to love, and a time to hate;
a time of war, and a time of peace."
(Ecclesiastes 3:1–2, 4–8)

Leader: Let us pray.

Father, throughout our lives, in all our times and seasons, you guide us through your Son, Jesus Christ, and through the Holy Spirit. We thank you for the Church's liturgical year, which helps us to appreciate your gift of salvation at all times. We thank you for this day, this year, and this moment. We ask you to bless all our days, in the name of Jesus Christ, your Son, who lives and reigns with you and the Holy Spirit, one God forever and ever.
Amen.

 Visit www.weliveourfaith.com for additional prayers and activities.

"Wait eagerly for the LORD, and keep to the way."

(Psalm 37:34)

♪ **Await the Lord with Hope**

Refrain:
Await the Lord with hope.
Await the Lord with joy.
Keep vigil for the coming of
the reign of God.

Verses:
Those who wait for God; they shall not be
put to shame. (Refrain)

Prepare a way for the Lord, a path of justice
for our God. (Refrain)

Let your hearts be strong, for the Lord is
coming soon. (Refrain)

Advent

Anticipation: It's looking forward to something that we're expecting to happen. Sometimes, when we're anticipating something, we almost feel as if the wait will never end. Things we might anticipate include time spent with friends, the end of a school year, birthdays, and holidays. How do you feel when you're anticipating something? Impatient? Hopeful? Anxious?

Activity Recall a few things that you anticipated when you were younger. When they finally happened, did they match your expectations, or perhaps exceed them? Would you still consider these things to be a cause for anticipation today?

Advent is a time of waiting and anticipation.

During the four weeks of Advent, the Church prepares to celebrate the birth of Christ while also anticipating his coming again at the end of time. Advent begins four Sundays before December 25 and ends at the Christmas Vigil Mass. During this season, in the Scripture readings proclaimed at Mass, we recall the long years the people of Israel waited for the Messiah, as well as the messages of hope they received from the prophets who spoke in God's name.

The people of Israel, whom God had guided and protected as his own, had been suffering and struggling for centuries. Their kingdom was conquered and divided, and they were exiled. With great anticipation they looked forward to the fulfillment of God's promise to send a Messiah—an "Anointed One"—to save them. God promised this through the prophets, who said that the Messiah would bring peace, justice, and freedom to the people of Israel. The Messiah would be a great leader and would protect the people from their enemies, restore their nation, and renew their covenant, or solemn agreement, with God. As the prophet Micah said:

"But you, Bethlehem-Ephrathah,
    too small to be among the clans of Judah,
From you shall come forth for me
    one who is to be ruler in Israel. . . .
He shall stand firm and shepherd his flock
    by the strength of the LORD,
    in the majestic name of the LORD, his God;
And they shall remain, for now his greatness
    shall reach to the ends of the earth;
    he shall be peace" (Micah 5:1, 3–4).

The prophets also said that the Messiah would restore people to health and bring justice and salvation. Because of him,

"All the ends of the earth will behold
    the salvation of our God" (Isaiah 52:10).

With hopeful expectation the people awaited the Messiah's coming. Then, in fulfillment of all these prophecies, God sent his only Son, Jesus Christ. Jesus, born in Bethlehem as prophesied, went

beyond all expectations about the Messiah, for it was in him that God truly became one of us. This truth is known as the Incarnation.

Jesus, being not only divine but also human like us in all things but sin, showed great concern for our human condition. He cared for those who were poor, sick, or physically challenged. He healed people and forgave their sins. He invited all people to follow him. And he gave his life for our salvation and rose from the dead. Before ascending to his Father in heaven, he also promised he would come again at the end of time. He said, "They will see the Son of Man coming upon the clouds of heaven with power and great glory" (Matthew 24:30). In Jesus, God began—and, at the end of time, will complete—his Kingdom, the power of his love active in our world and in our lives.

The Church celebrates Jesus' first coming, the Incarnation, at Christmas. It is during Advent that we prepare for this celebration, anticipate it with joyful expectation, and prepare our hearts and lives for God's presence among us in Jesus Christ.

The Advent wreath is a symbol of expectation for the coming of Christ. The wreath's circular shape recalls all the years the people waited for the Messiah. During each week of Advent, we light one candle on the wreath until, by the end of Advent, all four candles are lit.

Activity What are some ways to show your joyful anticipation for the coming of Christ? Share your ideas.

Advent is a time of prayer and reflection.

Advent is the time of the liturgical year that we as a Church prepare for and reflect on Christ's coming into our lives. In the hymns and prayers of the liturgy during Advent, we express our longing and gratitude for Christ's first coming, the Incarnation. The Gloria, or "Glory to God" hymn, that we usually sing on Sunday is omitted on the Sundays in Advent so that we will long to sing it more joyfully on Christmas. And, through the Scripture readings that are proclaimed during Advent, we share in the hope and joyful expectation of those who awaited the birth of the Messiah more than 2,000 years ago. From December 17 to December 24, the theme of these readings is anticipation of Jesus' birth and ministry.

Yet Advent is also a time to reflect on our readiness for Christ's second coming, his coming at the end of time, when he will fully establish God's Kingdom. When this happens, there will be no more death, no more sorrow, no more injustice—only rejoicing in goodness and love. As we proclaim in the Nicene Creed at Mass, Christ "will come again in glory to judge the living and the dead, and his kingdom will have no end." Though, as Jesus said, only the Father knows the "day or hour" of this second coming (Mark 13:32), the Church looks forward to it with joy and hope. We anticipate that "Christ will come in glory to achieve the definitive triumph of good over evil" (*CCC*, 681). Thus, Advent is a time to reflect on our lives and to prepare ourselves for the second coming of Christ. From the beginning of Advent until December 16, the focus of the readings is on Jesus' second coming and on preparation for the coming of God's Kingdom.

But we do not have to wait until the second coming to meet Jesus Christ. Christ is with us here and now. Through Baptism we live in Christ and Christ lives in us. And through the Eucharist we receive the risen Christ, who lives and reigns with the Father and the Holy Spirit, now and forever. Year-round, we ought to be aware of Christ's presence and his love. We should share that loving presence with others preparing for and anticipating Christ's coming: at Advent, in our own lives every day, at the hour of our death, and in glory at the end of time.

Activity Within the season of Advent, the Church celebrates the following feast days in honor of the saints. As part of your Advent preparation and reflection, learn more about one of these saints and attend Mass on his or her feast day. (Note: The feast of the Immaculate Conception is a holy day of obligation.)

SAINTS REMEMBERED DURING ADVENT	
December 3:	Saint Francis Xavier, priest, missionary
December 4:	Saint John of Damascus, priest, Doctor of the Church
December 6:	Saint Nicholas, bishop, patron of children
December 7:	Saint Ambrose, bishop, Doctor of the Church
December 8:	Mary, the Immaculate Conception, patron of the United States of America
December 9:	Saint Juan Diego, visionary who saw Our Lady of Guadalupe
December 12:	Our Lady of Guadalupe, patron of the Americas
December 13:	Saint Lucy, virgin and martyr, patron of Sweden
December 14:	Saint John of the Cross, priest, Doctor of the Church

RESPONDING...

✚ **Leader:** Let us listen to a reading from the prophet Isaiah about the promised Messiah.

Reader: A reading from the book of the prophet Isaiah

"The spirit of the Lord GOD is upon me,
    because the LORD has anointed me;
He has sent me to bring glad tidings to
        the lowly,
    to heal the brokenhearted,
To proclaim liberty to the captives
    and release to the prisoners,
To announce a year of favor from the LORD
    and a day of vindication by our God,
    to comfort all who mourn. . . .
For I, the LORD, love what is right. . . .
I will give them their recompense faithfully,
    a lasting covenant I will make with them.
Their descendants shall be renowned among
        the nations,
    and their offspring among the peoples . . . .
As the earth brings forth its plants,
    and a garden makes its growth spring up,
So will the Lord GOD make justice and praise
        spring up before all the nations."

(Isaiah 61:1–2, 8–9, 11)

Leader: Justice shall flourish in his time,

All: and fullness of peace for ever.

(response, responsorial psalm, Second Sunday of Advent, Year A)

Leader: Let us pray.
Father in heaven,
the day draws near when the glory of your Son
will make radiant the night of the waiting world.

May the darkness not blind us
to the vision of wisdom
which fills the minds of those who find him.

(Roman Missal)

All: Amen.

 Visit www.weliveourfaith.com for additional prayers and activities.

"Lord our God, with the birth of your Son, your glory breaks on the world."

(prayer for Christmas Midnight Mass)

♪ **Joy to the World**

Refrain:
Joy to the world, the Lord is come!
Let earth receive her King;
Let every heart prepare Him room,
and heaven and nature sing,
and heaven and nature sing,
and heaven, and heaven, and nature sing.

Verse:
He rules the world with truth and grace,
and makes the nations prove
the glories of His righteousness,
and wonders of His love,
and wonders of His love,
and wonders, wonders, of His love. (Refrain)

Christmas

Perhaps you've heard of the "seven wonders of the world." Since ancient times, people have put together lists of what they consider to be the most wondrous, magnificent constructions ever made by human hands. The seven wonders of the ancient world are usually said to include the pyramids of Egypt, the only structures among the seven to survive today. The largest pyramid consists of more than two million blocks, each weighing 2.5 tons. Also on the list of seven wonders is the hanging gardens of Babylon, which were destroyed. These gardens, mounted on terraces rising 75 to 300 feet above ground, were said to have been built by a Babylonian king around 600 B.C.

There are many other things in our world that we might consider to be wonders. What are a few that you can think of?

Activity Perhaps you've experienced the wonder of a special place—a great waterfall or canyon, for example. What are your top seven wonders of the world? In what ways do these remind you of the presence of God?

BELIEVING...

At Christmas we celebrate the wonder of the Incarnation.

The word *Christmas* originated from the Old English phrase *Christ's Mass*. *Christmas* is the name that most people use for December 25, the day that the Church celebrates as the "Solemnity of the Nativity of the Lord." But Christmas is actually an entire season, beginning on December 25 and ending in January on the Feast of the Baptism of the Lord. During the Christmas season we celebrate the birth of Christ, the Son of God, God with us, true God and true man, Emmanuel, who was born long ago in Bethlehem and is still among us today.

What comes to mind when you think about celebrating Christmas? What are some of your best memories of celebrating Christmas? There are so many wonderful things that we do when we celebrate Christmas. We give and receive gifts, a custom that may have started in remembrance of the Magi from the East who brought gifts to the infant Jesus (see Matthew 2). We decorate trees with ornaments and lights. And we sing Christmas carols, a way to express our joy while proclaiming the good news of Christ's coming.

Some people might say, "All this is nice, but the real meaning behind Christmas is that Christ was born." Yes, Christ's birth is the real meaning of Christmas. And, of course, as a Church we celebrate Christ's birth in the Christmas Day liturgy and the liturgies throughout the Christmas season, giving God praise and thanksgiving for his Son, Jesus Christ. But the things that we do with our families and friends to celebrate Christmas can also express the real meaning of Christmas and help us to understand it. God became part of our physical world, and our "worldly" Christmas customs can be very much a part of the celebration of Christmas—if we also understand that at Christmas we are rejoicing in the wonder of the Incarnation, God's Son becoming human. All of the things that help us to celebrate Christmas—the trees, the gifts, the carols, the parties—are to be connected to the truth that Christ came among us to bring us salvation. He came so that we might learn to live as he did, with love for God, others, and ourselves, and so that we might someday be with him forever.

Christmas, therefore, is not a time to make ourselves happy for the moment, in the here and now. That kind of happiness fades quickly. Rather, Christmas is a time to celebrate that the glory of God is right here on earth, in our own world, throughout our lives. At Christmas we can give praise for God's glory through the familiar things of our world. We can sing holiday songs. We can decorate trees. We can have festive gatherings with friends and family. These are ways of showing that Christmas is a special season. After all, what God did for us was truly special. He chose to live among us, to call us his brothers and sisters, and to make us his own family. As we profess at Mass, "For us . . . and for our salvation he came down from heaven: by the power of the Holy Spirit he was born of the Virgin Mary, and became man" (Nicene Creed).

Christmas is a time to celebrate, with thankfulness in our hearts, the wonder of God's becoming one of us in Jesus Christ. It is a time to remember to follow Jesus, to love and care for others, and to build a lifetime of joy.

Activity On a separate sheet of paper, make a questionnaire to share with others about their understanding of the meaning of Christmas and the ways to celebrate it. Use your questionnaire to survey yourself and others, and then share your results.

At Christmas we celebrate the wonder of God's love.

At Christmas we celebrate the great truth that each one of us is loved by God: "For God so loved the world that he gave his only Son, so that everyone who believes in him . . . might have eternal life" (John 3:16). Every human being is loved by God and has dignity and worth. We are called to recognize this, to love and respect ourselves, and to show the same love and respect to others—most especially those who are poor, weak, sick, or in need. If we can see such people as God sees them, we see people worthy of our respect and love. Likewise, if we see ourselves as God sees us, we also recognize that we are truly God's beloved children. At Christmas, as we celebrate the great love God has for everyone, we are reminded to see others as God sees them and to love others as God loves.

In the Old Testament we read a story that helps to explain how God sees each of his children. It is the story of the anointing of King David, the greatest king Israel ever had. When God wanted to choose a new king for Israel, he sent the prophet Samuel to the house of Jesse, a man with several sons. God told Samuel that one of the sons of Jesse would be the new king. One after another, the sons were presented to Samuel. And one after another, God rejected them.

At one point God said, "Not as man sees does God see, because man sees the appearance but the LORD looks into the heart" (1 Samuel 16:7). Finally, when it seemed as if there were no sons left to present to Samuel, Jesse told Samuel that he had one more son: his youngest boy, David, who was out in the fields caring for the sheep. As the youngest, David had not been considered important enough to meet the prophet Samuel. But Samuel asked to see David, and when David came before the prophet, God said, "There—anoint him, for this is he!" (1 Samuel 16:12). The son who had been over-looked, the one who seemed least important, was chosen by God to be king of Israel.

Jesus was actually called "the Son of David" because he descended from the family of King David. He was raised by his mother Mary, a humble Jewish woman, and Joseph, his foster-father, a carpenter. Thus, Jesus joined the human family as one who seemed unimportant as David did. And although Jesus was divine, he experienced human life the way we do, in all its stages: birth, growth, and death. Because Jesus was and is truly divine, his life, death, Resurrection, and Ascension bring salvation to us all. Jesus accepted, and continues to accept, everyone, and he offers them this salvation. In this way Jesus shows us the love that God has for people, a love that excludes no one. During the season of Christmas, we can celebrate the wonder of God's love and try to reach out to others with the same great love.

Activity There are many people in society who are overlooked or considered unimportant. In what ways can the Church see them as God sees them and reach out to them with God's love? Write your ideas below, and discuss them with your group. Vote on one idea for your group to put into action this Christmas season.

RESPONDING...

Leader: During the season of Christmas we celebrate that Jesus Christ, fully God and fully human, came among us.

Reader: A reading from the Gospel of Luke

"Do not be afraid; for behold, I proclaim to you good news of great joy that will be for all the people. For today in the city of David a savior has been born for you who is Messiah and Lord. And this will be a sign for you: you will find an infant wrapped in swaddling clothes and lying in a manger." (Luke 2:10–12)

The Gospel of the Lord.

All: Praise to you, Lord Jesus Christ.

Leader: Lord Jesus Christ, may we never lose sight of the wonder of your coming among us as one of us. That all people will be reminded of the real meaning of the Christmas season, the Incarnation, we pray:

All: Jesus, king of glory, help us and hear us.

Leader: That all people in need will be assured of God's love this Christmas season, we pray:

All: Jesus, Son of the living God, help us and hear us.

Leader: That people who are overlooked and alone this Christmas season will find the support and comfort of their communities, we pray:

All: Jesus, prince of peace, help us and hear us.

Leader: That each of us will experience the wonder of Christmas throughout the season, we pray:

All: Jesus, splendor of the Father, help us and hear us. Amen.

 Visit www.weliveourfaith.com for additional prayers and activities.

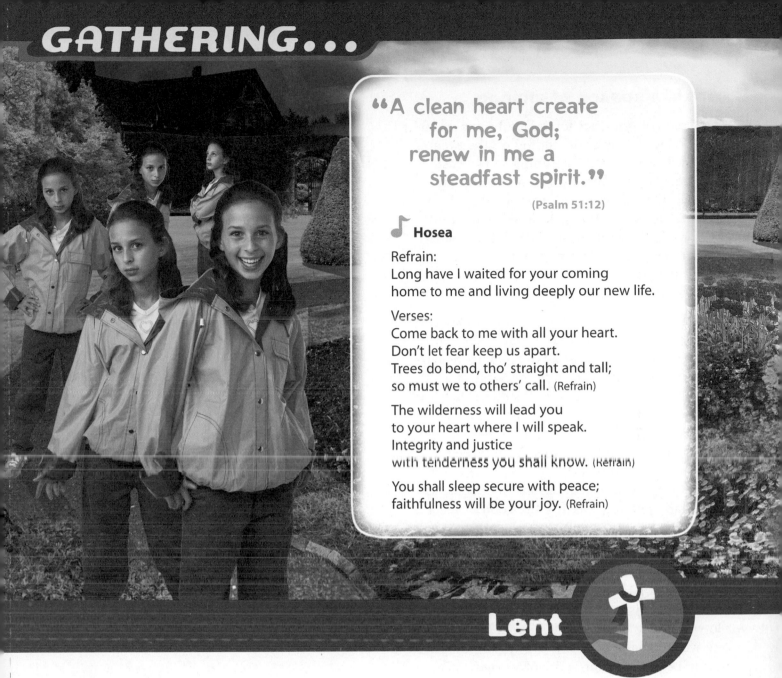

GATHERING...

> **"A clean heart create for me, God; renew in me a steadfast spirit."**
>
> (Psalm 51:12)

🎵 **Hosea**

Refrain:
Long have I waited for your coming
home to me and living deeply our new life.

Verses:
Come back to me with all your heart.
Don't let fear keep us apart.
Trees do bend, tho' straight and tall;
so must we to others' call. (Refrain)

The wilderness will lead you
to your heart where I will speak.
Integrity and justice
with tenderness you shall know. (Refrain)

You shall sleep secure with peace;
faithfulness will be your joy. (Refrain)

Lent

Have you ever wondered what life would be like if no one ever changed? You may not have considered this before, but all of us are constantly changing. Sure, our looks change as we grow older, but many times so do our interests, our goals, our opinions, our favorite things, our hobbies, and even our personalities and outlooks on life. Think about it: In these respects, are you the same exact person that you were two years ago? Probably not. Are the changes for the better? Or is that difficult even to determine? Why or why not?

Activity Think about your behavior and the way you treated others during the past month. What are some changes that you think you should make? Why? Write a prayer asking God to help you.

Lent is a season of change.

The season of Lent lasts forty days, beginning on Ash Wednesday and concluding on the evening of Holy Thursday, the beginning of the Easter Triduum. The number 40 is a biblical number. It is said that the Israelites wandered for forty years in the desert; the great flood lasted forty days and forty nights; Jesus fasted in the desert for forty days. The number 40 came to signify "a very long time" of preparation for something important and life-changing.

During Lent we are getting closer and closer to Easter and to the rising of our Lord Jesus Christ. The forty-day Lenten season is a reminder of journeying from death to new life. After the Israelites spent forty years in the desert, finally reaching the promised land meant a new life for them. In the forty days of the great flood, the world died, but a new beginning followed this death. When Jesus went into the desert, he was a carpenter from Nazareth. Forty days later, Jesus too began a new life, finally publicly sharing the good news of God's love.

Lent gives us an opportunity to "die" to our old ways and to "rise" with Jesus to a new way of life. Even though, as baptized Christians, we are already living the Christian way of life, our decision to let old ways die and to follow Christ in new ways is one we can make over and over again, especially during Lent. But doing so involves *conversion*, a turning back to God with all our hearts, a coming closer and closer to Jesus Christ, God's Son.

What are some of the "old ways" that we need to "die" to? Many of these are personal choices and attitudes that we have gotten used to: being selfish with our time or money, refusing help to others, saying hurtful things to get a laugh, or not putting effort into schoolwork or into our gifts and talents. Other "old ways" are attitudes and choices that we often share with the society around us: ignoring the needs of poor or homeless people, not caring for those who are sick or hungry, or allowing the most vulnerable among us (those who are elderly,

sick, disabled, or very young) to go without the help that they need. Lent gives us a chance to let these old attitudes and choices die. Lent gives us a chance, with God's grace and our best efforts, to change our minds, our hearts, and our lives.

Activity Name an "old way" or attitude in society that needs to change. Perhaps it's neglect of homeless people, elderly people, or the environment. Then identify ways to learn more about this problem, express your concern, and make an effort to help.

The "old way" or attitude:

Ways to learn more about this problem:

Ways to express my concern about this problem:

Efforts I can make to help:

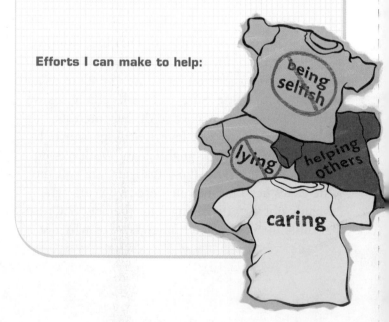

Lent is season of grace and renewal.

In our Lenten dying and rising, in making our choices and forming our attitudes, we are guided and strengthened by the word of God. Many of the Lenten readings at the Eucharist are from the prophets of the Old Testament, who spoke in God's name and advocated change and conversion. On the Friday after Ash Wednesday, we hear the prophet Isaiah speaking to us about the meaning of Lent:

"This, rather, is the fasting that I wish:
    releasing those bound unjustly . . .
Setting free the oppressed . . .
Sharing your bread with the hungry,
    sheltering the oppressed and the homeless;
Clothing the naked when you see them,
    and not turning your back on your own"
(Isaiah 58:6–7).

Isaiah's words are a great reminder of the Lenten practices that we follow in order to move toward conversion: *prayer, fasting,* and *almsgiving,* the giving of our time and resources to help those in need. What can you "do for Lent" in one or more of these areas?

Whatever you decide to do, it is also important to remember that Lent is a season of grace. Lent is not so much about what we *do* but about Jesus Christ's presence with us, calling us to come closer and closer to him each day. Whatever our failures or trials in responding to his call, we are never overcome. We can always renew our efforts with the help of the grace he gives us. And renewal is always possible for us, for we are following our Savior, Jesus Christ, who faced what we face yet leads us through death to new life.

 **Make a decision today, if you have not already, to do one thing for Lent that will help you to grow closer to Jesus Christ.**

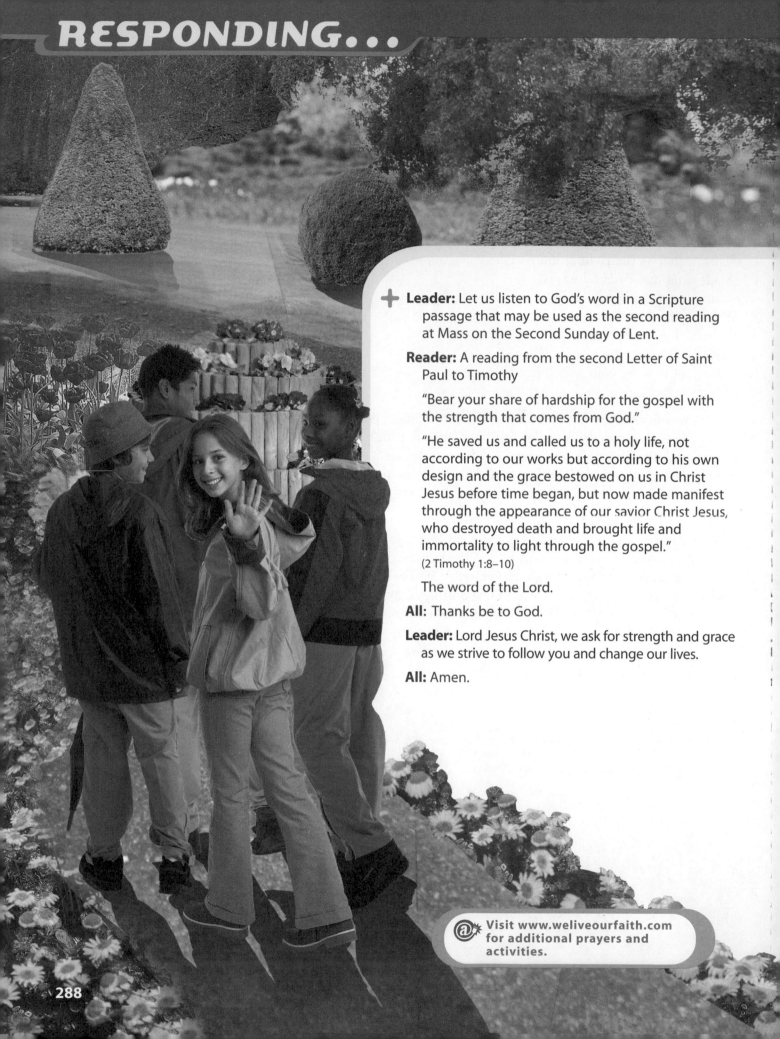

RESPONDING...

✝ **Leader:** Let us listen to God's word in a Scripture passage that may be used as the second reading at Mass on the Second Sunday of Lent.

Reader: A reading from the second Letter of Saint Paul to Timothy

"Bear your share of hardship for the gospel with the strength that comes from God."

"He saved us and called us to a holy life, not according to our works but according to his own design and the grace bestowed on us in Christ Jesus before time began, but now made manifest through the appearance of our savior Christ Jesus, who destroyed death and brought life and immortality to light through the gospel."
(2 Timothy 1:8–10)

The word of the Lord.

All: Thanks be to God.

Leader: Lord Jesus Christ, we ask for strength and grace as we strive to follow you and change our lives.

All: Amen.

@ **Visit www.weliveourfaith.com for additional prayers and activities.**

GATHERING...

"Lord, make us worthy to celebrate these mysteries."

(Prayer over the Gifts, Evening Mass of the Lord's Supper)

♪ Three Days

Three days our world was broken
and in an instant healed,
God's covenant of mercy
in mystery revealed.

Two thousand years are one day
in God's eternal sight,
and yesterday's sorrows
are this day's delight.

Though still Christ's body suffers,
pierced daily by the sword,
yet death has no dominion:
the risen Christ is Lord!

Triduum

In everyone's life, there are turning points—events signifying that a big change has occurred, that we are "turning" toward something new. Such events might include graduating from school, moving to a new home, gaining a new responsibility, or even experiencing a change of seasons. Sometimes people mark the turning points in their lives by gathering together for a special meal or celebration. For example, they hold "going-away," graduation, housewarming, retirement, or birthday parties.

And, at school or in your community, there may be spring festivals, winter dances, or other celebrations marking seasonal turning points.

Activity Recall a family gathering or celebration that had great meaning for you. What was the reason for the gathering or celebration? Why was the experience meaningful? Share your thoughts.

The Triduum recalls the turning point in the history of our salvation.

The Easter Triduum recalls and celebrates a great turning point—Jesus Christ's journey from death to new life, his offering of his life for our salvation. This event marked a turning point in humankind's relationship with God.

The word *triduum* means "three days." During the Easter Triduum we follow a practice for counting days that comes from our Jewish ancestors in faith: counting the period from one sunset to the next as one day. Thus, the Triduum begins on the evening of Holy Thursday and extends to the evening of Easter Sunday—a total of three days from sunset to sunset. And when we celebrate the Triduum, we are celebrating the three most important days of the year for Christians. The liturgical celebrations of these three days are seen as one connected liturgy during which we celebrate Christ's passing from death to new life. We focus our celebration on the Paschal Mystery of Christ—his passion, or suffering and death, his Resurrection, and his Ascension.

The Triduum begins with the evening of Holy Thursday, when we recall Christ's giving of his Body and Blood at the Last Supper. It continues through Good Friday, when we remember Jesus' suffering and death for humankind. And it extends through Holy Saturday, when we reflect and pray about his death and then celebrate the Easter Vigil. The Triduum concludes on the evening of Easter Sunday. Then the joyful season of Easter, in which we celebrate the Resurrection of Christ, begins. Each liturgical celebration of the Triduum heightens our awareness of and gratitude for Jesus Christ, who brought about the great turning point in the history of our salvation.

The Last Supper by Frans the Younger Pourbus (1569–1622)

On Holy Thursday, we celebrate the Evening Mass of the Lord's Supper. This liturgy recalls Jesus' last meal with his Apostles before his death. While he and the Apostles were gathered together to celebrate Passover, he shared the bread and wine with them, saying, "This is my body, which will be given for you" and "This cup is the new covenant in my blood, which will be shed for you" (Luke 22:19, 20). And he assured them that he would be with them always. This meal, the Last Supper, also marked a turning point: Jesus, on the night before his suffering and death, was offering to his disciples the everlasting gift of himself, his Body and Blood. Through his words and actions that night, Jesus gave us the Eucharist that we celebrate today. And through the Eucharist, Jesus continues to be with us always.

Jesus also gave us an example of love and service that night: He washed his Apostles' feet as a sign of his love for them. In the Mass on Holy Thursday evening, we not only recall all of these events, we celebrate in a special way Christ's giving of his Body and Blood, which he shared then and still shares with us today in the Eucharist. We praise and thank God for this great gift. And, as a reminder of the love and service that Jesus calls us to, a reenactment of Jesus' washing of his Apostles' feet takes place. We also contribute to a special collection for those who are in need.

Activity How will you and your family celebrate the Triduum this year? Make a chart recording the times your parish will gather for each day's liturgy. Include a prayer for each day in your chart. Display your chart at home. Encourage your family to pray these prayers and to attend the Triduum liturgies.

The Triduum leads us to the celebration of Christ's Resurrection.

On Good Friday, we remember Jesus' passion. By his death on the cross, Jesus demonstrated God's love for all humankind. As Saint Paul wrote, "God proves his love for us in that while we were still sinners Christ died for us" (Romans 5:8).

The liturgy of Good Friday of the Lord's Passion often takes place around three o'clock in the afternoon, in keeping with Gospel accounts of Jesus' death: "And at three o'clock Jesus cried out in a loud voice . . . . and breathed his last" (Mark 15:34, 37). This liturgy has three parts: the Liturgy of the Word, the veneration of the cross, and Holy Communion. In the Liturgy of the Word, we hear a reading from the Gospel of John telling of the Passion of Christ. "The message of the liturgy in proclaiming the passion . . . is to enable the assembly to see vividly the love of Christ for each person, despite their sins." (*God's Mercy Endures Forever, 22*) The Liturgy of the Word concludes with a special prayer of the faithful in which ten prayers for the whole world are prayed.

The veneration of the cross, the second part of the liturgy, is a ritual in which we show reverence, or honor and respect, for the cross, because upon it hung the Savior of the world. The cross is a sign of Christ's death, a symbol of the salvation that he offers to the world. To venerate the cross, we approach in a kind of procession. We genuflect before the cross or show another sign of reverence such as kissing it. The Liturgy of the Eucharist is not celebrated, so a brief communion service, the third part of the liturgy, takes place. Then all depart in silence.

On Holy Saturday, we gather in the evening with our parish for the celebration of the Easter Vigil. In the Church, a vigil is a liturgy celebrating Sunday or another solemnity, but which takes place the night before. The Easter Vigil begins after sunset on Holy Saturday, the night before Easter Sunday. It is the most important vigil of the year, and the high point of the Easter Triduum. It celebrates the new life Jesus has given us by his death and Resurrection.

The Easter Vigil liturgy has four parts. The first part is the "service of light." We assemble with the priest and other clergy in front of a fire that has been made outside of or in the back of the church. This fire is blessed, and the Easter, or Paschal, candle is lit from it. The lighted Paschal candle represents the risen Christ among us and our own passing with him from death to life, from darkness to light. The candle is carried with great reverence into the darkened church. We may light small candles from it. Then, the deacon, priest, or a parish member chants the *Exsultet*, or Easter Proclamation. The Exsultet is a joyful proclamation of our Easter faith. It announces that this is the most beautiful and exciting night of the year.

The second part of the Easter Vigil is the Liturgy of the Word. A series of Scripture readings encourages us to meditate on all the wonderful things God has done for his people from the beginning of time.

The third part of the vigil is the celebration of the Sacraments of Initiation. New members of the Church are baptized, confirmed, and receive the Eucharist for the first time. All present also renew their baptismal promises and are sprinkled with the baptismal water, a sign of new life in Christ.

The fourth part of the Easter Vigil liturgy is the Liturgy of the Eucharist. The whole Church is called to the table that the Lord prepared for his people by his death and Resurrection.

Then, on Easter Sunday, we celebrate the day that Christ rose from the dead. The Triduum concludes with the evening prayer on this day.

Activity Design an insert for your parish bulletin encouraging others to celebrate the Triduum liturgies.

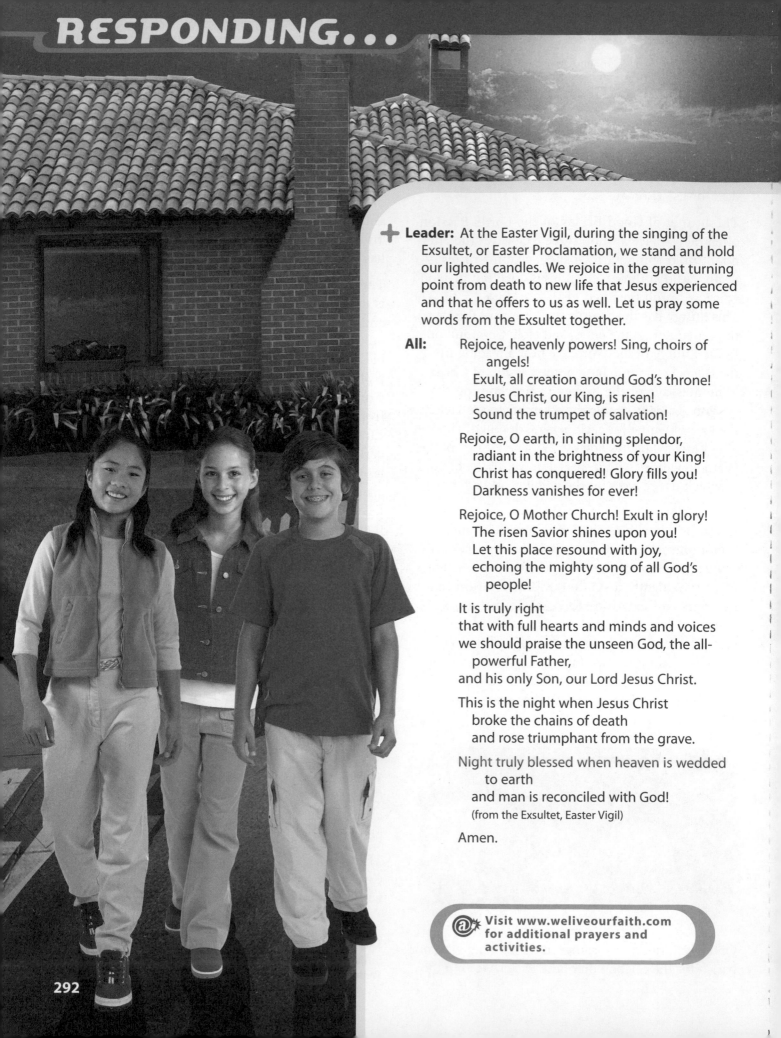

✚ **Leader:** At the Easter Vigil, during the singing of the Exsultet, or Easter Proclamation, we stand and hold our lighted candles. We rejoice in the great turning point from death to new life that Jesus experienced and that he offers to us as well. Let us pray some words from the Exsultet together.

All:
Rejoice, heavenly powers! Sing, choirs of angels!
Exult, all creation around God's throne!
Jesus Christ, our King, is risen!
Sound the trumpet of salvation!

Rejoice, O earth, in shining splendor,
radiant in the brightness of your King!
Christ has conquered! Glory fills you!
Darkness vanishes for ever!

Rejoice, O Mother Church! Exult in glory!
The risen Savior shines upon you!
Let this place resound with joy,
echoing the mighty song of all God's people!

It is truly right
that with full hearts and minds and voices
we should praise the unseen God, the all-powerful Father,
and his only Son, our Lord Jesus Christ.

This is the night when Jesus Christ
broke the chains of death
and rose triumphant from the grave.

Night truly blessed when heaven is wedded to earth
and man is reconciled with God!
(from the Exsultet, Easter Vigil)

Amen.

@✲ **Visit www.weliveourfaith.com for additional prayers and activities.**

GATHERING...

concert for PEACE

> "Jesus came and stood in their midst and said to them, 'Peace be with you.'"
>
> (John 20:19)

♪ Christ Is Here

Refrain:
Christ is here; the risen Savior greets us.
Here the body of Christ is revealed,
here in word and sacrament and people.
Here the wound of the world in Christ is healed.

Verses:
Strength from God above, peace and holy love:
these the gifts for us to share. (Refrain)

Earth rejoices; raise your voices:
celebrate God's Holy Day. (Refrain)

Easter

When peace is present in people's lives, they are able to come together as a community and experience harmony, acceptance, and love. They are able to reconcile their differences. Often we see the need for peace in various places around the world. Peace may also be lacking in situations in our own lives. When have you helped to promote peace? Think of times when you brought people together or helped to reconcile differences with people in your own life.

Activity Work in a group to make a map of the places in today's world where peace is lacking. In the key for your map include symbols representing different ways that people in each individual place can find peace. Sketch your ideas for these symbols here.

At Easter we celebrate our new life in the risen Christ, who shares his peace with us.

Jesus lived in the spirit of peace. He showed his disciples the way to spread peace to others. And, when he had risen from the dead, he appeared to his disciples and gave them the gift of his peace. "He stood in their midst and said to them, 'Peace be with you.'" (Luke 24:36) He calmed their fears, saying, "Why are you troubled? And why do questions arise in your hearts? Look at my hands and my feet, that it is I myself" (Luke 24:38–39). The risen Christ's message that day gave the disciples peace and comforted them with the knowledge that Jesus Christ was truly alive and would remain with them forever. This same message is meant for us today, at Easter, and throughout our lives.

When we celebrate Easter, we celebrate Christ's Resurrection and rejoice in the new life that we have because of him. With Jesus we have passed from death to life, from sadness to joy, from hopelessness to the fulfillment of our deepest hope: everlasting life. At Easter we celebrate that we too can share everlasting life with Christ—we too can rise from the dead and have endless glory with the Lord. And when that time comes, our peace will be everlasting.

The Church sets aside an entire season, the Easter season, to celebrate all the meaning that Christ's Resurrection has for us. The Easter season begins on Easter Sunday and concludes with Pentecost Sunday, which is the fiftieth day after Easter Sunday.

Between Easter Sunday and Pentecost, there are seven weeks of celebration. The first week of the Easter season, called Easter week, begins with Easter Sunday and ends on the Second Sunday of Easter. Thus, this week consists of eight days of celebration. For this reason, it is also called the Easter *octave*, a word that means "eight." Because Jesus Christ rose from the dead on Sunday, every Sunday is a *solemnity*, an especially important day of celebration in the Church. But every day of the Easter octave is also considered a solemnity. Easter week, then, is eight special days of celebrating the day that Jesus Christ rose from the dead.

The readings for Easter week give us a glimpse into the different ways that the Resurrection affects the lives of all Christians. For example, at Mass during the Easter octave, the first reading comes from the Acts of the Apostles, not from the Old Testament as is customary during the rest of the year. These readings from the Acts of the Apostles help us to meditate on various ways that the truth of the Resurrection was lived out among the Apostles and the early Christian communities. The second reading comes from the insights and observations written in the epistles, or letters, of John, known as the "beloved disciple" of Jesus. And the Gospel readings are accounts of the Resurrection as told in the four Gospels.

Activity These are the Gospel readings for the octave of Easter: John 20:1–9; Matthew 28:8–15; John 20:11–18; Luke 24:13–35; Luke 24:36–48; John 21:1–14; Mark 16:9–15; John 20:19–31. Read them. Illustrate the scenes in the panels below.

The Easter sequence celebrates the Resurrection of Christ.

Four special hymns are part of the liturgies of four important celebrations in the liturgical year: Easter Sunday, Pentecost, the Most Holy Body and Blood of Christ, and Our Lady of Sorrows. The words of these four special hymns, or *sequences*, as they are called, express joy over the events celebrated at each of these liturgies. Each sequence is sung, or may be read, immediately after the second reading in the Liturgy of the Word.

The title of the sequence for Easter Sunday is *Victimae Paschali Laudes*, which is Latin for "Praise to the Paschal Victim." This sequence describes the events that unfolded on the first Easter Sunday, when Jesus rose from the dead. The words at the beginning of the sequence are addressed to us Christians, calling us to offer praises because Christ, the "Prince of life," has redeemed us and now reigns as King forever. Then the words address Jesus' disciple Mary Magdalene, who found his tomb empty. Mary is asked to proclaim what she saw. The words that then follow are meant to express Mary's reply, giving an account of the Resurrection of Christ. The sequence ends with a proclamation and a prayer. Christ is risen from the dead and gives us new life, the sequence proclaims. We pray for Christ's mercy and end with, "Amen. Alleluia."

The music for this sequence, as well as the other three sequences, was originally sung in Gregorian chant, an ancient form of singing. Chant continues to be used for the sequences today. However, throughout the years, well-known composers have also set the words of all four sequences to their own musical scores.

We do not know who originally wrote the beautiful Easter sequence, or any of the other sequences.

We can only be grateful that this writer used God's gift of creativity to help millions of Christians throughout the ages celebrate the Resurrection of Christ and the peace and new life he offers to all who have faith in him.

Activity Celebrate the Resurrection of Jesus Christ. Write a song or a poem, or draw something, to help you to remember and celebrate the new life that Jesus brings.

RESPONDING...

+ **Leader:** Let us celebrate the Resurrection of Jesus by praying the sequence for Easter Sunday.

Group 1: Christians, to the Paschal Victim
Offer your thankful praises!

Group 2: A Lamb the sheep redeems:
Christ, who only is sinless,
Reconciles sinners to the Father.

Group 3: Death and life have contended in that combat stupendous:
The Prince of life, who died, reigns immortal.

Group 4: Speak, Mary, declaring
What you saw, wayfaring.

Group 1: "The tomb of Christ, who is living,
The glory of Jesus' resurrection;

Group 2: Bright angels attesting,
The shroud and napkin resting.

Group 3: Yes, Christ my hope is arisen;
To Galilee he goes before you."

Group 4: Christ indeed from death is risen,
our new life obtaining.

All: Have mercy, victor King, ever reigning!
Amen. Alleluia.

 Visit www.weliveourfaith.com for additional prayers and activities.

GATHERING...

> **"We celebrate that day when your Son, our Lord, took his place with you and raised our frail human nature to glory."**
>
> (Eucharistic Prayer I, Ascension of the Lord)

♪ **Gloria**

Glory to God in the highest,
    and peace to his people on earth.
Lord God, heavenly King,
almighty God and Father,
    we worship you, we give you thanks,
    we praise you for your glory.
Lord Jesus Christ, only Son of the Father,
Lord God, Lamb of God,
you take away the sin of the world:
    have mercy on us;
you are seated at the right hand of the Father;
    receive our prayer.
For you alone are the Holy One,
you alone are the Lord,
you alone are the Most High,
    Jesus Christ,
    with the Holy Spirit,
    in the glory of God the Father.
    Amen. (Roman Missal)

Ascension

Throughout our lives, we often receive some kind of help from another person. Such a person might help us in ways that are as basic as listening when we need to talk, or as substantial as giving us the courage to use our abilities to their greatest potential. When the circumstances of our lives lead us from this person toward new relationships with others, it helps to recognize all the gifts this person has brought to us. All those gifts can continue to help us as we go forward in life.

Activity Think of a person who has influenced you in some good way. Write a message thanking him or her. Deliver the message, or, if you can no longer reach the person, keep what you have written in a special place where it will remind you to pray for him or her.

On the solemnity of the Ascension we remember that Jesus Christ is with us always.

After Christ rose from the dead, he spent forty days with his disciples, helping them and giving them the courage to use their gifts to continue his work. Then, forty days after his Resurrection, he appeared to his disciples, ate with them, and talked to them. He promised to send the Holy Spirit to guide and strengthen them.

Then "he led them [out] as far as Bethany, raised his hands, and blessed them. As he blessed them he parted from them and was taken up to heaven" (Luke 24:50–51). This event is called the Ascension. In the Acts of the Apostles, we read that the Apostles then left for Jerusalem, where they awaited the coming of the Holy Spirit that Jesus had promised, and the Holy Spirit came upon them at Pentecost. Though they could no longer be with Jesus in the same way that they could when he physically walked the earth, his presence and love would

continue to be with them, through the power of the Holy Spirit. When we celebrate the Ascension, we can rejoice in this continuing presence of the risen Christ.

The Church celebrates the solemnity of the Ascension of the Lord about forty days after Easter. As we reflect on the Ascension, we are called to remember that the "heaven" to which Jesus ascended is something greater than a physical place. Heaven is a spiritual reality that human words cannot fully describe. The majesty of the sky—with the sun, moon, stars, white clouds, and beautiful and mysterious light—makes it a natural symbol for heaven. We say that Jesus was "taken *up* to heaven" simply because it is difficult for us to express in any other words what heaven is. Yet the *Catechism of the Catholic Church* explains heaven as "perfect life with the Most Holy Trinity" and "the state of supreme, definitive happiness" (1024). The *Catechism* further explains, "To live in heaven is 'to be with Christ'" (1025).

It is equally important to remember that the body of the risen Christ was, and is, a fully human body, but also a *risen*, *glorified*, and *spiritual* body. In other words, the risen Christ is not limited by time or space as we are. Because the risen Christ is not limited in any way, he can be, and is, with the Father and with us at all times. The Ascension of Jesus is an event that signifies to Jesus' followers that, from that moment forward, he is with the Father in heaven, and also with us forever, through the Holy Spirit. This is the joy of the Ascension.

Activity There are nine days between the solemnities of Ascension and Pentecost. Traditionally, on each of these nine days, the Church prays for the coming of the Holy Spirit. Mark your calendar and pray the prayer to the Holy Spirit (page 305) on each of these nine days.

In celebrating the Ascension we celebrate God's everlasting power and glory.

When we celebrate the Ascension, we praise God's power and glory. During the Easter season, which includes the solemnity of the Ascension, the Church, after having omitted the Gloria hymn throughout Lent, sings it again with renewed joy in the Introductory Rites at Sunday Mass. This hymn expresses our recognition of the power and glory of God—Father, Son, and Holy Spirit—which was revealed in an extraordinary way through the life, death, Resurrection, and Ascension of Jesus Christ.

In celebrating the Ascension, we celebrate the power and glory of:

- God the Father, who raised Jesus Christ from the dead and welcomed him to sit at his right hand in heaven. The image of Christ "at God's right hand" is a symbolic image representing the power that Christ shares with the Father.

- God the Holy Spirit, for it is through the Holy Spirit that Jesus Christ saved us and that God's Kingdom will be established on earth.

- God the Son, Jesus Christ, for he is Lord of heaven and earth.

The Ascension of Jesus Christ is a sign of his great and powerful love for us. In returning to the Father, Christ gave us the Gift of the Holy Spirit. The Holy Spirit unites us to Christ. With the Holy Spirit to strengthen us, we can actually live as Jesus Christ taught us to live. In the power of the Holy Spirit, we can be the disciples Jesus calls us to be. So, in leaving us, Jesus Christ is with us more than ever, through the Holy Spirit. And, at his second coming at the end of time, Christ will come again in glory. At that time, we, the members of his Body, hope to follow him in glory. Until that day comes,

the Church, with the guidance of the Holy Spirit and led by the pope and bishops, continues the work and mission of Jesus on earth. Together we pray and work for the Kingdom of God. While following the teachings of Jesus, acting with love and kindness, and working for justice and peace, we look forward to the day when Jesus Christ will come to establish his Kingdom once and for all. If we have lived as Jesus' disciples, then we can look forward to that day as a day on which the power, glory, and love of God will triumph forever.

Activity Reread the Gloria on page 297. Then work as a group to compose another prayer of praise for the glory of God—Father, Son, and Holy Spirit.

RESPONDING...

✛ **Leader:** Let us celebrate the Ascension of Jesus by praying a responsorial psalm from the Mass for the solemnity of the Ascension. The words are from Psalm 47.

All: God mounts his throne to shouts of joy: a blare of trumpets for the Lord.

Reader 1: All you peoples, clap your hands, shout to God with cries of gladness. For the LORD, the Most High, the awesome, is the great king over all the earth.

All: God mounts his throne to shouts of joy: a blare of trumpets for the Lord.

Reader 2: God mounts his throne amid shouts of joy; the LORD, amid trumpet blasts. Sing praise to God, sing praise; sing praise to our king, sing praise.

All: God mounts his throne to shouts of joy: a blare of trumpets for the Lord.

Reader 3: For king of all the earth is God; sing hymns of praise. God reigns over the nations, God sits upon his holy throne.

All: God mounts his throne to shouts of joy: a blare of trumpets for the Lord.

(responsorial psalm for Mass, Ascension of the Lord)

Leader: God our Father, make us joyful in the ascension of your Son Jesus Christ. May we follow him into the new creation, for his ascension is our glory and our hope. We ask this through our Lord Jesus Christ, your Son, who lives and reigns with you and the Holy Spirit, one God, for ever and ever.

(opening prayer for Mass, Ascension of the Lord)

All: Amen.

@ **Visit www.weliveourfaith.com for additional prayers and activities.**

GATHERING...

> **"Teach us to count our days aright, that we may gain wisdom of heart."**
>
> **(Psalm 90:12)**

♪ **This Day God Gives Me**

This day God sends me
Strength as my guardian,
Might to uphold me,
Wisdom as guide.

Your eyes are watchful,
Your ears are list'ning,
Your lips are speaking,
Friend at my side.

Ordinary Time

ave you ever counted down the number of days left until a special or important event—for example, the number of days until a holiday? until your birthday? until the last day of school? If you have counted days in this manner, you have been using an old technique to give meaning to time itself. By counting time, you have "ordered" it. Strangely enough, by counting the days and ordering them, you have turned "ordinary" time into a time of special meaning.

Activity Choose a special event that is scheduled to happen at some point in the near future. Beginning today, start counting down to that event. How can counting the days change your attitude toward the current day, or the event to come?

BELIEVING...

We celebrate the season of Ordinary Time.

When the Church observes Ordinary Time, it is "counted time" or "ordered time." The season of Ordinary Time has two parts. The first part is the time between the seasons of Christmas and Lent. The second part is the time between the seasons of Easter and Advent. The Sundays during these two parts of Ordinary Time are numbered, or "counted," so that we speak of "the Tenth Sunday in Ordinary Time" or "the Nineteenth Sunday in Ordinary Time." Yet even though the Sundays and all the weekdays of Ordinary Time are not part of Advent, Christmas, Lent, the Triduum, or Easter, they are not ordinary as in "average." Rather, they are ordinary as in "counted."

The days of Ordinary Time, especially its Sundays, "are devoted to the mystery of Christ in all its aspects" (*General Norms for the Liturgical Year and the Calendar*, 43). The purpose of Ordinary Time is to celebrate Christ in every way: his life, his teachings, his parables, his miracles. Sunday after Sunday, and each weekday too, we listen carefully to Scripture and learn from Jesus Christ and his teachings. We receive his Body and Blood in the Eucharist and are strengthened to share his life with others in word and action.

It is important to remember that the celebration of Ordinary Time revolves around Sunday, the day of Christ's Resurrection and is celebrated as a solemnity by the Church. On each Sunday of Ordinary Time, we are celebrating the saving love of God, expressed within our everyday lives, as we celebrate the death and Resurrection of Jesus and his Real Presence under the appearances of bread and wine.

Four other solemnities that are celebrated within Ordinary Time mark important times or aspects in the life and teachings of Jesus. Celebrating these solemnities helps us to reflect on our own lives and on our growth as disciples of Jesus.

Early Christian mosaic of Christ the King (16th century)

On the solemnity of Christ the King, the last Sunday of both Ordinary Time and the liturgical year, we rejoice that Christ reigns as a servant-king who makes God's love present and active in the world.

Activity As you celebrate these solemnities ask yourself these questions and pray these prayers.

Four Special Solemnities of Ordinary Time	Questions to Ask Myself	My Prayer
The Most Holy Trinity	Am I aware of the Father, the Son, and the Holy Spirit in my life? Do I make the sign of the cross with reverence?	Holy Trinity, help me to recognize you in my life.
The Most Holy Body and Blood of Christ	Do I receive Holy Communion reverently? Do I then spend some time with Jesus in prayer?	Jesus, thank you for giving me your very self.
The Most Sacred Heart of Jesus	Do I try to remember how much God loves me? How do I try to show love to others?	Jesus, help me to share your love with others.
Christ the King	Do I truly follow Jesus and honor him with my life?	Jesus, help me to live as a true disciple.

The season of Ordinary Time gives us a strong foundation in Scripture.

During the season of Ordinary Time, the Scripture readings at Mass are not focused on a theme in the same way that readings for other liturgical seasons are. For example, the readings for Advent center around the theme of joyful expectation. But during Ordinary Time, we read from various books of the Bible, from beginning to end, in a continuous way. This is a unique characteristic of Ordinary Time that helps to give us a strong foundation in Scripture.

In this season, the Church has also "ordered" the Scripture readings for Sundays. The Church has accomplished this by following "cycles" of readings. There are three cycles that the Church follows: Cycle A, Cycle B, and Cycle C. In each of these we hear, particularly on the Sundays in Ordinary Time,

readings from one particular Gospel. If the current year falls into Cycle A, on the Sundays in Ordinary Time we hear readings from the Gospel of Matthew; if Cycle B, then readings from the Gospel of Mark; and if Cycle C, then readings from the Gospel of Luke. The cycle changes each year—from A to B to C, and back to A again. This ordering of Gospel readings allows us, over the course of three years, to hear the life and work of Christ proclaimed from the point of view of each of the synoptic Gospel writers. And we hear the Gospel of John each year in readings during the seasons *outside* of Ordinary Time.

Activity Check a missalette or another resource to find out the cycle for this year. At Mass this Sunday, pay particular attention to the Gospel and to what you can learn about Jesus Christ. How can you act on what you have learned?

RESPONDING...

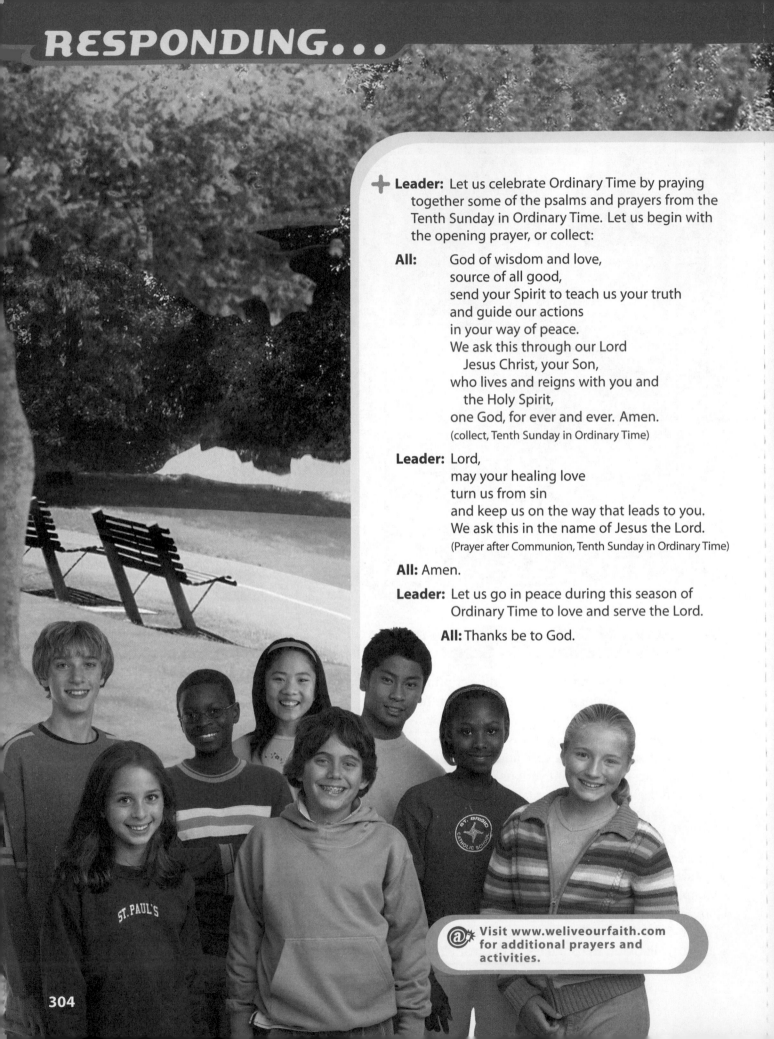

✝ **Leader:** Let us celebrate Ordinary Time by praying together some of the psalms and prayers from the Tenth Sunday in Ordinary Time. Let us begin with the opening prayer, or collect:

All: God of wisdom and love,
source of all good,
send your Spirit to teach us your truth
and guide our actions
in your way of peace.
We ask this through our Lord
Jesus Christ, your Son,
who lives and reigns with you and
the Holy Spirit,
one God, for ever and ever. Amen.
(collect, Tenth Sunday in Ordinary Time)

Leader: Lord,
may your healing love
turn us from sin
and keep us on the way that leads to you.
We ask this in the name of Jesus the Lord.
(Prayer after Communion, Tenth Sunday in Ordinary Time)

All: Amen.

Leader: Let us go in peace during this season of Ordinary Time to love and serve the Lord.

All: Thanks be to God.

@ **Visit www.weliveourfaith.com for additional prayers and activities.**

Glory to the Father

Glory to the Father, and to the Son,
    and to the Holy Spirit:
as it was in the beginning,
    is now, and will be for ever. Amen.

Our Father

Our Father, who art in heaven,
hallowed be thy name;
thy kingdom come;
thy will be done on earth
    as it is in heaven.
Give us this day our daily bread;
and forgive us our trespasses
as we forgive those
    who trespass against us;
and lead us not into temptation,
but deliver us from evil. Amen.

Hail Mary

Hail Mary, full of grace,
the Lord is with you;
blessed are you among women,
and blessed is the fruit
    of your womb, Jesus.
Holy Mary, Mother of God,
pray for us sinners,
now and at the hour of our death.
Amen.

The Jesus Prayer

Lord Jesus Christ, Son of God,
have mercy on me, a sinner.
Amen.

Apostles' Creed

I believe in God, the Father Almighty,
    creator of heaven and earth.
I believe in Jesus Christ,
    his only Son, our Lord.
    He was conceived by the power
    of the Holy Spirit
    and born of the Virgin Mary.
He suffered under Pontius Pilate,
    was crucified, died, and was buried.
He descended to the dead.
On the third day he rose again.
He ascended into heaven
    and is seated at the right hand
    of the Father.
He will come again to judge
    the living and the dead.

I believe in the Holy Spirit,
    the holy catholic Church,
    the communion of saints,
    the forgiveness of sins,
    the resurrection of the body,
    and the life everlasting. Amen.

Prayer to the Holy Spirit

Come, Holy Spirit, fill the hearts
    of your faithful.
And kindle in them the fire
    of your love.

Send forth your Spirit and they
    shall be created.
And you will renew the face
    of the earth. Amen.

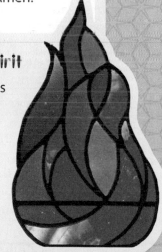

For prayers in Latin see
www.weliveourfaith.com

Nicene Creed

We believe in one God,
   the Father, the Almighty,
   maker of heaven and earth,
   of all that is, seen and unseen.

We believe in one Lord, Jesus Christ,
   the only Son of God
   eternally begotten of the Father,
   God from God, Light from Light,
   true God from true God,
   begotten, not made, one in Being
      with the Father.
   Through him all things were made.
   For us men and for our salvation
      he came down from heaven:
   by the power of the Holy Spirit
      he was born of the Virgin Mary,
         and became man.

For our sake he was crucified
      under Pontius Pilate;
   he suffered, died, and was buried.
   On the third day he rose again
      in fulfillment of the Scriptures;
   he ascended into heaven
      and is seated at the right hand
         of the Father.
   He will come again in glory to judge
         the living and the dead,
      and his kingdom will have no end.

We believe in the Holy Spirit, the Lord,
      the giver of life,
   who proceeds from the Father
      and the Son.
   With the Father and the Son he is
      worshiped and glorified.
   He has spoken through the Prophets.

We believe in one holy catholic
      and apostolic Church.
   We acknowledge one baptism
      for the forgiveness of sins.
   We look for the resurrection of the dead,
      and the life of the world to come.
         Amen.

Act of Contrition

My God,
I am sorry for my sins with all my heart.
In choosing to do wrong
and failing to do good,
I have sinned against you
whom I should love above all things.
I firmly intend, with your help,
to do penance,
to sin no more,
and to avoid whatever leads me to sin.
Our Savior Jesus Christ
suffered and died for us.
In his name, my God, have mercy. Amen.

The Precepts of the Church
(from *CCC*, 2041–2043)

1. You shall attend Mass on Sundays and on holy days of obligation and rest from servile labor.

2. You shall confess your sins at least once a year.

3. You shall receive the sacrament of the Eucharist at least during the Easter season.

4. You shall observe the days of fasting and abstinence established by the Church.

5. You shall help to provide for the needs of the Church.

The Rosary

A rosary is made up of groups of beads arranged in a circle. It begins with a cross followed by one large bead and three small ones. The next large bead (just before the medal) begins the first "decade." Each decade consists of one large bead followed by ten smaller beads.

Begin the rosary with the Sign of the Cross. Recite the Apostles' Creed. Then pray one Our Father, three Hail Marys, and one Glory to the Father.

To pray each decade, say an Our Father on the large bead and a Hail Mary on each of the ten smaller beads. Close each decade by praying the Glory to the Father. Pray the Hail, Holy Queen as the last prayer of the rosary.

The mysteries of the rosary are special events in the lives of Jesus and Mary. As you pray each decade, think of the appropriate Joyful Mystery, Sorrowful Mystery, Glorious Mystery, or Mystery of Light.

The Five Joyful Mysteries

1. The Annunciation
2. The Visitation
3. The Birth of Jesus
4. The Presentation of Jesus in the Temple
5. The Finding of Jesus in the Temple

The Five Sorrowful Mysteries

1. The Agony in the Garden
2. The Scourging at the Pillar
3. The Crowning with Thorns
4. The Carrying of the Cross
5. The Crucifixion and Death of Jesus

The Five Glorious Mysteries

1. The Resurrection
2. The Ascension
3. The Descent of the Holy Spirit upon the Apostles
4. The Assumption of Mary into Heaven
5. The Coronation of Mary as Queen of Heaven

The Five Mysteries of Light

1. Jesus' Baptism in the Jordan
2. The Miracle at the Wedding at Cana
3. Jesus Announces the Kingdom of God
4. The Transfiguration
5. The Institution of the Eucharist

Stations of the Cross

From the earliest days of the Church, Christians remembered Jesus' life and death by visiting and praying at the places where Jesus lived, suffered, died, and rose from the dead.

As the Church spread to other countries, not everyone could travel to the Holy Land. So local churches began inviting people to "follow in the footsteps of Jesus" without leaving home. "Stations," or places to stop and pray, were made so that stay-at-home pilgrims could "walk the way of the cross" in their own parish churches. We do the same today, especially during Lent.

There are fourteen "stations," or stops. At each one, we pause and think about what is happening at the station.

1. Jesus is condemned to die.
2. Jesus takes up his cross.
3. Jesus falls the first time.
4. Jesus meets his mother.
5. Simon helps Jesus to carry his cross.
6. Veronica wipes the face of Jesus.
7. Jesus falls the second time.
8. Jesus meets the women of Jerusalem.
9. Jesus falls the third time.
10. Jesus is stripped of his garments.
11. Jesus is nailed to the cross.
12. Jesus dies on the cross.
13. Jesus is taken down from the cross.
14. Jesus is laid in the tomb.

Hail, Holy Queen

Hail, holy Queen, mother of
　mercy,
hail, our life, our sweetness,
　and our hope.
To you we cry, the children
　of Eve;
to you we send up our
　sighs,
mourning and weeping
　in this land of exile.
Turn, then, most gracious
　advocate,
your eyes of mercy toward us;
lead us home at last
and show us the blessed
　fruit of your womb, Jesus:
O clement, O loving, O sweet
　Virgin Mary.

Memorare

Remember, most loving Virgin Mary,
never was it heard
that anyone who turned to you for help
was left unaided.

Inspired by this confidence,
though burdened by my sins,
I run to your protection
for you are my mother.
Mother of the Word of God,
do not despise my words of pleading
but be merciful and hear my prayer.
Amen.

Saint Patrick's Breastplate

Christ, be with me, Christ before me,
　Christ behind me, Christ within me,
Christ beneath me, Christ above me,
　Christ on my right, Christ on my left,
Christ where I lie, Christ where I sit,
　Christ where I arise.
Christ in the heart of everyone who
　thinks of me,
　Christ in the mouth of everyone who
　　speaks to me,
Christ in the eye of everyone who
　　sees me,
　Christ in the ear of everyone who
　　hears me.
Amen.

Prayer for My Vocation

Dear God,
you have a great and loving plan
for our world and for me.
I wish to share in that plan fully,
faithfully, and joyfully.

Help me to understand what it is
you wish me to do with my life.
Help me to be attentive to the signs
that you give me about preparing
　for the future.

Help me to learn to be a sign
of the Kingdom, or Reign, of God,
whether I'm called to the
priesthood or religious life,
the single or married life.

And once I have heard and understood
your call, give me the strength
and the grace to follow it
with generosity and love. Amen.

Prayer of Saint Teresa of Ávila

Let nothing disturb you,
nothing cause you fear;
all things pass.
God is unchanging.
Patience obtains all:
Whoever has God
needs nothing else.
God alone suffices. Amen.

Prayer of Saint Francis

Lord, make me an instrument of your peace:
where there is hatred, let me sow love;
where there is injury, pardon;
where there is doubt, faith;
where there is despair, hope;
where there is darkness, light;
where there is sadness, joy.

O Divine Master, grant that I may not
　so much seek
to be consoled as to console,
to be understood as to understand,
to be loved as to love.

For it is in giving that we receive,
it is in pardoning that we are pardoned,
it is in dying that we are born to eternal life.
Amen.

The Mass

Introductory Rites

Entrance Chant: Altar servers, readers, the deacon, and the priest celebrant process forward to the altar. The assembly sings as this takes place. The priest and deacon kiss the altar and bow out of reverence.

Greeting: The priest and assembly make the sign of the cross, and the priest reminds us that we are in the presence of Jesus.

Act of Penitence: Gathered in God's presence the assembly sees its sinfulness and proclaims the mystery of God's love. We ask for God's mercy in our lives.

Gloria: On some Sundays we sing or say this ancient hymn.

Collect: This prayer expresses the theme of the celebration and the needs and hopes of the assembly.

Liturgy of the Word

First Reading: This reading is usually from the Old Testament. We hear of God's love and mercy for his people before the time of Christ. We hear stories of hope and courage, wonder and might. We learn of God's covenant with his people and of the ways they lived his law.

Responsorial Psalm: After reflecting in silence as God's word enters our hearts, we thank God for the word we just heard.

Second Reading: This reading is usually from the New Testament letters, the Acts of the Apostles, or the Book of Revelation. We hear about the first disciples, the teachings of the Apostles, and the beginning of the Church.

Alleluia or Gospel Acclamation: We stand to sing the Alleluia or other words of praise. This shows we are ready to hear the good news of Jesus Christ.

Gospel: The deacon or priest proclaims a reading from the Gospel of Matthew, Mark, Luke, or John. This reading is about the mission and ministry of Jesus. Jesus' words and actions speak to us today and help us to know how to live as his disciples.

Homily: The priest or deacon talks to us about the readings. His words help us understand what God's word means to us today. We learn what it means to believe and be members of the Church. We grow closer to God and one another.

Profession of Faith: The whole assembly prays together the Nicene Creed (p. 306) or the Apostles' Creed (p. 305). We are stating aloud what we believe as members of the Church.

Prayer of the Faithful: We pray for the needs of all God's people.

Liturgy of the Eucharist

Preparation of the Gifts: The altar is prepared by the deacon and the altar servers. We offer gifts. These gifts include the bread and wine and the collection for the Church and for those in need. As members of the assembly carry the bread and wine in a procession to the altar, we sing. The bread and wine are placed on the altar.

Prayer Over the Offerings: The priest asks God to bless and accept our gifts. We respond, "Blessed be God for ever."

Eucharistic Prayer: This is the most important prayer of the Church. It is our greatest prayer of praise and thanksgiving. It joins us to Christ and to one another. The beginning of this prayer, the **Preface**, consists of offering God thanksgiving and praise. We sing together the hymn "Holy, Holy, Holy." The rest of the prayer consists of: calling on the Holy Spirit to bless the gifts of bread and wine; the consecration of the bread and wine, recalling Jesus' words and actions at the Last Supper; recalling Jesus' passion, death, Resurrection, and Ascension; remembering that the Eucharist is offered by the Church in heaven and on earth; praising God and praying a great "Amen" in love of God: Father, Son, and Holy Spirit.

Communion Rite: This is the third part of the Liturgy of the Eucharist. It includes the:

Lord's Prayer: Jesus gave us this prayer that we pray aloud or sing to the Father.

Rite of Peace: We pray that Christ's peace be with us always. We offer one another a sign of peace to show that we are united in Christ.

Breaking of the Bread: We say aloud or sing the Lamb of God, asking Jesus for his mercy, forgiveness, and peace. The priest breaks apart the Host, and we are invited to share in the Eucharist.

Holy Communion: We are shown the Host and hear "The Body of Christ." We are shown the cup and hear "The Blood of Christ." Each person responds "Amen" and receives Holy Communion. While people are receiving Holy Communion, we sing as one. After this we silently reflect on the gift of Jesus and God's presence with us. The priest then prays that the gift of Jesus will help us live as Jesus' disciples.

Concluding Rites

Greeting: The priest offers the final prayer. His words serve as a farewell promise that Jesus will be with us all.

Blessing: The priest blesses us in the name of the Father, Son, and Holy Spirit. We make the sign of the cross as he blesses us.

Dismissal: The deacon or priest sends us out to love and serve God and one another. The priest and deacon kiss the altar. They, along with others serving at the Mass, bow to the altar, and process out as we sing the closing song.

Introducing . . . the Bible

The Bible is a collection of seventy-three books written under the inspiration of the Holy Spirit. The Bible is divided into two parts: the Old Testament and the New Testament. In the forty-six books of the Old Testament, we learn about the story of God's relationship with the people of Israel. In the twenty-seven books of the New Testament, we learn about the story of Jesus Christ, the Son of God, and of his followers.

The word *Bible* comes from the Greek word *biblia*, which means "books." Most of the books of the Old Testament were originally written in Hebrew, the New Testament in Greek. In the fifth century, a priest and scholar named Saint Jerome translated the books of the Bible into Latin, the common language of the Church at the time. Saint Jerome also helped to establish the *canon*, or the Church's official list, of the books of the Bible. Many centuries later, in 1384, the first translation of the Bible into English was completed.

The chart below lists the sections and books of the Bible. It also shows abbreviations commonly given for the names of the books in the Bible.

OLD TESTAMENT

Pentateuch
("Five Scrolls")

These books tell about the formation of the covenant and describe basic laws and beliefs of the Israelites.

Genesis (Gn)
Exodus (Ex)
Leviticus (Lv)
Numbers (Nm)
Deuteronomy (Dt)

Historical Books

These books deal with the history of Israel.

Joshua (Jos)
Judges (Jgs)
Ruth (Ru)
1 Samuel (1 Sm)
2 Samuel (2 Sm)
1 Kings (1 Kgs)
2 Kings (2 Kgs)
1 Chronicles (1 Chr)
2 Chronicles (2 Chr)
Ezra (Ezr)
Nehemiah (Neh)
Tobit (Tb)
Judith (Jdt)
Esther (Est)
1 Maccabees (1 Mc)
2 Maccabees (2 Mc)

Wisdom Books

These books explain God's role in everyday life.

Job (Jb)
Psalms (Ps)
Proverbs (Prv)
Ecclesiastes (Eccl)
Song of Songs (Song)
Wisdom (Wis)
Sirach (Sir)

Prophetic Books

These books contain writings of the great prophets who spoke God's word to the people of Israel.

Isaiah (Is)
Jeremiah (Jer)
Lamentations (Lam)
Baruch (Bar)
Ezekiel (Ez)
Daniel (Dn)
Hosea (Hos)
Joel (Jl)
Amos (Am)

Obadiah (Ob)
Jonah (Jon)
Micah (Mi)
Nahum (Na)
Habakkuk (Hb)
Zephaniah (Zep)
Haggai (Hg)
Zechariah (Zec)
Malachi (Mal)

NEW TESTAMENT

The Gospels

These books contain the message and key events in the life of Jesus Christ. Because of this, the Gospels hold a central place in the New Testament.

Matthew (Mt)
Mark (Mk)
Luke (Lk)
John (Jn)

Letters

These books contain letters written by Saint Paul and other leaders to individual Christians or to early Christian communities.

Romans (Rom)
1 Corinthians (1 Cor)
2 Corinthians (2 Cor)
Galatians (Gal)
Ephesians (Eph)
Philippians (Phil)
Colossians (Col)
1 Thessalonians (1 Thes)
2 Thessalonians (2 Thes)
1 Timothy (1 Tim)
2 Timothy (2 Tim)

Titus (Ti)
Philemon (Phlm)
Hebrews (Heb)
James (Jas)
1 Peter (1 Pt)
2 Peter (2 Pt)
1 John (1 Jn)
2 John (2 Jn)
3 John (3 Jn)
Jude (Jude)

Other Writings

Acts of the Apostles (Acts)
Revelation (Rv)

Finding Your Way Through the Bible

The Bible is divided into books, which are divided into chapters, which are divided into verses. Below is a page of the Bible with these parts labeled.

Book
Chapter

Matthew, |13| 28

Verse

The Demand for a Sign |38| ʳ*Then some of the scribes and Pharisees said to him, "Teacher, we wish to see a sign from you." ³⁹*He said to them in reply, "An evil and unfaithful generation seeks a sign, but no sign will be given it except the sign of Jonah the prophet. ⁴⁰*Just as Jonah was in the belly of the whale three days and three nights, so will the Son of Man be in the heart of the earth three days and three nights. ⁴¹*At the judgment, the men of Nineveh will arise with this generation and condemn it, because they repented at the preaching of Jonah; and there is something greater than Jonah here. ⁴² ˢAt the judgment the queen of the south will arise with this generation and condemn it, because she came from the ends of the earth to hear the wisdom of Solomon; and there is something greater than Solomon here.

The Return of the Unclean Spirit ⁴³ ʳ*"When an unclean spirit goes out of a person it roams through arid regions searching for rest but finds none. ⁴⁴Then it says, 'I will return to my home from which I came.' But upon returning, it finds it empty, swept clean, and put in order. ⁴⁵Then it goes and brings back with itself seven other spirits more evil than itself, and they move in and dwell there; and the last condition of that person is worse than the first. Thus it will be with this evil generation."

The True Family of Jesus ⁴⁶ ᵘ*While he was still speaking to the crowds, his mother and his brothers appeared outside, wishing to speak with him. [⁴⁷*Someone told him, "Your mother and your brothers are standing outside, asking to speak with you."] ⁴⁸But he said in reply to the one who told him, "Who is my mother? Who are my brothers?" ⁴⁹And stretching out his hand toward his disciples, he said, "Here are my mother and my brothers. ⁵⁰For whoever does the will of my heavenly Father is my brother, and sister, and mother."

CHAPTER 13

The Parable of the Sower ¹ ᵛ*On that day, Jesus went out of the house and sat down by the sea. ²Such large crowds gathered around him that he got into a boat and sat down, and the whole crowd stood along the shore. ³*And he

Passage title
Titles are sometimes added to show the themes of the chapters, but these titles are not part of the actual words of the Bible.

Passage
A passage is a section of a chapter made up of a number of verses.

This passage shows Matthew 12:46–50, which means: the Gospel of Matthew, chapter twelve, verses forty-six to fifty.

Chapter number

When you are given a Scripture passage to read, here are five easy steps that will help you to find it! Follow these steps to look up the passage given in the example below.

Example: Lk 10:21-22

1 **Find the book.** When the Scripture passage that you're looking up contains an abbreviation, find the name of the book for which this abbreviation stands. You can find this information in the chart at left or on the contents pages at the beginning of your Bible.

2 **Find the page.** Your Bible's contents pages will also indicate the page on which the book begins. Turn to that page within your Bible.

3 **Find the chapter.** Once you arrive at the page where the book begins, keep turning the pages forward until you find the right chapter. The image above shows you how a chapter number is usually displayed on a typical Bible page.

4 **Find the verses.** Once you find the right chapter, locate the verse or verses you need within the chapter. The image above also shows you how verse numbers will look on a typical Bible page.

5 **Start reading!**

almsgiving (p. 231) the sharing of our resources or time to help those who are poor or in need

angel (p. 81) a creature created by God as a pure spirit, without a physical body. Angels serve God as messengers, helping him to accomplish his mission of salvation.

Annunciation (p. 81) the announcement to Mary that she would be the mother of the Son of God

apostasy (p. 248) a total abandonment of one's faith

Apostles (p. 108) twelve of Jesus' disciples who shared his mission in a special way

Ascension (p. 129) Jesus' return in all his glory to his Father in heaven

Assumption (p. 250) the truth that at the end of her earthly work, God brought Mary body and soul to heaven to live forever with the risen Jesus

Beatitudes (p. 100) teachings that describe the way to live as Jesus' disciples. The word *beatitude* means "blessed" or "happy."

bishop (p. 197) a man who has received the fullness of the Sacrament of Holy Orders and continues the Apostles' mission of leadership and service

bless (p. 260) to dedicate someone or something to God or to make something holy in God's name

Blessed Trinity (p. 34) the three Divine Persons in one God: God the Father, God the Son, and God the Holy Spirit

candidates (p. 166) those preparing for a sacrament (e.g. Confirmation, Holy Orders)

canon law (p. 210) the name that we give to the body of laws that govern the Church

catechumenate (p. 156) a process of formation for the Sacraments of Christian Initiation that includes prayer and liturgy, religious instruction based on Scripture and Tradition, and service to others

catechumens (p. 156) adults and older children of catechetical age who have entered the catechumenate and are participating in the Rite of Christian Initiation of Adults (RCIA)

Catholic social teaching (p. 240) the teaching of the Church that calls all members to work for justice and peace as Jesus did

celebrant (p. 156) the bishop, priest, or deacon who celebrates a sacrament for and with the community

celibacy (p. 210) the state of those who have chosen to remain single, promising to devote themselves to the work of God and the Church for the sake of the Kingdom

charity (p. 194) a gift from God that enables us to love him and to love our neighbor

chrism (p. 165) perfumed oil blessed by a bishop

Church (p. 17) the community of people who believe in Jesus Christ, have been baptized in him, and follow his teachings

common good (p. 240) the well-being of every individual person and of the whole society to which everyone belongs

common vocation (p. 208) our call from God to holiness and to evangelization

communion of saints (p. 249) the union of all the baptized members of the Church on earth, in heaven, and in purgatory

conscience (p. 185) our ability to know the difference between good and evil, right and wrong

consecrate (p. 89) to make sacred for God

conversion (p. 184) turning back to God with all one's heart

covenant (p. 45) in the Bible, a solemn agreement between God and his people

creed (p. 220) a statement of belief

deacon (p. 197) a man ordained to share in Christ's mission by assisting bishops and priests in the service of the Church

deposit of faith (p. 27) all the truth contained in Scripture and Tradition that Christ revealed and entrusted to the Apostles and thus to their successors, the bishops, and to the entire Church

diocese (p. 165) a local area of the Church led by a bishop

divine inspiration (p. 24) the special guidance that the Holy Spirit gave to the human authors of the Bible

Divine Revelation (p. 15) God's making himself known to us

ecumenism (p. 248) the work to promote the unity of all Christians

epistles (p. 25) letters found in the New Testament to the early Christian communities about God's Revelation in Jesus Christ

eternal life (p. 118) a life of happiness with God forever

evangelical counsels (p. 208) poverty, chastity, and obedience

evangelization (p. 37) the sharing of the good news of Jesus Christ and the love of God with all people, in every circumstance of life

faith (p. 16) the gift from God that enables us to believe in God, to accept all that he has revealed, and to respond with love for God and others

free will (p. 78) God's gift to human beings of the freedom and ability to choose what to do

Gentile (p. 56) non-Jewish

Gospels (p. 25) the accounts of God's Revelation through Jesus Christ

grace (p. 17) a participation, or a sharing, in God's life and friendship

heresy (p. 248) a denial after Baptism of a truth of the faith

human dignity (p. 238) the value and worth that we share because God created us in his image and likeness

humility (p. 258) the virtue that enables us to acknowledge that God is the source of all good

Immaculate Conception (p. 81) the truth that God made Mary free from original sin and from all sin from the very moment she was conceived

Incarnation (p. 54) the truth that the Son of God, the second Person of the Blessed Trinity, became man and lived among us

infancy narratives (p. 88) the accounts of Jesus' birth and childhood found in the first two chapters of the Gospels of Matthew and Luke

intercession (p. 260) a type of petition in which we ask for something on behalf of another person or a group of people

Kingdom of God (p. 99) the power of God's love active in our lives and in our world

last judgment (p. 231) Jesus Christ's coming at the end of time to judge all people

liturgy (p. 146) the official public prayer of the Church

Liturgy of the Hours (p. 261) the official public prayer of the Church celebrated at specific times, or hours, throughout the day

Magisterium (p. 27) the living teaching office of the Church, consisting of the pope and the bishops

marks of the Church (p. 220) the four characteristics of the Church: one, holy, catholic, and apostolic

Mass (p. 176) the celebration of the Eucharist

mercy (p. 46) God's forgiveness and love

Messiah (p. 64) the person God planned to send to save the people from their sins. The word *Messiah* comes from a Hebrew word that means "Anointed One."

mortal sin (p. 184) very serious sin that turns us completely away from God because it is a choice we freely make to do something that we know is seriously wrong

original sin (p. 78) the first sin committed by the first human beings

parable (p. 56) a short story with a message

Paschal (p. 175) a word that means "of or relating to the Passover"

Paschal Mystery (p. 129) the suffering, death, Resurrection, and Ascension of Jesus Christ

Pentecost (p. 66) the day on which the Holy Spirit came to Jesus' first disciples as Jesus promised. Pentecost marks the beginning of the Church.

petition (p. 260) prayer in which we ask something of God

praise (p. 260) prayer in which we give glory to God for being God

prayer (p. 258) the raising of our minds and hearts to God

priest (p. 197) a man who is ordained to preach the Gospel and serve the faithful, especially by celebrating the Eucharist and the other sacraments

prophet (p. 64) someone who speaks on behalf of God, defends the truth, and works for justice

providence (p. 47) God's plan for and protection of all creation

Real Presence (p. 119) the true presence of Jesus Christ in the Eucharist

Resurrection (p. 25) the mystery of Jesus' rising from death to new life

righteousness (p. 238) conduct in conformity with God's will

Sabbath (p. 108) a day set apart to rest and honor God

sacrament (p. 144) an effective sign given to us by Jesus Christ through which we share in God's life

salvation (p. 15) the forgiveness of sins and restoration of humanity's friendship with God

sanctify (p. 147) to make holy

sanctifying grace (p. 145) the grace that we receive in the sacraments

schism (p. 248) refusal to submit to the leadership of Peter's successor, the pope, or a lack of unity with the members of the Church

Scripture (p. 24) the written account of God's Revelation and his relationship with his people. Also referred to as Sacred Scripture or the Bible, it is God's word, written by human authors under the inspiration of the Holy Spirit.

sin (p. 78) a thought, word, deed, or omission against God's law that harms us and our relationship with God and others

social justice (p. 238) opposing every form of injustice in society and working to promote justice for all people

sponsor (p. 166) a Catholic who is at least 16 years of age, has received the Sacraments of Initiation, is an example of Christian living, is respected by the candidate, and is involved in the candidate's preparation for Confirmation and will help him/her to grow in faith

synagogues (p. 25) gathering places in which people of the Jewish faith study Scripture

synoptic Gospels (p. 56) the Gospels of Mark, Matthew, and Luke, which present the good news of Jesus Christ from a similar point of view

thanksgiving (p. 260) prayer in which we show our gratitude to God for all he has given us

theological virtues (p. 218) the virtues of faith, hope, and charity, which have God as their source, motive, and object

Tradition (p. 24) the Revelation of the good news of Jesus Christ as lived out in the Church, past and present

venial sin (p. 184) less serious sin that weakens our friendship with God but does not turn us completely away from him

virtue (p. 218) a good habit that helps us to act according to God's love for us

vocation (p. 208) a call to a way of life

vows (p. 210) deliberate and free promises made to God

Word of God (p. 57) Jesus Christ, the Son of God, the most complete expression of God's word

Works of Mercy (p. 229) acts of love by which we care for the bodily and spiritual needs of others

The following is a list of topics that appear in the pupil's text. Boldface indicates an entire chapter or section.

Photo Credits

Cover: From top left, clockwise: Ken Karp; The Redemptorists; Richard Mitchell Photography; Art Resource, NY/Nimatallah/Galleria Palatina, Palazzo Piti, Florence; Richard Mitchell Photography; Art Resource, NY/Scala; Getty Images/Photodisc Red/Chad Baker/RyanMcVay; Ann Ball; Neal Farris; frpat.com; Neal Farris; The Crosiers/Gene Plaisted, OSC; Punchstock/Rubberball; The Crosiers/Gene Plaisted, OSC; Image State/Matthew Donaldson; Roman, Inc. 1981/Frances Hook, The Carpenter (St. Joseph); Ken Karp; Cynthia Large. Bridge: Corbis/Royalty Free. Interior: akg-images: 35 bottom. Alamy: 235 bottom right; Design Pics Inc./Don Hammond: 209 top; Jeff Greenberg: 168 top; JG Photography: 140 lower center, 177; Brad Mitchell: 255 background, 256 background, 262 top. Ann Ball: 168 bottom. AP Photo: 102 bottom; Charles Rex Arbogast: 27; François Guillot/Pool: 248; Lee Jin-nan: 221 top; Tia Owens-Powers: 220 bottom left. Art Resource, NY/Giraudon: 121 top; Erich Lessing: 155, 290, 232; Erich Lessing/Israel Museum, Jerusalem: 80; Erich Lessing/Musée d'Orsay, Paris: 143 bottom; Nimatallah/Galleria Palatina, Palazzo Piti, Florence: 132 bottom; Scala: 18 bottom, 37, 74 bottom, 130, 222 bottom; Scala/Collezione d'Arte Religiosa Moderna, Vatican Museums, Vatican State/© 2006 Artists Rights Society, New York/ADAGP, Paris: 55 right; Nicolas Sapieha: 250. Aurora Photos/IPN/Michael Freeman: 181 background, 182 background, 188 top. Lori Berkowitz: 62 left, 245 background, 246 background, 252 top, 279. Jane Bernard: 204 lower top, 220 right, 231, 244. Anthony Boccaccio: 101. Breaking the Cycle, www.breakingthecycle.us: 183. The Bridgeman Art Library/Two folios from the Gutenberg Bible, printed in the workshop of Johannes Gutenberg, 1455 (parchment), German School, (15th century)/ Universitatsbibliothek, Gottingen, Germany, Bildarchiv Steffens: 10 lower top, 25; St. Jerome (tempera on panel), Theodoricus of Prague (fl.1359-c.1381)/Narodni Galerie, Prague, Czech Republic: 28 bottom; The chair of St. Peter, detail of the stained glass window behind, 1665 (detail of 158488), Bernini, Giovani Lorenzo (1598-1680)/St. Peter's, Vatican, Rome, Italy, Joseph Martin: 66. Bridge Building Images/Fr. John Guiliani: 10 upper bottom, 55 center. Karen Callaway: 36, 140 upper bottom, 140 bottom, 146 top right, 186, 197, 210 bottom, 261, 291 bottom. Catholic Relief Services: 58 inset, 178 bottom, 220 top left. Christie's Images Ltd: 191 background, 192 background, 198 top. CIVIC/J.B. Russell: 158 bottom. Corbis/Alessandra Benedetti: 198 bottom; Bettmann: 13 top right, 173; Digital Stock Corporation: 39, 49, 53 top center, 93, 113, 123, 133, 149, 159, 189, 199, 233, 263; Danny Lehman: vi, 259 top; Michael S. Lewis: vii; Gabe Palmer: 274 center; Carl & Ann Purcell: iv, 215 background, 216 background, 222 top; Royalty Free: 18 top, 156; Stapleton Collection: 14 center top; Zefa/G. Baden: 163 bottom. The Crosiers/Gene Plaisted, OSC: 10 upper center, 14 center bottom, 15 center left, 15 center right, 31 background; 32 background, 34, 38 top, 48 bottom, 74 top, 74 upper bottom, 78, 91, 119, 140 lower top, 154 top, 218, 278, 291 top, 294, 299, 305, 306, 307, 308, 309. Don Bosco Publications, England: 232. Neal Farris: 6, 7, 8, 9, 67 bottom, 75 bottom, 85 bottom, 106 left, 115 bottom right, 124. 134, 141 bottom, 142 left, 150, 166, 170, 174, 180, 185, 219, 224, 225 bottom, 226 left, 234, 235 bottom, 236 left, 245 bottom, 246 left, 254, 255 bottom, 256 left, 257, 264. Franciscan Brothers of Peace, Minneapolis, St. Paul: 210 top. frpat.com: 188 bottom. Getty Images/Blend/Ariel Skelley: 204 top, 209 right; Brand X Pictures/John Anthony Rizzo: 131 top left; Brand X Pictures/SW Productions: 24 bottom, 108 bottom; Comstock Images: 103, 152 top right, 154 bottom, 282; Dex Images/Yoshio Sawaragi: 19; Digital Vision: 80 background, 272 left; Digital Vision/Michael Cleary: 28 top; Digital Vision/Ivano Confalone: 243; Digital Vision/Jay Freis: 33 top right, 33 top left, 33 center right, 33 bottom right, 33 bottom left, 116 lower center, 209 bottom; Digital Vision/David Loftus: 253; Digital Vision/Fernando Palma: 151 background, 152 background, 158 top; Digital Vision/Michael Saint Maur Shell: 14 center; Digital Vision/Stockbroker: 153; Digital Vision/David Tipling: 35 top; image 100: 179; The Image Bank/Barros & Barros: 43 bottom; The Image Bank/Peter Cade: 61 background, 62 background, 68 top; The Image Bank/Color Day Production: 122 bottom; The Image Bank/GK Hart/Vikki Hart: 24 background; The Image Bank/Harald Sund: 295; Mark Mainz: 247 bottom center; National Geographic/Sarah Lee: 99; Photodisc: 22 left, 152 top, 152 center right, 152 center bottom; Photodisc Blue: 21 background, 22 background; Photodisc Blue/Tracy Montana/PhotoLink: 55 left; Photodisc Green: 86 left; Photodisc Green/Neil Beer: 14 bottom, 223; Photodisc Green/Martial Colomb: 213; Photodisc Green/C Squared Studios: 207 center; Photodisc Green/Don Farrall: 157 bottom, 237; Photodisc Green/GK Hart/Vikki Hart: 152 center left; Photodisc Green/Spike Mafford: 194 bottom, 195 center right; Photodisc Green/Ryan McVay: 43 top; Photodisc Green/Derek P. Redfern: 63; Photodisc Green/Donovan Reese: 115 background, 116 background left, 122 top; Photodisc Green/Kevin Peterson: 215 bottom left; Photodisc Green/StockTrek: 10 top, 14 top; Photodisc Green/SW Productions: 117, 258 top, 116 upper center; Photodisc Green/Jeremy Woodhouse: 163 top; Photodisc Red/Chad Baker/Ryan McVay: 76 left; Photodisc Red/Ron Farrall: 29; Photodisc Red/Akira Kaede: 59; Photodisc Red/Ryan McVay: 247 top left; Photodisc Red/Eastcott Momatiuk: 169; Photodisc Red/Kevin Peterson: 247 bottom left; Photodisc Red/Photomondo: 50; Photodisc Red/Trinette Reed:104; Science Faction/CMSP: 209 left; Stockbyte: 195 right; Stockdisc Classic: 147; Stone/Martin Barraud: 40, 42 background, 48 top; Stone/Ron Boardman: 142 bottom center; Stone/David Burder: 142 top left; Stone/Giuseppe Cacace: 58 bottom; Stone/Andrew K. Davey: 26; Stone/Sean Ellis: 122 top; Stone/Amanda Marsalis: 125 background, 126 background, 132 top; Stone/Bruce Rogovin: 85 background, 86 background, 92 top; Stone/David Scharf: 142 top right, 142 bottom right; Stone+/Ryan McVay: 16; Taxi/Paul Avis: 146 bottom right; Taxi/Lester Lefkowitz: 51 background, 52 background, 58 top; Taxi/Dick Luria: 84; Taxi/David Oliver: 77; Taxi/Olivier Ribardiere: 53 top right; Taxi/Ulf Sjostedt: 143 top; Taxi/Arthur Tilley: 114, 204 upper center, 230 top right; Thinkstock: 64; Thinkstock/RonChapple: 124; Time Life Pictures: 54; Time Life Pictures/François Lochon: 68 bottom; Workbook Stock/Sarah Stone: 121 bottom. The Granger Collection: 207 background. Greene Uniforms, Hackensack, NJ (sweatshirts): 95, 96. Index Stock Imagery/David Carriere: 69; DesignPics Inc.: 311; Diaphor Agency: 61 bottom; John Dominis: 10 lower center, 44; Omni Photo Communications Inc: 75 background, 76 background, 82; Jacque Denzer Parker: 26 inset; William Rogers: 272 background; Thinkstock: 238 top; Zephyr Pictures: 240 lower center, 241. Image State/Matthew Donaldson: 42 left; Robert Llewelyn: 200. Jesuit Volunteer Corps: 242 bottom. Jupiter Images/Botanica/Simon Watson: 171 background, 172 background, 178 top. Ken Karp: 95 bottom, 96 left, 160, 190, 205 bottom, 206 left, 214, 271, 273, 276, 277, 280, 281, 283, 284, 285, 287, 288, 296, 297, 300, 301, 303. Courtesy of Regina Kelly: 194 top . Kobal Collection/ITC/RAI: 15 right. Kröller-Müller Museum, Otterlo, The Netherlands: 228. Cynthia Large: 38 bottom. Madden: 176. Mary Evans Picture Library: 148 bottom. Masterfile/Bill Brooks: 238 bottom; Steve Craft: 95 background, 96 background, 102 top; Kevin Dodge: 40; Ron Fehling: 21 bottom. Celebration of Saints by Michael McGrath. Copyright © World Library Publications. www.wlpmusic. All rights reserved. Used by permission: 204 upper bottom, 249. Mercy International Association: 252 bottom. The Missionaries of Mother Laura, Antioquia, Columbia: 212. Richard Mitchell Photography: 105, 115 bottom left, 116 left, 125 bottom, 126 left, 131 bottom, 141 background, 142 background, 148 top, 151 bottom, 152 left, 171 bottom, 172 left, 181 background, 182 left, 191 bottom, 192 left, 215 bottom right, 216 left. National Gallery, Washington, DC/Duccio di Buoninsegna: 108 top. The Norman Rockwell Art Collection Trust, The Norman Rockwell Museum at Stockbridge, Massachusetts. Printed by permission of the Norman Rockwell Family Agency Copyright © 1961 the Norman Rockwell Family Entities: 229. Panos/Dieter Telemans: 240. Picture Desk/Kobal Collection/MGM/Samuel Bronston Productions: 175. PictureQuest/Banana Stock: 195 left; Comstock Images: 50; eStockPhoto/IT STOCK INT'L: 208; Photodisc/Mel Curtis: 116 top; Thinkstock Images: 20. Photomosaics/Runway Technology, Inc.: 47. PonkaWonka/Pavel Chichikov: 146 bottom left, 235 background, 236 background, 242 top. Punchstock/Digital Vision: 195 center left;Image Source: 258 bottom; Photodisc: 33 center, 51 bottom, 52 left; Rubberball: 161 bottom, 162 left. Zev Radovan: 89 top. The Redemptorists: 112 bottom. Roman, Inc. 1981/Frances Hook, The Carpenter (St. Joseph): 92. Shutterstock/Richard Paul Kane: 247 center right. Superstock/age fotostock: 6 background, 8 background, 30, 94. teresadelosandes.org: 262 bottom. University of Notre Dame Archives: 207 right. Veer/Alloy Photography: 7 background; George Diebold: 272 center; Digital Vision: 11 background, 12 background; Photo Alto: 11 bottom left, 23; Photodisc: 53 top left; Rubberball: 53, 70; Stockbyte: 11 bottom right, 12 left, 31 bottom, 32 left, 33 center left, 116 bottom center, 116 bottom, 247 top right, 247 bottom left. Soichi Watanabe, Japan, The Coming of the Holy Spirit. www.asianchristianart.org: 10 bottom, 67 top. W.P. Wittman Ltd: 17, 36 inset, 57, 128, 131 top right, 140 lower center, 146 top left, 146 center, 167, 187, 211, 230 top left, 230 bottom, 259 bottom, 303.

Illustrator Credits

Mike Arnold: 172, 256. Diane Fenster (photo collage art): 87, 105, 107 Darren Hopes (photo collage art): iv-v, vi-vii, 271, 273, 276, 277, 280, 281, 284, 285, 288, 289, 292, 293, 296, 297, 300, 301, 304. Jacey: 205. W. B. Johnston: 218. Robin Kachantones: 193. Michel LaRose: 217. Joe LeMonnier: 79, 165. Dean MacAdam: 206, 216. Diana Magnuson: 81. Greg Morgan: 127. Frank Ordaz: 65, 88-89, 90, 98, 109, 110, 111, 118, 120, 128, 144, 164, 184, 251, 260, 298. Gary Phillips: 279. Leah Palmer Preiss: 56, 57. Zina Saunders: 45, 286. Phil Scheuer: 97. Peter Siu: 82, 86. Jessica Wolk-Stanley: 227. Jane Sterret (photo collage art): 247